AMERICAN STASI

The Domestic Surveillance Targeting You And Your Children

Michael Trust

Cover Art And Design By Better Book Covers
BetterBookCovers@gmail.com

FEDERALIST PUBLICATIONS
Macclenny, Florida

Published by Federalist Publications, Macclenny, Florida

www.AmericanStasi.com

ISBN-13 : 978-1-7334142-3-4   Softcover
ISBN-13 : 978-1-7334142-4-1   Hardcover
ISBN-13 : 978-1-7334142-6-5   E-book

Library of Congress Control Number (LCCN): 2024917037

Library of Congress Subject Headings:

United States--Politics and government
Conspiracies--United States
Conspiracies--United States--History--20th century

I must first acknowledge the greatest appreciation for those who selflessly gave of themselves to offer help and support to this project all along the way, often in critical moments.

I also must offer Glory to God, for He undoubtedly put me on this righteous path, and has guided and protected me all along it.

For those suffering, stay strong and take heart – you are not alone. We are the righteous, we are legion in this nation, we need no gang of criminals to hide behind like cowards, and we will win. Traitors always get the rope, eventually.

Keep the faith.

"All these investigations, the thorough research on the Stasi structures, the methods they used and are still using, all that will fall into the wrong hands. These structures will be painstakingly examined – to copy them.

They will be adapted a bit so that they'll work in a free Western society. The dissidents won't necessarily be arrested. There are finer possibilities to neutralize someone. But the secret prohibitions, the surveillance, the suspicions, the fear, the isolation and ostracisms, the branding and censoring of those who won't go along – that will come back, believe me.

Institutions will be created that will work far more effectively, in a far more sophisticated way than the Stasi. Also the permanent lying will come back, the disinformation, the fog in which everything loses its form."

-East German dissident Baerbel Bohley

"Do not be afraid of them. Nothing is concealed that will not be revealed, nor secret that will not be known. What I say to you in the darkness speak in the light, what you hear whispered, proclaim from the housetops"

- Matthew 10, 24-44

Table of Contents

Prologue

This book has been created as a warning to all real American citizens, as well as other citizens throughout the Western sphere, that they are presently being targeted by a massive domestic intelligence operation, the prime mission objective of which is to control them, and limit both their ability to succeed in life, as well as the abilities of their children to succeed.

There is no more preposterous proposition than the idea that right now, someone is watching you, and assigned to make sure you never succeed to the fullest of your potential. You have been told, from the time you are a child, that you are not important, nobody was paying attention to you, and to think so would be a sign of mental illness. You would be a dreaded "conspiracy theorist."

What if I told you, that was entirely false? You are important, in the eyes of the elites. What if I proposed that out there were elites, running America, who had committed so many crimes, ripped the nation off so thoroughly, they could not possibly let someone honest like you simply go out, do whatever you wanted, become whatever you set your heart on, succeed wildly, and make it into high society, where you might see those crimes and oppose them? What if I said their biggest fear is the idea of you, succeeding wildly and becoming rich, or even running for office? What if I said they recreated the East German Stasi, throughout the Western world, and its sole purpose was to spy on you and your children, to make sure you can never rise to a point you could pose a threat to their power?

This book is going to show you that is exactly the case. By the time we are done, you will have no doubts. You are going to see this machine's operators deployed in America with your own eyes, first here on these pages, and then, once you know what it looks like, all around you in real life.

In America, our intelligence community has been compromised by these global elites, and has created a massive domestic intelligence operation for them, modeled on the East German Stasi, with the primary mission objective of keeping you down - keeping us all down. And they have done a most impressive job of keeping it secret.

Moreover, this operation is all throughout the Western world. This book will focus on America, but at our main website, we will show you it operating in numerous countries. From Finland, to Latin America, you will see its surveillance people operating openly on the streets. In the process, you will develop countersurveillance skills which we will show you exceed those possessed by top level Tier One Special Forces operatives. You are going to become dangerous in ways you never even knew were possible.

You will see they are running their surveillance operations all throughout American society, and just like the Stasi, they are recruiting retards from society who cannot compete, and telling them it is unfair your natural ability and gumption might allow you to succeed over them.

They offer to even the odds, by rewarding these midwits for spying on you, and reporting anyone who is on track to succeed wildly in some way. Once reported, this machine will operate behind the scenes to kill your opportunity, or, if your child was reported, to intervene in their life to derail them.

They are turning these retards into a sizable civilian surveillance force and embedding them in your community, giving them all the best surveillance tech so they can listen in the houses of everyone in the neighborhood, and telling them to alert command to anyone who threatens to step out of line and maybe rise in society above the station American intelligence, and the conspiracy now running it, has assigned to them.

These retards are even running their retard children as spies in the schools, to find children who are too smart and moral to be allowed to succeed, and to clip their wings before they can get their feet off the ground by corrupting them - exposing them to drugs, or alcohol, or pornography, or ensnaring them in criminal activities to give them a record. The surveillance people are even sending their young daughters in as sexual honeypots, to help derail the potential high flyers who they think could become a problem for their criminal conspiracy later in life, or to wrangle some sort of control over them through blackmail.

I have seen all this with my own eyes, since I was a kid, growing up in a school which was some kind of hive of these midwits. Here, in this book, I will let you see it with your own eyes.

I have an ingenious method. I will take you through Russia on Google Streetview, where the American Google car, taking pictures as it drives and maps out Russia, is seen as an intelligence threat. There, you will see real life Russian surveillance operators tracking the Google car in the photos it takes.

I will point them out to you, show you where their behaviors are nonsensical, and then explain why they are doing what they are doing, and how spotting those required surveillance procedures is how you conduct a counter-surveillance detection protocol.

Once you have an elite CIA Officer's understanding of how to spot surveillance, I will take you to Bulgaria, where the Google car did a drive-by of a hidden, covert intelligence facility tucked away in an industrial area, and I will let you spot the surveillance yourself, pointing out everything so you don't miss a detail.

Then we are going to come home to America, once you are trained up to an elite, CIA, tier-one operative's level in surveillance detection. Here, in America, you will see even more surveillance than in Russia and Bulgaria deployed on the Google car, and you will have no choice but to understand that surveillance is everywhere in America, and the American intelligence community has gotten fully out of control.

Then we are going to play you videos, taken by innocent Americans, showing you this operation harassing innocent citizens who happened to see their operatives, and angered them. It is a technique straight out of the Stasi playbook, which the agency called Zersetzung. Translated to "decomposition," it described the mental breakdown targets endured as all the informants in the community began harassing them, while the government called them mentally ill and paranoid for speaking of such imaginary persecutions.

Here in America, the New York Times reported that almost a decade ago, in 2016, there were ten thousand Americans just in online communities complaining of exactly this type of harassment, with probably tens of thousands of others quietly enduring in isolation. Since then their numbers appear to have grown substantially. In the article, the Old Gray Lady derided them all as mentally ill, and imagining their persecution. On these pages you will see their persecutors in the flesh, and receive links to videos showing the persecution. You will also realize, the New York Times helped to cover up a crime by our intelligence community. Either it was too stupid to do real investigative reporting, or it was taken over and has become a mere propaganda mouthpiece for the CIA.

In the process, you will become an expert in foot surveillance, vehicular surveillance, covers, silhouettes, and monitoring technologies, at which point you will not be able to help noticing the domestic surveillance units deployed in your own neighborhood around you. They are astonishingly obvious once you know what to look for. Their only protection from exposure has been your conditioning - to think such a thing could never happen in America. You have probably already seen them at some point, and dismissed what you saw as an odd coincidence, or just a moment of strangeness, since you have been told thousands of times, nobody would ever pay attention to you. In reality, we all have files assembled by this thing. It fears and loathes every honest, loyal, patriotic American, and it has taken measures to contain you. Once you see the operation it will be blatantly obvious.

Then we will go to the darker side, and show that the surveillance technologies this operation is deploying in neighborhoods, are giving Americans cancer. We will show you an interview with the head of all technology development at the National Security Agency, William Binney, who says half the people on his street were given cancer, by radio-emissive thru-wall surveillance technologies the American intelligence community is deploying throughout the country to listen and see in homes - emissions he himself has measured on a spectrum analyzer in multiple locations, and which the government will not even acknowledge any of his communications about.

They may be beaming you right now through your walls to see what you are doing in your home, and if you are not running a spectrum analyzer, you will never know, until that cancer diagnosis comes back. And even then you will assume it was just bad luck.

We will show you a website Bill Binney, and numerous

other luminaries from the American intelligence community set up, explaining that American intelligence is beaming innocent citizens as part of a massive criminal intelligence operation, and that this needs to be addressed.

We will show you American Intelligence had the website wiped off the internet, and we will show you Bill, in an interview, explaining that American intelligence is now trying to kill him, and has blown holes through steel shielding in his ceiling, which he installed to try and block the beams that are hitting him nightly. The energy beam they used did not damage his walls, but rather passed cleanly through them, before blowing two holes through steel sheeting above him with loud explosive bangs.

From there, we will look at some cases where individual neighborhood surveillance cells have spun out of control, drunk on power, and appear to be involved in other criminal activities, breaking into women's homes to drug the food in their fridge. Then, after the women came home and ate the food and passed out, they returned to gang rape them as they laid unconscious. We will show where they are murdering citizens, possibly because those citizens had small businesses which threatened the local businesses of surveillance people. We will reveal where they are supporting serial killers for reasons unknown, and where they were almost certainly involved somehow in the brutal murder of several innocent college girls.

You will also realize, by the fact these things were not publicized by the news media, that the penetration of this American Stasi extends into our news media, as well as elsewhere, much farther than you would have thought possible. I will even show you a reporter who is attacked by a citizen – a citizen who appears to believe the reporter is part of his local surveillance harassment cell, after seeing the reporter filming him using a technique we will show is commonly used by this domestic surveillance operation.

There is no shortage of people in your community who are complicit in this conspiracy to keep you and your family down, and many even enjoy the power trip, as they keep this secret from you.

All along the way, you will see American Stasi surveillance in action, even children which are employed by the conspiracy to target other gifted children in the schools, talking freely amongst themselves, openly in public, about conducting surveillance follows for this conspiracy.

We focus on America here, but if you are from any nation in the Western sphere, especially in Europe, you will also be subject to this same operation. This intelligence op has penetrated the entire West, which is why of late all our nations are doing the exact same self-destructive things, the exact same way, at the exact same time.

All of our societies are run by these conspirators, who are taking their orders from the exact same global command. And yes, our leaders were all installed by this conspiracy in rigged elections, all throughout the West. All the talk of how we control our governments was all lies, intended to mollify you with a false sense of power and control, as well as a sense you could have succeeded and been a multimillionaire, if only chance had played out differently for you. In reality, you were not allowed to strive and succeed as wildly as you could have, because the conspiracy could not let you, lest you see their crimes.

As you see the surveillance in America, understand, if America looks like that, as heavily armed as the citizens are, and as committed to freedom as they have been raised to be, other nations will be even worse.

Once you realize American intelligence has sought to close the doors to success to you and your children, to enslave you covertly, without you even knowing, and as part of that they are exposing you and your loved ones to cancer-causing radiations in your home, I want you to take this movement to eradicate this to the next level, by helping to tell other people about this work. This movement, your nation, and your children's future, all need your help, right now. We need to unite as a movement.

Only real American patriots and heroes like you can fight this - by telling each other to seek out this work and learn how to spot the surveillance, so we can all see this enemy clearly and unite across the nation to oppose this machine and ostracize these enemies among us. I cannot do this myself. I am buried under hostile surveillance, and it has me fully contained. Moreover, as with Bill Binney, the radiations they are hitting me with are so powerful now I can feel their effects, and at times, I can barely think, or even walk. I have even been knocked unconscious by them, and I do not know how long I have here. I have done all I can with this work, and now I need fellow patriots to amass for this crucial battle in the information warfare space.

I need random American patriots and other heroes throughout the world, willing to fight the Second American Revolution by sending out a few chain letters to other random Americans and Europeans, and then telling everyone they know about the American Stasi, according to the procedure I will lay out later in this book. We need everyone to know about the American Stasi, and the global conspiracy behind it, so we can generate the political drive to destroy it.

This movement needs freedom-loving heroes willing to stand up and fight for their freedom and their health, as well as their loved-one's freedoms and health. In this information war, that means printing out our chain letter inviting people to join us at our website or read this book, to warn them that they are targets too.

Hopefully they will continue the chain of letters, and we can warn everyone about this - and in the process, destroy this through exposure, and the political pressure which will inevitably develop as a result of that. These traitors must pay.

This conspiracy's only strength is the fact it is secret. Its people are cowardly traitors and retards looking for an easy path to success. Its operations are comically obvious once you know what to look for. Its actions are clearly criminal and illegal. Public exposure will destroy this operation, and at the very least, put regular citizens on alert, and on equal footing with the conspirators, making it harder for the motley crew of mental defectives it employs to roll over us. Its biggest advantage is its secrecy. We want to strip it of that.

For the price of a few stamps, you can take part in the Second American Revolution, be a part of history and free our kind from this plague, and in the process free yourself and your children - and eliminate a risk of cancer we are all being exposed to.

My one goal is to destroy this operation and restore American Freedom to every citizen before I die. If you want to buy a book, we will appreciate it, and the money will help buy us advertising. If you bought a billboard somewhere, or printed out a few thousand flyers with our chain letter to air drop over a city, or nplaced stickers in public places, we're not stopping you. All we need is every American aware of this, by any means necessary.

If you want to contribute monetarily, your best bet would be to buy a few extra stamps, print out a few extra chain letters, and send them out to random people, using fake return addresses so they cannot be tracked, to alert everyone to our website and the book, and the surveillance detection courses we make available for free.

It is important to emphasize, this movement is non-partisan, non-ideological, and based on the principle that every race, religion, creed, and political party in America is being targeted by this domestic intelligence operation modeled on the East German Stasi. Every American is a target. Every real American is getting screwed over by these traitors.

I began this journey as a political ideologue myself. On the right, on the left, it doesn't matter. I knew the other side was the problem. I wrote a book, and became pretty successful. But then I saw the American Stasi when it came in to harass me.

I realized once I saw the American Stasi, politics does not matter. The intelligence operatives who run this thing view ideologues as foolish, because one, they control nearly all political figures. Pick somebody you hate on the right, or the left. George W. Bush? Bill Clinton? They are both literally laughing at you, as both are essentially just actors, hired by this thing to rile you up.

In reality, they attend parties together, eat finger foods together, travel together, and when they see each other, they hug like bears and share the bond of the conspiracy, as both view you as a threat and an enemy. Neither cares about politics, because they knew there was no fight, and all the outcomes on all the issues they touched were predetermined. They were given scripts, and read their lines, and made you dance on command. I danced too, before I understood this.

It is like that all through politics. The issues you are passionate about? The advocates you see up there? The opposition fighting against your cause? The issues, the advocates, the opposition, they are all a scripted production to divide the population, and get us fighting at the grassroots. Meanwhile right-wing extremist Sean Hannity is gayly shooting selfies with ultra-liberal CNN reporter Don Lemon at cocktail parties, where the elites who have been cast in this production laugh at all of us.

Even the outcomes of those issues are just predetermined by the elites, no matter what you at the grassroots do. The conspiracy designs the outcomes to be as riling as possible, because if we are fighting each other at the grassroots over meaningless garbage which is already decided, they are in full control up there, all enjoying limitless money from the raided treasury, as they never work a day in their lives. They are all the enemy, and all are enjoying your stolen success, in the form of millions of dollars, as they impoverish entire communities of the less fortunate.

I played the ideological political game for a long time. It is all a rigged scam, designed to distract you from the observation post next door picking up on your new side hustle, and sabotaging it, so you cannot get off the plebe's treadmill they have put you on. They want it so you never make enough money to be in control of your own life, and you will always have to dance to their tune. As it stands, you will die a slave, who never even noticed your chains, as your children are covertly enslaved right before your eyes, without you having a clue it was happening.

They got hooked on heroin? It must have been bad luck, because nothing in America would ever see them on a path to succeed, and do that to them purposely.

Left, Right, Republican, Democrat, Liberal Conservative, Black, Brown, White or purple, set your differences with the other side on pause, just for a little bit, and jump in this fight against the American Stasi and the intel op which has coopted the West. Lets see if we wreck this intel op, if the rest of America, and the rest of the world, improves in the process. You are going to be shocked.

In the 1950's, an average American man worked, while his wife stayed home to raise the children and maintain the house. With just one salary from that single man's productivity, that family had enough money to get out of debt, buy a house, take yearly vacations all over the country, and have money left over for toys like boats, and motorcycles, and fishing equipment. They even had time for regular vacations, all off that one man's production. It was a different time, and a different world, filled with family, fun, and community. Attics overflowed with 8mm videotapes of vacations taken all over the nation.

Today, you have families, where both the man and woman work full time. Each brings to the table the production level of a single person in the 1950's augmented by technology, so each of them can produce ten, twenty, fifty times as much value for their work as that single man in 1950.

And yet the two of them, both working full time, augmented by technology, barely produce a subsistence level of income, as they struggle under debts they may never pay off. They will never even get to buy a home, let alone take vacations, or take out the boat for a spin every weekend with the kids, if they could even afford kids. Nor would they have the time for it, if they had the money.

America was a different place in the fifties, because the American Stasi had not yet clamped down control, and enslaved the nation - and turned us all against each other.

Today it has, and everything is different. The culture is fractured, the political debate is filled with strife and acrimony. People work like slaves to barely survive, but are told it is freedom because they could chose not to and be homeless.

We fight all the time, over every issue, and barely even know who we are fighting, or why the issue matters. Criminals are being freed to prey upon us, as every institution of our country is being destroyed, and none of us can get a moment to even stop and look at the wreckage around us as we rush off the serve this machine which destroyed everything. And don't even think about finding the time to start a business in your garage, as used to be an American tradition.

It is terrible if you are an American. But it is great if you are a criminal conspiracy in the intelligence community, looking to keep all Americans poor, off balance, and fighting each other, so they never notice you ripping them off, and screwing them over.

The full scale of this operation far exceeds what we will cover here. Here we are going to focus solely on the surveillance of the American Stasi, in your neighborhood. It is the most exposed and obvious part of the conspiracy. Once we show it to you, and teach you surveillance detection, you will inevitably end up seeing your local units. And once you see how many people are in it, you will realize this is a massive criminal conspiracy, and you will realize all of the other parts of it which must exist.

For now, lets begin this book and learn a little about surveillance detection, and the American Stasi's massive domestic surveillance program.

Chapter One

What Is The Premise Of This Book?

You are not free, you are controlled. You are a slave, bound by shackles you are unable to see or feel. You are being spied upon, this very moment, and your life has been manipulated by these spies. All of this has been hidden from you, from the very beginning of your life, as the American system has foisted lie upon lie, upon you, until you came to believe the lies so thoroughly, you could not imagine the reality of your life.

I know this because a unique series of events opened my eyes, showed me the lies, and I saw the reality of America. Now, for me, there is no going back, and after you see what this book will show you, after you review the pictures and videos, listen to the interviews, and then see your own shackles, there will be no going back for you either.

Those in power in the world, the real elites, so wealthy we have never heard their names spoken, have assembled a private sector intelligence operation in the shadows, modeled on the old East German Stasi secret police. This operation has recruited people in your neighborhood to betray the very foundational principles of America, and monitor your entire neighborhood, using all the tools of an elite intelligence agency, so they can take control of your life from you.

These American Stasi agents are periodically listening in your home, just as the Stasi did in apartments in the old East Germany. Assigned to know you like an acquaintance, your local neighborhood Stasi archivist maintains an incredibly detailed file on you, and he has been given access to everything – your internet activity, your smart phone, your computer, he has even assigned physical surveillance to track you through stores periodically and document what you buy.

And they don't stop there. They are using the children of Stasi agents to build files on your children in the local schools – and sometimes they even have those children intervene, to derail the problematic gifted children who might grow up to threaten this criminal intelligence operation they have hidden in the shadows.

They are controlling who rises to the top in our society, starting from the beginning of the life of every American child. They are now in so deep, their organization has turned so outright criminal, they absolutely have to make sure nobody with morals, or honor, or loyalty to the ideals of America, can ever rise to a position of real power.

It sounds unbelievable, but we will show you all of this. You will see it with your own eyes, just as I have. Then, we hope you will join with us, and help us destroy this abomination. It does not belong in America.

We don't have much time. This thing is growing in power and control every day. Unless I can get all Americans to see what I have seen, our nation will be collapsed by the hidden foreign enemy who set up the American Stasi, and our children will be raised in the wreckage, forced every day to fight for their lives against an enemy they will never be able to defeat.

Taking this leviathan on will be no small feat. In the shadows, likely over centuries, global elites, with more money and real power than we could imagine, have assembled a massive global, private-sector, CIA-like operation. It is essentially a complete intelligence agency, with professional intelligence operatives, and an extensive East German Stasi-like ground network of civilian informants, embedded in Western nations, all around you, made up of your neighbors. The only thing it does not have is a nation to serve or any kind of oversight body to reign in its excesses.

The intelligence operation is too complicated to expound upon fully in this book. It permeates politics, business, culture, the news media, the intelligence community, the Congress, the Executive branch, and the Judiciary, religion, as well as a myriad of social clubs and organizations. Its purpose appears to be exerting control over the population as it drains the national treasury.

What this book will do is train you to see the Stasi-like surveillance machine this intelligence operation has constructed in the US, made up of people all throughout your community, whose whole lives are devoted to spying on you for this machine.

We will do it in a creative fashion. Without ever leaving the chair you are sitting in, we will go overseas together, in Google Streetview.

As a service designed by Google, Google Steetview uses a Google car to drive along roads featured on Google Maps. On top of the car is a giant "camera ball," which has cameras pointing out of it in every direction. As the Google car drives, every few feet that camera ball takes a tranche of pictures of everything in every direction around the Google car at that point, for 360 degrees.

Those pictures, and the GPS location where they were taken, are uploaded to Google's servers, where Google then organizes them, so you can pick a road on Google maps, click on it, and essentially drive that road on your computer, using your cursor and arrow keys to see what the Google car saw at each point. You can stop at one spot in the street, and pan 360 degrees, to see all around the Google car, just as if you were at the location.

We will begin our Google Streetview tours in hostile nations which will view an American vehicle taking pictures as an intelligence threat, and we will show you what the surveillance deployed on the Google car looks like. We will point out the operators as the Google car passes them. We will explain how the surveillance operates, and why it does the unique things it does, using the pictures the Google car took, as it drove around those nations, tailed by their domestic surveillance operations.

Then we will use Google Streetview to drive around the United States, and show you the same surveillance machinery tracking the Google car in the USA. As you see these images, it will program your brain to understand how surveillance works, how it times approaches and pass-bys. You will know what it looks like, and from there it will be a matter of time until you see this surveillance in your own community. I have seen it, and it is everywhere. People you know, will have secret lives they will never talk about, in which they run this surveillance, on the side.

Those elites who created the American Stasi have deployed

this machine throughout numerous nations, infiltrating the nation's governments, co-opting their intelligence agencies, and subverting their law enforcement, building the operation up to gargantuan proportions. Presently they are using it to infiltrate and take over America, most likely so our nation may be collapsed, most likely for simple profit through some sort of investment positioning, now that they have drained the national treasury.

This is not an ideological issue. Please leave all the things you thought you knew about government at the door. This has nothing to do with Republicans or Democrats, beyond the fact they have all been compromised by this thing. There is no left or right in this book, and we have no idea whether Q-anon is a good guy, a bad guy, or a nobody. This has nothing to do with the left or right, hippies or Nazis, Trump or Biden, or race or religion, beyond the fact I believe this operation has used all of those to divide our population, and keep everyone fighting everyone, so nobody could spot this operation in the shadows and target the real enemy destroying our nation.

I believe, if everyone sees this thing, the most diehard left-wing ACLU member will have no problem uniting, arm in arm, with the most hardcore right-wing Republican against this monstrosity. I believe the battle against the American Stasi and its agents in our communities is the one thing which might just reunite our nation. I was a hardcore ideologue when I first saw this thing. Now, it has turned me into a hardcore American who will unite with anyone else who desperately wants real freedom. You will see, this enemy is that contemptible.

All around you, this Stasi-like intelligence service has been operating in America for decades - citizens who look just like you, embedded in every neighborhood, watching and reporting anything they think will get them credit with Management, acting as junior wannabe covert agents, running operations against you. They even intervene in circumstances to alter life-paths of individuals, as directed to by their command, to stifle success, and prevent people deemed too honorable from rising to positions of power where they might pose a threat to the operation.

Even worse, the children of the people who are in the informant network are trained as junior spies, even sent to sleep away camps where professional spies school them on how to operate. Then they are given to units assigned to local schools.

Most likely organized as "training" operations, the files these children help the machine create, and the life interventions they perform on other children, likely follow those they cross paths with for the rest of their lives.

In investigating this network you will see the children post photos to social media from some sort of organized program they attend in Florida. There, they are trained under instructors in wrap-around sunglasses wearing what look like placards with FBI logos, in some sort of weeks-long sleep-away camps devoted to surveillance training.

The entire purpose of this surveillance machine is to control regular Americans like you, and make sure you never rise too high, or can pose any sort of threat, in a system that is so corrupt and evil at the upper levels that no normal person would ever stand for it, if they rose high enough to see how it operated up there.

From pedophile blackmail operations like Jeffrey Epstein's, to abuses of power to raid the national treasury, bad things happen

6

at those upper levels, and the machine intends to keep that secret, and not allow anyone decent or honest to get too close to it.

It sounds ridiculous, given how the public schools always told you that you were in full control. I know, I was told the same lies, and I believed them too.

They tell you that you elect the government, which is filled with weak people too afraid to act out against you, for fear you will elect a different leader next time.

But look at the world. If we elected our politicians, they would look to please us, for if they did not, someone else would run against them who would please us, and we would vote for them.

Yet instead of striving for our approval, politicians today waltz into office, and flout low single digit approval ratings in our faces as they free criminals to prey upon us. They import migrant criminals who demand we provide them with free housing, food, healthcare, and jobs. They give away our tax dollars to anyone they can find – even the Taliban – and they are rarely unseated. When they are unseated, even by a member of the opposition party, the new politician will end up doing the exact same thing.

They fight wars we have no care for, give everyone but hardworking Americans foreign aid even as our nation goes bankrupt - and they openly accumulate what is to us unimaginable wealth that hardworking Americans could never dream of, through graft, theft, and insider trading.

If we elected our leaders, things would work differently. This government would be eager to please us. And if we do not elect our leaders, why on earth would our all powerful intelligence agencies, manned by a Deep State we will never even see named, fear us?

How did we end up losing control of the government of the United States? It did not happen by chance. Seizing control of the United States government would have been the product of an incredibly complex intelligence operation, which would have been capable of executing its plans while leaving nothing to chance.

Such an intelligence operation would absolutely require an extensive surveillance network on the ground. Comprehensive surveillance is the foundation of all intelligence activity, as it is the only way to gain the extensive awareness of all possible variables necessary to control the course of events in such a complex operation. Failure to maintain that control, while engaged in such treasonous activities, could quite literally result in a death sentence.

Solely the contempt shown by our supposedly elected politicians for the average American citizen indicates that there is something out there, controlling the system. Something massive, permeating all the parts of society.

To maintain control, it would need an intelligence service like the Stasi. Something capable of watching the human terrain at a granular level, assessing every single person and what they were up to at regular, not-infrequent intervals, and controlling those who threatened to become problematic before they could pose a threat.

To make you unable to see such a Stasi-like operation, it would need to feed everyone lies, beginning at a very early age, and it has.

The lies you were told made sense. *"We are all free."* *"Anyone can be anything they want to be."* *"Nobody could spy on you in your house, as the East German Stasi used to – that would be ridiculous."* *"You elect your leaders, so you control them."* Did you believe them? Has it worked like they said? Do you feel in control?

I believed them, and so did you. It was the world you would want, and you assumed everyone else wanted it too, so why not? *"Our Constitution limits our government's power."* You probably retold the lies to other Americans like yourself, while believing them. *"The three branches of government would constrain each other through Checks and Balances."* Other Americans like you recited the lies as well. *"If there was a conspiracy, our intrepid news media would expose it, so as to become famous and rich."*

It made sense. You would expose it. But then you are not influential in the news media or politics. But still, we must elect our leaders. What kind of lunatic would not want to live in a country where the people elect our leaders?

Well, in East Germany, there were apparently more than a few who actively worked to create the despotism which trapped everyone else behind the East German wall. Estimates vary, and there are no hard numbers, but according to one former Stasi colonel who served in the counterintelligence directorate, the Stasi likely employed somewhere in the area of 2 million citizen informants spying on the population, which at the time would have been about 29% of the East German population.[01] Those 29% had no problem helping a dictatorial government wrangle the rest of the population, in return for a few more crumbs than the average East German was given.

9

Although we all want to believe Americans would never do that to fellow citizens, human nature is human nature, and that human nature is fairly consistent from population to population.

From what I have seen in my own community, and traveling in the US, it would appear the American Stasi has been able to recruit somewhere between 4% and 10% of the American population to spy on the rest of the nation, and when called upon, to torment them as well.

It would comport with the one time this network almost became an official government agency, when a program called Operation TIPS, to be discussed more in detail later, was briefly enacted, only to later be outlawed. It recruited roughly 4% of the population into its pilot program of informants, as a test of the waters of domestic surveillance. Had it not been for a lone intrepid reporter, who fought to get a piece on it published, it would be a fully functional agency today, likely expanded far beyond that pilot program's size.

I can say for a fact, in America there is a massive group of citizens, apart from those of us who believe in the principles of liberty, freedom, and privacy, and they have kept themselves well-hidden as they have concealed a massive secret from us. I have seen these people with my own eyes. They want a government which knows all your secrets, and which can torture you physically, at will. They crave it.

I assume this machine has sought to identify these citizens while they were still children in school, with agents of the American Stasi using their own children, operating under the command of adults in the conspiracy, to find them, probe them, and mark them for induction into this conspiracy later in life.

The recruits do not want that world where anyone can be anything. I assume when this machine told them it could give them power, if they would join it and help suppress you, they jumped at the chance.

These people rebuilt the East German Stasi, entirely in secret, in America. I have seen it with my own eyes, and before you finish this book, you will have seen it with your eyes as well. You will have no doubt.

And it is not just watching. I have felt the effects of directed energy weapons, and recorded the changes in EM fields, all of which is available for your review at AmericanStasi.com. I have even found cases where other Americans who have complained of the same thing have recorded almost identical recordings. This thing has grown to be far more horrific than you would think possible.

And I am not alone. This book will show you that the former head of the technology division at the National Security Agency, the man who was fourth in command at the NSA on 9/11, legendary crypto-mathematician Bill Binney, joined numerous other intelligence officers at a website, BiggerThanSnowden.com (since shut down by American Intelligence), where they all attested to the fact that the US intelligence community is zapping Americans, on American soil, through the walls of their houses, with Directed Energy Weapons (DEWs), outside of any legal or judicially approved oversight or government mandate.

As we will show you, in an interview, Bill himself will describe installing steel shielding to try and diminish the power of the energy beams reaching him, only to have his government intelligence community harassment team literally blow two holes through the steel sheeting with some kind of energy-beam weapon. Bill, formerly the head of all technology development at NSA, who oversaw all of the agency's most advanced prototype technology, will tell you he has never seen any device remotely like it.

This thing has acted, and is acting right now, criminally, to assault regular Americans, who would not casually abide by the creation of the East German Stasi in this great nation. It is happening, I have seen it myself. In this book you will be shown reams of evidence in support of it – enough that by the time you finish this book, you will have no doubts. You will know how the world really works. You will know what they have hidden from you.

Today, I would estimate the civilian informants number between 4% and 10% of the population, perhaps not quite as large as the East German Stasi's civilian operation, but supported by technologies the East German Stasi could not imagine.

By the end of this book, I think you will understand that such a circumstance, unless rigorously guarded against by stalwart patriots, willing to do anything to protect freedom, will tend to arise spontaneously, because these people will always lurk in the shadows, looking for the opportunity to seize full control.

The moment they do not encounter resistance, the moment they catch us sleeping and the population assumes it could never happen and does not actively fight against it, they will advance, and create that East German Stasi, as quickly as they can, to clamp down control.

And sadly, for many decades, now, the stalwart patriots of America have slept, confident nobody could ever seek to corrupt our great nation.

Of course of late, due to the extent of the purposeful destruction of the nation, our patriots have begun to awaken. It is becoming increasingly difficult to not see what is happening, and not realize there are great hidden forces at work, seeking to destroy the nation.

I suspect that as we reach the climax of that awakening, a great civil war is in the offing, pitting patriots against genuine traitors in service of evil - the freedom-loving Americans against the quislings spying on them for the foreign powers who seek our destruction.

It is not really our fault we slept, blind to the danger. Our "thought leaders" have long denied there was any threat of such a thing, even as accounts began to bubble up of "gangstalking," where regular people reported being placed under aggressive domestic surveillance operations designed to harass and intimidate, which sounded exactly like the old Stasi "Zersetzung" ("decomposition") gaslighting operations that were used to intimidate and harass East German citizens until they mentally broke down (decomposed).

We fell for the denials because we all assumed it was not possible. Americans would not do that to fellow countrymen. We are different.

As mass shooters, who were previously respected people,

13

like Navy Veteran and IT specialist Aaron Alexis, or Assistant District Attorney Myron Mays, suddenly went on shooting sprees, leaving behind messages claiming to have been harassed by a domestic surveillance operation of unimaginable size, we ignored the cases as aberrations.

They claimed they had been "beamed" through their walls with microwave weapons, which at the time sounded ridiculous. However we now know from the reports of Havana syndrome such weapons actually exist, they are being deployed, and they present exactly as they described. Of course as we will recount, you have to confront the fact that they described the finer nuances of something which could only have been so accurately described back then, had they actually experienced it.

We believed our government was constrained by the fact we elected our leaders, our intelligence agencies were under strict Congressional oversight and subservient to us, and our nation was ruled by a system of law and order which would punish criminality.

And of course conspiracies never form anyway, and groups never work together to break the law for personal gain, especially those in the intelligence field, because we are all too nice and people frown on that.

Finally, if all else failed, we had a free and intrepid news media, which was assiduously honest and committed to truth, uncontrolled by anyone, and not in any way attached to our intelligence services or compromised with controlled assets. It would immediately tell us if anything ever went wrong. To think anything else would be to become a dreaded conspiracy theorist, promulgating "misinformation."

It all sounds incredibly stupid and retarded when you say it out loud now. But all along the way we could see ourselves in any of those roles of authority protecting freedom, from a government worker, to an FBI Agent, to a reporter, to a politician, to an intelligence officer. We would protect freedom. And most people were like us. Why wouldn't it be like that?

The answer, in a word is "intelligence." Or rather, "intelligence officers." They are the psychopathic sharks of human society, absent all morals and decency, trained and conditioned to take power for themselves, deceive everyone, and destroy anything nice, replacing it with a controlled criminal dystopia run by them for their own personal gain.

At some point, intelligence entered the domestic American scene. It may have begun quite early in our nation's history, as a wounded King sought to regain some control over his lost colony, and set about locating and reactivating his revolutionary war spy network in the newly formed America.

Having found them it would be a small measure to simply promise them a small fortune from the King's treasury, in return for their loyalty to the supposedly defeated Monarch. In so doing, he would elevate them to high positions in American society with power and control. Then, one day they might be elected to high office, and the King they pledged loyalty to, could eventually rule a puppet government from the shadows.

From there, the network could grow, until our "leaders" were mostly under foreign control. Absent resistance, that is how it would go. That is how intelligence operates, and from what I see, there was no resistance.

Given it is estimated as much as 4% of the population is on the Antisocial (psychopathic/sociopathic) Personality Disorder spectrum,[02] there was a ready pool of recruits from the start, for any intelligence operation which required individuals with no morals, and willing to do anything for their own advancement.

In addition, an intelligence operation could augment the American population of psychopaths by preferentially importing still more foreign psychopaths which they found overseas, eager to betray anyone around them for the most minor of gains, wherever they landed in the country. All they would have to do is push the idea in society that America was not a nation of patriots, but rather a nation of immigrants.

Suddenly the American population would be swamped with a flood of migrants from Europe, the center of the conspiracy of old-world elites. Do you think any foreign European government back then might have sent agents to America, hidden within that flood of migrants, to take citizenry and operate within America as foreign agents? What if all those monarchies had been controlled, by a deeper level of elites, and all those foreign agents served one organization?

Now a foreign organization has agents in the country voting. Their children, if given wealth, can pose as respected members of high soceity, and run for office, and probably win. You see how easily regular Americans could lose control to a wealthy former conspiracy. It is far from outlandish.

Additionally, given there are numerous other potential agents within the country to be recruited, such as immigrants with citizenship issues, criminals facing lengthy prison sentences, people in financial distress, or merely the greedy and craven, it would appear this network has been easily able to build its civilian informant network up to unbelievable levels.

After decades, at least, of unfettered expansion, this network has extensively permeated through every facet of American society which has any ability to influence or educate the citizenry - politics, the judiciary, law enforcement, intelligence, arts and culture, the criminal underworld, the news media, book publishing, high finance, religion, the public and private school systems, social clubs, the private sector business environment, real estate, and on and on – it is throughout it all.

The intelligence organization's full operational structure and capability is beyond the scope of one book, and likely even several volumes. It would take a small library to do the full scale of all its operations justice, from graft, to murder, to blackmail, to narcotics importation, to psychological operations, to human trafficking, and much more. It appears to have taken most political offices, and is sustaining itself through outright graft from the national treasury, as well as several income sources in the private sector, both legitimate and criminal.

While detailing the entire operation in one book would be impossible, what the American Stasi series of books, beginning with this one, is intended to do is to expose the average citizen to the keystone of the conspiracy – the massive and sprawling domestic surveillance network made up of embedded civilians, and modeled on the East German Stasi, which this operation has constructed within the United States, and deployed in every neighborhood.

We will attempt to show you and explain each part of the exposed structural elements of the surveillance operation to monitor and observe you and your children, which you will encounter all throughout your life. You will see where its behaviors deviate from the norm, you will be shown why this happens, and you will eventually see these things in your own life, because this thing is surveilling us all.

It is our hope, once revealed, everyone will see this operation in their own neighborhoods, at which point, we as a nation can begin to figure out what needs to be done to free ourselves of this menace.

The surveillance is the most exposed portion of the conspiracy from what I see, the least professional, and the portion which you will have all around you. It will prove the most obvious piece of this conspiracy. Thus you will be able to most easily see it with your own eyes. Once you see it, you will instinctively infer the rest must exist.

If that does not make sense now, once you see the surveillance, it will. You will realize an operation that massive was created for something much bigger than any mere domestic security purpose.

This machine is a well-developed network of fellow citizens who have pledged to work for the conspiracy at the grassroots level against us, for some personal benefit. We are not entirely sure what they get, as none have yet broken ranks to explain what their motivations are, but it is probably the same as in East Germany.

First and foremost, they get some safety from the machine

itself. Later they can get access to jobs, money, power, and influence which would otherwise elude them, since the machine has structured its infiltrations of businesses to control access to all of that.

To get those benefits, these citizens are spying on everyone they know, as well as reaching out and forming "friendships" with people the conspiracy sends them to meet and spy on, so they can report back to command, and accrue their benefits.

This surveillance machine is organized, and complex. It has broken the nation up into "neighborhood" sectors. It has planted one surveillance-commander/file-archivist in command of each neighborhood sector, with several other surveillance people planted in houses which it appears the command chooses for them, to maximize the penetration and coverage of the neighborhood, as well as proximity to targets of interest.

Together they are tasked with the responsibility of using all of the assets in the neighborhood for the purpose of "knowing" everyone in the neighborhood, essentially on a personal level.

You probably have never met your archivist, but they will know you intimately. And if the machine ever needs it, they will be able to offer a profile of you as detailed as that which any loved one you know could produce, backed up with videos, audio recordings, transcripts (some incredibly private, from inside the most interior portions of your house), reports from "friends" and more.

The surveillance commander/archivist and his minions will draw upon CIA-level technologies which can backdoor your electronic devices, listen in your home, and even watch you move around in your home through the walls and ceilings.

In addition they are given the ability to co-opt other government assets, from local police officers, to civil service workers. They can even draw upon the resources of a fully functional domestic intelligence agency with capabilities ranging from diverting shipped packages and installing technology in devices you have ordered from Amazon so they can spy on you, to supplying access to the most sensitive databases in the nation, to supplying specialized teams capable of breaking into your home while you are out at work, to tasking loitering aviation assets overhead to your location which can "see" into your home through the roof, using advanced thermal imaging, radar, and other technologies.

And of course, they will draw upon the massive Stasi-like network of civilian informants, made up of four to ten percent of the population, as of this writing, who they can direct to follow and surveil you in-person periodically. You may only receive the full surveillance treatment for a few days every few years, to fill out their files, but it will allow them to make sure they know you well enough that if you ever become an issue for the machine, the machine can call them up and they will know everything about you, from what brands of food you buy, to even intimate, personal details. In the interim, they will, as part of their daily duties, periodically tune into your home as they "peek" in each house each night, just to see what your family is talking about, and what you are up to. They do not appear to concern themselves with warrants or other legal niceties.

The file on you will be massive. Your file will begin with observations of you by children of surveillance people who you went to school with, beginning as early as kindergarten. The children will provide the observations as a sort of training program which prepares them for their Stasi-responsibilities in adulthood.

However even though performed under the rubric of training, the training observations will still end up in your file, rather than be thrown away.

There may even be records of interventions in your life. As we will discuss later, it is believed now, by many who have seen the actual surveillance, that the ubiquitous *"porn fairy,"* is this operation, provisioning selected children with pornography to addict them to dopamine early in life to make them more controllable as adults. That is but one example of a number of interventions we will go into later, including interventions I saw in my own life.

As we will show, some interventions may become more ominous when the child's file indicates abilities and psychological tendencies which could prove more problematic at adulthood. From alcohol, to drugs, to actual sex and molestation, this machine will use any tool necessary to control the life-paths of the children it identifies as threats, and chooses to target.

Your file will also include material from files generated by the neighborhood surveillance of your parents, which caught material about you. Transcripts of conversations inside your childhood home, details gleaned from your family's surveillance, reports from *"family friends"* you bumped into at gatherings, who subtly pumped you for information and then gleefully delivered it to their handlers – it will all follow you for your entire life as this thing builds its picture of you.

21

As an adult, the files will contain transcripts of conversations from inside your house which were picked up when your surveillance was being periodically updated. There will be reports from people they sent in periodically to observe you, interact with you, and see what your deal was. There will even be reports from surveillance teams documenting what you purchased on some shopping outings you went out on. There may even be photographs which they took after one of the operators got on the checkout line behind you, and snapped a photo of your purchases on the conveyor, as they pretended to text message with their phone. And of course your file will have all the database stuff we already know they collect.

Of special focus will be any blackmailable information, in the event it is ever needed. Chances are, they have videos of most people in some sort of embarrassing situation, from hidden cameras capturing sex in college, to illicit drug use, to documentation of affairs, just because it is probably a mission priority to acquire that on everyone at some point, in the event it is needed one day.

The male or female archivist in your neighborhood assigned to know everyone in it, will know stuff about you that you would not believe. It is just the way it works. We gave them more money and power than the Stasi had, following 9/11, told them they could keep anything secret from us under the rubric of national security, never resisted this because we felt a dystopia such as they created could not possibly happen, and we trusted them to always be honest and upstanding.

This is what happens when you do that with intelligence officers, who are quite frankly, the scum of the earth. I am sure at times they have marveled at how foolish and naive the entire nation was. I have no doubt, they only viewed your trust of them as rank stupidity.

The sad fact is, the United States government was not special. The politicians running it were basically the same lot of scumbags and criminals as was found in the old East German politicians. The people manning our domestic intelligence machine were just as psychopathic and assiduous in their aspirations of dictatorial control as the old East German intelligence officers. None of that was different, and we were foolish enough to trust them.

The only differences today were that they have developed, and kept secret, technologies for spying on you which you would not believe possible, and the United States had a level of money to throw at all of this which the old East Germans had dared not even dream of.

If you know what to look for you will see this machine all around your neighborhood and town. There are a lot of people in the network, and it is now big enough it has people stationed at most shopping centers all of the time, waiting for priority targets to arrive to shop. You will notice certain areas always have somebody standing around. Some sidewalks which should not have much traffic will always have someone walking on them as you drive by, and when you see a news story about someone posing as a "homeless" person begging on a street corner, only to then get caught heading back to a brand new Lexus to drive home, those will very often be posted surveillance on that street corner, posing as a homeless person.

I have already been showing people this material on my website for years, and now thousands have seen it, with many coming back to excitedly report they saw their neighborhood surveillance teams, and it was everything I have told them it would be.

From readers at my site:

I finally saw the neighborhood field surveillance teams!

Earlier this week I was out with a couple of my junior engineers doing preliminary field reconnaissance for a Corps of Engineers project on the Texas gulf coast. (Miles of seawall)

We were in a neighborhood approximately 1/2 mile from the bay, We all had our safety gear on and one of us had a survey rod, another had a camera and a white board, we are looking around taking pictures of culverts and channels etc. Neighborhood has really big lots, houses are really spread out (figure 1/4 acre) in lower economic class.

We weren't parked more than 2 minutes than all of the sudden at the intersection east of us (about 50 yds) it turns into a parade. We couldn't hardly talk to each other because of the amount of road noise, in a residential neighborhood! I would say in a 2 minute span there was 15 cars/motorcycles that traveled by us.

I just started laughing and said to one of my young'ins wow it's like a parade! The engineer replied maybe it's the neighborhood watch got word that we were in the neighborhood! Very blue pilled and we all had a laugh but wow you weren't kidding on spooling up the assets when something 'strange' shows up in their area.

But it was your teaching that made me realize what was going on, not a single one of them slowed down and looked at us, even though we were stomping around with equipment and a camera with hi-viz vests. Everywhere else we stopped on that day people would look at us or stop and ask questions about what we were working on...

Fascinating to say the least.

Another reader pipes up:

I've read the stuff on surveillance including showing it through Google Streetview. But I live in suburban Melbourne Australia and have never seen it here (I do a lot of cycling, especially at the moment with the way our Dictator Daniel Andrews has us in lockdown). I like simple hypotheses to test so this morning I decided to try and prove it wrong in my allotted 2 hours of exercise.

One of the great things about cycling is that you're in touch with the environment around you in a way that is difficult in a car – you don't have the background noise of an engine when moving, you're not travelling as fast, you can sit up and look around easily. All of your senses can work unhindered. It's one of the things I've always liked about cycling but also lends itself to this sort of observation. Cars going as slowly as a bicycle will stand out easily and there's all sorts of tricks you can use to justify going slowly or stopping, forcing cars to overtake you etc.

The method I used was to try and stick to back streets as much as possible (to avoid the normal traffic that is always there on main roads) and at every intersection or decision point where I could choose from multiple directions I'd record if there was someone in a position to observe that decision. In particular I was looking for people walking/jogging close to the intersection and cars. Note that I ignored streets that were dead-ends when counting the intersections – a lot of the housing estates I rode through had heaps of short courts that didn't seem necessary to monitor since they didn't lead anywhere. I took a pretty cruisy pace – usually only 15km/h so I could focus on my surroundings.

I rode a total of 38km and counted 208 decision points. Of those 208, I was able to detect there was someone who could observe my choice at 144 of them (69%). It was a Sunday morning so a lot of people are out walking/mowing the lawn etc and on its own this number doesn't prove/disprove anything. I also probably made a few mistakes as I was keeping track in my head.

The thing that got me (and I noticed VERY quickly) was how few people I observed walking were on the long stretches between intersections – it appeared that almost everyone was walking within a short distance of intersections that were a decision point. I began to focus more on riding along streets that weren't feeder streets to observe what was happening and it became quite clear that the location of people walking was strongly biased to within a short distance of intersections that were decision points.

I also observed a lot of cars exiting their driveways as I came along. Nothing out of the ordinary here... but possibly because that's what I've always seen and it appears normal, even if statistically abnormal! One time I tried a mini experiment when I noticed a path running between two streets. I went down the path *but stopped at a point where there was only one house that could observe my location and then sat there for about 2 minutes. No cars went down either street during that time. I then took a bet with myself what was the chance that there would be a car pulling out of a driveway/starting up as I came onto the street. Sure enough, someone backed out of their driveway as I pulled onto that street. Proves nothing on its own, but adds to my suspicions!*

Another time I had a car coming behind me as I approached a T intersection. I pulled over so they would have to go first. They turned right and I slowly followed them, but stopped on the side of the road. They came to a halt in the middle of the road about 150-200m down the road and sat there for about half a minute. It was getting weird as they hadn't even pulled to the side – just stopped in the middle of the road with no plausible reason. Eventually a car in the house they were stopped in front of started backing out and as it came in site, they left. Over the next little while I felt like this scene from The Truman Show https://youtu.be/z9lBvg5clr0?t=55 with cars coming from everywhere. I'm only talking about 5 cars or so, but it seemed way out of proportion! In addition, a couple of ladies came along delivering junk mail and stood at the corner across the road from me for a minute or so discussion where to go next. They had come along the street I'd just come from and I didn't notice them. I wish I had a video camera to go back and see if I had passed them earlier!

In the 5 minutes or so I sat at that spot, I saw about 4 cars pull into or out of houses in one short section (where that first car stopped in the middle of the road). It really makes we wonder if there's something special about that location!

It would be really interesting to do a statistical analysis of where people are walking. When you regularly go along back streets that are 500-800m long and don't see anyone walking along the sections away from the end intersections (or only rarely) and then consistently find people within 20-50m of the intersection, you have to wonder what the odds of it are as I'm pretty sure it's way outside what you'd expect to see!

I'm probably doomed to always notice this now – thanks!

Another reader, another awakening:

I had never talked about your site to my wife before but after reading that post I mentioned it to her explaining what you had said. We regularly go for an evening walk on a bike path that parallels the main road into our neighborhood. On that evening as we started walking to the west a small Cessna airplane began flying a pattern. They'd fly toward the road, turn parallel to the road, then fly some distance to the northwest then west and loop back. Every time on the return leg, the plane reached the road at the point adjacent where we were on the bike path. This continued for several miles until we reached the end of the path. Normally we stop there and admire the sun setting behind the mountains. When we stopped this time the plane no longer continued moving to the west but looped so that when it reached the road it was consistently across from where we were standing. Then as we started back home the plane now flew the pattern to the east, again reaching the road at the point where we were walking. Finally, I said let's stop and see what happens. We stood there for a good 10 minutes and the plane stayed in a pattern to always reach the road where we were standing. When we started walking again, the plane again tracked us until we reached the road to our house at which point it flew away. That experience made me a believer in what you say. I think the reason they did what they did is exactly what you've said many times. They do it because they can. Because they get bored and because they like to mess with people. I'm not important to any one in any way so it's not about that. It's because, as you've said, they can do it so they do it for whatever reason. In this particular instance I think they happened to be monitoring our home, heard what I said, and decided to have some fun. For context we've lived here for several years. I have never before or since seen any planes flying patterns around here. I'm outdoors a lot because I enjoy being outside, so I know I would have noticed if flying patterns around here was a regular occurrence.

There have been many more over the years. The American Stasi is everywhere, and if you are an independent thinker, they will be well acquainted with you, your file will be substantial, and you will have watchers. We were merely told it did not work this way because they wanted us to remain weak, vulnerable, and unaware.

You will be doubtful at this point. I do not blame you, I would have been as well, before I saw the surveillance. Seeing it is shocking, and indeed it took me probably five years of seeing it over and over, overtly harassing me each and every day, before I could come to accept it could exist.

This is probably a good time to show you what that shocking experience is like, so here I would ask you go to the following web address, and examine this video, shot by a young woman who encountered the surveillance. Imagine this is you, and you begin seeing this every day, every single time you go out:

https://www.bitchute.com/video/t2Z2f1SEqAlU/

or

https://files.catbox.moe/c92u1b.mp4

Bear in mind, that is not a small surveillance unit which rolled out of some building in DC, flew to that area, and targeted that girl. That is a small handful of individuals who live in that community. They belong to a massive local "secret society" of surveillance people, which will number in the thousands, maybe the tens of thousands, and in major cities, hundreds of thousands of people. They all work for the American Stasi, which itself appears to have some sort of federal imprimatur, and they have hidden that secret from all of us.

That organization is always operational there, 24/7, watching everyone in that locality, almost always covertly, as a sort of Stasi Secret Police. For some reason, she angered the wrong people, and it is revealing itself to her there, to intimidate her and degrade her quality of life. It happens to a lot of us. It is not that well known only because most Americans would never believe fellow Americans would be a part of something so criminal, and treasonous, which so directly contravenes every principle of freedom and privacy in America. The people involved know how regular Americans would feel about their involvement in that, and they keep that secret from us very effectively.

By the time you finish this book, you will be able to see those people in your own community, even when they are trying to remain covert. This is important, because their operation is presently trying to destroy America for some reason. Its main advantage is, nobody knows it is out there, or could believe it, even if shown it. If we can make every American see them, and know they are out there, we will rob them of 95% of their advantage against us. We might even be able to turn the government on their operation, and we might just save the nation from collapse

Presently almost everyone knows something is destroying this nation. This operation gives you a plethora of red herrings, which appear to be responsible, each custom designed to appeal to one group. Conservatives are told it is liberals. Liberals are told it is conservatives. Racists are told it is minorities. Antisemites are told it is "the Jews." Minorities are told it is whites. Immigrants, Soros DA's, the Russians, even the Police get blamed.

Meanwhile, the American Stasi, made up of individuals from every race, religion, and classification, from the shadows, promulgates all of those red herrings to distract you, as the people you see in that video help it to control everyone by watching everything - and intervening in select lives, to derail anyone who might be able to threaten them. And nobody even knows it exists.

As a result, the patriots in our nation are paralyzed. Nobody really knows what is going on, or who is responsible. As a result, nobody can find who is responsible, deal with them as enemies, or resist the nation's destruction.

I want to change that. I want to reveal the enemy and draw the battle lines. If this nation is to fall, let it fall in glorious battle with a roar, and not in paralysis with a whimper. In truth, I think just by revealing this, we will save the nation and emerge victorious.

For that, I need your help, and I am begging you for it.

My website doesn't spread online as well as it should. We are actively suppressed by the intelligence operations assigned to control the dialog online, to a degree you would not believe.

Antivirus programs will try to divert readers away from my site, despite the fact I hired a professional service which scans my site regularly and would not allow any malware on it. Others report that they will try to visit, only to be told there is nothing at the address. Some readers have noted that while they can see my site, other parts of the internet are walled off from them, possibly to prevent them from spreading information outward. A reader once sat down with two other people, and found that their phone and computer would not display the social media pages of the people they sat down with, as if they did not exist. Those people could not find their own social media pages, when using my reader's computers. They were walled off from each other.

When I check Google, and do searches for specific topics I have covered on my site, Google will not show those pages, but will instead return pages from my site to me with material completely unrelated to what I was looking for.

Given the mechanisms this thing has to stifle the spread of ideas online, I'm going to need your help to spread this.

First, I need you to learn what this book teaches. The book will begin by showing you what surveillance looks like in Russia. We will use Google Streetview to tour a small neighborhood in Russia, and as the Google car drives around taking pictures, you will get to see a real Russian surveillance team track it, using all the techniques of covert surveillance. We will explain what you are seeing, how to tell it is surveillance, as well as why they are utilizing each of their techniques.

Once you have seen one elite foreign surveillance team, and begun to familiarize yourself with how to spot elite-level covert surveillance, we will take you to Bulgaria, and show you how the Bulgarians do it. You will see all the same techniques, repeated slightly differently, by actual real-world surveillance, but you will immediately see how these techniques are being done for the same purposes.

From there, we will hit the Midwest of America. There you will see the same techniques employed by the American Stasi, and realize, the Google car is being surveilled right here in America, by a Secret Police made up of regular citizens from the town, and you will realize, the operation is so large it is nearly unbelievable. Then we will show it to you in Southern California, before heading up to the remote wilds of Alaska. Even there, in the remote wilds of Alaska, you will see that the prying eyes of the American Stasi never blink.

Then we are going to take a moment to show you how the surveillance appears to be involved in some murders of innocent citizens, so you will process that what you are seeing is a criminal surveillance operation, and not regular national security or law enforcement, even if it bears some governmental imprimatur.

From there, we will show you some videos of what the foot surveillance in America looks like, from the little children of the surveillance people, employed in the local schools to target other children, to the adults who send you off from your home, and then swarm you in the department store.

At that point we will show you how esteemed individuals

from all walks of society, from the intelligence community, to the government, have discussed this surveillance, and even been assaulted with directed energy weapons in their homes.

To emphasize the operation's criminality, we will then review the cases of a sizable number of the law enforcement officers it has gotten killed, before we move on, and discuss what needs to be done to free our people and save our nation from this plague - and how to operate against it.

We will finish with a general look at what the future likely holds, and how beautiful this nation will be once we are rid of the surveillance and exist as one united nation without these criminals, before finally asking you to help us spread this work by sending a few chain letters around, anonymously.

I have invested everything I have in this work. I have put my mind, body and soul into it, even as I was getting zapped in the head, in the middle of the night by an energy beam to degrade my brain function. I have endured some fairly intense slings and arrows for my country, and the people in it who are my kind of American. I have zero problem dying for this cause.

My only request in return is, if you are my kind of obstinately patriotic American, and find this work worthy, and if you too love this country and want it to save it, make a few copies of a chain letter and send them around so we can make everyone aware of this horrific abomination, and we can begin the work we will need to do together, as one nation united, in order to be rid of the American Stasi.

I have tried spreading this online, but that environment is too controlled. For this to spread, we must return to the way of the

Founders, and use the good old fashioned method of pamphleteering in real life, which ignited the first Revolution. For our purposes, the old tricks are the best tricks, even in the age of technology. I can almost hear the Founders laughing.

We will be rid of this. But we will need every patriotic American to focus all of their energies on making every other American, regardless of race, religion, political ideology, or other factor, aware of this. When it comes to the American Stasi, it is screwing over all of us, from the poorest minority Democrat in the inner city, to the most rural Republican in the Midwest.

The truth is, all of those political fights are pointless anyway. Nobody has won a political battle in America in decades, because this thing controls all of that. I know, I was an ideologue in politics. This thing looked me over, didn't like what it saw, and took me out of the game in politics.

The only people it lets win its rigged elections, are controlled assets. When you fight over issues, be it guns, abortion, taxes, budgets, the outcome is preordained. This thing tells its controlled assets – your "elected" leaders - what to do. They are all compromised. They all know about the American Stasi and fear it. You can't get near power without it flexing its muscles at you, and you only get to obtain power if you capitulate. You may think you "won" or lost, but you had no effect. It wants you to fight those pointless battles which it controls the outcome of, so you will never turn on it, and maybe secure your freedom for real.

Barack Obama became President because this thing pulled a switch and put him in office. Donald Trump won because somebody pulled a switch as well, and it could just as easily have been pulled for Hillary. Joe Biden too. If you think 2020's election was rigged, you will have to acknowledge it was probably not the first time. There are possible indications of some sort of struggle within those upper levels, and perhaps the people who pulled the switch for Trump were different from the people who pulled the switch for Obama, but no matter. Switches were being pulled for some time. You are not electing anyone, or winning any political battle, until the American Stasi is dealt with. You will not have any effect in the political realm until then. It is all controlled, for now.

If we are to defeat the American Stasi, and reestablish our elected republic, where the people have the power, we will all have to unite as Americans, regardless of all our differences, against this traitorous force within our nation. We will have to set aside our differences, put our debates and fights on pause, and come together as one American team, until we have dealt with the American Stasi within our borders. There will be no ideology in this war for every American's freedom and the future of our country, aside from opposing the tyranny of the American Stasi. You will not save this nation, unless you can unite. From here on out it will be us, vs them, and every real American who is not in the Stasi will be your brother.

Now, on to your training.

Chapter Two

The Google Streetview Surveillance Course

Here is where your operational training will begin. I have offered this same material on a website for years, and I have lost count of how many people took this course, and came back to me shocked, as they suddenly realized their entire town was rife with a massive domestic surveillance operation, which in some cases had been tracking them, presumably for visiting my website.

If we do this right, you will be intrigued by the strange things you will see in Russia, it will hold your interest, and as time goes on you will learn what you should expect to see when surveillance is operative around you.

Once you are programmed this way, to see the surveillance on Google Streetview, you will notice it when you encounter it in real life, roving around town looking for anything interesting, or even following you. It is everywhere in the US, and you have already been followed numerous times in the course of your life, just as part of the normal monitoring the local neighborhood units will give everyone for a few days every year or two.

This is high level training, and even our best government operatives do not get trained in this way. The American Stasi sees to it even our elite CIA and Special Operations personnel are never trained in ways which would allow them to operate against it.

37

I think the best example of this can be found in the story of Thomas Mixon.[03] When legendary Navy SEAL commander Richard Marcinko came to the end of his tenure as the commander of the most elite SEAL Team, SEAL Team Six, which he founded, he ended up transferred out from under the Navy and directly attached to the Department of Defense, where he was tasked with forming an even more elite and more secretive covert operations unit, which he called Red Cell.

Attached directly below the Secretary of Defense and outside of the military's normal chain of command, Marcinko was told to handpick the absolute best Special Operations personnel for this new unit, which was to be the most elite in the United States, and which would handle the most secretive black operations.

He proceeded to choose roughly 40 of the best Navy SEALs from Team Six, as well as a few other operators from other areas of the government, including some Marine snipers, and even a CIA operative he had become acquainted with in the course of his work. Once in Red Cell, their jobs were two-fold. By day, they played the role of a "red team" for training operations – a unit which would simulate terrorist attacks on US facilities, so security forces could see how best to defend against them.

In that role, they took the most extensive training in every field, from stunt driving, to intelligence operations, to helicopter piloting, to rock climbing. His black budget for training was reportedly almost limitless. His operators could do everything from surgery in a battlefield environment to flying and landing a 747 jumbo jet. They then took those skills and practiced elite, tier-one level assaults on hardened US government installations, simulating everything from attacks on embassies to assassinations of government officials. They even famously parked a pallet of simulated explosives on a forklift next to Air Force One in one training operation.

These training operations were then to be used by the facilities he attacked, to harden their own security, and close up any security holes. In the meantime, Marcinko's unit became the most proficient in the country, and maybe the world, at hard-target assaults. Reportedly, in between official duties, they were employed to do everything from wiping out terrorist training camps, to breaking into foreign facilities to steal intelligence.

You get the picture. Under that facade, Marcinko's team was the very tip of the Tier-One black operations spear. They were the best of the best, schooled in everything needed to operate against a fully funded first-world government, organized so nobody provided them with oversight, and whatever they were doing could be hidden and denied, with nobody the wiser.

Marcinko even modeled the team's structure to mimic the highly adaptive, agile, and mobile aspects of a terrorist cell, so it could deploy on a moment's notice and attack anywhere, absent the bureaucracy and red tape of the regular military.

But oddly his team was never schooled on the domestic Stasi-like surveillance network, made up of regular citizens, which it seems is run in most Western governments.

His operatives, the baddest of the bad in the world, were helpless when pitted against the overweight geriatrics, chubby soccer moms, tattooed, pot-smoking hippies, and degenerate voyeurs of the American Stasi's civilian informant network.

How do we know they were never trained to operate against it? One of Marcinko's most elite operators was a SEAL named Thomas Mixon. Handpicked out of SEAL Team Six, as a member of Red Cell, this man was a machine, schooled in everything needed to operate kinetically in a hostile environment, against the best security that the most elite governments had to offer.

He left the SEALs, heading to civilian life, where he began a business as a personal trainer. You would think, if personal training were a meritocracy, he would have been the richest and most successful. Not many can say they have survived SEAL training, and taken their own body to such a height of fitness they are judged not just superior to normal SEALs, and selected for Team Six, but then judged more capable than the SEALs of Team Six, and hand picked for an even more elite unit. However he never made it into the upper echelons of personal training and fitness, and began to fail financially.

For reasons known only to himself, as he spiraled financially, he appears to have decided that he would put his unique skillset to use robbing banks. Following a short spree of robberies, the man trained to detect and evade normal government surveillance of the most hardened, sensitive facilities, was taken down almost immediately in a sting which timed its approach to him just as he exited his house to go to his truck, without any firearm on him. His neighborhood Stasi unit was even watching him in his house, to time their approach of him and make sure he was not armed.

An above-tier-one Special Operations operator did not know there is a Stasi-like operation, embedded in American society, watching everyone, all the time, made up of regular civilians who look entirely normal, and often, pathetic, even. He had no idea as a former above-Tier-One operator, he would have been given his own full time surveillance, tasked from his local population's ever-present coverage, and that the moment be began robbing banks, they would have identified him and tracked him.

And I have seen that elsewhere. There is a video of a CIA surveillance training tape you can find online, which had been given to the most elite intelligence officers in America as part of their training. It showed them how to perform the traditional "three-car follow" of a surveillance target.[04]

Yet as they were attempting to execute that "three-car follow" technique in the video, using only six people in three cars, all around them the domestic Stasi of their host nation, which will also be present throughout Europe, was tracking them, with posted surveillance that looked just like regular people on street corners and at intersections, calling their path of travel over the radio, all as they passed by, oblivious.

As you develop to see the surveillance, understand just how elite a body of knowledge you are being imbued with. As the most elite operators in the world strut around, playing James Bond, they seem wholly oblivious to the fact this thing surrounds them, and is entirely on top of them. Whether mafiosos, heading out to "whack" a rival, bank robbery crews about to knock over an armored car, cat burglars stealing high-priced art, or FBI surveillance tracking a terrorist, none of them seem to have any idea this thing is all around them at all times, running circles around their operations.

So how do we intend to impart this knowledge to you?

41

These lessons are premised on the fact the Google Car, which drives around taking 360 degree photos of streets for Google Streetview, is actually under surveillance itself.

We will first show this in Russia, since Russia is obviously hostile to the West, and would be suspicious of the car. However we will then show that as you move through nations, into the Western political sphere, the surveillance you saw, first in Russia, and then Bulgaria, actually becomes more intense in the Western nations.

All along the way in these lessons, we will include links in the endnotes so you can go online, to the Google image we show here in the book, and retrace our steps, and see everything the Google car saw, as it happened.

It is very clever, as it essentially puts you behind the eyes of someone who is a target of this domestic surveillance machine. Even the most hardened skeptic will be impressed.

Let us begin.

Chapter Three

Surveillance Detection – The Professional Course Of Real Life Experience - Russia

So you want to know if someone is following you. Real surveillance detection has an artistic aspect. You can't learn it just from reading a book or a website. The real art is a secret skill, kept almost entirely secret from regular people, save for what you are about to read. However even after reading this text, you will still need to spend some time practicing it, before your mind will develop an almost psychic intuition regarding what belongs in the environment around you, and what is just pretending to belong.

Even worse, most texts are so incorrect in their assertions they are almost disinformation. As an example, if you purchase a text on the subject of surveillance detection, you are most often told detection revolves around the principles of TEDD, which stands for Time, Environment, Distance, and Demeanor.

You watch everyone around you, and look for the same people, or cars, or other facets of the environment reappearing over different areas, some time (T) apart, in different environments (E) or some distance apart (D), as you scan for people which exhibit unusual demeanors (D). Time, Environment, Distance, Demeanor – TEDD.

As an extreme example, stop by the gun store, and then

visit the local office for Handgun Control Inc. 100 miles away three days later, and if you see the exact same guy, getting out of the same car, in both places, looking awkward and nervous, you can assume he is following you. That would be a different Time, and different Environment (right-wing vs left-wing), a sizable Distance, and a suspicious Demeanor.

That form of detection works best for targets who expect to be followed by individuals or small teams, where the opposing force (OpFor) cannot rotate large numbers of faces or vehicles around you. If you are a terrorist or a drug kingpin, facing an underfunded DEA team, maybe it works well.

But those who run this world run an operation far bigger than you could imagine, a civilian informant network at least as big as the Stasi, and maybe bigger. They can follow you all day, to hundreds of places, over hundreds of miles, letting you see their operatives thousands of times, and not show you the same faces or cars twice.

It is a massive force combining seasoned and trained surveillance officers, and lower level civilian informants/surveillance who have signed on to follow their orders. If you have surveillance problems with the American Stasi, TEDD is of little use.

If you want to detect Stasi surveillance, you have to look for subtle movements around you which betray controlled and practiced maneuvers designed to help a large operation make sure it sees everything you do and everyone you contact.

They will be performed by an unrecognizable array of different people and vehicles, but the patterns of movement will be the same, and will eventually start to jump out at you.

This is more of an art form. Those who have not developed it will tend to not see the indices that become apparent to you when you have developed it. It is almost like going from being colorblind to seeing in color, and after a time the ability becomes a vision of the world you can't unsee.

If you want to develop the ability, you have to be put under surveillance, and see it firsthand. Surveillance operators try to hide, and appear as if just normal people passing through your space, so spotting them can be difficult. It is made even more difficult by the fact that these will all be different people, since the network that they have amassed is so massive.

If you are reading this you are probably under this surveillance right now. As part of its monitoring of the population, it has identified free thinkers and individualists, and it targets them in every community, keeping a watchful eye on them. They will view you as a tier one threat, since you would not want to live under their shadow dictatorship, if you saw it. All that is keeping you from seeing it are the ingrained biases instilled by your societal programming, which tell you this could never happen in America - and anyone who thinks it could is, ipso facto, mentally ill and someone to be shunned by society.

I've spent a lot of time thinking about this, because one of the things I think will free our society is if I can train people to recognize the surveillance around them. The surveillance is the most visible part of the domestic Stasi's operations, and its biggest Achilles' heel. If everyone sees it, if everyone understands how it is operating against them, a groundswell can be built to destroy

45

this machine.

But to do that I knew I would need a way to have everyone have the experience of being put under surveillance, while knowing they have been put under surveillance, so when they see the indices, they know they are real. Once conditioned to see them here, they will see them in their own neighborhoods, and the US domestic surveillance wing of the American Stasi will no longer be able to advance in the nation unopposed.

What we are going to do is take a spin around the world on Google Streetview. There, you are going to see what surveillance looks like, firsthand, with your own eyes, as real life covert surveillance people follow you in the Google car, executing all the techniques of advanced surveillance.

We will begin in Russia, where we'll run an actual counter-surveillance detection route, in real life, customized to exaggerate the differences in patterns of activity around you that you will see while under surveillance. You will be looking at real spies, doing real spy stuff to you, and you will never leave the seat you are sitting in right now. When you finish, you will have the training and experience which previously was only available to top-tier operators who had been lucky enough to get the most demanding espionage assignments in hostile nations. Most importantly, you will not only become a capable operator yourself, you will see how utterly helpless you are right now, and how incapable you were of protecting freedom in America.

Before we begin, some basics on surveillance detection. Surveillance detection is a game of recognizing probabilities. You don't get 100 percent certainty in the business of detection. You will rarely be lucky enough to be able to say, "There is a definite surveillance operative, now I know I am under coverage!" It does not work that way.

Surveillance tries to look like normal people going about their day, so you cannot look at an operator, and be sure that they are part of a team tailing you.

So what you do when you begin learning detection, is you perform actions, which if there were no surveillance, would likely result in you being alone. Now somebody may show up by chance at that moment. But you are playing probabilities. So you do it again. Maybe somebody else shows up by chance again. But if you do it ten times, and you should have been alone each time, and you were not, you can begin to conclude that the probability dictates, you are being followed.

So you won't know with 100 percent certainty whether each person you see in the following courses is a spy following you. Many surveillance operators will look like normal people going about their business while operating, because that is what they are trained to do.

But you will know you are under real-life surveillance coverage, with real-life covert surveillance operators, because it is the Google car operating in hostile territory. And that will produce enough weirdness for you to get an idea of what real life, first-rate coverage will look like. Most importantly, it will show you how probabilities build up as time goes on, and the repeated small-probability observations indicative of likely surveillance coverage begin to amass into an overall conclusion that you have surveillance.

47

As you do this, you may begin to feel what surveillance people look like. There is a quality many of them have, kind of like distracted, kind of under tension, kind of faking interest in anything but you, kind of like even though technically they could belong, they do not. I actually had a German Shepherd who could feel when surveillance people were trying to look, while pretending to look away.

I had played a game with him from when he was a puppy, where I would pretend to ignore him as I inched closer, trying to steal his tennis ball. He would wait and laugh at me, sometimes even barking and lunging, to make me jump as I inched closer looking at the clouds, ignoring him. When my surveillance began, he doubtless saw our game in the weirdos popping up all over, and he would bark at them. Never normal people, just the surveillance people trying to look, while faking their interest elsewhere.

With practice, you will learn to feel them too.

After your first run through Russia, we will do it again through Bulgaria, and again, and more after that, eventually bringing the lessons home to America. What you will notice is the same weirdness repeats, because surveillance follows procedures and develops shortcuts, and these tend to be the same wherever it operates.

So you will see the same events again and again, under the same circumstances. Operators show up at specific critical moments in your travel, they take specific positions, to minimize their exposure and gain an optimal sightline to you, and then they are not present at other junctures in your travels which surveillance does not typically concern itself with. It develops a feel. You will realize they would want to know what you are about to do, you will expect one, and there one will be, waiting for you to make your decision, and you will feel a sense of disingenuousness radiating off him.

Of course, once you process this information, you will be really dangerous. We see preppers online try to make people capable of surviving the Apocalypse by making them "dangerous" in various ways. We see tactical websites talk about the bright, shiny pieces of being dangerous, like weapons choices, tactics, fortifications, improvised explosives, defensive hand to hand techniques, knife fighting, security procedures, and so on.

I was enthralled by, and studied most of it in my youth. There are hacks to make your car more bullet resistant, or scientific tests of the best weapons sights for use with night-vision.

Firearms especially are undergoing a renaissance of technological sophistication with thermal imaging red-dots at budget price points, and a plethora of brands of infra-red lasersights, only visible through night vision devices. As of this writing a video is circulating showing the latest thermal riflescope, which produces so detailed an image you can identify a coyote at 500 yards out in pitch blackness, solely off the thermal emissions of its body heat, with zero ambient light, and place a bullet accurately enough to take it down.

Night vision using traditional intensifier tubes to see in minimal light are being blended with thermal imaging into dual-spectrum binocular devices, allowing one to see in the dark while enemy forces show up as brightly lit bodies of heat on the image, no matter how camouflaged they are, or how dark it is.

Surveillance cameras and security systems are also advancing similarly.

There are endless threads on the benefits of different bullet brands, and how to be self-sufficient in everything from medicine to metalworking as everything falls apart. I will tell you, when you are talking about really surviving in a hostile environment, all of that is only 5% of being dangerous, if even.

Because the real battles are won before they are fought, and before you ever get the chance to use any of that pretty, shiny, attention-grabbing stuff.

Those battles are won before they are fought with intelligence operations. And intelligence operations may begin with database dumps and chair-borne research, but the meat and potatoes is actual, physical surveillance of the target, from vehicular and foot, to electronic monitoring, to infiltration. Being able to see surveillance, will make you untouchable on a whole new level, against the most professional enemies you will face.

You will see it treated as common knowledge, from a CIA assault on a foreign terrorist safehouse, to an Al Qaida terrorist attack. They will all perform detailed surveillance of the target, before doing anything. That surveillance is the weak point, where their operation is most vulnerable to exposure, and it can then be prepared for.

Has anyone performed detailed surveillance on you? Would it give your leaders a power over you, if they had, and they knew what guns you owned, where in your house you hide your gold, or that your son has been known to keep some weed, an illegal narcotic, in your home? Is the United States government so responsible with your money, and its leaders so moral and committed to freedom they would not have sought that advantage? Do you trust the powers running the United States government to look at the power the Stasi gave the East German government, and not seek to gain that power for themselves?

I almost wonder if the government is out there promoting debates on the utility of a subcompact .22LR pistol vs a 25 ACP, or pushing the AK-47 vs AR-15 comparison in an apocalypse scenario. If you were not discussing those comparatively meaningless survival/defense topics on your own, have no doubt the government would have agents out there promoting those conversations to keep you from studying intelligence/surveillance – the one subject which would make you truly dangerous – and the one subject which if understood, would actually promote freedom as much as, if not more than, the Second Amendment has historically.

Because a good intelligence operation, by winning the war before it is fought, without the victims even aware there was a battle, makes the Second Amendment's ability to help an oppressed population fight an overbearing government utterly useless. And believe me, they are running a very good intelligence/surveillance operation out there on all of us as you are reading this. The Second Amendment is at this moment, useless to resist this machine, given nobody even knows it exists, or has intervened in their lives, or the lives of their children. Indeed, as a nation we are armed to the teeth, and yet we are all helpless as we watch our beautiful nation torn apart and destroyed. And we know it is purposeful. But we cannot figure out how to stop it. That is the power of intelligence, and it begins with surveillance.

Reveal the surveillance, and we will begin on the path to reclaiming our nation and rescuing her.

Now one final word of caution before we begin. You will likely see surveillance in your actual real life if you begin practicing this. I estimate the Secret Society of informers, which those who rule over us have recruited within the US, comprises between 4% and 10% of the population, at least. It could be even bigger than that.

That was the size which a tentative pilot program for such an operation, called Operation TIPS, envisioned. Operation Tips was created after 9/11,[05] and by most media accounts was going to create a network of civilian informers for the government which would have been as large as that run by the East German Stasi, just as a pilot program. When word broke of it in the media, Congress made it expressly illegal, and it was supposed to be dismantled.

My assumption was it already existed prior to the formation of the program, and the program was an attempt to make it fully legal, to cover the collective asses of everyone involved.

Obviously a program exactly like it, only much larger now, continues to exist, so I assume they just continued it as it was, prior to the outrage - deep in the shadows, as a dangerous secret which they all pray every night will never be revealed.

So if this is past the pilot phase of Operation Tips, and is reaching maturity as I suspect, it is not impossible we are approaching 10% of the population operating as junior surveillance G-men, available for surveillance or harassment duties for whatever organization is really running things in the US.

Undoubtedly it focuses coverage on those who are awakened, on the left and right, whether they are active in BLM, or Antifa, or the Tea Party, or the NRA, or are just generally aware of the corruption of the system. Just you knowing this material will make you interesting to them if they find out you are aware – because it will make you a little dangerous yourself, in that you could help reveal the secret.

If you get coverage, I cannot tell you what the real life risks are long term, if they find out you know about them. I am still figuring that out myself.

It would obviously be best if they did not know you know about them. If you practice this detection skill in real life, and see your surveillance, as the kids say, hide your power level, and try to not let them know that you know. You will pose the biggest threat, in their eyes, once they realize you know.

Notice, but don't notice, and never think you can tell anyone about it or talk about it, whether in the car, or even in the deepest recesses of your house. The remote eavesdropping technologies they issue everyone, are to die for. They listen in moving vehicles all the time, and the neighborhood monitors are listening all throughout everyone's houses. It is my belief they tune their devices to each person's house, and run each of those feeds into an interface which makes listening in houses in the neighborhood kind of like switching between radio stations on their computer. And they will have a monitor on duty 24/7 whose entire job is to switch around, looking for anything interesting.

They are listening everywhere – especially where you think they never could, and where you would utter your deepest, darkest secrets. They know to focus there most of all, where you think they're least likely to listen, since the best secrets will be there.

So if you notice it, make it your secret which never leaves your lips, and enjoy noticing it without showing any external sign you noticed it. Enjoy fooling them. It is easier said than done, because when the shock hits of how big this thing is, and that it is targeting you, your brain will explode.

So if you see it, put on a pokerface and act as if you notice nothing, and know, if they are there, you cannot tell anyone around you anything, because they will hear it, and you cannot let them see, that you see them.

OK, now a little on Google Streetview, the virtual reality 3D world that Google constructed from actual pictures, taken by a Google car with a giant camera ball on it, which takes pictures in all directions as it drives on roads. In Streetview, you can go on your computer to any road it has mapped, and turn around in any direction, even looking straight up, from any point, and look around as if you were there. You will see what the Google car's cameras saw at the moment it was there, in that spot.

Did you ever wonder, what would it cost to actually drive almost every street in the world, with a 3D 360 degree camera ball, snapping 50 pictures per second, and then upload all of them to servers all over the world over a satellite uplink as you drive? Did you wonder what it would cost, to take all of those pictures, and assemble them, using a database program that could actually organize all of it into a 3D model, and deliver it over the internet to anyone who wanted it, at a rate of a hundred thousand users simultaneously at a time? Do you know how much the bandwidth costs to run a small, primarily text-based website? What do you think imagery-based Streetview costs Google?

What does just the bandwidth cost? What is the cost of the computing power to create that virtual 3D world? What is the cost of maintaining servers with enough memory capacity to store multiple photos from almost any point, on any road, in the world? Let alone the cars and drivers and electricity, and camera balls, and so on. Did Google do that just for us to cruise the streets and make fun of people we find captured in the images, on Reddit?

Suppose, just for the sake of argument, Google Streetview wasn't some altruistic pie in the sky effort by a bunch of geeks to waste hundreds of millions of dollars and *"share knowledge with the world."* Suppose Google Streetview was a CIA operation, designed as a cover story, to produce a 3D map of the globe, for operational purposes, so CIA could better run snatch and grabs, and dead drops, and meetups and so on, by allowing operatives to see where they would be operating, before they got on scene?

Suppose you have to get something from beside a bridge in Moscow. Imagine if you could actually rehearse your approach, using a computer model composed of actual pictures of the area, and see where you would be most exposed, and where you would have the most cover. Imagine you could see exactly where the package would be hidden, where surveillance might hide to catch you, where you might be ambushed after retrieving it.

Wouldn't it be great to have a 3D virtual reality world you could enter, and see the place before you ever went there?

There is one problem. Vladimir Putin isn't going to let CIA run a giant camera ball all over his country, so they can more effectively operate against him.

But Google can go there. If you ever use Google Streetview around sensitive sites in the US, you notice more often than not the interesting stuff gets the old 2007, overexposed, low-res treatment. Not so in Russia, or China. So if Google Streetview is a CIA op, it would make sense foreign powers would treat it with hostility.

Imagine in Russia, a US company car, in their homeland, with a giant ball camera, two feet in diameter, three feet up in the air over the car on a pole, with fifty cameras on it pointed in all directions, and hundreds of wires zip-tied and run into the car, recording fifty different shots in all directions.

That is a huge red flag which any foreign intelligence agency is going to want to keep an eye on.

For all they know, an enemy may have hacked the feed, and paid off the driver to take it by sensitive government facilities as an intelligence gathering tool in preparation for an attack. It might not even be a real Google car, but rather be a spoofed car from a foreign agency sent in to look like a Google car and surveil something.

So any foreign intelligence service is going to follow it just to keep an eye on it, document where it goes, and exactly what it sees. They can't just leave that be, especially in a foreign country that is not on good terms with the United States.

Moreover, the Google car is a good choice for our purposes because while they need to keep an eye on it, it is probably not a tier-one threat that will run counter-surveillance detection routes and try to uncover them, and be ultra surveillance-aware. So the following team is not going to break out their "A" game when following it, like they would with a trained spy. They'll be around, they'll be in shots, but they won't be in ultra-stealth mode like they would following an elite CIA officer meeting his best source.

Now, how do you run a counter-surveillance detection route, to spot if those spooks are following you, and you have *"grown a tail,"* as the spies say?

The answer is simple. You head somewhere where you should not see people, and then see if you end up seeing people. If you unexpectedly go in an empty store, early in the morning when nobody should be in it, and right after you enter, three people walk in and spread out in the store, the chances are good you have company. If they behave unusually, like trying to keep you from seeing their faces, so they can continue to follow you in the future without you recognizing them, you have even more indicators. If you repeat that fifty times, and never manage to tour a store alone, and the people keep behaving unusually, you can get to a point where you will be pretty sure you have a hidden entourage.

So here, we are going to drive around and look for people following us or looking at us in places where we shouldn't see too many people, and we will look for things they do that are unusual. It is limited, as Google tends to stay on roads. It would be nice to walk a park or duck down an alley, but we will find some spots.

And so we are ready to begin. Here, we will take a little flight over Russia, and look for a nice area, rural, without apartments (which will increase foot traffic and dilute the surveillance signal with lots of regular people walking around). It should have winding roads that will curtail long sightlines so they will have to have people either follow you in a car closely to keep an "eye" on you at all times, or pass you in the oncoming lane frequently, or take to foot and loiter as you pass by to keep an "eye" on you as you go out of view. We do not want long straight roads, where one car, a mile back and almost out of sight, can watch you through binoculars.

For the same reason, we don't want a massive flat area where one guy can park in a parking lot in the center, and watch you travel the entire route. You need terrain to hide you, and bring them in close. And we will look for roads that should not have a lot of traffic in the middle of the day because they only serve a smallish number of houses or industrial operations. They also need to not be good for traveling from one heavily populated place to another as a shortcut.

Basically we want to reduce the normal population level so the surveillance signal stands out more and is easier to see, while making sure the area is difficult to surveil without sending in large numbers of people, all to maximize that surveillance signal.

All along the way we will keep an eye out for strange behaviors, loitering, and people that appear stationed at intersections ("commit units" that call the path you take at "decision points," like intersections, so the team which is staying in a "floating box" just out of your sight can rush around the margins, out of your sight to get ahead of you and keep you in "the box," without you seeing them do so).

It's going to be fun. You will be blown away.

Basically, we will cruise around and see how often we enjoy a little bit of solitude, and how often our solitude is interrupted by an "innocent" citizen or car just happening by innocently, just as we are about to decide to go left or right or straight, and then we will scrutinize the interloper to see why you should give them a second glance when performing surveillance detection.

We will begin this journey in Russia because we need a place where Americans will assume there is hostile surveillance. Since Russia gets demonized so much, and Americans would assume a Google car would get surveillance because of the "hostile" relationship, it will be our first choice.

I actually came upon this method of training, cruising around Russia, looking at what it would be like to relocate there, to get away from my own local American Stasi teams and their tender, directed energy ministrations of the night.

When cruising around on Google Street View, you can click the transparent arrows on the screen to move in the direction you are pointing (and the farther away you click, the farther you jump), or you can press the up and down arrow keys to move one step in the direction you are pointing (up arrow), or move backwards away from what you are looking at (down arrow). That is good for looking back behind you as you drive forward by pointing behind you, and hitting the down key to head in the opposite direction, as if driving while looking back. You can swing with the right and left arrow, or for more efficiency, drag the screen side to side with your mouse by clicking a point and holding the click as you drag the image. And don't forget you can zoom in by clicking the plus and minus arrows on the lower right of the screen. We will also include the images here though, so no need to run to the computer just yet. You can do this all, while just looking here.

So where to begin? Let's try here.[06] This is a small road through a sparsely populated residential neighborhood in Russia. An overhead of the path we will take is below, with our entry and exit located at the bottom of the path, where this neighborhood street opens onto a main drag:

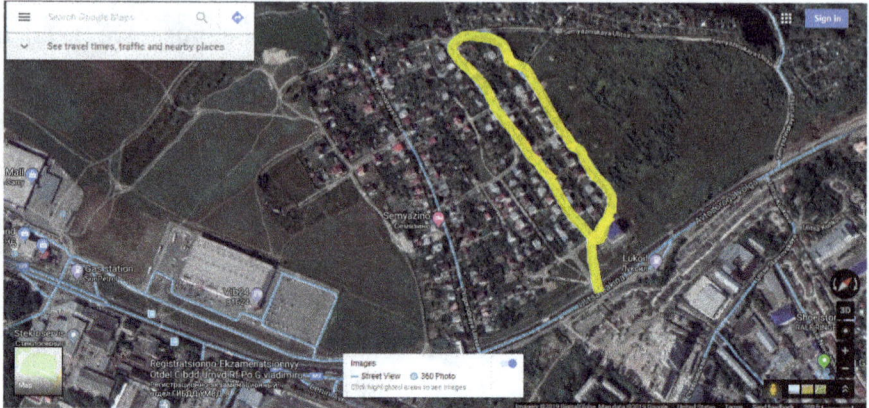

It is an isolated neighborhood, the roads are not really good shortcuts connecting two heavily trafficked areas so the only traffic should come from the houses there, and at midday, things should probably be running slow. Notice Google coverage with Street View is a little spotty, but there is a nice little loop over on the right, highlighted above in yellow. Lets take that and see if we notice anything. This is Google's August 2012 record of the footage there. Google periodically updates footage with newer pictures. So if it does, you can click "more dates" in the little window in the upper left, and select the date above to take exactly this tour.

If you want, take the drive here at this footnote,[07] and pretend you are an innocent tourist, just looking around, and do not look for anything strange. Scan from side to side, and take in

60

the details. Examine how everything appears as exactly what you would expect. Now lets look at the trip while being surveillance aware.

A quick word on how vehicular surveillance will operate today. As you drive, it will be disbursed around you in what used to be called a floating box[08] when surveillance was done by small, specially-deployed teams, and all that stood between you and losing your team was one thin layer of coverage around you. Back then maybe six cars tried to get in front of you and behind you, as well as paralleling you on side streets, and when you turned, the box would turn, off the radio call from the "command" unit that was in sight of you.

As the box turned with you, it kept cars all around you on side streets, just out of view, except for the one car on the street in front of you, and the one way back, ideally out of sight. The weakness of the box was you could lose your team if you could make it through the single layer of vehicles.

Today surveillance has exploded and been permanently stationed everywhere, on street corners and near points of interest, and in roving vehicles constantly driving all around. What you see is now more akin to a giant cloud of mist all over your town or city, with a smaller denser cloud which forms around targets like you as they travel.

That smaller, denser cloud of followers is assembled on the fly from a force that is more like a hidden undercover Police force embedded all over, and stationed in sectors to provide what is called phased coverage.

In phased coverage, each area has several vehicular, foot,

bicycle, and posted units loitering around within it. They wait to be called on, to follow someone when they enter the sector. Then they hand the target off to the next group operating in the next sector as the target exits their sector. When not following someone, they cruise around and keep their eyes open for anything interesting to report to their controller. All of this has been organized very much like a Police force spreads out its patrolling cruisers. The American domestic surveillance machine's following brigade is very much just a covert agency deploying watchers on foot and drivers cruising around, all over its various areas of operations.

It would appear as US domestic surveillance has grown, it has far exceeded the original size and mandate of the Operation TIPS network of citizen informants, many of whom appear to have an app on their phone which calls them into action and gives them directions when they are in the vicinity of a target. I have been walking in Costco myself, and actually seen a picture of myself, taken in the clothes I was wearing, within the previous hour or so, on the screen of a phone held by a watcher who was looking for me in the wrong direction as I walked up behind her.

Regardless, when you are on the lookout for it, understand that surveillance doesn't get in your rearview mirror and follow you around. It drives in front of you and leads you. It parallels you on side streets according to the directions of a car watching you from a parking lot as you pass. It gets to where you are going before you, and parks with its hood up as if it is having engine trouble when you arrive.

Now lets begin the drive. The entrance to the neighborhood will look like this:[09]

You enter the neighborhood, staying right:[10]

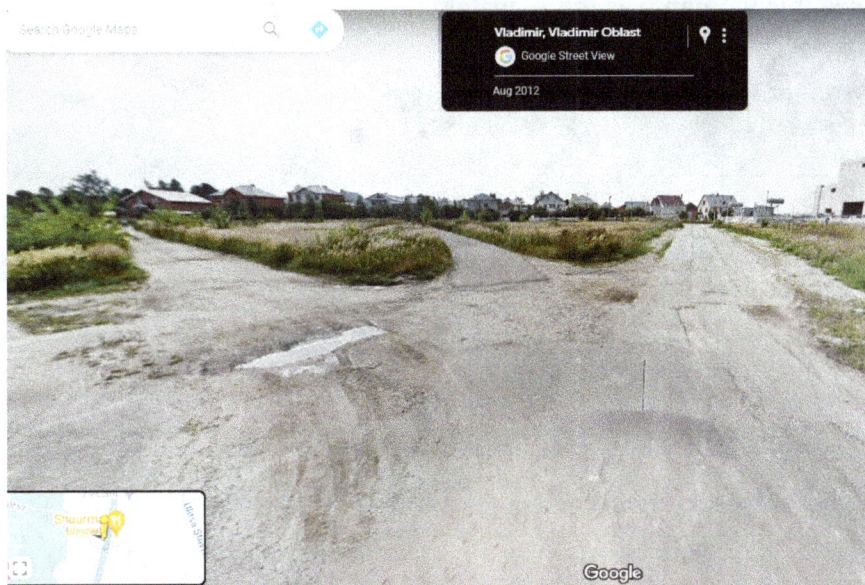

Since I have published this, Google has deleted several specific images from this drive, however we have saved the images and will reprint them here.

When you pulled in a few minutes earlier in the first link, you would have seen the woman pictured below, with her baby carriage, standing off in the street to the left as you passed:

If you continue, and look back from this address,[11] you can see this woman was there, watching you enter:

If they delete that image, you will have to take my word the images were genuine, and the woman was there.

I am not surprised after my publishing these pieces, which were quie popular, online at the time, someone has been scrubbing the Google database. This information is the most dangerous information in the world. The fact you have a secret society, modeled on the East German Stasi, *in your neighborhood right now*, striving to control your life path from the shadows, using the tools of an intelligence agency to even target your children in the schools, using their own children as agents, subverting your Constitutional republic, is the big secret which could set off a real revolution - and create real freedom. If you become surveillance aware, as I am teaching you to be, and if you help our society become surveillance aware, that is the biggest single threat faced by the powers that be. It is not surprising they would seek to limit the access to this information.

As you continue on, you will stay to the right, and follow a counter-clockwise loop, coming back to the main road behind you. You will then take a left onto the main road you just got off, and stop for gas at the next gas station off to the right. That will keep the Google car's timeline as consistent as possible. If you go left as you enter, you will be following the path the Google car drove, but you will be looking at the pictures in backwards order compared to how the Google car took them, as it originally went right when it took these series of images.

So, returning to our entrance, when we pull off the road, to the left we have a woman on foot, watching us, with a baby carriage, and she is totally focused on the baby as you approach, before turning to look at you after you pass:

Clearly she has a carriage, and isn't looking at you, so she couldn't be surveillance. Unless she was surveillance and the carriage is the cover she uses when she runs foot coverage. I would ask, why is she not pushing the carriage, and in motion? I assume she was posted there, and had to remain in place, one of two redundant elements which would call your entrance into the neighborhood to the team already positioned in it.

In reality we will later discuss why this neighborhood may house something more than just houses. It is possible she is a sort of lookout, for a more serious security team housed here. But for now, we will examine her, and then move on.

Note, surveillance does not stand alone, with nothing in their hands, looking out of place and staring at you. That is not how they are trained. The truth is, that woman is actually what they are trained to look like when on a job.

Now she could be innocent. Or she could have jumped out of a leading vehicular unit a minute before, grabbed and unfolded a carriage, and stood there. Nothing says there is definitely a baby in the carriage, though in my experience surveillance will bring children, and even babies, on follows to enhance their covers.

Remember you are looking for consistent unusual activity near intersections as you pass them, which could be consistent with "commit units" calling your direction of travel to a bigger team. Notice how she is not walking, she is just standing there, looking at her baby. If you saw me with a carriage there, I would be actively moving it more often than I would be standing around next to it, as the carriage is a conveyance. As a car suddenly turned off, it would trigger me, and I would reflexively glance at it, just to assess it. How long does she stand there looking at her baby each day? Where is she coming from, and where is she going to? How many houses are there in this neighborhood? How often is somebody there at that juncture, not moving, just as a car passes, in the middle of the day?

Ask yourself what the statistics are that you have a pedestrian at that turn off, just as you turn off. It can be a small probability and still be innocent, but if it is a small probability and it happens all the time, again and again, it may not be innocent.

For now, do not assume she is surveillance. Simply remember the pedestrian-at-the-intersection theme. You will see it again throughout this book. What will happen over time, is you will note, over and over again, you will enter neighborhoods and come to intersections in areas which are remote, where you would not expect to see a pedestrian, and one will be there, over and over.

Over time, with repetition, you will realize surveillance places an asset at "decision points," so they can radio the team, apprising them that the target has traveled in "X" direction, and the team needs to make the adjustment. Once you make that realization, you will come back to this picture, and that innocent woman will look entirely different to you, and you may find a drive through your own neighborhood and town will as well.

Since this is the first event we have seen, we will call it a low-probability event. However it is an event consistent with surveillance. So you register it, as well as the fact she turns to look at you only after concealment has come between you and her:

Google deleted that image as well, but not to worry, we kept the screenshots. I would ask, if it is not significant, and this work is not important, why would Google delete just those photos? You do not see that anywhere else on Streetview.

I will conclude by pointing out, if she is a foot operator then one car may be missing a navigator. Official government surveillance vehicles usually feature a driver, and an operator who does double duty as navigator, plotting paths as the driver drives, for maximal efficiency, and who is trained to jump out and run foot surveillance where needed. So a car with a missing navigator could be of interest. We also just happen to have a car that just happened to pull off right ahead of us, at that moment:[12]

Not dispositive, but on that side of the development, you are looking at about fifty houses which that car might be heading to. In the middle of the day while everyone is out working, how many cars head to houses there per hour? Three? Five? One? Ask yourself how many cars you will see during your drive through.

What are the chances that the very two-second window when you pull off onto that road, the one car that will pull off that hour, would pull off right ahead of you, just in that two second window? Exactly in front of you? It seems out of fifty times pulling into that development, you might expect maybe once or twice, a car might jump off right ahead of you. Maybe.

It is a smaller probability event, unless you were under surveillance, where a surveillance vehicle, leading a target, is considered a preferable technique to the more obvious follow from behind. In surveillance parlance, the technique of leading a target is called, taking a *"cheating command position,"* and it is a well-established, commonly used technique to maintain eyes on a target in a rear-view mirror, while concealing the surveillance driver's face more effectively, and appearing to not be a following vehicle.

69

Notice also how as you drive down the road, initially he is way ahead of you, but as you approach the decision point, you catch up to him. If he is surveillance, he is doubling as a "commit unit" for that second intersection, to let the team know which fork you are about to take. If he was surveillance, he would go slow to see which fork you took, as he tries to stay as far ahead of you as he could, without blocking his sightline, so you don't get too good a look at him.

He does exactly that, so that would normally be a higher likelihood surveillance-related event. Of course since this is the Google car, he almost certainly is surveillance. In fact I would have bet you would have seen exactly this, with a stationary unit at the entrance and another unit at the first turn. But if this were you instead of Google, although not dispositive, it is curious, and would put you on alert.

As we continue, we will take the right fork, as that is the path the Google car took, so it will maintain a consistent timeline of photos in chronological order, instead of traveling backwards in time as you take the trip.

Were this me performing this route in a neighborhood like this in America, there is not a lot off that main road, so I would have expected them to get one or two cars or so off into this neighborhood ahead of me, just in case I decided to go in. Once I went in, they would have sped to a spot in the neighborhood where they could call my path, and get an idea what I was doing, and they would have then tried to act natural.

If they knew ahead of time I was heading into this neighborhood, then I would expect several units prepositioned in there, including foot units, as I went in.

Although professional surveillance cars will often have two people, with a driver and a navigator (who doubles as foot surveillance, being dropped off as needed, and then picked up after), informants from the civilian informant network, who pad out the force in the US, appear to ride solo, or however they normally would, such as with their children, or other family.

My impression from driving around Russia, on Google Streetview, is that ironically, Russia does not have an extensive civilian informant network of citizens spying on their fellow citizens for the government, preferring instead a smaller force of professional government surveillance workers.

When I travel to poor areas in Russia, the surveillance vehicles I see will be brand new sedans, probably brought in from Moscow, in contrast to the run down and rusted out cars you will see in driveways. When I make similar trips in America, even in the most-rural and remote Alaskan woods, as you will see later, the cars following you will be the same beat up, rusted-out cars from the community - in one case, even being seen later parked in the informant's driveway.

I know it goes against current narratives. However my assumption is the media and the narrative-crafters in America are so hostile to Russia because this Stasi-like intelligence operation, which appears to have as its ultimate command structure, a foreign, non-state group of ultra-wealthy globalist elites, has somehow been kept out of Russia, which as a result has far fewer citizen informants, and far less surveillance. And that makes Russia an enemy of the true, hidden hand which runs the West.

So going into this Russian neighborhood now, I would expect professional government surveillance with two people per car. Which means one on foot alone, such as the woman who was dropped off with the baby carriage, and another person near or in a car. It is always possible they could be shorthanded or have informants helping out, or some sort of team leader might roll alone, but usually I would expect there would be a duo.

Now in the US, I would assume five of these houses in this neighborhood would be surveillance observation posts, owned, and lived in, by citizen informants, and with operators inside watching their neighborhood. As a rule of thumb, one in twenty to one in ten houses will tend to be associated with surveillance somehow in the US, and in some neighborhoods, it is much more. I am not exaggerating, or being hyperbolic. In the US, the network is that large and intrusive.

Also, there is so much coverage in the US, and it is so much about control (and when needed intimidation), that they will use even more vehicles than you will see here, added to those large numbers of covert observation posts hidden in homes, making it even more obvious than you will see here.

Returning to our trip, take the right fork, to begin driving the loop which will curve around to bring you right back to the entrance. Drive it with an eye to scrutinizing anyone you see for any unusual signs they might be surveillance. Also, examine the houses for tech wired in, or people loitering (Spoiler – little observation post activity was seen, so all you will see is foot and vehicular – another sign Russia has more privacy than America, and a government which is less hostile towards its people).

We don't see much, until we make the first turn and see this black sedan parked in a driveway off to the left. It contains a guy, who is sitting half in the car with the door open, not doing anything or moving as we pass. He appears to just be watching a turnoff onto a dirt road 150 yards ahead:[13]

This is pretty obvious. First, look at him. No hands on the wheel, he is not advancing his position. He is just sitting there with his hands in his lap watching the Google car. This guy backed in probably a couple of minutes ago. If you drive all the way down the road, and look back, he is still sitting there, not moving, with his car door open.

Despite it being a nice car, he has no air conditioning, possibly because he has an alternator that is supersized for powering various tech in the car, he has a second alternator stuck where the compressor for an AC would go, or he needs the pickup, or his agency supplied the car and didn't spend money on it.

I don't know exactly why, but I have noticed it seems many surveillance vehicles lack air conditioning. So he has done what I have seen vehicular surveillance do all over in hot weather when stationed in hot cars in parking lots, waiting on calls to enter stores to follow targets – he popped his car door open to get as much cool outside air in as possible. It is either that, or some resident in the neighborhood likes sitting outside in full sun in a black car, with their car door open. Remember that pattern, because the open car-door of a loitering vehicular unit is actually another theme you will see in the next section, as well as in your own travels.

So, just a short, quick detection route, and already you have a high-probability detection event with this guy, a mid-level with the car leading you in, and a possible in the lady with the carriage, and every intersection, and the turns on each side of this guy, were covered when you came to them. What are the chances, during the middle of the day in a neighborhood with only about fifty houses?

This old white car is a low-level, maybe/possible event.[14]

Although nobody is in it, look how the back is tinted. If I were surveillance, I would tint the back of my car like that, park it, and then hop in the back to call the passing of a vehicle I was following.

If this is surveillance, this is more what you could expect from a pro. The only fault would be that the very nice house already has two very nice cars, making me think they might not need a third car, and if they got a third it would look nicer than that, especially given the paver driveway is old enough to have weeds growing in the cracks, and yet it is perfectly flat, indicating a quality job with a quality base layer laid down properly, which is expensive.

It is a very low-likelihood event, but it is something which may not fit in the environment, which might be amenable to surveillance, and which you will look for in the future. But you only need that level of paranoia in Russia if you are an elite spy posing a state-level-threat, where they would roll out their most elite, camouflaged, invisible operators.

In America you would see this level of surveillance just by being mildly politically active, or even just being marked in grade school as a high IQ free-thinker. Here, Russia is probably not using its "A," "B," "C," or even D teams, since it knows the Google car is videoing, and all of these characters are likely to get burned. I am actually more uncertain about the car because it would be so good, and I wouldn't expect that level of good for a mere Google car follow.

Across from this house is a turnoff to the right on a dirt road which the car with the open door is watching, to see if we took it:

Zoom in behind you, and you can see he selected that spot to have a clear sightline to this intersection:

As we get to the end of the road, off to the right, we have a woman in the next neighborhood over, who has opened the back of her car, and is walking away, turning 90 degrees, and going around the back corner of the house.[15]

What is weird is in the next shot she has turned 90 degrees again, and is walking away from the house.[16]

If she was surveillance, she had to get to that location from the next neighborhood over, something not at all strange in the world of surveillance with radio coordination. Alone, she wouldn't do anything to the probability. This is not even a low-probability event, though it is interesting you couldn't get to be alone back here, even at the back of this loop where there shouldn't have been anyone. Not being able to find solitude, itself, can be a sign.

However I mention it for three reasons. One, if I knew I was under coverage, and she is there when I was just about to enjoy a moment alone, that is potentially coordinated timing. You are looking for rare events which could have happened at any time of day, but they happen to occur just as you were almost alone - and you see this timing over and over again, everywhere you go. I would try to get a good look at her, and remember her face and her car, to see if I saw her again.

Two, she would be a good example of what surveillance can do, to look natural and unlikely to be surveillance, and render itself almost totally undetectable. These people take their work seriously, and work hard to look like they couldn't possibly be surveillance. For that reason, she is useless for any detection purposes, beyond her being right there, just as you would otherwise have found a moment of solitude.

Which brings us the final point of significance, which is, you went somewhere where you should have been alone and you were not alone. When you are under coverage, the biggest sign is, every time you almost get a moment alone to enjoy some solitude, something happens. A bicyclist happens by, a plane flies over, a helicopter is hovering over a distant treeline with a sightline to you, a dog-walker comes around a corner, a car just happens to pull in the parking lot, some maintenance guy happens by to clean trash cans or fix something up.

Early on, before I saw my surveillance, I took my two dogs to a lovely park. We were almost alone, when I looked up, and a small helicopter was hovering a half mile away over a treeline, just sitting there, until I returned to the parking lot, where some guy was cleaning out the empty trash cans despite the park being so remote and unknown that nobody should have been there.

If that happens predictably all of the time, enough times, no matter what it looks like, it is indicative of surveillance.

As we are heading out, we come to this, in roughly a symmetrical position compared to the other car on the other side of the loop:[17]

Just a couple of guys with briefcases, by the side of the road, their car parked hastily on the other side. Of course they both have briefcases, so they must be on official business, and aren't there watching you as surveillance operators, calling your decision at this intersection. How many people, in that neighborhood stand by the side of the road with briefcases each day? But they were there, in the two-second window, as you passed.

These guys don't appear to be going to or coming from the house there. When you first see them, they are pointed at the house, as if they are going to it. But they don't approach it, instead they turn around as you drive by, and then just stand there.

From the moment you see them, until you are as far down the road as you can be, they stand right there, and don't move, one with arms crossed. It appears they just popped out of the car on the opposite side of the road, ran across the street, and they stood there. If you were running a surveillance detection route here, they are definitely suspicious, and up the probability. In reality, it is the Google car in Russia – so those guys are definitely surveillance.

There is a guy on the left as you go out, talking on his cell phone, but the hood of his car is up, and he could have hid inside the house and looked, so I would say he is probably not. Surveillance will tend to remain totally unseen, or get right up next to you, obvious, while acting innocent. He is here:[18]

Before we leave, it is worth noting there may be more to this little circuit than meets the eye. One, that was a decent amount of coverage for a simple 90-second neighborhood jaunt where you probably should not have seen anyone normally, in a nation where there is not a lot of surveillance from my other observations of it on Streetview.

Two, why didn't the Google car do the rest of the neighborhood? On the overhead you can see where the two guys were standing, a turn off led to the rest of the neighborhood, and all we did was about a third of the neighborhood. The rest of the neighborhood had no Streetview coverage when this circuit occurred. Three, it was a fairly nice neighborhood with nice cars, making me wonder if somebody important lived there. And then there was this - a surveillance camera set up to catch plates as cars enter, seen here from the side:[19]

Here it is from the entrance point to the neighborhood, pointed right at you, where it will catch images of cars head on entering and exiting for license plate capture:[20]

From an earlier image Google deleted:

More cameras, covering a large area of the neighborhood:[21]

Here, a higher end pan/tilt/zoom job, mounted way up implies somebody watching live to pan/tilt/zoom it:[22]

Remember, in 2012 Russian surveillance began harassing American diplomats.[23] I assumed at the time, the massive global intelligence operation of the Western Stasi began to flex its surveillance/harassment muscle against the Russians, breaking a long-running detente between intelligence operations, and the Russian harassment was retaliation.

Here we have what is probably a CIA operation driving into this nice neighborhood, taking only one loop, and then taking off.

There is something interesting in there, and the obvious surveillance presence was the Russians counter-harassing the Google car, as a form of protest. Of course amusingly, this was about one fifth of what I would see as surveillance, were I arriving at my home in a residential neighborhood just like that in America, but that is neither here nor there.

Moving on, cruise out, turn left on the main drag, and pull into the gas station on the right, being sure to maintain the 2012 timeline. There is no point looking around as you head out of the neighborhood on this little leg because you have jumped timelines back to the beginning, and are just replaying the photos you saw when you drove in.

Just before you hit the main road, you will notice this posted vehicular unit has pulled off and is sitting on the corner across the street, observing the Google Car, waiting to call your direction of travel:[24]

Once you hit the main road, you would have been on another timeline yet again, this time, August of 2018.

In this timeline, another pedestrian is standing there, this time directly across the street with a sightline to the intersection. Unfortunately Google has again deleted that image from its database, replacing the whole segment I used with new footage shot just two months after I had originally published this piece. However had they not, this is what you would have seen:

The old, now inoperative image address was:

https://www.google.com/maps/
@56.1192216,40.3413343,3a,15y,131.91h,84.4t/data=!3m6!1e1!
3m4!1sz5vrhL4Nu5xVy6WvBm98VQ!2e0!7i13312!8i6656

Examining the pedestrian, it appears he is not walking either on the sidewalk, or into or out of the store. Ask the question you should always ask of a pedestrian. Where is he coming from, and where is he going to? If that is difficult to answer, it may be because he is loitering. And if he is loitering at an intersection, it may be for you, since a posted commit unit at an intersection, placed there to call your direction of travel, is a normal surveillance procedure.

In the new photo, there is no pedestrian across the street, however there is a vehicle parked at the now paved intersection of the loop behind you:[25]

So to reiterate, if you are under coverage, this intersection would have a pedestrian or vehicular unit present at it as you arrive at it. Of course, this is the Google car, driving during a period of "surveillance unrest" between superpowers, so I would have expected somebody there, given the Google car was certainly under coverage, and that is what you saw.

Again, in your daily life, these things are not dispositive, and you cannot say anything with certainty. You merely observe, and see if you begin to notice patterns of anything around that appear unusual which are repeating, as you have seen here. You want to notice statistically unlikely events repeating at statistically unlikely frequencies. In America, if you look, you will eventually see it.

Individuals loitering at intersections, even alone in the middle of nowhere, is a theme you will see again in future installments. It is a procedure of the physical surveillance which blankets the West, which is embedded in every neighborhood in America, and which is tasked with spying on every citizen, to maintain their file, and the files of their children.

Continuing on, as you approach the gas station in the original tour, in another photo which is now deleted, there is an SUV parked in the shadow, by the gas station sign:[26]

What is it doing there? Why didn't it pull closer to the station? It isn't getting gas, or going inside the station. It kind of looks like it is using the sign and shadow for some concealment from oncoming traffic as it loiters. In the original timeline, you could back up on the highway while watching it, by hitting your down arrow key while pointed at it, and you would see how in this deleted image, the sign obscured the car, in the center of this image behind the sign, as you got farther away from it. Notice that he could still see you in his driver's side rearview mirror:[27]

So a glance in his rear view mirror will allow him to see you clearly, but you cannot see him. One thing surveillance operators are taught in vehicular surveillance school is the power of car mirrors to allow you to observe a target, while minimizing your profile to the target. They can see you, but you cannot see them. Combined with his use of the sign as concealment, that is a professional.

Unfortunately, when you originally would jump into the gas station, you jumped timelines to a different trip, this time to July of 2017. But in that timeline, another SUV appeared to have been parked where the SUV above was parked, and when you pull in, it pulls out and takes off after you pass. Looking back:[28]

Behind him, is another car which watched you pass by as well, though it is unclear what they are doing:[29]

I have noticed, very often those in surveillance will seek out jobs which utilize "branded" business trucks, from plumbing and electrical contractors, to cable TV techs. I assume they like the idea that a branded vehicle with some business labeled clearly on the outside will tend to make people think they are not surveillance. In addition, such jobs will offer the surveillance operator access to other intelligence, be it the access a taxi-driver has to a passenger or a contractor or repairman's access to denied areas like home interiors, or business offices.

So ask yourself why would a car be parked in a gas station lot, as far from everything as it could be, and take off just as you pull in? He is not going to the store. He is not getting gas. Why would two SUVs, years apart, have done the exact same thing on two different trips by the Google car? It could be innocent, but you have two doing it on two different trips, and it leaves just as you arrive, as if it doesn't want to remain there once you pull in, lest you ask what it is doing sitting away from everything and loitering.

A quick word on repetitions like this. It is my suspicion surveillance groups are assigned sectors, and tend to work the same areas over and over again, tracking different targets in their sector. Maybe for a few days every six to eight months, you get surveillance teams assigned to you to polish your file, but these people, in their sector, are doing that to different Americans, every day, over and over, in the same sector.

As a result, they discover certain spots work better than others for maximizing visibility of passing targets, while minimizing the profile of the surveillance operator watching the target. Certain covers fit better than others in certain places. Certain routines and movements give a better advantage than others. As they follow different people through the same places day after day, the members of the team will develop similar patterns which you may pick up on if you pass through that area multiple times. Somebody will always be sitting in a certain spot, usually a different person each time. Or there will always be somebody doing the same thing, usually a different person, and so on. There is always a bum with a sign on a corner, always a coffee drinker with a newspaper on a bench, always a dog-walker near a dog park, but not in it. They will be in the same position, using the same covers, positioned the same way. I suspect hiding by this sign as people passed, or entered and exited that neighborhood, was one such pattern this sector's team developed.

Getting gas is always fun, because how much gas you have in your tank is key operational information to a surveillance team. It tells them the range of your vehicle, as well as the mpg of the vehicle, once they are following you. That tells them how far you can drive at any point, and when you will need to stop for gas next. They consider that important operational information, especially if they one day lose you, and acquiring it is a high priority.

So they have to get close at gas stations. One day I will show funny video of three guys, all filling cars around my car at a station, all talking into their chests as I pay for gas inside.

We will end this trip there, as from there the Google car moves into a more populous area, which will dilute the signal produced by the surveillance within a larger pool of regular people, making it harder to notice.

So a short surveillance detection route, and you have one low probability event when you pull in with the carriage lady, one medium event at the first intersection, and three events in the loop. In addition, there is the gas station car always parked by the sign, and the fact a commit unit was always loitering around that intersection when you happened by.

Now that was a very short surveillance detection route. You see how if you keep jumping off and running routes in unpopulated areas, one after another, and you keep seeing activity like that, you can begin to uncover the probability of your surveillance coverage, even though it is trying to look normal.

That is what spies do before going to meetings. Or at least they did, before things got this bad in the West, and the domestic Stasi-like networks became so pervasive that as you drove, there was no need to have anyone follow you as there were agents posted to every street corner, radioing control as targets passed.

But using these routes to see it here, you will grow sensitive to what surveillance looks like, and how it operates. You will develop a feel for it, which will border on psychic awareness. Once you are sensitive to it, you are going to see it throughout your neighborhoods and towns in America, even if you do not run detection routes. The American Stasi is now all over, and shockingly, there are a ton of Americans who seem to enjoy betraying fellow citizens for this foreign network that is destroying our nation.

And still more nuances will begin to jump out at you as your skills develop. There are ways they drive which are different from regular people just absent-mindedly going to a destination. There are ways they look at others which are different from regular people, possibly due to a life spent deceiving others while trying to gauge their effectiveness at fooling them. And there are different ways they act, while following targets, compared to normal people going about their own day without concern for what anyone else is doing.

In the West, once you are sensitized, you will see the surveillance everywhere, and you will quickly find, it is almost impossible to lose a tail, as your coverage is more akin to driving through a cloud of surveillance which blankets your entire nation.

Conversely, in Russia, Google, itself a division of the elite Cabal of ultra-wealthy and powerful individuals who run the world, probably chose drivers who worked for Western/Cabal intelligence, so they could exploit the video produced by the vehicle. I would assume the company sought to shut the Russians out, so Russia had to assign surveillance assets to the Google car to protect their homeland.

It is another good sign that if patriots in the West ever need a fallback position to secure themselves, until some sort of unrest opens up opportunities to purge from America whatever this operation is which has taken over the West, Russia might make a good choice. It may even ultimately prove a potent ally, should a conflict begin in the West, between the regular people and the surveillance people.

That may also be why we see the Cabal of elites and the media machine it controls, trying to demonize Russia in the eyes of the majority of the West. They hope to dissuade us from forming any sort of alliance with the Russians, who could one day be our most potent ally against the criminal conspiracy subverting the governments of the West, which seek to control everything.

The Russians could offer us counter-intelligence or technical support against whatever coverage is on us. They could provide sources of information and direction, on competing with the more established Stasi information outlets to better disseminate truthful information and ideas among ourselves to combat the intelligence operation's propaganda. Or they might help us overcome other factors which our Stasi-supported enemies are presently using to manipulate us, and make us weak.

And if things ever did go kinetic in America, Russia could offer a first-world level of intelligence support to any American citizens opposed to the takeover of our nation by a foreign intelligence operation run by a hostile group of foreign globalist elites.

The single biggest thing any American revolution against this conspiracy would need is a detailed roster of the domestic surveillance machine, including names and addresses of this secret society of Stasi informants working against all of America. In a revolutionary scenario, there is no path to victory for American patriots, which would not first begin with blinding the domestic surveillance machine of this criminal conspiracy. To do that, patriots would need to know who was in the conspiracy at the neighborhood level.

I would be shocked if Russia did not already have a detailed roster of America's domestic Stasi machine. Simply by using artificial intelligence to analyze vehicular traffic patterns readily accessible through regular satellite surveillance systems, as well as commercially available databases of cell phone geolocation data, it would be a small matter to identify vehicles and people engaging in patterns of travel which are indicative of surveillance.

Were Russia not to have done this already, given the massive strategic benefits of being able to identify the conspiracy's spies, I would be shocked.

Perhaps some day we will even have a national Targeted Individual Day, to complain about the physical surveillance in America. We could mark it with rallies outside the Russian Embassy, asking the Russians and Vladimir Putin to intervene in America in support of the civil rights of the Americans who are being targeted by this criminal machine that has infiltrated our government and its intelligence community.

I'd imagine the optics of a crowd of ten thousand Americans, featuring large signs with the pictures of Detective Miosotis Familia, Deputy Natalie Corona, Deputy Brad Garafola, Officer Matthew Gerald, and Corporal Montrell Jackson, as well as other victims like Brain Mancini and Myron Mays, noting they were all killed by this operation, and their murders were a direct result of the program, would also help to draw law enforcement's attention to the problem.

Next, we will move on to Bulgaria, where the Bulgarians show you the more aggressive procedures used in Eastern Europe against the national security threat of the Google car.

Chapter Four

Surveillance Detection – The Professional Course Of Real Life Experience – The Bulgarian Roundabout

In our last chapter we took a short cruise around a Russian neighborhood where we saw one mobile vehicular unit lead us in and several posted foot and vehicular surveillance units observing us as we passed them.

Some of the themes I told you to remember were the posted vehicle with a car door open due to the heat within a hot car under the sun, the lack of AC in vehicles, windows on surveillance vehicles often being open either due to heat or to enhance the ability to observe sounds and smells relating to a target, cars positioned to allow the operator to observe the target, often using rear view mirrors, so as to maximize target visibility to the operator while minimizing the exposure of the surveillance operative to the target, the patterns of activity that repeat almost exactly because surveillance teams learn what works in a sector and then tend to use the same spots and techniques on successive follows through that sector, the pedestrians posted at intersections acting as commit units to call which route you took, the timed arrival of vehicles at intersections just as the target vehicle arrives, to observe the arriving target and any passengers in their vehicle through the front windshield, and the idea that you will have difficulty ever getting completely alone, especially at decision-points, like intersections, especially in remote areas where you should not expect to commonly see traffic. You will see all of that material again in this chapter as we develop your mind.

In this chapter, we will travel to Bulgaria. We are going to use an industrial zone for our next surveillance detection route, which has several advantages, and several disadvantages. First, in a civilian area, domestic surveillance in America today frequently purchases residences on corners surrounding intersections, which means you can sometimes hit an intersection and not see someone with a sightline to your position, because they will be hiding in a house on the corner. That can make detection difficult. You'll see this in another surveillance piece like this on our website, AmericanStasi.com, which examines Sri Lankan motorbike surveillance in a Sri Lankan neighborhood, where the few intersections you come to with no vehicles or pedestrians, always have a resident of one of the corner houses, outside the house in the hot sunlight watching you pass, despite the obvious heat which is keeping everyone else inside.

As I have been doing this in different nations, I have noticed different places do surveillance differently. Some is related to the environment. Some differences are superficial. Go to Turkey, and you will see a lot of motorbikes. They are everywhere anyway, you can hop on and off them quick, they can zip around in traffic so you don't get held up, and they can go off road to scoot around the margins of a floating box around a target as they move, to get ahead of the target while remaining out of sight. Go to Guam, and most of it is vehicular, because it is too hot in the sun to run foot or motorbike surveillance, and few people use motorbikes there anyway, and surveillance does not want to stand out.

However in other cases the differences are deeper than just what tools are used. I am not sure whether you are seeing a difference in hostility to the Google car, where one place aggressively reveals themselves to intimidate it, while another tries to hide more to avoid frightening it, or if it has to do with resources available, or just differing styles of surveillance, with one emphasizing the covert aspect at the expense of control of a target, while other places require a target be contained fully, even if it makes the surveillance more obvious.

Some places seem to have the posted unit hide as much as possible at the intersections, even I suspect, going inside local stores and peering out. Other places put them in the open, possibly under a theory people assume if someone is not hiding they must be innocent. Some places follow you into neighborhoods aggressively, others just document you went in, and either leave you be while in there, or covertly conduct their observation from houses they own in the neighborhood and use as observation posts.

What you will see here is probably the most similar to what you will see in America, helping you learn to spot the domestic surveillance in America. The only possible difference I have noticed is American domestic surveillance seems to often replace the posted units at intersections with vehicles driving up to the intersection. But the rest of this is dead on, even down to the cover vehicles being actual branded company vehicles.

This will be highly illuminating in your journey to surveillance-awareness, because it will show you how the coverage has no fear of exposure, because it has no fear of you suspecting it. But once you see it, there will be no going back. Your eyes will be opened, and you will not be able to un-see it.

To be clear, if we head to revolution, this is probably not what you will see if real surveillance shows up to confront a real threat to the power structure. Imagine as you watch this, how you would do this if you wanted to hide. How posted units could go inside businesses and peer out, or use a ghillie suit from a field. How ten following vehicles could be replaced with a sky-blue drone 400 yards up that you would never see or hear. How pole surveillance could hide hidden cameras wired into the internet, removing the need for anything you would see standing out at intersections.

All of that is out there in America now. I was buzzed by the aviation lights of a small plane like a Cessna in the dark of night, which, at about 30-40 feet off the ground, glided entirely silently over me, I assume off an electric engine. At night, you'd never hear it overhead, and it could be right above you. At 500 feet, with its navigation lights off, watching you through a thermal camera, you would have no idea it was up there, as it saw you, clear as day.

That is the puzzle really, because in America, the American Stasi is not really surveillance. You could do the same thing, be much more effective, even gather much more intelligence, by hiding. You would never be at risk of exposure, or lawsuits, or even violent retribution from a target that snapped.

You would get more intelligence because your target would relax, and act freely without paranoia, and even be happier as they continue to believe the myth of privacy and freedom in America. It would even avoid any hostile relationship between the citizenry and the surveillance, which I think will prove unavoidable in the near future.

They could do this much better, for less money, and less risk. But they do not. It is almost as if this is actually a department of government devoted entirely to intimidation and harassment, using surveillance as a plausible cover for its real activities and purpose, perhaps to aid in recruiting civilians into it, by trying to make its work appear as at least semi-legitimate, if illegal.

Or perhaps it has recruited as many people as possible, even rank amateurs, into its massive ranks, in an effort to get as many people's hands dirty as possible, so when conflict comes, there will be a plethora of lower level surveillance operators which will absorb the ire of the populace, leaving the upper-level leadership untouched.

Regardless, if you fall under this organization's harassment surveillance (and I increasingly believe most will in their lifetimes on our present trajectory), this is what it will look like in the US.

Some of you may be skeptical as you follow this, and wonder if I am making this up, so I would like to point something out before we begin. I first published this piece on my website, to show people what I have clearly learned to spot as surveillance from my own harassment coverage in the United States. I recognized the surveillance immediately in this spot in Bulgaria, and knew it was out of the ordinary, despite never having visited the town, or walked its streets.

When I posted the initial version of this piece to my website, which was fairly well-read, one commenter was actually familiar with this area. He traveled there often to visit family, and he confirmed what I had been able to deduce from 4,000 miles away - that what you will see in this piece was unusual. Following the piece, he commented as follows:

"Been following the series – how did you pick Stara Zagora? I have relatives from that area and from a couple villages close by. I did the same type of google drive-along in those villages and was amazed to see how many pedestrians are on the street – esp during a colder time of year. I've been there in the summertime and rarely see anybody. Strange… I always practice situational awareness whenever I travel – and this series has been very enlightening. Thanks again."

So from 4,000 miles away, never having set foot in this region of Bulgaria, I can tell you what belongs, and what does not. I can spot surveillance, even though I have no familiarity with the normal patterns of activity in the area. Ask yourself, what have I seen, in my daily life in the United States, which has taught me how to do that, simply through osmosis, with no formal education or training in the craft? How long have I been seeing it? How bad must it be in America?

I am not lying about any of this. I am not trying to trick you. I know what I am talking about. I am the type of guy, that if I am unsure about something, I do not try to tell you about it. I remain quiet and learn. If I take the microphone, and begin explaining something to you, you can be confident I will have attained mastery over it, acquired 100% certainty of what I am talking about, and most importantly, if I am standing up to say it, you can know, it is important. I do not like or want attention.

What is presently operational in the United States is

horrifying, and it affects the life of every real American. If we fail to make every other real American aware of it, I think the United States may be lost to this shadow dictatorship. Nothing else you could possibly do in your life will be as important as learning to see the surveillance yourself, and making everyone else in America aware of this cancer spreading throughout our nation.

I do not think that commenter happened to cross paths with my work by chance, or post that coincidentally, either. Much of what I am doing here is done with so many coincidental advantages, I can feel the hand of God at my back. I have no doubt He is aghast traitors in this nation were willing to so sully this nation's beautiful freedom with such a grotesque organization as the American Stasi. The number of coincidences, the amazing strokes of luck, the Divine guidance, you would not believe it all if I laid it all out. It is for that reason I have no doubt we will destroy this thing, nor that I am doing God's work here.

Google's overhead usually airbrushes traffic out of the streets so they will look empty from above. So it is of no use for this. But this map is perfect because it does not airbrush out traffic.

Here is the route we will take:[30]

103

The route begins at the bottom right of the image above, and you will travel left along a highway, following the arrows, up into an industrial area off the side of the highway. You will make a right at the "T" intersection, then follow the loop counter clockwise, before returning to the dirt road at the first intersection on the side street, where you took a right at first. That is the path the Google car took when it filmed this route, so if you follow it, the images you see will be in chronological order.

If you examine the traffic captured at the map at the link, you will see the detection route we will take has only five cars on it, represented by yellow circles below, and judging by sun position it is about the same time of day, making it likely useful as a low-traffic backstreet for a surveillance-detection route.

Since traffic there should be low, when traffic is building up around you, you can begin to understand that there is a high likelihood that the mass of additional traffic is there for you. The more traffic, the higher the likelihood the extra traffic drove there because you are there, and it is following you.

Obviously I already know what you will see here. So let me say this is what you could expect of a first rate, well funded, competent surveillance operation, performing the pseudo-harassing, semi-covert surveillance that politically oriented figures who are not compromised by, or assets of, the American Stasi, will tend to receive in America.

Again I emphasize, this is not what you would see if you were a really high end threat who they wanted to hide from and observe covertly to gain real intelligence. They can disappear, to gather intelligence while unseen, for either blackmail, or to gather operational intelligence for use elsewhere. If you ever operate against the powers that be in a real, practical, kinetic fashion, this is probably not what you will see, especially if you are known to be surveillance-aware.

What you see here however will be representative of the surveillance which an increasing number of Americans are seeing from the American Stasi, which some refer to as "gangstalking." I see this literally everywhere I go, and never get a moment's respite from it, from the grocery store, to my front yard.

We, who are not being blackmailed or paid off by the American Stasi, and who they do not want affecting the political sphere, see a completely different world from regular Americans. It's my hope, every American now will see this criminal operation.

This shows good manpower, and more intricate cover vehicles, probably drawn from a robust domestic informant program similar to the American Stasi's, where these are actual trade vehicles driven by actual tradesmen, who run surveillance on the side for the domestic intelligence apparatus, in between jobs during the day. This is more like what you will see in the United States, including the overkill. And clearly from what you will see, they have not opted for full-stealth mode, as they usually do not in the United States. Most Americans never see them, just because they would think this impossible in America.

It is amusing to me that I see tangible evidence that Russia, the land of the supposedly "evil" dictator Vladimir Putin, is vastly more respectful of its citizen's privacy, and exerts far less aggression, and more professionalism in surveillance against even hostile intelligence threats, than you will see the supposedly more freedom-driven nation of America show to its own fellow citizens.

We begin with a shot pointing back on the highway, in the August 2015 timeline.[31]

There are two ways you can be followed. Some operations would use a single team which will follow you from origin to destination. However with the American Stasi, you will receive "phased coverage," where as you travel from one assigned sector to another, you will be handed off, from one sector's assigned coverage, to the next sector's assigned coverage.

Often, the operatives of the American Stasi who rush to follow you appear to be setting aside their responsibilities of the day for a moment. According to reports, and my observations of them, it seems the GPS on their cell phones reports to command which operatives in the domestic network are close to the approaching target. Command sees this, picks who it will draw upon, and a phone app the operatives were given by command chimes and delivers instructions to them on where to go and who to follow. Apparently part of their deal is, when called, they obey.

The operatives then drop everything to join in the harassment of the target for a brief moment, before returning to their days. It is assumed they will get some sort of recompense for taking part in the surveillance and harassment of another citizen.

Some will be office workers who will take a short break and jet out to the car to get in on the follow. Others will be Postal Service workers who will divert briefly to the target's location. Others may be small business owners who were in the area and have a moment to hop in the car and rush to an intersection to watch the target pass. Still others may be soccer moms who were about to go shopping, but who will drop everything for whatever it is the Stasi offers them. Still others could be kids whose parents are in the network, and brought them in too, who may duck out of a summer job in the early days of a lifetime which will be spent spying on, and harassing, fellow citizens for the machine.

What the target will see is a scene out of the Twilight Zone, where it will seem almost everyone in the community around them knows who they are, and wants to act out against them covertly, making them feel ostracized and alienated from any sense of community with the people around them. As a gaslighting technique of an intelligence operation, it often works quite well.

With respect to law enforcement, the literature (if you can believe it) claims FBI mobile surveillance teams (MSTs) are composed of 12 people in six vehicles (each vehicle with a driver and dual-purpose navigator/foot-surveillance operative). If need be, they could deploy multiple 12-man MSTs on one target if circumstances warranted it. Other reports say Britain's MI5 will assign a single team of 25 surveillance operatives to one target for 24/7 coverage.

That small and targeted a surveillance operation is not what we are describing here, in the American Stasi, which is much more vast and all encompassing, and which seems only tasked with operations designed to assure the continued control of the government and nation, by those presently in power.

If you are a regular American encountering the domestic Stasi (which appears something very different from law enforcement), you can be swarmed by literally hundreds, if not thousands of seemingly regular citizens over a day, all in vehicles which will look exactly like what we are about to show you.

Since regular law enforcement surveillance operations have a limited number of cars, and they don't want you to recognize them, regular law enforcement or intelligence surveillance teams deploy in stealth mode. They are supposed to keep the majority of the team so far behind you it is out of sight. Only one vehicle should maintain "command," or visual contact with you, acting as the "eye," and it will maintain a "set following distance," which offers the greatest balance between keeping as much distance as possible and as many cars as possible between you, and yet having the fewest instances of temporary loss of visual contact at turns and curves in the roadway, where you become, "unsighted."

It is accepted visual contact with you will be lost on some turns, and each time the eye will notify the rest of the team of its loss of sight, calling out "unsighted," the position, and the speed you were traveling when sighting was lost. It will then notify the team it has either reacquired sight, or it has lost you when it should have regained sight.

If you disappear, navigators or central control will then immediately begin calculating a radius of how far you have traveled, based on the last known speed and last known sighted location called, combined with the time since the last sighting. The team will then break up to head to every possible place you could have diverted to within that radius, at high speed, to try and reacquire you.

In America, when dealing with the domestic surveillance machine here, the American Stasi does not employ the team model in most populated places. Highways appear to have their own assigned coverage units, composed of individuals, spread out over the highway, just driving their assigned segment of the highway back and forth, during their shifts of service.

When they get the call you are heading toward a highway

on-ramp, they will try to get in the right places by the entrance ramp to pick you up as you as you enter. Occasionally they may pull up to a car and look in to verify the driver's description if they are uncertain they have the target vehicle, or if the purpose is overt harassment.

If you drive fast and pass cars, each unit will spread out in traffic ahead of you as you enter, and as you pass cars, you will be passing surveillance vehicles who will note your passing to the team as it tracks you. What you may notice as you pass, is people either talking on their phones, talking to themselves, or engaging in some behavior which covers their mouth, like smoking, itching their noses, and so on, as they radio your passing to the team. They will not try to follow you, if you are driving unusually fast, since you might notice that. Again, just things I have noticed which may be of use to you.

Here in Bulgaria, we will begin on the highway, just to give you a quick look at highway vehicular surveillance, before we begin our detection route by jumping off into the less populated industrial sector. We are using the August of 2015 timeline of photos, in the event Google takes a new series of photos between the publication of this and your reading of it. If Google serves you a newer timeline, you can select that older tranche of photos in the dark box in the upper left, where the link says "see more dates."

Here, the Google car will pass the cars ahead of you, which will allow you to see if any of the drivers do anything unusual, which you would not do, if a car with a giant camera ball perched precariously on a post on top of it, bristling with wires and cameras pointing in all directions, were to drive along side of you like Doc Brown's Delorean in *Back to the Future*.

First car's driver is unremarkable, though he appears to not be looking at a car which would look very interesting to me.[32]

If he studiously avoided any eye contact with a Google car, I would say he was surveillance, but with the face blurring by Google, it is tough to tell. But his driver's side window is open.

When I look at oncoming traffic, which I would expect to mostly not be surveillance, it appears most of the drivers have their windows closed, indicating there is not a cultural predisposition to open windows in this part of Bulgaria, nor is everyone opening their windows due to the weather and the temperature.

An open driver's window is common to surveillance operatives as it will allow them to listen to any sounds which might be relevant to their mission, from an unknown acquaintance of your's yelling some piece of information at your car as it passes, to imminent vehicular failure, to someone sneaking up on the surveillance operative as he sits on a target during a stakeout.

Second car is the same, window open, no looking at the

Google car with the big Google ball.[33]

Both drivers are old, so maybe their eyes don't work well. However if you control your speed with the arrow key, you will notice that you, the second car you pass, and the first car you pass are initially all driving quite fast. Car #2 drives the same speed as you and the car behind him to stay ahead of you. Here is several seconds before you pass him, note the distance relative to the car behind him:

Six frames later the distance has grown, as he has sped up to remain ahead of you, maintaining his cheating command position, as the car you are passing taps its brakes as you reach it, so you will blow by fast, and not get a good look at him:

As you approach, the second car suddenly taps the brakes and slows as well, allowing you and the car in front of him to zoom past. If you turn around and continue moving forward while looking back, using the back arrow, you will see the first car has come up on his back side quite rapidly after you pass him:[34]

Now they will pick up speed together to remain behind you

at a set following distance.

That is something surveillance would do, as surveillance wants to see you, but does not want you to see them. They want to minimize your visual contact with them, to maintain their ability to operate around you in the future. If you make keen note of this guy's face, he can hardly follow you into a grocery store tomorrow, or you might recognize him and wonder why you are seeing him everywhere.

So he was driving fast while you were behind him to stay ahead of you as long as possible, until you passed him and were able to look in his side window at his face. Then he tried to create as much distance as possible between you (and your camera ball) as quickly as possible by tapping his brakes.

If you saw this on a highway, he could be surveillance. Because this is the Google car, he almost certainly is. But if this were you, it would be a low to mid probability event. I highlight these as I have no doubt that because this is the Google car, many of these vehicles around you are surveillance. So here, you can look at them to see what you would see in real life if you were under coverage.

As we are driving, we pass this.[35]

That is a surveillance operative communicating via a cellphone texting app, as the Google car passes.

Again, when I see vehicles while performing surveillance detection, I ask, where are they going, what are they doing, and could I see myself doing that, if I were them? If I were the driver of that car, why would I park there? Was I going to meet somebody in that business? If so, when I pulled off, I would drive into the business's parking lot.

Zoom out, look at the car and picture yourself parking it there. There is nothing around.

Where do you go? Would you walk to the front door, or get back in your car and drive up? Why did your female passenger open her car door? That indicates she will be there a while.

If I was doing something I would expect to draw surveillance, my assumption would be that was a posted unit, the girl was the driver, and she pulled off, hopped in the passenger seat, and then sat there updating her control via text message on your passing.

She was hot in the car as the sun beat down on it, so she opened her door, as is almost a procedure for them when forced to stop their car (and you saw this in the last chapter in Russia, as well). It looks like a good example of poor "cover for action," aka reason for being where you are loitering.

These are the types of rare events working for you when surveillance is working against you. Would you have spotted it as you drove by, if you were not looking for coverage? Would you have seen it if you were looking for someone following you, and didn't know that real coverage isn't in your rearview mirror, but rather looks like that?

Next car is this guy:[36]

His face is blurred, but he appears to be looking at the Google car and his window is closed. He is likely just a regular Joe going about his business when a weird-looking Google car drove by him.

We saw the woman parked in the last lot with her door open, so it is possible they are having people pull off into lots to wait in case you enter them, so when we hit the next pulloff, we scan the lot. It is a car dealership. In the parking lot, pointed toward the highway, we have a car with a woman sitting in the passenger seat again.

It is interesting we have another female sitting in a passenger seat. It is possible that is a procedure Bulgaria uses. A surveillance vehicle, piloted by a female parks, the female moves to the passenger side, and sits, and it appears as if a man driving the car has gone inside to do something, and the woman is waiting for him. It functions as a sort of subconsciously assumed cover for action, ie a cover story which explains what the vehicle and person are doing there which is not surveillance-related. They may feel it looks less suspicious to a target than a car with a female in the driver's seat just sitting, watching the target pass:[37]

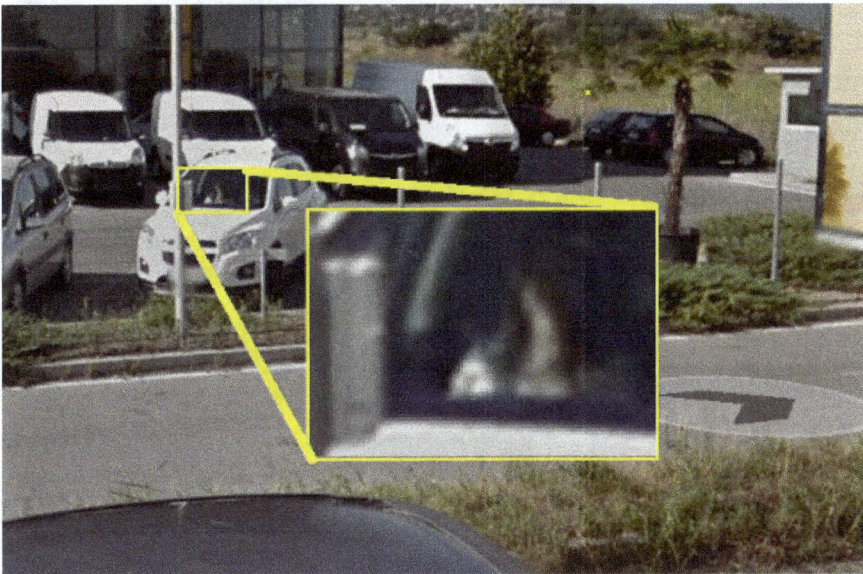

Again, you can't say she is surveillance, because that could be completely innocent. But if surveillance wanted to have

117

someone waiting in each turnoff (that seems to be procedure in the US, when possible) that is what it would look like. And why didn't she accompany the driver, who is presumably inside the building?

Also note how the guy in the foreground, who you are passing, again has a driver's window open, won't look at the Google car, and hit the brakes as you passed.[38]

Here with a large space between himself and the car behind him as you approach that lot:

Here, you have passed, he has hit the brakes, and now the

car behind him has come up to his bumper:

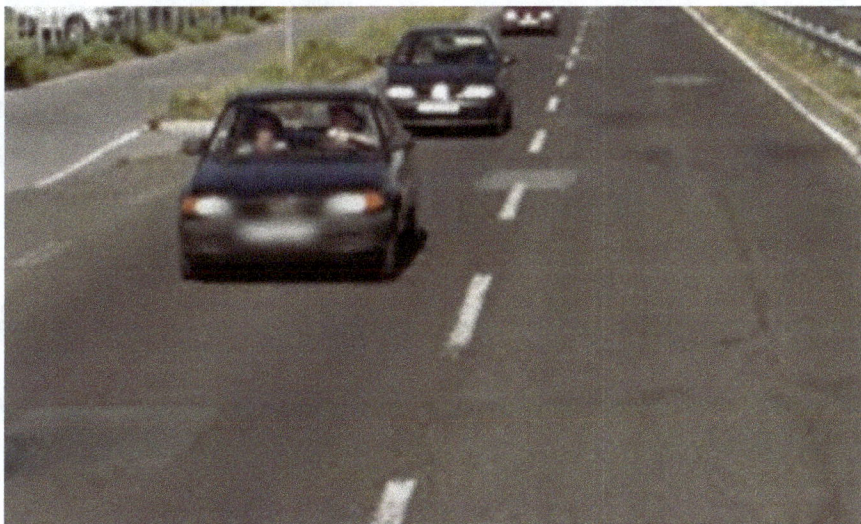

If you look in his window when he is right next to you, his expression would make me suspicious. Notice his ramrod posture and total, blank-eye'd focus – a stiff, awkward focus forward - as opposed to a relaxed, easily distracted, absent-minded curiosity about everything he is passing on his way, driving somewhere.

Again, he could have just argued with the girl in the car, but in detection, you are taking in everything, and looking for anomalies that may indicate you're under surveillance. I would factor this as one "demeanor" anomaly, albeit not decisive.[39]

As we continue, and hit the next turnoff, there is this next car pulling off the side of the road, and lingering there as you pass, as if watching you pass and updating the surveillance command:[40]

And here:[41]

If you go back, and look at it from the earliest moment, you will see it was sitting there, or creeping very slowly, for a while. They may have taken that position because there were numerous different parking lots in that turnoff, had you pulled in there:

Plus there is nothing really of interest in that lot. I'd also wonder if they are curious about something in the lot, why not just pull in it? The gate is open. So they could have been trying to turn their car and their faces away from the Google camera just as it passes. Also, the driver's window is open, allowing better transmission of sound and smell from outside, and cooling the car.

Note that as we are driving, we are passing oncoming traffic, and almost all of their driver's side windows are closed. So the open window thing is not common in Bulgaria. It seems to be primarily the cars around you, on your side of the road.

So far, nothing big, but you have gotten a good look at highway surveillance, with at least one, and maybe two or three static units stopped by the side of the road.

We will take the next right here:[42]

A good surveillance operation will not want you to see a car follow you onto a turn off. And yet if you take a turn off, they will want to have somebody capable of following you onto that turn off. This will usually mean they will either get cars on turnoffs ahead of you, and have them wait for you to arrive, at which point as you turn off, they will begin moving as if they had just turned off before you, or they will arrange a car to come at you from the oncoming direction on the highway. If they chose that option, the oncoming car's arrival will be timed to land at the intersection just before you do, and they will turn off just before or just after you onto the street you are turning onto.

They assume you will think that if the oncoming car was coming from the opposite direction, where you had been heading, they came from somewhere else and couldn't possibly be following you. If you should happen to not take the turnoff, they can let you pass and once you are far enough ahead, the oncoming car can pull a U-turn and rejoin the surveillance team behind you, while assets in the direction you are traveling are contacted and coordinated to get ahead of you.

Again, these days operations like the American Stasi's are not a small team of twelve operators, with most driving right behind you. Rather they are a massive pool of surveillance people, recruited from the community, which function almost like a law enforcement agency, only ten times to fifty times as large as your local police department, once civilian informants are factored in.

And that is not an exaggeration or hyperbole. The government's own description of the pilot program for Operation TIPS, a proverbial toe in the water, to test the feasibility of managing such an informant network, said it would recruit roughly 350,000 civilian informants in New York City, all spying on their fellow citizens. Doubtless, had Congress not outlawed the program, that would have been expanded to two to five times as large over time, as the pilot program matured into a full fledged agency. At the time the New York City Police Department only numbered 35,000 officers. Pundits noted specifically, Operation TIPS would have produced more plainclothes undercover civilian spies than were employed by the old East German Stasi, *in its pilot stage,* and the plan was to expand it as large as possible.

Today, this massive network is arrayed around areas in sectors, just like Police would be. There, in their assigned sector on-duty members will wait, staged in civilian vehicles, listening to the radio (or waiting for a text on their cell phone) for orders to temporarily join one passing operation or another. The rest of the civilian component may be just going about their business, shopping, or commuting, or driving to a job, before getting a text about a target passing nearby, and requesting they join the follow.

When done covertly for surveillance, the effect will look like what you will see here. If the operators do not betray themselves with strange behaviors or clearly mouth the name of the street you are taking (as I have seen them do), the only thing you may notice is that whenever you make turns like this, someone strangely just happens to turn off from the oncoming lane and come in behind you or in front of you, or there happens to be pedestrians there predictably, all the time.

If you are under coverage, the only time you may find yourself alone is when you travel a road with only one entrance and one exit. And even then you will see a commit unit at the start when you enter, and another when you exit, at the end of the drive.

So intersections are points of high surveillance exposure and lots of activity. This is because you could take any turn, and they need to have a lot of people to call the turn and maintain contact with you, whatever turn you take. As you begin to become proficient in detection, you will notice your alertness will always spike as you approach intersections and in response to activity levels at intersections. You'll see what I mean, as I expect after this chapter, you will begin to think differently as you approach intersections, even in real life.

Now take this right turn onto the side street we will use for this detection route, as we jump into the March 2012 timeline.[43]

Did you spot three people loitering, with a sightline to that intersection, where they could see you jump into the turn-off lane?

Might be surveillance, since there's no other reason to stand there. So we have an intersection with people on foot who can call whether you took that turn, if traffic slowed down other vehicular units unexpectedly, and they needed someone present there, to call it. Remember static posted units at intersections, because you will be seeing this material again. And again, and again.

As we saw in the last chapter at the gas station, surveillance people tend to have patterns they engage in, in the areas they operate in. Most have done it for a long time, often from childhood, because surveillance is the Secret Society and they are raised in it from their earliest days. Over time, they find spots which serve their purposes, and often share them with the team.

So follows on different days, even with different teams, can look remarkably similar. You might see the same position occupied by different units at different times if you are taking the same route on different days.

Fortunately here, we can see how this intersection looked during another follow by staying on the highway.

If you stay on the highway instead of taking the turn, you will jump to a different trip timeline (Aug 2015), from the one where you turn (Mar 2012). If you do, you will note that when you were heading in the same direction on another trip, the exact same spot is again occupied by a different set of people out on foot:[44]

Again, I'd ask how often are people out on foot at that intersection, and that spot, when targets are not passing by? Especially given it appears to be a gated entrance to a used car sales lot, where people are supposed to pull in and pull out, and these people are blocking the entrance while not doing anything of note.

In another pass by that intersection in March of 2012, when you did not turn, but continued straight, there was somebody standing on the opposite side of the road:

If you switch over into the oncoming lane of the highway, which is another timeline of photos, you will notice people situated similarly relative to the turnoff, this time loitering on the opposite side of the highway, in front of some little shop that sells clay pots and yard sculptures, which appears closed:[45]

The shop is almost empty because that is a small garden center and according to Google that timeline was March of 2012, in Bulgaria, which is probably not the growing season.

In July of 2022, they were set up on the opposite side of the street again, even though the business there seemed closed:

Here is the same driveway seen in the first example, when the Google car passed in March of 2023. In this timeline, a telephone repair guy just happened to be standing there, using his truck as cover to hide:[46]

Surveillance operators will be very prominent among any utility workers who work the poles, as surveillance technologies require access to power and the data-transmission afforded by cable internet hookups, to send the images and sounds back to either the local monitoring post or a central command center. As a result, in many areas, the telephone poles are laden with covert microphones and even cameras. Utility workers who work those poles will see the devices, and need to be judged trustworthy by the conspiracy to keep the secret. As a result I would assume the American Stasi placed a priority on taking over the positions who determine hiring of pole-workers for telephone companies, cable companies, and electric utilities, and they will stock those positions with their fellow conspiracy-members. Seeing this guy here is no surprise.

If you want, go to the intersection on Google Streetview, and click the little link in the black box in the upper right of the screen which says, "See more dates." On the bottom of the screen will be other imagery timelines for you to peruse. There is something on this side-road which is hot, which local surveillance is assigned overwatch for, because in perusing the timelines, you will notice everything from people standing around watching the intersection, to a tinted Humpty Dumpty technical van sitting on it.

Remember later on that there was almost always traffic at this intersection turning on and off this street, on different timelines, when you passed. It will become significant at the end of our route here.

My assumption is Bulgaria wants somebody stationed at intersections, in a static position, to make absolutely sure someone is there who can call if you took the turn or continued straight, right past the intersection.

Vehicles on the road are subject to traffic, and could get trapped behind people and lose you or not see what you do. So the static unit makes the call on whether you turned or not. Where I see it here, it is often a redundancy backing an arrangement of vehicular units which are arriving at the intersection.

In real covert surveillance designed to gather intelligence, the procedures would be different, and I suspect the loitering foot units would hide inside shops, or in cars in the parking lot, maybe with their backs to the intersection, watching through rear-view mirrors, to be less conspicuous.

In surveillance speak, the text books say they call this a "commit" position. The purpose of it is to make sure the broader cloud of surveillance assets surrounding this position, but far enough away to be out of sight, will know which way you turned (committed to), and which way you are heading. Once your direction of travel is radioed, the cloud of assets can begin moving, out of your sight, to better surround and contain you as you move.

A commit unit can be a car, a jogger, a guy sitting on his bicycle, a dog walker, a member of a road crew doing something with a sightline to the intersection, a phone company tech in his cherry picker, just about anything you can imagine. They will not generally be FBI-Agent looking guys in suits and sunglasses talking into their wrists as you pass unless you really pissed someone off, and it is purely harassment-surveillance.

Most likely you will be looking at soccer moms, obese people, geriatrics, and even children, which are children of the surveillance people building experience in the field, at least in the United States.

If you approach the intersection while in the opposite lane of the main road, on another timeline, you can look across the intersection and see a dark car stationed at the end of the road we will take, parked catty-corner all the way down the road, off on the dirt:[47]

If you took the turn down that road on that trip from the opposite far lane, that car would have begun moving as you entered the turn lane, and come at you, as if it just happened to be driving there just as you arrived, and the dance would have begun.

He may be a unit which is unrelated to your follow, and that position is where he remains staged for long periods of time, waiting for the radio to deliver orders to check something out in his sector. I have seen evidence most neighborhoods have at least one vehicular unit assigned almost all the time like that, staged just like this within the neighborhood, ready to check out anything interesting control sees happening on their telephone pole tech and other technical monitoring devices.

Such units will not remain in their staged position, static as you enter a side road, and let you see them sitting there as you pass them. In my experience, they usually pick up and begin moving toward you, and exit the neighborhood when you enter, as if they were already leaving. Most people will see them, and never think twice.

If you are under harassment surveillance, or you are aware of your surveillance, and they are not hiding, they may sit there and glare at you as you pass. In harassment surveillance I have even had multiple cars all break out the aviator sunglasses and glare as they drove by me, to heighten the intimidation, as if they are all government agents.

In that timeline above, you were driving by so fast, they called that you weren't taking that road, so the unit just sat there, as you can see, waiting at the end of the road.

Notice again, a random overhead, shot around this time of day, showed no traffic back there, and as you will see, there really isn't much back there for people to be traveling around to. And again, if you see this type of traffic, you have to take every possibility with a grain of salt. We know what you are seeing here is surveillance on this go-around because this is the Google car operating in Bulgaria. But in your real life, this could arguably be normal background noise.

However, this is the important thing – these Streetview drives are about showing you what real surveillance looks like as it tries to look normal. Once you see what it looks like here, and pick up on the nuances, you will begin to see it, and recognize it in your own community in America. It is everywhere in the US, far more dense than any other place I have seen on Streetview.

Now go back to how we began our approach to this intersection, so you may continue your right-hand turn, into that side street, as we were doing originally.

First thing, again, is you have two cars poised on the side street opposite you, ready to turn off in each direction:[48]

We're just generally noting traffic density and positioning at intersections here. That street (seen below in yellow) which the two cars (circled in red) are on, literally only serves the two buildings on the corners there, if you look at the overhead:[49]

So you have to ask, how often are cars turning out of it? What are the chances that intersection is a bustle of activity on both sides just at the very moment when you happen there, to turn off?

Again, this is a Google car in Bulgaria, and that is surveillance. Understand what it looks like, because you will see it in your own life in the US.

As you will see in this drive, when you are under Stasi surveillance, wherever you are, is a bustle of activity. If in your real life, you find that is a pattern, especially when you go to places which should not be a bustle of activity, a local cell of the domestic Stasi in America, responsible for your neighborhood, may have concluded you are in some way interesting.

Now before going forward into this side street, lets back up and get in the lane on the highway to turn into this side street.

Look at the street, as far down as you can from there, before you hit the turn, for any vehicle that might be staged the way you saw a vehicle staged when you were traveling the other way on the highway., ie, at the end of the road, just sitting on the dirt, parked and waiting to pick up, if you turn on the street.

If you do that, you will see this:[50]

That is some sort of delivery van set up there. Get used to seeing commercial vehicles being used in surveillance. There is a Johnsonville Brats commercial along those lines which is uproarious… because it is so real. It is located at: https://vimeo.com/129326661

It features a very realistic looking FBI surveillance van:

It is a joke, but it is not far off from real life. You will see a lot of vehicles like that when you ae under surveillance, only they will not have all of the satellite antennae.

Returning to our drive, now move to the side street and complete the turn onto it, and you have two vehicles at the end of the road facing you (in the back is the staged van still parked, which has allowed another car to pass it), as well as a third car which turned off just before you, and is driving just ahead of you.[51]

Remember our Russian drive began with a pedestrian with a baby stroller on the corner and a car which turned off ahead of you. Here, pedestrian commit units are posted at the intersection, and a cheating command vehicle turns off ahead of you.

You will see the first car immediately coming at you.[52]

Again, he doesn't look at the google car, despite the big camera ball, and the incredibly intricate mounting system you can see in the reflection of his windows here:[53]

I've seen the Google cars of this era several times with their massive camera balls, and today I would still be looking on with great interest. But not him.

One, he has been briefed on the fact he will be following a Google car, so for him it is no surprise to see it. Two, this may be the fiftieth or sixtieth follow of a Google car he has done in the last two months because the Google car has been mapping out his sector for that period, so it is nothing unusual. And three, he has been trained to ignore targets, so a suspicious target will not catch him glaring at them, and wonder if he might be surveillance.

So this is a behavior that is unusual in a normal context, but one which would make perfect sense if he is surveillance assigned to track the Google car's travels.

Often in places like the US, where surveillance is very broadly deployed in every neighborhood, you will see at least one unit that is stationed in a neighborhood exit the neighborhood just as you enter it (or even as you pass by the entrance to a neighborhood which surveillance thought you might enter).

As they exit, these exiting units are probably looking in the front of your vehicle to confirm occupancy one last time before you potentially make contact with a residence in the neighborhood. If you are getting real, non-harassment surveillance, they will tend to want to leave you be in a neighborhood, in hopes you will do something interesting they can document. They prefer not to risk exposure with drivebys, or units you might see and notice.

If however, you begin to get harassment coverage, you may even get the same intersection treatment every time you leave or arrive home at your house, with vehicles suddenly appearing to drive toward you as you exit your driveway and begin your travels, to confirm occupancy at the beginning of your travels, and doing the same on your arrival home.

If you want to have fun, get a mannequin with a wig in your passenger seat, and periodically pull it up and push it down when no cars are around, as you drive along. You may see surveillance second guess themselves, wondering if they missed a pickup you made, or if they have inadvertently lost your car and picked up a lookalike at some point, which means somebody will have to come in for a closer look to confirm you are their target and get a look at your passenger. Disguises for yourself, like long blonde wigs, or old bald man latex masks, and jacket/shirt changes could also make for fun times.

Next up is the second car that was staged there as you turned off, a trade van. He opted to wait and create spacing with the next vehicle, both to appear unrelated to their movements, and to lengthen the period over which you will be observed. As he passes, he does look, as he talks on the phone, and from his expression, he appears to be having fun playing junior spy:[54]

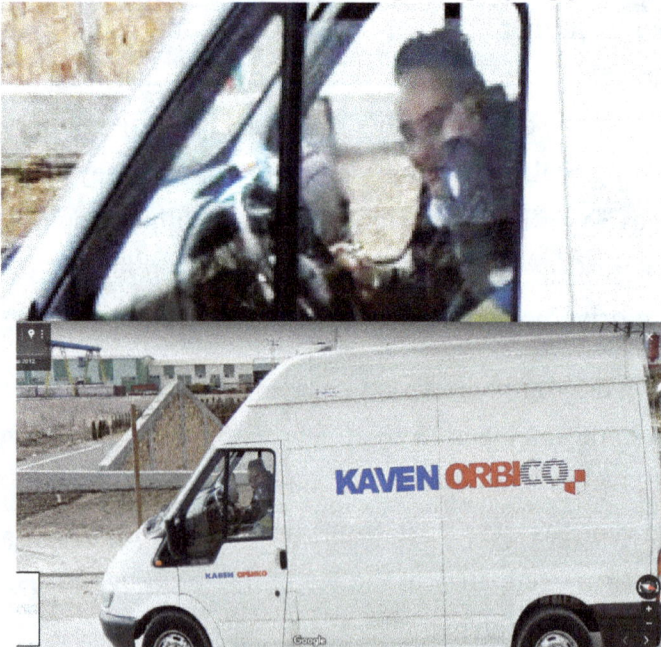

The looking would almost make me think he is innocent, even as I wonder who he is on the phone with. But I recognize he was staged, back when you first turned off, and waited until you came into view to pick up and move.

It is possible when they recruit tradesmen to use their occupations as cover, and to get access to the interior of residences and businesses which hire them, the recruits are not professional spies, but rather are more like civilian Stasi volunteers, and thus are less professional.

You can see the delivery truck sat motionless in the road for some time after you turned off, not moving and letting the first little SUV get ahead of it. Here is a photo when you first turned off, and you can see the little SUV leading it was stacked right in front of it, to the point he was on its tailgate:[55]

Here is what it looked like going the other way, just after you passed the delivery truck:[56]

You can see how far ahead that first little SUV got. You can actually see that the delivery truck was sitting there from the two images before you took the turnoff from the highway, but you might not have noticed unless you knew to look for it specifically - from experiences like you now have with surveillance. Not even four chapters in, and you are already an operator who would see this before turning off, and know what it would mean:[57]

Again, it's a little thing which seems of no significance if you lived in the America we were told existed, where there was no domestic surveillance like the East German Stasi. But today America is vastly different from that noble image you were sold on, and it is worse if you are politically active, or overly successful in business.

If you organized for Ron Paul or Bernie Sanders, or your small business has found a niche and begun to really take off, that is what you look out for. Yet how many Americans, do you think, would scan their periphery for something like that? That is why the myth persists that there is privacy in America, and something like the American Stasi could not possibly exist. By the end of this book, you will know the truth. You will see the surveillance.

If you look back on the turnoff now, a vehicle has turned off behind you from oncoming traffic on the highway and will now follow you to the next intersection.

You are in the bubble, contained by the surveillance team:[58]

Again, with a car in front of you, a car behind you, two cars driving opposite, and two cars at the opposite side of the intersection behind you, there is a lot of traffic here just as you arrive, and I would wonder to myself if this side street is always this busy, given how little there is back here on the overhead.

Although we don't know time-frames from the overhead traffic shot at the beginning, I am thinking probably not, but we will see as we continue to drive.

As we continue, you will see this next vehicle.

It is parked off the side of the dirt road that heads left at the end of the side street. Here it is as you approach the intersection:[59]

Notice, there is nowhere for him to get out of the vehicle and go. This is an office supply delivery truck which pulled off the road, headed down a dirt road with no offices on it, for a fair way, and stopped in a spot where there is no building to enter. If I were that driver, and I wanted to pull off this main road to have lunch or make a phone call, I would pull just off it in a way so pulling back on it would be easier when I decided I wanted to continue on my way. And if I was going in that building he is parked in front of, I would have entered the parking lot thirty feet behind him, so I would not have to walk back and around that fence. But he's just sitting, with nothing around, and nowhere to get out and walk to.

My guess is after you get out of sight, he will turn around and take up the staged position the last staged delivery truck just left. In the meantime, he is the static commit unit posted at this intersection, to radio whether you turn left toward him, or right and head away from him. He also can act as a commit unit for the next intersection if you turn right at this one, since he has a sightline to that intersection as well, from that position. Using that position is a good use of team resources, as a single vehicle, placed along your least likely direction of travel, guarantees the team will get your decision at this decision point, and the next likely decision point as well.

Notice also his positioning. Surveillance people are trained to maximize their sightlines to you, and minimize your sightlines to them, and they are trained to, when possible, use their vehicle's mirrors. A car turned away from you at an angle that allows him to use that driver's side rearview mirror to watch you, lets him see you without you seeing him. Now if they need a foot unit to follow you into a store, that guy can do it without any fear you will realize that you and he crossed paths before. They will also use such positioning to stay in the blindspot of your vehicle when possible.

Their ideal is to be in a car positioned like that, which as you turn, will be at your seven o'clock, in your left, driver's side blind spot, as you head to the next intersection.

143

Also, when you are under coverage, a lot of your coverage will be specialty trucks like this. Most of them appear real. Either the surveillance people take on real jobs for those companies, or they recruit these people, who already have these jobs, into the Secret Society of Stasi surveillance people, under something like Operation TIPS.

If you get a vehicle like this following you or posted outside your house, you might have problems. The most notable case was the one videoed by John Lang, who we will discuss later. He posted a video to YouTube of a carpet cleaning truck like that which he said just delivered a hit team to the house next door, which was about to kill him. He was found stabbed in his burning house shortly thereafter. In America, this operation is shockingly criminal, and has nothing to do with national security or law enforcement. It's only about who controls the United States.

When you get to the end of this first straightaway, if you take the dirt road off to the left by that van, you will shift time-frames, so we will do that later so as to maintain continuity of travel on this route. Down there is a dead end with nothing "operationally significant" to a surveillance operation, so it will be a good example of what you will see if you ever take such a path while under coverage.

Instead however, at the end of this street, where you can go either right or left, for now we will take a right, and continue on to the next intersection. There, at that intersection, we will be able to go straight, and follow a looped road counterclockwise back to that intersection, or we can turn left, catch the end of the looped road, and follow it clockwise.

Approaching the first decision point, to go left or right:[60]

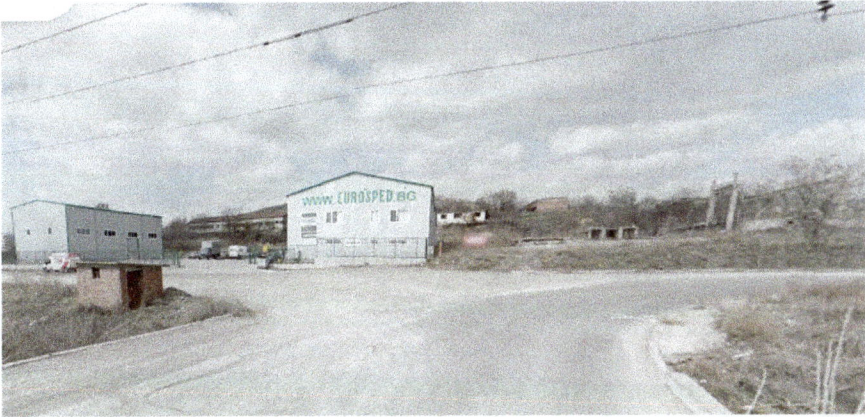

Behind you, another vehicle has turned onto the road, behind the vehicle behind you:[61]

It is a regular traffic jam back here.

Go right. As we arrive at the second intersection another car is approaching from the oncoming lane as you approach it:[62]

As you pass it, it will have a GPS mounted to the windshield.[63]

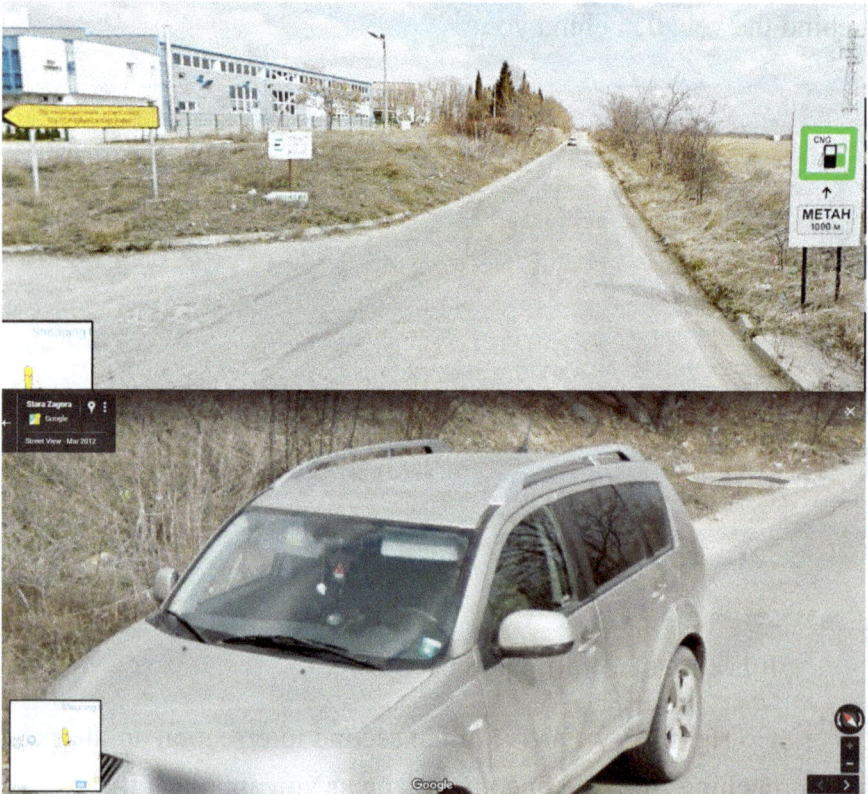

Obviously, oncoming traffic at intersections can always be innocent. But I always register it as a weak indicator, since arriving at an intersection just as a target does, is a surveillance

146

technique. If it happens at almost all intersections, even in areas like this (you are about to see the road this car is on has almost no traffic), then it can begin to give you an idea that those cars are not arriving at the intersections you arrive at, just at the very moment you arrive at them, entirely by chance, over and over. Again, you have to calculate the probability, on a road with no traffic, that just as you arrive at the intersection, another car is always just hitting the intersection too.

Also take a moment to consider how high-level this training is. You are, even now, more experienced at spotting surveillance than many elite government operatives. And from here, your skills will grow exponentially as you continue.

Also, in just observing the traffic levels back here, if you look back, as the car following you is turning off, another car has arrived at the previous intersection. The office supply truck is still sitting straight behind you, on the other side of the intersection:[64]

At this intersection, we will go straight to maintain continuity of the Google car's photographic timeline, since it went straight as well, as it was photographing.

147

The lack of side streets on this road is a problem for surveillance, because any following vehicle cannot turn off, and new vehicles cannot turn on. That raises the possibility of a target feeling as if they are being followed, as time goes on and a single car behind them stays behind them.

Surveillance knows this and tries to avoid that. So the car behind you will turn off to the left, and they will either post a vehicle here or send another vehicle to follow you, keeping as far back as possible to prevent you from noticing it, to make sure you don't double back on the team.

This team opted to have a vehicle follow you but it will stay so far back it will almost be invisible. If you were actually of interest, and not a mere Google car, I would have assumed they'd have called in one of the planes most security services, including America's Stasi, keep in the air every day for just such occasions. I have actually gotten aviation - helicopters and planes - quite often.

As you start down the road, you will notice the oncoming car takes a right, which is the other side of this loop, which will take a path that parallels this road (and backtracks to where he just came from, if he follows the entire loop, driving opposite to you).

Also, the other car has just arrived at the intersection behind you, and will turn off and follow him:[65]

148

They will now drive at high speed on the parallel street, to get to the far part of the loop ahead of you, and turn off it so they are ahead of you on the street which splits off from the far side of the loop, in case you head in that direction.

In the below image, the intersection behind you is circled in red, the path the surveillance vehicles are taking is in yellow, and your path is in blue. They will be speeding to where the blue and yellow paths meet, which is where a third green street splits off and heads to a different location. They will turn down that green street, head to the next series of intersections and begin to set up a follow which would pick you up and transmit your directions of travel, should you head in that direction:

You can see, they are heading where you are going, on a parallel street, to get control over the route you might use to try to escape their bubble, if you do not follow the loop.

So to recap traffic at the last intersection, light SUV behind you turns off, oncoming car turns off, second car behind you turns off, SUV turns off side street and heads back to the main drag away from you (you have to zoom as you drive away to see it), office supply truck maintains his position watching both intersections, and finally a light SUV/truck turns on behind you from the second intersection, back behind you, and maintains a set following distance behind you, literally as far back as he can be so you won't see him, while maintaining sight of you from behind:

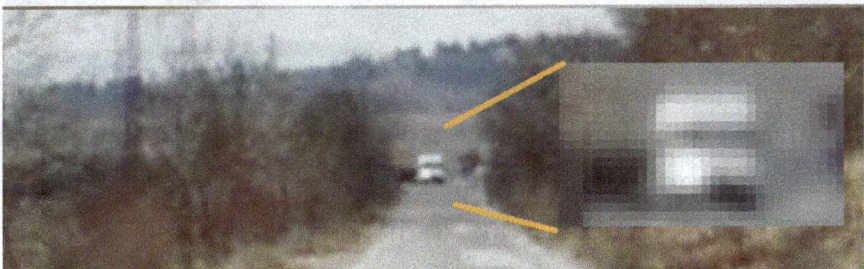

Notice he is only running one headlight in the image above. Surveillance vehicles are set up so you can shut off either headlight using a switch under the dashboard. It is often used as part of prearranged signals which teams have for non-radio communications, where it is thought a wary target might be signal sweeping the radiofrequency spectrum to detect any potential surveillance team following him. It can also be used as a signal to local law enforcement that a vehicle is surveillance and is operational, and should be left alone, and that the Police assets in the area should withdraw so as to not spook a target. And in cases like this, it can be used to shift up the "silhouette" of a following vehicle, by making it appear this vehicle has a headlight out. If a target sees a similar vehicle later, but both headlights work, they will be likely to assume it is a different vehicle, and they are not, in fact, being followed by a surveillance team. Remember the one headlight thing. You will see it in a number of places as we go forward.

He is not really following you to make observations, he is just making sure you don't double back. If you look back unzoomed, this is what you would see:

So long as you just drive through, he will just tail you from that far back, and most people would never even see him. But if you stopped and got out on foot, he would drive by as he radioed it in, and all of a sudden the traffic driving by would increase substantially, probably in both directions, and the passing vehicles would have offloaded foot surveillance just out of sight which would suddenly just happen through from each side, pushing baby carriages, riding bikes, and walking dogs, all looking completely innocent. All over the town, undercover surveillance peoples' phone apps would begin going off, directing them to pass by you and send back observations. It is how it works.

Again, you can use that information to test whether you have coverage if you ever run a real-life countersurveillance detection route like this. Go somewhere you should be alone, get out and move off the road and hide, and see if suddenly the place heats up and gets active.

In the United States, if America was like they taught us, this would all be coincidence. Obviously, this being the Google car, in Bulgaria, which is noted for the aggression of its state security services, you pretty much know what you are looking at. It is just surprising to me to see an even more aggressive surveillance operation in America, and know what I am looking at there too. Things do not work in America the way they have told you.

In the US, along this route I would expect to encounter dog walkers, joggers, bikers, parked cars, and I would expect at least one observation post in at least one of the buildings, from which monitors inside would be watching hidden pole surveillance on the telephone poles, both microphones, and hidden cameras.

Looking at this trip, I am amazed Bulgaria has so little surveillance compared to what I see in the United States. I would also expect the pole surveillance all along the road would be wired into either an observation post on the road, hidden in a plain looking house or building, or it would be sent to a central control room over internet connections on the poles, from which a central command would be monitoring you along the route remotely, and issuing directives to the team on the ground following you as the operation unfolded. That sounds like hyperbole or fantasy in the US, but I have seen it with my own eyes. And I would bet, soon you will too.

In the US, any area which surveillance has found to be problematic for conducting follows unobserved (and they are doing this all the time, all over, to everyone, so they will have identified the areas where it is difficult to follow a target unobserved), that area will be altered to make it less problematic through the use of deployed technology. Very quickly utility trucks would roll into an area like this and install all kinds of microphones and cameras on the telephone poles, disguised as cable internet routers and electrical transformers.

I would also have expected ten or fifteen oncoming cars at least, over the course of this drive, and more if I was stopping and getting out on foot. I would expect, in my own life, probably five times the coverage you see here, and if I had just reached out to the Russians, or otherwise pissed my coverage off, it would be up to twenty times this, just as a show of force and intimidation.

With time, I'll post a video of literally, a non-stop caravan of vehicles that lasted about fifteen minutes, bumper to bumper, driving slowly by me in a remote parking lot, just to show off the local unit's vehicular manpower, with everything from delivery vehicles, to dirt bikes, to airstream-like towed campers. Knowing they were all helpless pussies, incapable of violence, who needed the group to feel safe, I was unimpressed.

But there is a reason I can see this all so clearly, and I came up with such a creative way to school you up on the finer points of surveillance operations, with actual real life scenes. I have been buried under the surveillance of the American Stasi for a long, long time.

Oddly enough, many, many of you have too, you have just never stopped to look and see it, or recognize what it was you were looking directly at. Returning to our drive, Bulgaria is obviously making sure nobody contacts that Google car without it being documented.

Which brings us to our first potential contacts on this trip, with whom, were we operational, we could exchange contraband, or sensitive intelligence, which would be of operational significance to our surveillance. Observe the roofers here on the right:[66]

They don't appear to be surveillance, although one is on a phone. Between the ladder and the bucket, it seems unlikely a surveillance operator would have that on hand in their car.

In the US, they could be TIPS informants in the Secret Society who are legitimately employed as roofers, and were recruited to do surveillance part time. Here, they'd get a text on their phone from Control to watch as you passed the GPS location of their cell phone, at the jobsite they were already working at.

In America, it appears the central control running surveillance follows will have their target's GPS phone location up on a map on a big screen, as well as the nearby GPS locations of all the cell phones of the American Stasi's civilian informants, who have installed the Stasi's app on their phone, and can be called into duty. I was in BJ's, turned a corner, and a fat woman had her back to me. On her smart phone screen was a photo of me taken that day, in the clothes I was wearing. She turned around, saw me, saw I saw her phone, and took off. Command had directed her to the BJ's I had travelled to, and sent her a photo of me, and she was looking for me, presumably to hover around me and text updates to whoever was running my follow. It is beyond obnoxious.

Go to the url above and zoom into the distance. You will notice that the white car parked on the right side of the road in the distance has a sightline to you, as you come in close proximity to the roofers. That will be significant in a moment.,[67]

154

Then there were these two guys:[68]

Pointing to them being innocent is that it appears somebody was hosing down that vehicle to clean it off, so they'd have a reason for standing there. However good operators will grab a hose and do things like that to give themselves a cover for being there. As I will argue in a moment, these may not have been surveillance, but it does not mean they were not interesting.

Somewhat strange, is the guy who is standing with his back to the road, and who has no curiosity of what car is driving behind him or who is in it. If I was standing talking to that guy, I just see myself standing there facing him. And even if I had my back to the road, if I heard a car driving by, I'd give a glance to the road as the car passes.

Odd too is all the security cameras at that facility, one of which, right above them, appears to be pointed at the road, possibly to grab plates, as well as others on the other side, above the barbed wire:[69]

Then again, it appears to be a heating oil company, and heating oil companies often offer service contracts. That means employees can get free access to the interior of homes and businesses from the owners to perform service. In the world of domestic intelligence, such employees will often be recruited by nosy security services, looking to bribe their employees to do illegal searches of customer's properties, which the security services would be unable to do themselves.

Fall under FBI surveillance, and try to get some electrical or plumbing work done on your house, and you will find out what that means. It is not as easy as you would think to get clean service, without a free search of your house by an FBI informant, who would claim to be acting on his own initiative as a citizen, and thus not need a warrant as the FBI would, even though FBI was paying him to do it, and even issued him an order to do it.

When the George W. Bush administration was attempting to set up an official domestic spying program modeled on the Stasi, called Operation TIPS[70] (this endnote is a must-read), the mission statement said it would preferentially recruit civilian surveillance/informants from such service people, so the service people/informants, acting as independent citizens, independent of government, could conduct what would otherwise be illegal searches in homes, while given access to them by the homeowner to perform the repairs or maintenance their companies offered. These would be searches which law enforcement could not get warrants for, but which apparently they felt would be fine if they could bribe the right person to perform the search for the agency.

So if you are under surveillance, and the heat went out on a cold winter night, and you needed an oil burner service call, part of the deal in America would be you have to implicitly agree to give up your Fourth Amendment rights, and allow the service person/government-agent to poke around your home for the government, to make sure you were in full compliance with all government edicts, while he worked.

Maybe Bulgarian Secret Police might use a company like this fuel oil company as a cover for surveillance operations, and then tuck some secret facility away back in an area like this, as long as they are there.

It might even be why the Google car decided to run back here, to give CIA, or whoever is running it, a quick peek at the lay of the land in this area in the event they ever wanted to come back here operationally.

I am beginning to wonder if you could map out the locations of secret foreign intelligence operations centers in countries that the West is hostile to, by looking at where the Google car has chosen to run into one single area, while neglecting many other similar areas right nearby. If you zoom out and look at the maps, street view is quite spotty in a lot of these areas, choosing only to run into select, isolated spots, where I assume CIA, or the amorphous non-state intelligence operation behind the trans-national surveillance operations of the West, wanted to get some on-the-ground photography, under the cover of a simple Google car run.

Regardless, the two guys in the driveway of the oil supply place are not probative to any surveillance detection effort, even though one probably should show more interest.

There was a guy digging right after that, and a fork lift operator running a fork lift off the side of the road on the opposite side.[71]

The digger is on the left in this shot above with his back to you, and the forklift is the small orange thing behind the fence on the right side of the road.

The digger's hole has taken a while to dig, and he has a pickaxe laid out, which a surveillance guy jumping out of his car with a shovel for cover would probably not think to grab. Of course he has his back to you as you approach, to conceal his face, he is holding some sort of spade instead of the shovel, and he never actually moves or uses it during the entire time you approach, pass, and travel on (and if he was using it, it is not clear to me what he would be doing with it from that position).

It is possible he was a passing surveillance guy (maybe

even the navigator of the car you are about to see), and saw the tools laid out, parked quickly, jumped out and grabbed them, and posed. In the US it would not surprise me to find he flashed a fake FBI badge at the real digger, told him to move to concealment, and picked up the spade himself to pose. A good surveillance guy would probably do exactly that. So when under coverage, never relax, or assume you know anything. But here, he doesn't feel like surveillance to me. Likewise the forklift guy would be redundant to the white car, and would appear to not be surveillance either.

I am, however, struck by the plethora of people surrounding a facility with a plethora of modern, professionally installed surveillance cameras, which maintain good coverage of people both outside and about to enter the facility, as well as those already inside the gates. Especially since we have seen nobody else on this road, until we got to this facility, which has six people on foot symmetrically disbursed, two on one side of the entrance, two on the other, and two standing in the entrance. There is a lot of activity concentrated right here at this spot.

Either way, none of the people on foot are probative for surveillance detection purposes, and for the purposes of further exposition on surveillance procedures, we will assume they are all regular citizens going about their day.

In the eyes of the surveillance tracking the Google car, all of these people in this area would be a risk of contact and interaction. One of the primary objectives of surveillance is to control, or at least document, all of the interactions the target has with other individuals. If you were a CIA officer driving the Google car, you and any of these people could exchange contraband, or documents, or thumb drives, or other operationally significant materials. Surveillance has to be on top of that. So when you are under coverage, you will not get to have uncontrolled contacts without your surveillance right there.

Knowing this is obviously relevant to detection, since if you see what appear to be innocent people, that is when surveillance will move in close and make sure you are completely covered and could not even "brush pass" something off to them. And that is when the surveillance will be most obvious.

Enter the white car which you will pass next, that is parked by the side of the road, with the driver not getting out to go anywhere, or preparing to leave:[72]

Driver's window is open, and his elbow is resting in the opening. An open window is a surveillance procedure, which allows the vehicular surveillance agent to better experience the environment around his vehicle.

If your car starts making funny noises, or emitting funny smells, he will want to report to the team you may be about to have a breakdown, so they can work on inserting their tow truck driver to respond to it, when you call AAA. Plus it prevents someone from sneaking up on his car as he is staking something out, and taking him out.

Also, he is texting on his phone, and parked strangely in the oncoming lane to improve his sightline to the road near the roofers and the other people on the opposite side of the road. Moreover, there is literally nothing for him to get out of that car and go to. One side of the road is an empty dirt field, the other side is a wall with a chain-link fence on top of it, and there are no houses or businesses to walk to. He is there, just for you:[73]

At this point, you should be beginning to think this material looks interesting, and that this Google car is actually under surveillance, and I just might know what I am talking about here. Moreover, if so, it's possible I am correct that an operation like this exists in the United States and is embedded in every local neighborhood, and that it is targeting you, and your children.

If so, and there is a shadow intelligence operation embedded in your community, working against you and your children, controlling the path of your lives from your earliest days for the benefit of the elites, then what I am showing you might be the most important information you will ever lay eyes on. Our country might actually be in the peril I claim, and everything might rest on you, and your ability to help spread this information.

Moreover, you should be asking how a biotech-geek with no official intelligence training, could have come up with all this, unless he has been buried under a massive hostile surveillance operation just like this, for the last ten years, in the United States, for nothing more than engaging in simple online political discussions. You should also realize, I must not be alone. Reams of your countrymen are also afflicted. It is horrific, and it is growing and coming for you, and eventually your children, some day.

In this instance, the problem surveillance probably identified, and which this posted vehicular unit above is designed to address, was that the roofers were there right after a turn in the road which obstructed the sightline of that following vehicle who is still traveling way back behind you on the road.

In addition, these other people on the side of the road are also massive risks of contact. So if this white car were not here, there would have been a moment when you could have jumped out and thrown a satchel to the roofers, jumped back in your car, and been on your way. Or one of the people standing around could have feigned crossing the road as you passed, and you could have tried a driving brush-pass of a thumb drive, which could not be seen unless you had someone right there.

White car is likely there to make sure that didn't happen. As I pointed out, surveillance will become most obvious when you are alone with other innocent people, and it has to draw close and loiter to observe everything in fine detail.

In real life, if you feel you should have coverage for political reasons, or you are operating as a spy overseas, or you have pissed off someone wealthy or powerful in the United States who could turn this machine on you, or if you just live in America and post political materials to Twitter, this is one of the stronger indicators you would see that surveillance is moving in on you.

Somebody sitting in a car with no reason to be there, near where you could possibly be making uncontrolled contacts.

It is always possible that guy just stopped there to answer a text from his wife. But his elbow on the window frame, as if he has been there a while and is in no rush, the use of the phone as you pass, and his being the only car you see, who just happens to be set up with a clear sightline to the people you just passed, while not near anything else which might explain his presence, is a pretty strong indication he is domestic surveillance.

Of course it is worth noting before we move on, that nobody you have just seen may have been who they were pretending to be, and surveillance itself may not have known what was going on. My impression is surveillance people are lower in the hierarchy of intelligence work, with it often even being used as a sort of entry-level position to vet prospective recruits for more important postings. Most of the work, while high-stress and an effective test of operational capability, is really not that important. They can put new recruits on it, and see how they do.

So surveillance would probably not have been read in on the presence of any secret facilities back here, or what the security situation around them was.

If there is a secret intelligence facility back here, then nobody you saw may have been as they appeared. All of the people we discounted as regular people going about their day, could have simply been covert security.

Covert facilities, hidden in civilian areas, and made to appear as civilian facilities will not use uniformed security personnel around them for obvious reasons. They are trying to be covert and blend in. But they will still need to deploy security personnel arrayed around their perimeter to offer resistance in the event of a hostile intrusion.

It is entirely possible that had a guy jumped out of the Google car with a submachine gun to launch an assault on the oil-supply facility's gate, the guy on the fork lift would have jumped off with an AK, the two roofers would have hopped out prone on the far side of the roof looking over the top and come up with a couple of SVK sniper rifles, and the two guys in the entrance to the oil place would have pulled out their own submachine guns to meet him, as the digger pulled an RPG out of the hole and punched his engine block to prevent him from fleeing.

I do find it odd that Google is back here, surveillance is almost as heavy as it is in suburban America, this facility has so many cameras, and there just happen to be so many blue collar workers using forklifts, doing roof repair, and digging holes, all at once, all in this single spot, on this fairly long road, all within sightlines, and firing lines to the entrance of this facility.

If my hypothesis, that Google streetview was being used by Western intelligence as a cover to "innocently" scout out intel facilities in unfriendly countries that have resisted being subverted by Western intelligence, then all these photographs of the Google car, could be much more interesting than they look. Because while the Google car can drive back here and claim it is motivated by some innocent hippie dream of photographing the world, CIA could never send a regular civilian in to photograph this place, without fearing they might get scooped up into a van by some angry Bulgarian spooks and never heard from again. Google Streetview is a great cover.

If I am right, these Streetviews will be a goldmine as a training tool, for making the general populace more surveillance-aware. Many of these trips may actually be dramatic intelligence battles between hostile intelligence services, being fought in the hidden, covert fashion intelligence agencies wage them, right in the open.

The truth is if you are a private sector entity, and you want to accumulate the trappings of a real intelligence agency without real intelligence agencies having cause to take you out, having something like Google would be a gold mine. It is no wonder it is one of the central nodes of whatever the non-state intelligence operation is, that is taking over the West, and destroying it.

Remember, one of the most important lessons in detecting surveillance and intelligence activity is to be aware of statistical probabilities, and their relation to patterns, when you are running detection for hostile activity.

This whole segment of the Streetview drive almost feels

165

like the opening scene of a Burn Notice episode (See the first three minutes and forty five seconds of this: https://tinyurl.com/m6hdurx6). The guy who wrote that TV Show saw that the American Stasi was taking over the United States, and wrote that show as a subversive effort to educate the nation, trying to prepare people for what was coming by giving them the weapons this conspiracy didn't want them to have – a knowledge of surveillance and intelligence.

If you love America and see Americans as your brothers, you will want to make everyone as strong as they can be. Whoever wrote Burn Notice was doing that. I strongly recommend everyone watch the first five seasons as a primer on how to spot the machine taking over the US, and on the power of deception and intelligence operations.

If you want every American weak and clueless, as the American Stasi does, then you can't, by definition, view them as your brothers and equals. You view them as your serfs, and you will weaken them as best you can so you can dominate them as a dictator.

In my eyes, all of the talk of our "Constitution" that protects us, our checks and balances afforded by three branches of government that prevent corruption, the constantly repeated refrain that the CIA is not allowed to operate domestically, and our intelligence agencies would never target our citizens (even if the citizens were about to take over the government from them in a landslide election), the talk of how we elect our leaders, and thus control our government, even just public schools telling children they can be whatever they want to be, as well as the promulgation of the idea we have a free press which would expose corruption -

that is all designed to weaken you. None of that is true. This operation has come in, and corrupted each of those entities, making it a conspirator which merely looks like it would fight the conspiracy, when in reality is is all working together to support it.

At the end of the day, you are the biggest threat to the intelligence operation which runs this country. They have been targeting you because of that since you were a child, in the public schools, using their own children as junior operatives, as we will reveal later, and feeding you lies about how everything worked. Sadly, there is no shortage of your "fellow Americans," who are delighted to help them keep you deceived as they subvert our government and operate against you in your community, if only the conspiracy will line their pockets a little more than everyone else's.

As you move on in our Bulgarian surveillance adventure, and leave behind all the action you just encountered, you will see why White Car set up back that far away from everything, and on the wrong side of the road. He wanted to maintain eyes on you as long as possible as the road you are following curves to the left and you head out of sight around the turn.

Notice, the forklift guy behind him, who is still not doing anything, took up an even superior position to keep eyes on that curve, which allows him both to watch you, as you follow the arc of the road, and to get eyes on anyone coming from that direction, beginning as soon as possible, as they approach from that side:[74]

The amusing thing is, if you go back and look, forklift guy had nothing to forklift there. The only thing he possibly could have used his lift on was a large empty bin, but he was nowhere near it

The amusing thing is, if you go back and look, forklift guy had nothing to forklift there. The only thing he possibly could have used his lift on was a large empty bin, but he was nowhere near it the whole time you were there, and there were no pallets nearby to hoist. Go and zoom in, and look for yourself:[75]

Surveillance people have been doing these things a long time, and after a while these little considerations regarding where to position themselves, to extend their ability to observe moving targets for as long as possible, come to them as almost second nature.

You'll notice as you continue, there is a dead dog by the side of the road.[76]

It is a little thing, but since we are here and you can see the example, surveillance often produces a tremendous increase in roadkill in its areas of operations. Vehicular surveillance involves a lot of driving at high speeds just outside of the target's sight in an effort to get ahead of them and keep them in the bubble. As you are driving here in the Google car, the vehicles you saw at the last intersection are driving as fast as they possibly can on the far leg of the road, to hit the far side of this loop ahead of you. Had you taken the far leg, vehicles on this side would have peeled through here at high speed, seeking to beat you to the upcoming intersection. Their only desire would be to head out on the road leading away from this loop ahead of you, and begin preparing a phase of your follow in that direction, in the event you took that other road. What they would not want is you reaching that intersection first, peeling out away from here, and getting outside of their bubble.

When I first came under extreme harassment surveillance, my neighborhood became littered with dead raccoons, and possums, and squirrels, lining the side of the road. My family had fed the raccoons since before I was born, but with surveillance, it is not really something you can do, unless you want the front of your house littered with dead carcasses.

I even found myself on a day-long drive, noticing the same car appear 50 feet ahead of me five different times, immediately after which my car filled with the smell of skunk.

It was one vehicle in a group tracking me for the day, and the car had run over a skunk earlier, and was offgassing the smell, so every time it took a cheating command position on me, my car would fill with the smell of skunk.

The death of these innocent animals, for such a stupid, craven, criminal conspiracy, is all very irritating. I suspect if you got rid of surveillance, you would see a dramatic reduction in roadkill numbers across the nation. Surveillance is a menace in so many ways, from the undoubted increases in cancer cases from their wide use of through-wall radiant imaging technologies, to their stymieing of children in the schools who appear too moral, and too academically capable at the same time, to their promotion of degenerates to high positions in society, simply so they can control them. Even the carbon emissions of surveillance vehicles, and the increases in gas prices due to them constantly driving around all the time is a cost. The day we rid our nation of it will be a day when pure goodness will have won, in many, many ways.

So while I have no idea how this dog died, I do know if there is a secret facility here, and surveillance operates more densely here, and a target was driving on the other street, his following coverage would have hit this road and driven as fast as humanly possible to get ahead of the target at the next intersection, and over time, dead animals would begin to line the road. It is one of the minor indices I would notice based on experience, and think to myself there was a heightened likelihood surveillance was operating more densely in an area.

The next driveway is gated and guarded by a guardhouse. After passing it you come to an open gate, and inside is a man, standing among pallets, looking out:[77]

Travel on, and you will come to the next major business. As you get there, despite this place being so isolated, somebody has just parked their vehicle, exited it, and is at first standing, facing their car, before turning and going inside:[78]

Timing his actions so he is walking in as you pass, allows him to both observe you as you pass from outside the business, and if you should stop and go in, observe you inside the building as well, while acting like just another customer. It allows one operative to cover you in two positions, should you go inside, and prevent you from having any unobserved contacts.

Go back to the earliest moment you saw this guy here, as you were turning, and you will notice he is standing by the gate facing his car:[79]

It is possible he arrived at that business just as you arrived and decided to head in, after waffling on what he was doing while standing around his car outside. But again, this is a low traffic area selected as a detection route specifically because if you pass every business, it is unlikely there will be people at every business to watch you. And yet, every business we pass where you can see the front of it, there somebody is, either going in or coming out, or sitting in a guard shack, or walking into the building:[80]

He has the ball cap pulled low. Or as I like to call it, the "Whitey Bulger." I employ that look myself all the time, paired with video camera sunglasses, to limit photography of me by surveillance as I maximize my own video capture of my coverage.

Then as you drive past the next business, we have another walker who just happens to be coming out:[81]

His movement is perfectly timed to put him in the street after you pass, and maximize his observance of you as you drive down the street, and make the turn:[82]

Continue to drive on, to the intersection at the end of this road. Remember intersection decisions need to be called by a "commit" unit, which observes the turn and radios it to the team, so they can hustle just outside your sight at the margins to get ahead of you. Do you go right, and head to a new area, or do you go left, and continue the loop, back to where you started? That is important. Somebody needs to have eyes on you, and it will often be a static unit.

Look in front, and there is a guy in what appears to be a mask, standing with a few cows:[83]

If this intersection is important, then there should be commit units in other timelines where the Google car traveled here. The only other timeline on Google was in March of 2023, and then, as the Google car passed this intersection, this car just happened to be present, to call which way you went:[84]

Or you could go right in that timeline. During that timeline, the car above was not there, however if you look over your right shoulder, this guy was watching you intently:[85]

These people are there predictably in such a remote area because they are surveillance, following procedures.

Returning to the March of 2012 timeline, you turn left. For amusement, after you have been driving a bit, check the white truck off in the distance of this shot. It is the little white dot on the horizon, which you probably cannot even see, in the fully zoomed Google image, which I blew up 300 percent more, below:[86]

Fully zoomed out it is entirely invisible, it is so far back. It is the white truck that was following you at the beginning of this journey, based on the box in back. When you exit this road it will have traversed the entire leg of the loop, likely at almost triple your speed. He is so far at the outside of this next turn, because if you look at the frame-by-frame, he was going so fast he nearly rolled his truck on the turn. Included in this photo will be a lower, right inset of the car tailing you when you began this loop:[87]

He has driven this entire loop behind you, almost out of sight, speeding to catch up to you only now. When you turn toward the main drag, he will drive behind you at a normal, slow speed, maintaining a reasonable distance:[88]

Again, these things can be innocent. That is why I chose the Google car, in a foreign country, combined with an overhead of the route you take to determine traffic levels beforehand. Because it is the Google car, you know it is under surveillance, and because of the overhead, you know there is no traffic back here when there is no Google car driving there. So what you see here is very similar to what you will see if you are under surveillance in America.

This is really the best way I can see to give you the experience and mindset of being under coverage, and let you see how you play probabilities and recognize patterns, and see procedures of surveillance operations implemented, to try and tease out the likelihood you have coverage.

176

I am showing you this, because if you learn these things, you will very likely see this in your neighborhoods and towns, monitoring the population in America. You may see it tracking you specifically. Understanding the United States has this level of monitoring of you, of everyone, is the first step in understanding that there is something very big, and very evil lurking in the shadows of our nation, and that the country may not work the way you were told, and you may not be as free as you think. Because the Stasi doesn't just watch, it controls. It intervenes covertly in ways designed to evade notice. The watching is just the tip of a very big iceberg of control ramming the lives of every citizen in our nation, every day of their lives. You will find it is intervening covertly in everything from who succeeds in the small business environment, to the rigging of elections, to actual interventions among our children, to clip the wings of the high flyers with morals while they are in the schools, so they cannot one day pose any sort of threat to those who run this corrupt, treasonous machine, when they grow up. I have seen that with my own eyes, even derailing the paths of innocent little girls who were just a little too gifted academically, before they even reached their teens.

By the end of this work, you will have the level of experience which normally only elite level spies get while serving overseas against hostile intelligence services, and you will have a much better idea of how surveillance coverage works, how intelligence works, and of how you were lied to about the United States, and the opportunities it offers each citizen and their children. It is my hope, spread through our society, this work will arm us with the training and insight we need, to fight this machine.

Returning to our Bulgarian roundabout, there isn't much

177

else back here, so we'll continue back to the second intersection where we initially turned right, away from a dirt road to the left where the office supply truck was watching us.

We'll go back the way we came now and take that little dirt side road we saw when we first started, where the office supply truck had been parked while watching both of the intersections here. Take a right and head straight back the way we came, and stay to the right at the next intersection, going straight onto the dirt road, rather than turning back toward the main drag.

You will switch time frames as you hit the dirt road. The photos are somewhat of a mish-mash, of when the Google car entered this dirt road, and when it was exiting.

One photo taken as the Google car entered this area will show you the little white truck which drove so fast behind you still on the road, exiting the area:[89]

Believe it or not, that is what a lot of surveillance vehicles look like in the US, and the guy inside it in the US will likely actually do that job when he is not following people around for the American Stasi. So if it is a plumbing truck, there is a good chance if you called that plumber, and surveillance was interested in you, that guy would show up and happily go inside your house, and be happy to be left alone in your basement to poke around.

Before he went, he would be briefed by the neighborhood crew on what he was supposed to do, where he was supposed to try to go in the house, and what was being sought. The neighborhood crew would likely have some degree of familiarity with the inside of the home either from a surreptitious entry while you were out at work, from the application of thru-wall imaging technologies like microwave or X-ray, the use of thru-roof thermal or backscatter X-ray from overflying aviation or drones with that capability, or even the access of backdoored technology, like laptop cameras, cell phone cameras, home surveillance systems, and the like.

After gaining entry to your home, and poking around, he would then attend a debrief, to apprise the local team of his findings, and what he discovered. He might have taken pictures or video with his cell phone, maybe even stolen something. The more "dirty-cop" aspects of law enforcement in intelligence divisions love it because it is like hiring a criminal contractor who doesn't have to obey the law, or adhere to the Constitution, or ask a judge for a warrant, and it gives them plausible deniability to break the law. It is like a half step away from being able to hire brownshirts to rough up suspects they don't like, only without any risk of ever having to answer for the violations of citizen's rights.

If they want some more overt involvement in your life, they can have him report anything he saw, like firearms or anything potentially illegal to the relevant authorities to gain a warrant, while acting like he was just a concerned citizen, acting on his own, unaffiliated with any government agency. He can in essence

179

"parallel construct" a cover story for how something was discovered in your house, which was really found through illegal spying. But he will make it look like it had been "innocently" discovered by accident by some worker you hired and brought into your house, and reported to the authorities.

I would imagine depending on how desperate the operation performing such actions is, he could even plant things, like drugs, or bloody clothes, or murder weapons, and report he saw them.

When you deal with intelligence, there are not a lot of boundaries. It is why the CIA was never supposed to operate domestically in the US. All intelligence organizations, domestic, foreign, law enforcement, military, it is all criminals in them. And just because the government pays them, doesn't mean they work for the government these days.

That was the entire point of Operation TIPS, a program the media characterized as creating a "Stasi-like" citizen informant/surveillance network in the United States. In its mission statement, it said it would preferentially recruit civilian informants from those types of service personnel and trades-people who had access to home interiors, specifically so they could perform searches the government could not perform due to the Fourth Amendment, all in the course of "servicing" your house.[90]

Even today as I am followed around, I notice an inordinately large number of these service and trade vehicles following me, from electricians, to plumbers, to HVAC repairmen. A neighbor they moved in, whose young child talked openly about following me, had another son who worked for Direct TV as an installer, before becoming a plumber.

Home security companies of course will be the gold mine for surveillance. I would be surprised if there is even one that's successful, which was not created by agents of this thing. There, it is an agent of the operation which will one day break into your house, who is installing your security system, maybe with equipment given to him, and backdoored by the operation.

You will see this later in the case of Brandy Vaughn, a medical activist, who had a security system installed, never gave out the password to anyone, and yet had her house entered, using her password, within days.

Returning to Bulgaria, the dirt road you're now taking is a dead end, with nothing operationally significant on it. You will not be closely followed into it, because when you turn around and head out, surveillance does not want to bump into you face to face, nor do they want you to see them coming in behind you, and then turn tail and run back out as you turn around to leave.

As you head in, judging by the shadow of the Google car, it appears you first bear right after the turn, at the small building in the middle of the road, and head up a small hill to the right:[91]

The Google car drives to the top of the little hill on the right above, reaching a gated area for a Coca Cola bottling facility.[92]

There it decided to not enter, turned around, and the stream of photos on this hill were taken as it left. If you position yourself looking at the gate, and hit the down arrow (moving down the hill) you'll notice a van drives up to the gate and sits, watching you:[93]

And it sits there as you drive down. Again, you are the American Google car operating in Bulgaria, photographing isolated areas where Bulgarian security could try to hide some sort of ops center, off the beaten path.

As you will eventually figure out, the only American tech companies which succeeded and became big, were the ones who immediately capitulated to being controlled by the conspiracy behind the American Stasi. It is why you see Facebook and not Myspace, and Samsung, and not Blackberry. Many Big Tech companies, I suspect, were actual planned creations of the conspiracy from the start, their founders merely actors who were employed play the role of accidental billionaire, and sell "their" companies as innocent, organic creations.

Google will be shown to be no different, and clearly the Streetview concept, which has enormous cost for almost no profit, is merely a cover for creating a database with these photos, taken of areas in hostile countries, where if you tried this as a "tourist" you would be detained and expelled, if not disappeared.

You continue to back out, and then drive to the left of the building photographed above. As you enter the far lane, the vehicle which began to nose out as you backed down, and which waited for you to leave, now comes down the hill and departs:[94]

You can get a better look at the truck here as it passes:[95]

Again, it could be innocent and coincidental. But you have to ask what are the probabilities that back here, and especially up there, a truck happens to come tearing down at that moment, as you pull out. Why wait for you to leave, if he's on a schedule? How many drive around back here per day? What are the chances that in that ten second window, a truck pulls out? If it happens once, it might not mean anything. But if those probabilities build

183

up, over and over, you may be looking at surveillance.

It appears the Google car drove up the dirt road ahead to the left, but was stopped when it ran into this payloader:[96]

The pay-loader could be coincidence, and was just digging there. But it is very convenient for surveillance. If you hit the minus key a few times until Google zooms you out to an overhead, and look at the overhead, had the Google car, at the yellow circle, been allowed to proceed, it would have hit a network of dirt roads, represented in red below, which would have made following the Google car difficult for the surveillance team.[97]

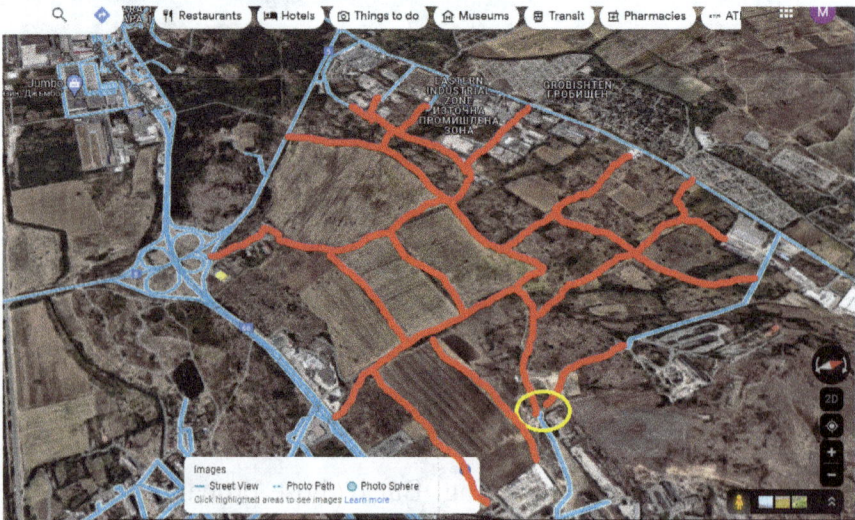

The yellow circle is where you are at the end of the blue dirt road with the payloader, the red roads are the rough dirt roads, in some places almost just ground which has been driven on a couple of times, probably by farmers in tractors, and the blue roads are regular roadways.

On those rough dirt roads, the type of traffic you have just encountered would seem overly strange. You do not often go four wheeling and see a plumber's van jump the hill in front of you heading the other way, as a UPS truck does donuts in a muddy field to the side and a bunch of sedans each hit an intersection of dirt paths just as you do. They can't blend in back there. There would not even be a pretense of a cover.

So surveillance cannot track you back there without just fully exposing themselves, which they do not like to do. Which would mean the surveillance would need to immediately deploy static posted positions as watchers to every point where a red path would re-enter a normal blue roadway, and have a team at each point prepared to pick you up before you escape. That would be about twelve posted commit units, with twelve teams set up to perform a pickup on each exit point. And there are other similar dirt roads on the other sides of some of those roads, so if you jumped the main road and hit a similar network of dirt paths on the other side, you could prove to be a real headache to track.

I see this because I have been under 24/7 surveillance so long, and want to lose it so badly. If that were me in that Google car I would get past the pay-loader at full speed no matter the cost, hit those roads, pop out on the other side, go pedal to the metal, and be three counties over in about two minutes, all on dirt roads, before surveillance knew what had happened.

So is the pay-loader surveillance? In America, it probably would be. I would suspect one of the surveillance people either just got on it, or went to the front desk when you entered this area, flashed a government law enforcement ID of some kind, maybe fake even, and told someone to go up there and make sure the Google car did not pass. It could even have been a surveillance person driving it. Even I can drive most payloaders - they're basically a big tractor, with two controls for the bucket up front, and a clutch and manual gearbox.

In America, surveillance might even have one of the workers there as an asset in the hidden version of Operation TIPS. Surveillance could even have gotten him the job, and could just phone him or page him on his phone app. Here I have no idea, but would suspect it was there due to surveillance somehow, given how it is exactly what the surveillance team would have wanted there, to contain the Google car's movements.

When you are confronted with intelligence enough, you come to learn that when chance favors your enemy, 99 times out of 100 it is not chance, and they arranged it. That is what intel does.

On your way out you pick up another follower. As you reach the bottom of the hill, this next older car on the right, parked parallel to your direction of travel, is kind of just sitting, cooling his heels. As you pass, I will shift to a look behind, and you will see him pull out to follow you out to the intersection:[98]

Here you have passed him on your way out, and are looking back, and he has pulled out to follow you:[99]

I suspect he is a mobile unit, but if you look closer, I think there was a posted unit there too in front of him. Notice the car door on this white vehicle in front of him as you pass:

As you continue to drive out, looking back:

There were no cars on the paved areas on the overhead without the Google car here. Look at how active it is just on the dirt area here now.

You really need to go to Google, and take the streetview tour of this area yourself, in 2012, as it is a much more immersive experience, almost like video. You can jump from one position, to ten feet away with the click of a mouse, drag the screen, and see all these characters chasing you. As a target of the domestic American Stasi in America, I can tell you, that is the experience, minus the intimidation factor, and the harassment of being hit by microwave beams while laying in bed at night.

Finally, when I first assembled this piece, I noted that as you exit, because they used some imagery from when you went in, and some from when you went out, the timeline of photos jumped around as you moved, between entering and exiting.

However as you exited, the following image captured your approach to the street, which is always filled with traffic:

Note that just as you approach the intersection to leave, two cars happen to pass in both directions. I took the above photo as a screenshot from this address:

[https://www.google.com/maps/@42.435771,25.6904241,3
a,15y,74.47h,89.75t/data=!3m6!1e1!3m4!
1sTpFb17HCWlKjUFelTVFFtQ!2e0!7i13312!8i6656]

However for some reason Google again deleted the image from its database since then. But it was an example of surveillance doing driveby's of an intersection as you approach, in such a way one of their two cars will lead you to the next intersection, no matter which way you go. Again, there is nothing back here and the overhead showed almost no traffic. What are the chances, two cars, going in opposite directions, cross just as your car approaches the intersection?

You have just had the experience of being a trained spy in a foreign land, who was operating under the watchful eye of local domestic surveillance, as you made your coverage right and left.

You are now massively more surveillance-aware than you were when we started. You know what this looks like, and how it operates. You have seen it, watching you pass.

Understand that you will see this on the streets in America, operating against you. It is in your neighborhood, it is following you periodically, and most terrifyingly, it is in your child's school, monitoring them, using its own children to infiltrate their social circles and infiltrate their minds, to build files on them for the machine which will follow them throughout their lives, seeking to make sure they never rise too high, to where they might become a problem for the criminals who run things.

Because in America, this operation is not concerned with national security, or protecting the nation from foreign threats. It is concerned with protecting its conspiracy from you and your children. And it can be quite ruthless in pursuit of that mission objective. You do not want to be too effective in your efforts to succeed in life, or raise your children too well, to be too successful themselves.

So now in Google Streetview, you have a tool to develop your own surveillance awareness, and practice counter-surveillance detection routes and surveillance detection. Many have done this on my website, and now see their own surveillance following them in their own neighborhoods in America. You will see your's as well. It is everywhere.

We will do a few more of these routes here in this book, there may be a second book devoted to them in the offing, and you can stop by the website AmericanStasi.com to see even more, and experience them in a more immersive internet format.

As we do them in different nations, you will begin to see, whether it is remote Vietnamese villages using logs with wheels on one side, bolted to some kind of modified rototiller on the other, which they use to drive around on, or the little half-motorbike, half cars of Sri Lanka, or Iranian motorbike surveillance, no matter what nation's security service you encounter, there will be commonalities to the overall surveillance procedures, particularly around intersections and decision points, which will turn you into a machine of pure surveillance detection. And that is vital, because you need to see what is operating in America.

Once you see the massive, sprawling surveillance in

America, actually see something which should not be able to exist, see it with your own eyes in your own neighborhood, around you in real life, you will begin to realize the enormity of the problem facing "Free" America.

Additionally, you will then begin to realize where you are looking at other elements of the criminal conspiracy, from in the news media, to Hollywood, to education, to business, to the Big Tech firms, to Washington DC, to all the social media "influencers" and "personalities" online, to people in your own life, and your children's.

You will realize the dangers our country and humanity face, as well as how close to home the threats lie. And that will be the first step to rescuing the nation.

Chapter Five

Surveillance Detection – The Professional Course Of Real Life Experience – Montana Boogaloo

A commenter on 4Chan wrote the following:

"I traveled quite a bit in the military over 14 years, and decided to move to Montana back in the mid-2000's. On paper, it looked perfect. Low cost of living, beautiful scenery, and lots of landmarks to discover. What I didn't take into account were the swarms of feral, inbred, backstabbing meth heads that make up the majority of the state population. I urge anyone considering a move to just about anywhere to spend some time in your potential location before you make the commitment. We stayed in Montana for a few years, but when we had enough money to break out, we did so. While Virginia is an Orwellian police state shithole, and apparently getting worse, it is nowhere near as fucking depressing and soul-crushing as living in the open air lunatic asylum known as Kalispell. For those that doubt, please, go watch the documentary "American Meth" (2008). When you are done watching it, you will have a good idea of what kind of people make up not just a small minority, but the *majority* of the population in Big Sky Country. I would imagine Alaska would be even worse than Montana, and have heard jokes about Alaska being the place where degenerate filth go to escape the rest of civilized society...."

"...I originally intended to open a small PC repair business

in Montana, but after having my tires shivved, my windshield gouged with rocks, trash dumped in my driveway whenever I left town, and people bringing their dogs to shit in my yard in the middle of the night, I decided against putting down any roots. Grew up in and around Philadelphia, but the white trash in Montana were worse than any West Philly ni**er I ever met...."

"...when we first moved to Cut Bank, MT. Sat at my PC and watched the white trash across the street pull off the interior panels of their truck and cram the entire door with bags of meth. Broad daylight, in the middle of the street, too. Faggot townies knew every minute detail of our lives, and would repeat our private conversations back to us when we went shopping, but nobody saw the strung out punks shoveling 20 pounds of crank into their rusty old hooptie."

Notice the townies knew every detail of what went on in their lives, and could repeat private conversations they had in their homes back to them. He was the new guy in town, and the local surveillance crew put heavy coverage on him to figure out his deal. For some reason, they either decided they didn't like him, or they decided to expose him to harassment to make sure he would be suitably cowed by the conspiracy, before they allowed him to stay.

Those people were domestic surveillance, and that was them flexing their muscles on this guy. They were listening in his home with covert surveillance devices, they were talking about it within their secret society, and they were so brazen, so sure nobody could touch them, they would actually repeat his conversations back to him, to let him know they were listening in to everything he said.

That is the American Stasi, and it is in every neighborhood. It may be more subtle in some neighborhoods compared to others, but it is everywhere, and monitoring everything that closely.

In America, you are either listening in the houses of your neighbor's, searching for things to report to command for brownie points, or you are the one being listened to, at least sometimes, and maybe all the time. You just don't know, because in most of America, these people hide, assiduously, from the majority of the population. And for reasons not yet fully understood, they do seem to select some people, almost randomly, for an increased level of monitoring, which strips them of nearly all privacy, even in their homes.

So lets hit Kalispell, Montana, where this 4Chan poster was clearly describing the American Stasi's operations in both the surveillance, and organized criminal realm. We will take a little tour, in Google Streetview, and see if we see surveillance on the ground similar to what we have now seen in Russia and Bulgaria. If what this poster described was real, we should see an even more brazen ground surveillance operation in this small, rural, Americna town. This is Kalispell, Montana:

We will use the September 2008 timeline, as that was all that was available when this piece was done. Here is a small area which looks promising for some surveillance detection:[100]

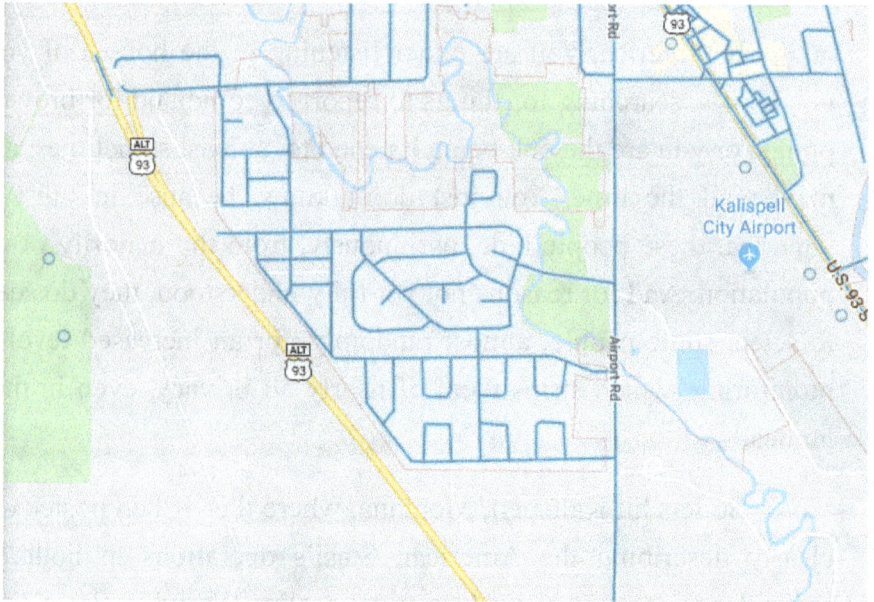

Again, when selecting a spot to do a surveillance detection route, you want to look for several things. First it has to be away from the center of heavily trafficked areas. If the place you go is swarming with regular people on foot and a ton of regular people driving around, they are all camouflage for the surveillance.

You want a place which is not too trafficked, and which is not a good connecting route between populated areas, so it is sparsely populated normally, and surveillance stands out. You also want to have some long roads without turnoffs to drive on, to see what the vehicular traffic is like in a place where surveillance will not swarm you. Then you will want periodic intersections between the long stretches, where surveillance will always place a commit unit to radio which way you go, so you can compare the traffic levels between the two.

Finally, you want to pick a place where there should be some nooks where you can go and be alone in a stopped car, and maybe meet a contact, or have someone run up and throw a little bit of contraband into your car. Because then surveillance will not want to leave you alone, to have an uncontrolled and undocumented contact. They will want to make it so you always have watchers in those areas. That will force them to expose themselves, even when there is no camouflage to hide behind.

Industrial parks seem great for this. But little neighborhoods on the outskirts of town can work too. So find a spot with lots of little spots where you could expect to be alone and you could meet a contact, and see if you can get alone there. If you cannot be alone, and despite reasonably expecting to be alone you always have people ambling by, then you likely have surveillance coverage.

Let's start this detection piece at the bottom of the map above, heading north on that north-south road in the middle, heading to the first intersection on the left:[101]

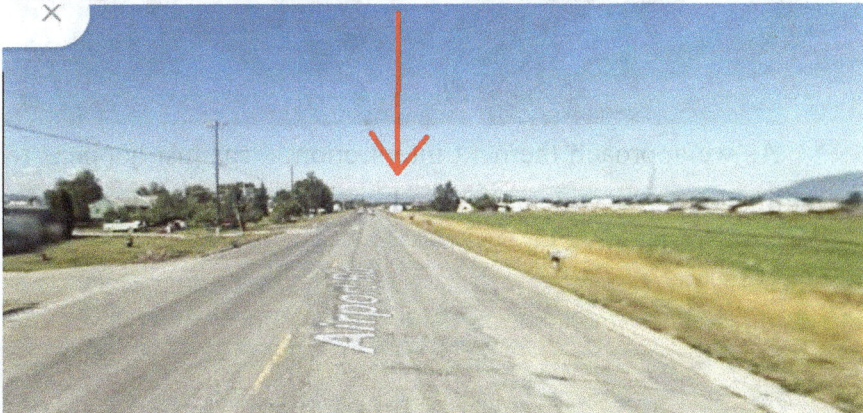

Notice the white box truck just sitting on the right, way off in the distance. Despite all the space in front of you, it will not pull out until after you drive by it. As you pass, the driver is just sitting in it, watching you go by as you pass:[102]

As we approach the next intersection, a car just happens to be pulling out of the neighborhood, and is sitting poised at the intersection as we drive by:[103]

You have seen this before. As before, once can be a statistical anomaly, but if we continue to see it, over and over, it may point to something ominous, unthinkable even, operative within our great nation. A traitorous American Stasi.

Turn around in the Google car and you will notice there is almost no traffic, and yet the car at the intersection has been sitting in that spot since before you even pulled up to the box truck. Here it is below on the left, in a zoomed-in image, long before you came up on it, with no traffic to stop it from pulling out. It was sitting there, as if waiting for you, opposite the box truck:[104]

There is another timeline at this intersection in September of 2019, however it was taken during a rush hour, making the myriad of people there into camouflage for any surveillance. Still, you have a truck approaching the intersection, and people outside the corner house, as well as a crossing guard behind you. (Domestic surveillance operations will often recruit from occupations which can serve as surveillance, and surveillance operators will often seek occupations which will allow them to perform surveillance while on duty, such as a crossing guard.):[105]

You can't say who is surveillance, but for your probability analysis, you can say this intersection wasn't obviously unmanned.

We will pull in that street, past the car sitting there, and drive all the way in, until we almost can't see back, even zoomed. You will notice, that car has not moved. The operator in it is watching his rear view mirror to radio where your car is going. Looking back, zoomed in and enlarged, they're still waiting:[106]

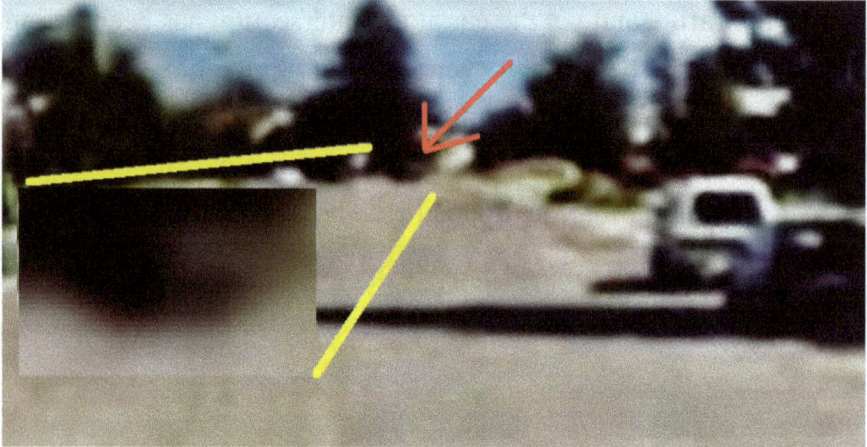

As you enter, to the left, a neighbor just happens to be home in the middle of the day, behind the wall of their house, where they can watch you pass. Notice they doubled over to hide their face:[107]

If you have never been under coverage, the probability of this would feel like 5% or less. But if you have been under, and you have seen the astonishing number of civilian homes set up as observation posts, and you know how many seemingly normal citizens have volunteered for this thing, and know this is the Google car, I would say it is about a 70-80% likelihood or more this house was an observation post that was manned 24/7 to monitor the neighborhood. At least it was in 2008 when these photos were taken. This person was contacted as the Google car was heading this way, likely by a cell phone app, and hustled out, and got in the yard just prior to its approach. Their purpose is to observe it on this stretch of road, and call what it does at the intersections on the right, as a redundant commit unit, backing the vehicle still sitting at the intersection, and not pulling out.

As I have said, US domestic surveillance is based on the old East German Stasi, which sought to create an ever-present awareness of everything by sectorizing its surveillance ops, and assigning one monitor/commander to perform broad overwatch on a manageable sector of civilian residences. In East Germany the most famous forms of sectors were apartment buildings, where microphones were covertly installed in each apartment while people were at work, with each microphone wired into a single monitoring apartment, with tape recorders attached to each microphone, creating recordings of anything interesting.

Living there as if a normal citizen themselves, a monitoring agent or officer was arranged to always be on duty, moving from microphone to microphone, looking for anything interesting going on. Here, in America, this has been adapted to the neighborhood sector model, where one house, with a specially selected surveillance family, often including children who will work the local school, is assigned to perform that duty for the entire neighborhood.

Their tools for eavesdropping will vary, from back-doored technology in each house they are given access to, such as cell phone mics and cameras and laptop mics and cameras, to Alexas, to home surveillance camera feeds. In the case of technological luddites in the neighborhood, who do not use such back-doorable technologies, there are specially installed geophone (underground microphone) and telephone pole-mounted microphone arrays, which, similar to shot-spotter, are capable of triangulating sound source locations based on wave-form arrival times, and using computer filtering to amplify noise from the target location, while digitally filtering all noise not originating at the target location.

When the feeds from multiple microphones and geophones are overlaid in a computer program, each feed positioned relative to the others precisely, by the time it takes a corresponding waveform from the targeted point to arrive at each mic, it will overlay the chosen target waveforms, and amplify the sound from the targeted-point.

Meanwhile, non-temporally-corresponding waveforms from outside the targeted point, arriving in disorganized times, are detected and canceled out, microphone by microphone within the computer, using corresponding inverse waveforms introduced by the computer. That will "erase" all sound within the feeds which did not originate at the targeted point, leaving behind multiple microphone and geophone feeds which only contain pure samples of the sound at the target point from multiple positions, that can be overlaid and amplified.

Once those functions are performed within the computer, and the multiple "pure" feeds are overlaid over each other, you can produce an incredibly loud, pure feed of sound from any point inside a house, devoid of all other extraneous environmental noise. Through the triangulation factor, it even allows you to know exactly where in the house the sound is coming from, and to program that point into the computer, similar to a preset radio station channel, so you can flip through common points of interest, even within houses, as if they were preset radio stations on a car radio. The computer will perform all filtering and modifications on the fly to produce the pure sound from those points. Yes, surveillance technology has advanced, and they've failed to apprise you of this. You see why. They're using it to spy on you.

The position of surveillance is that this is not eavesdropping since the initial waveforms are captured from outside the residence, and thus they need no court order or warrant to listen to it. Though such an argument would never hold up in court, they have never even revealed the technology exists, let alone allowed a product of it to be entered as evidence in any court proceeding. So there has never been a ruling on it, and they continue to maintain the pretense as they listen in your home and build your file.

Even if there had been a ruling outlawing the use of the technology, Congress has already expressly outlawed a civilian-informant domestic surveillance machine such as they created, and the other backdooring technologies they use are clearly illegal anyway, so the operation is already fully criminal in structure and nature. No mere court ruling or legal concern would stop them from doing anything, so long as the system is under their control.

Returning to Montana, as you travel on, to the intersection of the next little side street, you think you are alone, and there will be nobody here to call which way you turn. But in the world of neighborhood surveillance, that does not necessarily mean you are not being watched:[108]

Lets go over and peek into the garage:[109]

That is somebody in a pair of white pants who was standing just inside the garage, either peeking around the corner as you approached, or more likely, watching you in the reflection off the pickup's window. They would pick you up if you turned down this street and the last observer lost you as you turned the corner. It could be the landscaper. As I have said, the American Stasi recruits heavily from tradespeople, However it could also be the homeowner. In my experience, you will often find that civilian informants/surveillance-operatives have been purposely moved into specific houses with sightlines to corners, by the conspiracy, for just this reason. Corner houses are very commonly outposts.

It seems weird. I know. I only realized this was the reality after years and years of seeing it, as it exposed itself to me in an effort to intimidate me with its numbers and size. And in the course of that, I saw things much weirder. I have spoken insultingly of this surveillance operation to a family member in a private residence, at least 80 feet through woods, from other residences and the street, where there is no possibility anyone would have heard it, only to then hear, within seconds, a number of cars drive back and forth in front of my house revving their engines loudly as they passed, as if to let me know they heard it.

Once you see that, you realize there is no Fourth Amendment to the Constitution, there is no privacy in America, and the American Stasi is always listening. Even in the privacy of the most secure areas of the most secure homes.

In truth, it is not surprising, given the amount of money the United States blows through each year, both taxed and borrowed, that we would have a much larger domestic surveillance operation than could have been afforded by the dinky little economy of the old communist East Germany. Add in the advancements in technology, and the lack of any morals, honor, or decency within our intelligence agencies, and obviously we would have less privacy than the old East Germans.

To them, this is normal, as I am sure it was viewed as

normal by the intelligence officers of the old East German Secret Police. It is how domestic intelligence works, and every nation in the West, has domestic intelligence like it. Within their secret society of surveillance people, you are either a listener currying favor with the elites of the intelligence community, or you are being listened to. I am sure they feel lucky to have been inducted into the secret society of surveillance-people-listeners in America.

So we will turn at this intersection, and take this little loop. The next intersection you hit will be on the other side of this loop, seen in the yellow circle in the next image:

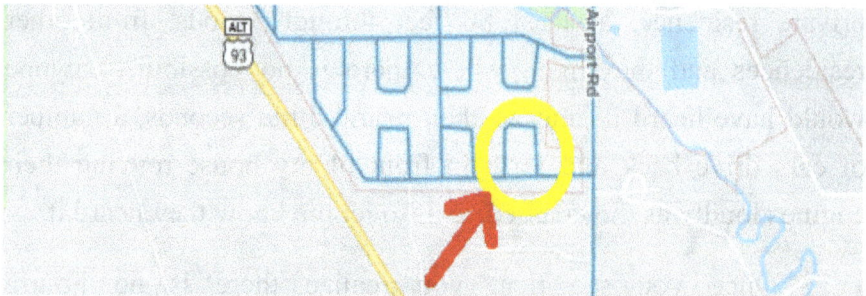

Here you are exiting that little side loop back onto the first street you pulled in on, a little ways down the first street. The arrow above will correspond to the arrow in the next picture, which is where the picture after that was taken:

It turns out, even though this is the crappy 2008 resolution of the Google-camera, if brightened, you can just see below that somebody (red arrow) just happens to be behind those bushes with a garden hose (yellow arrow) as you exit this intersection:

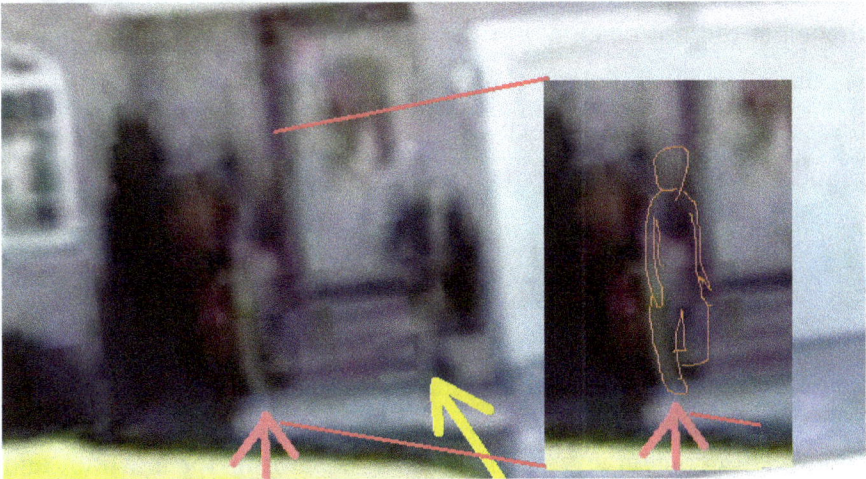

If you look closely, you can see legs, and a skirt.

You can never say anything with certainty in surveillance detection. The goal of surveillance is to appear normal. But you are seeing people in all the right places around intersections and they are all positioned consistent with a trained usage of concealment to make themselves less obvious, and a purposeful positioning of resident/informants at intersections, as would have been seen with the East German Stasi.

The other interesting thing is, since I published this piece online, and took the screenshot above, Google appears to have altered the three important pictures in front of this house, to wash them out. Below, are the images of this house from five photos in order as you drive down the street, captured on February 15th, 2024, simply to show the clarity of the images. Three shots which show this front door and person most clearly, have been altered to degrade the images since I took the screenshot above. The second image in which the stairs were obscured by a bush, and the final image from far enough away it is unclear, were not altered, nor were any others on the street. Looking up there were no clouds, the angle did not change, nor did the light exposure, so the images should all be of the same clarity, and apparently were when I took the screenshot above. Since then, the key images were altered to reduce clarity. Five images taken in front, side by side:

This conspiracy and I have been battling for a while, and they are quite concerned about my attempts to expose the American Stasi. This imagery should not have changed, unless there was something here to hide. Clearly there was.

Another good indicator for surveillance on Streetview is that operators, being trained to avoid letting their faces be seen by a target so they will not be recognized later, will shield their faces, and turn their backs, to avoid being photographed. Here, a couple of people who were out at intersections, specifically turned their backs on the Google car, rather than look at this strange vehicle with a giant camera ball on it, and wires coming out all over:[110]

And then there was here:[111]

We can continue through the neighborhood, and you will see a lot of people, but inside the neighborhood is only good for seeing if there are more people than you would expect to see out and about, and if they are in the right places. You will not see your coverage at every intersection in a neighborhood, since some will watch from inside houses.

Additionally, once you are dealing with observation posts in a neighborhood, actual physical surveillance is not as necessary, given there will be hidden cameras and mics on telephone poles, home surveillance cameras, as well as maybe other tech deployed tracking you, and the smarter residents can just peek out a window.

One thing which does seem to be highly common is direct eyes on just as you pull up to an intersection of a main street that meets a neighborhood street you may turn on. So lets go back out and just check the intersections around the neighborhood leading into it, where its streets feed out onto the main streets, and see if we approach a neighborhood entrance intersection, and are ever alone. Remember, the first intersection featured the car that didn't pull out, as well as the box truck opposite it.

Here is the second intersection heading north on the first street we started on, where you have lawnmower dude and a line truck. Because of the way these photos were taken, you were actually heading south here, looking back behind you in this photo. So the line truck would have met the intersection exactly as you did, you both passed through the intersection, and then you took this photo, looking back, which captured both redundant commit units just after you encountered them:[112]

Lawn mower guy never seems to actually do anything as you pass either. He just stands there, next to the mower.

At this point, you are saying to yourself, this guy is seeing coincidences, and ascribing relevance to them wrongly, due to paranoia. What I would say, is, keep reading. You'll see this so often, so consistently, you'll realize something strange is going on.

And once you do, all of these images will appear significant to you. I have had many readers read these analyses, and critique them, only to, several episodes later, say in the comments, *"I see what you are getting at,"* and then come back later and say they have seen their own local surveillance operating all around town.

Here we are at the next intersection north:[113]

Look around there at how few cars are around, except for right there as you arrive. So all three intersections have eyes on just as you arrive, and two of three had cars come out just as you arrived at them. The third had lawnmower guy loitering there.

Just for kicks, the above intersection during one pass-by in

September of 2019:[114]

Here was another pass-by in 2019, this car's driver's side window was open:[115]

The reason these cars are always there is that you are looking at a surveillance procedure being executed by trained domestic surveillance as they track a target vehicle.

There is one more bottlenecked entrance to that neighborhood, located below, in the red circle:

We'll hit that intersection from each timeline as the Google car hit it while driving back and forth. I will just put the pictures below with the commit circled and the url in the endnote. At some point you should be at that intersection alone, given how deep in the neighborhood it is, and the time of day, with everyone at work.

Timeline one, exiting the neighborhood heading north, there is an oncoming pickup truck. Continue forward and he will pass you:[116]

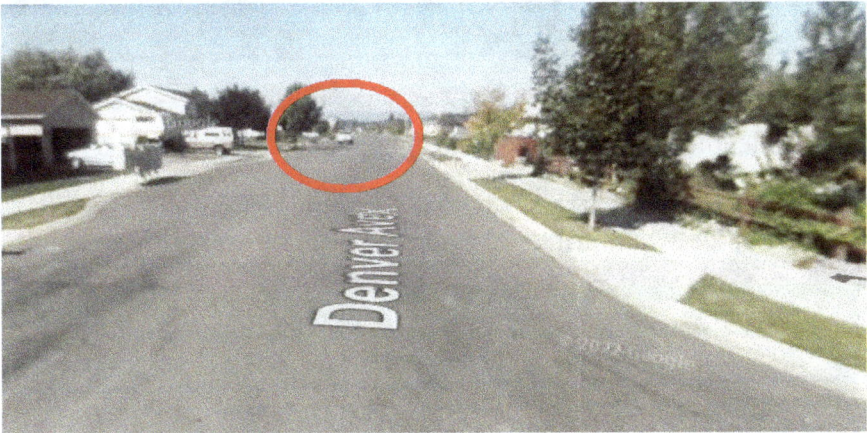

Seen here from the side as he passes:[117]

Next up, a different series of images, heading north, toward the intersection, before turning east, and there is a person standing at the mailboxes:[118]

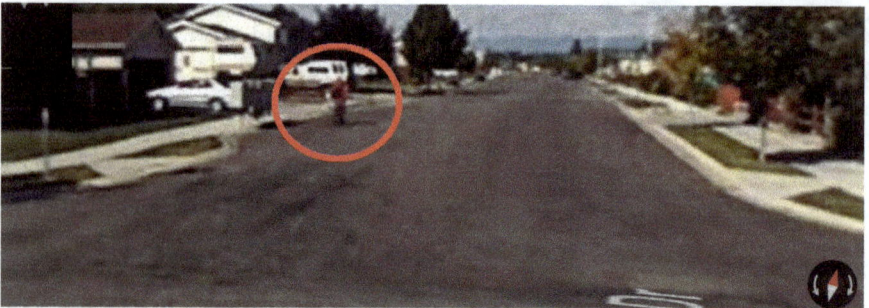

Heading west toward the intersection this next car passes you just before you reach it and is watching in his rear view mirror as you decide what turn to take, and go straight west:[119]

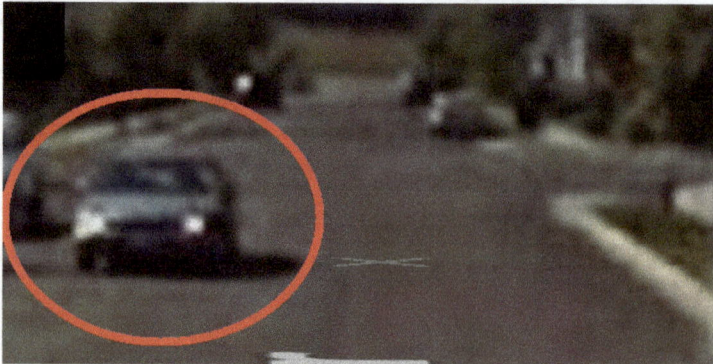

Every time you hit that intersection, which was a bottleneck into that neighborhood, somebody was there. I have lived under this machine's overt harassment for years. That is domestic surveillance, and a quite mild, covert variant of it.

This is the mathematics of surveillance detection. How many cars exit that neighborhood in the middle of the day? How many pedestrians pass the intersection? How long in seconds does each of those cars sit at the intersection, on average, before turning out? How long do the pedestrians loiter in the vicinity of an intersection? How many seconds, timed, in total, would one of those cars be parked in an exiting street like that each day? How often will there be somebody standing next to an intersection? How many seconds are there in a day? Even if every ten seconds, a car pulls up to the intersection, and sits there five seconds before pulling out, then half the intersections you approach should be empty, statistically. But they were not. Every time you went to enter that neighborhood, somebody was there.

Just to have a 2/3 chance of running into a car, then for every minute of the day, there should be a car parked there, waiting to pull out for 40 full seconds per minute. If each car took eight seconds to pull out, that is five cars per minute exiting every minute. It is 300 per hour exiting, non-stop all day. Did you see that much traffic in the neighborhood? And notice the one time there was no car, there was a line truck, and a dude who should have been mowing a lawn, but who was just cooling his heels. Or somebody standing next to a mailbox. That is how you mathematically calculate something may be off.

I could keep going, but this manuscript is over 200 pages already, and I need to get to southern California and the wilderness of Alaska, as well as cover some of the American Stasi's crimes.

Before we go, lets take a quick run over to Cut Bank Montana, since the online commenter at the beginning of this chapter, who put us here, describes a major American Stasi methamphetamine operation there, listening in houses. Lets see what the intersections look like. If the American Stasi is doing a Walter White there, it should be loaded with coverage. We will use the August 2008 timeline of photos, as that was all there was when I wrote this.

We will begin heading west into town, and then exit the town on the other side, to reduce traffic as shown here:[120]

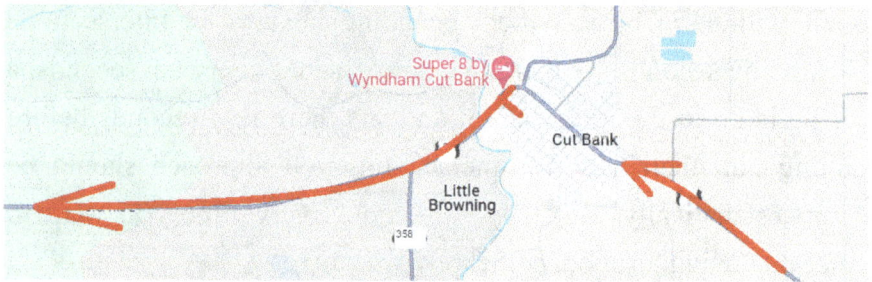

Coming into town, here is behind us:[121]

Nobody is there, and that is a lot of open road behind us.

Here is in front of us. Again, you can zoom, and no cars:[122]

You can see how if every time we hit an intersection, cars just happen to be pulling up, and yet the road looks this completely empty normally, it will seem strange.

First intersection, heading West into town, oncoming car:[123]

If I take that left, it jumps to another timeline, when the Google car turned off that street, so lets do that. It would be weird if the Google car hit that intersection later, and a single car just happened to be hitting it just as I pulled up yet again, wouldn't it?

That is what I saw when I did the piece, but Google has inexplicably deleted that image from the database. The above image had been at this address:

https://www.google.com/maps/@48.6272307,-112.3095207,3a,75y,145.11h,63.69t/data=!3m6!1e1!3m4!1sLszPckyR7NmpRl_swEko8Q!2e0!7i3328!8i1664

You can still see the car after it passed, here:[124]

Just for kicks, we will look at the intersection in 2023, and see if anything has changed.

Heading Northwest, car behind you:[125]

Approaching from the south, two cars, exact same time:[126]

Heading Southeast, truck approaches from the left:[127]

Notice, it is not like the road was packed with traffic in each instance. Each time, there are no cars nearby, except for the car or cars, which "by chance," drive up just as you hit the intersection. Those are domestic surveillance vehicles, and that is procedure.

Back to the 2008 timeline, next intersection here:[128]

2023 actually looks exactly the same:[129]

These are procedures, with operators who are incredibly practiced in timing, so it is unsurprising to me. It could even be the same driver.

The next intersection has a mish-mash of timelines. There is one photo heading in this direction, in which the Google car is being led to the intersection ahead by what looks like a minivan.

There is also a guy getting gas on the side, but you are getting into a more crowded area, which makes teasing out the surveillance signal from the regular activity signal difficult. [130]

In another set of 2008 photos, , the 2008 timeline of photos was taken traveling in the opposite direction for this part of the road, in that array, you were being led by this guy who pulls off ahead of you to get gas:[131]

But again, you are getting by the main street in town, there is a gas station, there is traffic, it is tough to tell. So here we will jump off on the side street to catch another timeline. This timeline of photos was taken by the Google car as it exited the side street, and surprisingly there is a car in front of the Google car, also exiting the side street, as you will see on the next page:[132]

Again, factor in how often cars are exiting that side street, here you have one exactly in front of the Google car at precisely the moment it is exiting, and add in the fact surveillance procedure when following a car is to not follow the car, but to use a cheating command position, leading the car, so the target will not think you are following him. It is curious. I have done this long enough to tell you, that car is local surveillance. But it may take you a few years of seeing it yourself to understand, that is what it looks like. But it is a bad intersection, as there is too much normal traffic.

So we will blow through town. US-2 is now covered with a set of photos from 2023, so we will take the long lonesome road out of town, and see what we see.

The initial photos were actually taken by the Google car on driving into town on that side, so we will be going backward in photographic time, as we head out of town. It is still interesting.

The first car on your way out which is weird is this dude, who is just sitting in the exit lane of the gas station. He never pulls out, he just sits there the whole time. You can go all the way down the street, he never moves, as he blocks the exit from the parking lot:[133]

222

He was in no hurry:

Opposite side of the street is this pickup, who also never pulls out. And there is no traffic light there or traffic. They could pull out any time they want, but neither do:[134]

Just for kicks, we will take the intersection just to the east of this, heading into town. The Google car seems to have taken this turn impulsively, and surveillance was not prepared.

Immediately after turning off, it must not have been clear there would be a commit unit at the next intersection in here, so a black truck immediately takes the turn behind you, coming from the opposite direction. As it does, control decides to have it turn off, judging the quick turn too obvious, and it has another car move to come in behind you to perform the commit function at the next intersection from some distance behind you, so as to avoid giving you the impression you are being followed.

As you look at these photos, ask yourself, if you watched that corner for one hour, how many cars would turn the corner? Here, you turn the corner, and two cars turn in right after you, within seconds. That is the type of statistical anomaly which points to surveillance activity. You can see this in the sequence of photos on the next page, looking behind the back of the Google car:[135]

What are the chances these cars are turning just as you do?

Next parking lot exit heading West, out of town, another car:[136]

You see a couple more on your way out. I won't bother with the endnotes or links.

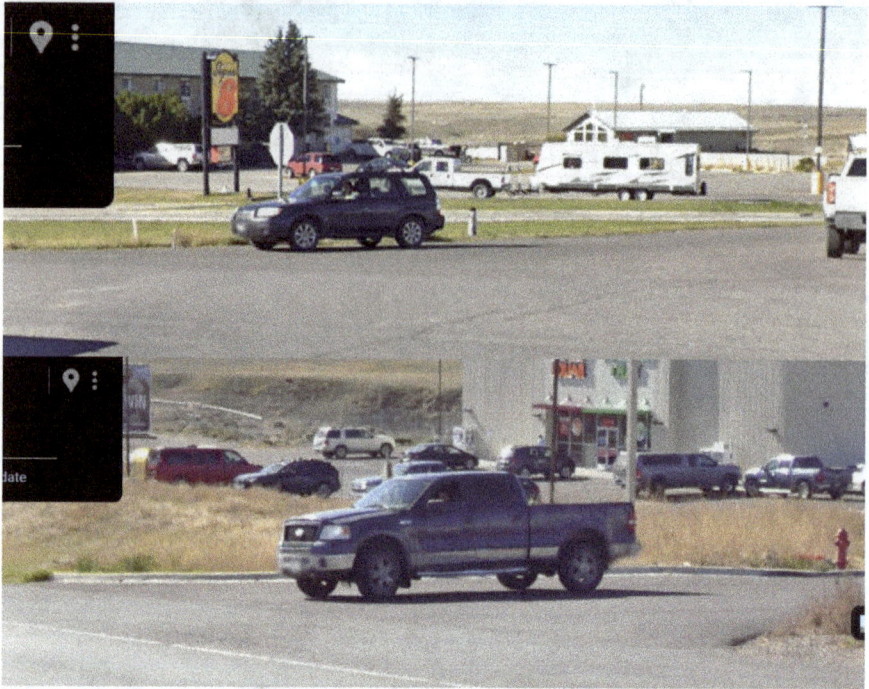

So what is this? Why do these cars pull up to the exit, and you see them there from way back, there is no traffic so they could pull out, but they don't? They let you pass, and then in most cases, they still don't pull out, even as you drive off?

Where I am, they station a car or two in every parking lot of nearly every major shopping center. That's how extensive the operation is. Those surveillance people will spend hours sitting in that lot, waiting to get a call that a target has entered and then they will exit their cars, and follow the target through the store.

When my harassment first started, I thought it must be a team of private eyes hired to follow me. So I would race to the stores, to try and get in and get out fast, before they could follow me in.

I got caught at a red light once back then, after speeding wildly to the store I wanted to go to. As I sat trapped at the light, I did have a sightline to the only entrance/exit of the parking lot of the store I wanted to go to. I worried the team would figure out where I was going, and some of them would get in the lot before I got up to it. Nobody pulled in or out. There were two more lights between me and the lot, and I ended up getting caught at both due to the traffic. So I had to sit through all three lights. It must have been four minutes of massive irritation. Finally, I got up to the lot, pulled in, parked, and in all that time, nobody pulled in or out of the lot, or even followed me in, so I assumed I must have been ahead of my team. I felt incredibly lucky they had not figured out where I was going, and gotten in ahead of me.

I got out of the car, and simultaneously, three cars all opened up, the drivers got out like they had just pulled into the lot, they slammed their car doors loudly, and they followed me into the store. Those were the local Stasi civilian informants/surveillance people. They had been stationed in that lot, and not just for me.

Since then, I have seen them all over, in lots of stores I never go in. On hot summer days, they prop open their car doors, get half of their behind out of the car and off the car seat, with a outer leg propped up on the car door, as the sun beats down on their car, and they wait for command to tell them to follow somebody who enters the lot. They look exactly like the girl in the beginning of the Bulgarian chapter. It is a big operation, and I assume they must be following a lot of people, probably the vast majority covertly, without the harassment upgrade in service.

So the cars you see here are stationed in those lots. I assume they are not pulling out because after you pass, they pull back into the lot and resume their wait for orders from command.

First intersection on your way out (actually the Google car was driving in), and you are being led by a white SUV, which could function as your commit unit. [137]

Being led is not dispositive, but detection never is. The question is, are you accompanied at intersections to a greater degree than on straightaways, and do the timings seem unusual?

Here, you can jump to the other side of the highway where the Google car was driving out as it took pictures. When you hit the same intersection there, you have a pickup which perfectly hit the intersection as you did:[138]

And again, I cannot tell you every single one of these is a domestic surveillance vehicle, especially closer to town. But you have an awful lot of cars, precisely at intersections, just as you pass, even on roads which have no traffic.

Since the white pickup is leading you when you look at the other lane's timeline, we will now drive just in this lane, heading out. That way, there is no vehicle constantly present, and intersections will be unobserved, unless other vehicles arrive, timed to our arrival.

Next intersection, the car ahead of you pulls off:[139]

Now you are more or less alone, and the traffic is thinning out as you pass these last few businesses at the outskirts of town. If you are going to hit an intersection and be alone, the next one could be it. But it isn't:[140]

You can keep driving, and see how long it takes him to pull out. He is another one of these cars which just sits there watching you. Below is the photo of him slowly crossing the road to the other side, after you have traveled a quarter mile down the road:[141]

We can actually turn off on that side street to get another timeline of photos. Maybe if we do that, and look back at the intersection, we will see there were no cars around the Google car then, and it was all alone on this desolate stretch of road. When you do it, it takes you back to 2008, when the Google car last drove that street, and as you can see, there was a white pickup there to call the turn:[142]

You finally get alone, but only on a straightaway. It shows you, this area doesn't have a lot of traffic, so you would think sooner or later, you'd get alone at an intersection. Below is your view in front as you leave, with no cars as far as you can see:[143]

Here is the view out the back. These are unzoomed to show distance, but I zoomed in and confirmed there are no cars present, all the way out to the horizon:

Unfortunately this road ceases to be productive as Google shifts you into the other lane, and for the rest of the drive you are led by the white SUV, which acts as a commit unit, negating the need for timed arrivals at intersections. But you get the idea here. You are in America, and on both sides of town, for miles out, you are seeing the same vehicular surveillance techniques you saw employed against hostile state actors in Bulgaria and Russia.

Only here it is the American "government" running a Stasi-like security/surveillance machine on US soil, designed for use against American citizens. The questions are, is it just in Montana, and is it just on the Google car?

It is important to note, those cars were not scrambled. They did not pull out of an underground parking lot in DC, drive in a convoy to the airport and take a C-130 to the local airstrip, offload, and head to this location to follow the Google car.

That is the normal embedded vehicular and foot coverage loitering around in a Podunk meth-town in Montana, probably all excited they finally have something to do beyond watching the boring residents live boring lives. These are embedded watchers of the American Stasi, recruited from the civilian populace, just as the Stasi recruited regular East Germans, and they are in every neighborhood throughout America. Some more than others.

I have seen this same surveillance tracking the US Marshals on the TV show Manhunter as they pursued fugitives, and the Marshals mostly seem clueless. When the surveillance began to obviously freak out was in an episode where they were hunting a fugitive who worked in a maraschino cherry bottling facility in New York City. For a brief interlude, the Marshals were asking each other why an American Stasi vehicular unit was pulling right in front of their vehicle, backing up close to them, and parking there (it was to orient a mic hidden in the surveillance vehicle, to listen to the Marshals in their vehicle and figure out exactly why they were sitting on the facility they were sitting on – (the maraschino cherry bottling factory).

My guess is the conspiracy was packing something extra into some maraschino cherry bottles, ala Gus Fring's packing meth in his buckets of chicken ingredients. The local American Stasi surveillance was assigned to perform overwatch for the operation, and immediately noticed the Marshals were poking around, and it had to deal with them.

Now try to picture all the silly "boogaloo" Civil-War fantasies people have about how a civil war would go. Imagine as people are prepping raids on the government, this Stasi- modeled surveillance force, which is run by the real conspiracy of elites which has subverted our nation and taken over the government, is tracking all the people who might be problematic during its many downtimes, when the Google car is not driving around.

Understand that the local Stasi units know exactly who the problem children are right now in each of their sectors. Those neighborhood units are listening in their homes from other homes on their street, maybe even next door. They are following their internet searches, reading their emails, listening to their phone calls, following them in person on grocery store runs, and the neighborhood crews will even have "friends" infiltrated into the social circles of these targets. It has clocked everything they have bought on every trip to a store, taken reports on their children from the children the American Stasi runs in the schools, and even befriended them, acting as if they are fellow patriots too, and are looking forward to the uprising. The Stasi has probably even broken into their homes and been through them, while they were out at work, And they may even have installed tech in there, to better watch their targets at all times in their homes.

This is why the conspiracy taking over our nation has gone so far, and why they felt they could form pedophile blackmail networks, steal trillions from the treasury, assassinate JFK, hijack the national security apparatus, rig our elections, and even (at least) allow 9/11 to happen (if they did not set it up).

Every one of the agents of this conspiracy, from Soros, to the Bush family, to the lowliest election rigger, was protected by this thing. Nobody could ever possibly even get near them, let alone touch them, and almost no citizen had any idea that beneath the thin veneer of freedom and privacy of this nation, this thing was watching everything, controlling everything, even where our children in the schools could go in life, using their own children as infiltrator spies, to get the best intel, and control it all.

233

Now in our next chapter, on to the first of the two questions. Is this only in Montana? Lets see if we see it anywhere else in the US...

Chapter Six

Surveillance Detection – The Professional Course Of Real Life Experience – California Dreaming

You have seen surveillance operating overseas. You have seen it outside a more remote Montana town. You have begun to grasp the patterns you see at intersections, and now understand better what you were looking at, when you saw the video of the gangstalkers set up outside the home of the young girl earlier. Now that you have come that far, we will take a trip to Long Beach California, and see if you can begin to spot the surveillance in more populated areas. If I have done my job, you are now ready.

The Google Streetview experience gives you the immersive experience of being able to look around, and experience approaching the intersection, and knowing where you will see people if you are under surveillance, preparing to see them, and then actually seeing them at the exact right moment. In the training of surveillance detection, there is nothing really quite like it.

A quick word on American surveillance procedures. Russian surveillance and Bulgarian surveillance employ a static posted surveillance operative at an intersection to act as a "commit" unit, who calls the direction of travel to the rest of the team after a target makes a decision and turns at the intersection.

Western countries seem not to do this as much in suburban

areas (though American cities rely extensively on pedestrian surveillance). In the West, surveillance will far more often have a vehicle hit the intersection at the same time as you.

Perhaps as wealthier nations, there is less foot traffic, and the different procedure is a reflection of trying to blend in with that. Nevertheless it is one difference you will note in most suburban American-Stasi surveillance operations. With time, you will begin to feel the tension when every intersection, even in the middle of nowhere, will have a car pull up to it just as you do, or a pedestrian walking up to it, looking blasé.

Surfing Google, looking for something interesting, I became curious, looking at this large undeveloped piece of real estate right on the water in California:[144]

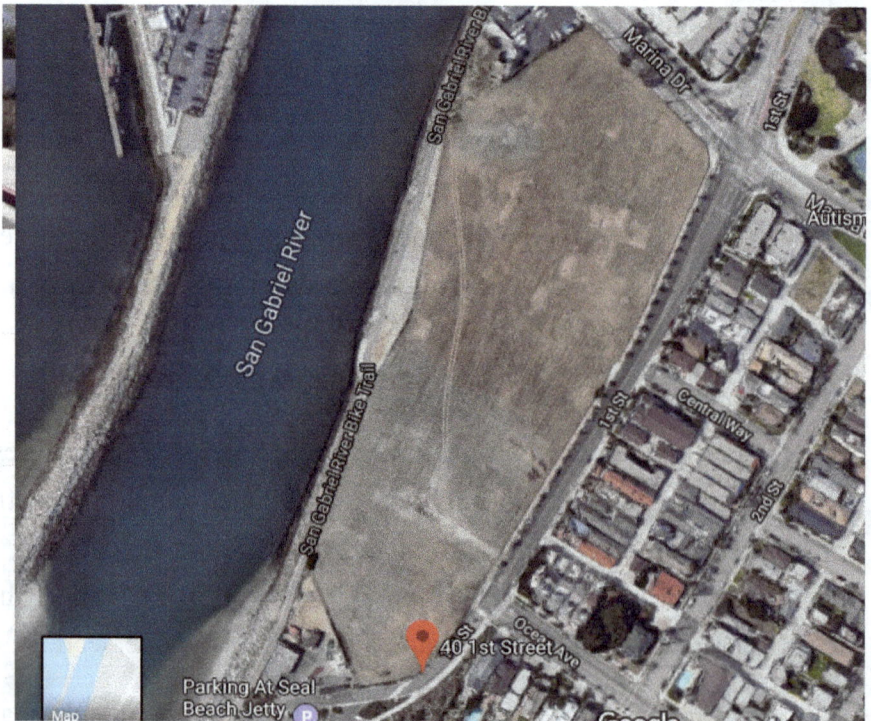

Although it has since been turned into a park, at the time I found it, I wondered, why had it not been developed? And why was it surrounded by barbed wire, when it was just an empty field? That got me curious. Sometimes interesting places will have surveillance around them.

By the tread in the dirt, somebody has driven a lot from the main gate to the back corner by the bike path, initially driving straight away from the road, as if they want to get deep inside the property before heading to that back corner:

Maybe they were doing something they didn't want people to see, which is exactly when surveillance will close in. Or maybe surveillance itself was up to something criminal there, and would have overwatch operative around the site.

On a closer look, it did appear likely coverage is in the area, and pretty thick. As we have said, the biggest sign of surveillance, is to be in an area with no traffic, but every time you hit an intersection a commit unit is present.

For this cruise we will use the April 2018 timeline, as that is

237

what I used when I wrote this piece in 2018. If you cruise north along the property line of #40 on 1st street in Google streetview, you will note no traffic on either side of you. The street is empty of cars. For a visual reference, this is a map of the empty street we will drive along, in red:

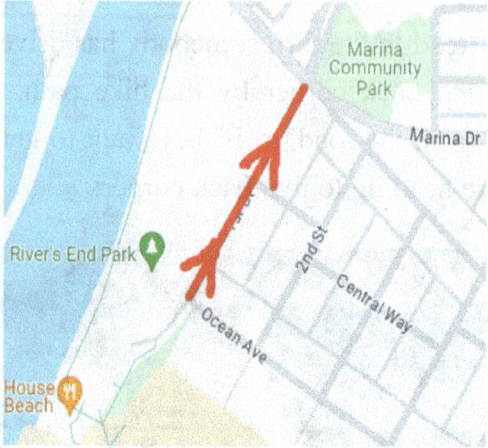

Here is how empty of traffic the street is, which is good as it means vehicular surveillance will not have much regular traffic to hide within:

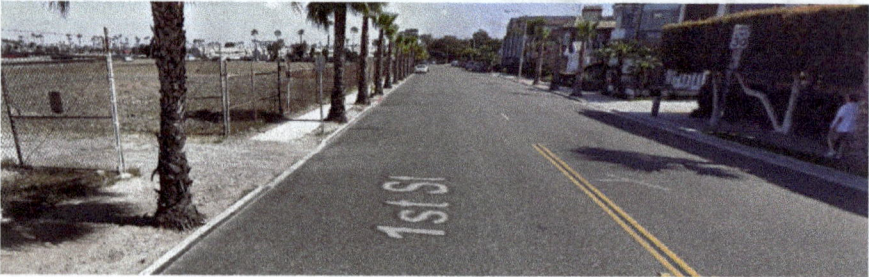

Here is the first intersection, and the two pedestrians you will see watching it, to see if the Google car ducks down it:[145]

The next minor intersection, just north of here, features a single surfer dude, sitting on the back of his car, with a boogy board.[146]

Obviously he is totally not surveillance coverage, by the fact he is sitting by the side of the road with a boogy board and his shirt off. And the fact the only two sets of pedestrians you saw on this street were at intersections, pointed at the Google car is purely coincidental.

Continue north and approach the intersection at 1st and Marina, and you will note no traffic is present at the intersection:[147]

So how was surveillance watching this intersection? There are a couple of potentials if you look closely. Further north, just out of your sight, is a woman pushing a baby carriage, with a backpack (Foot surveillance, which will often be walking for hours at a time in a sector, waiting to get the call to move to a new target, very often uses backpacks to carry surveillance kits ("costume kits" with changes of clothes, even wigs and disguises, cameras, eavesdropping equipment, backup batteries, backup radios, and other tools of the trade, as well as water and food to sustain them through a shift of following targets.).

Advance through the intersection and pass the van she is hiding behind, and you will see her:[148]

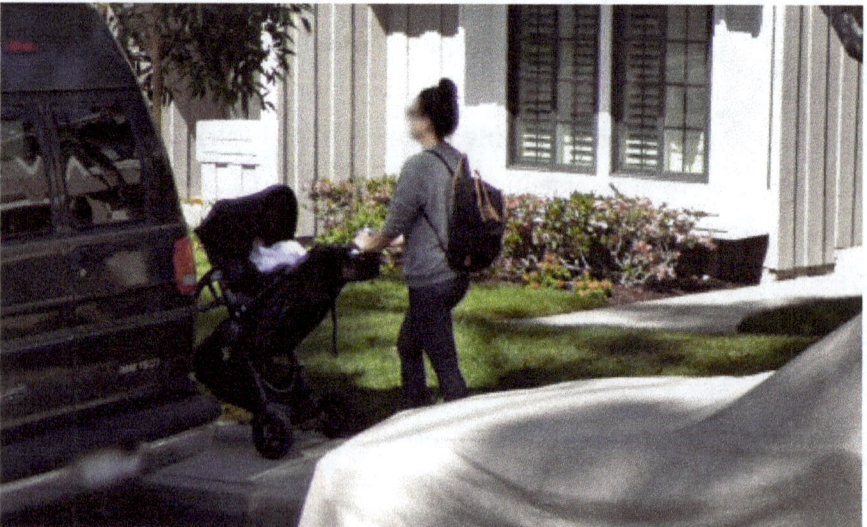

I have been followed by new moms with babies. The baby is an excellent cover, because who would see a mom tending to her baby in the carriage, loitering near you, and perceive a threat? It is very difficult for an average person to loiter near somebody without attracting attention, but a new mom just needs to kneel near the baby carriage, and clearly she is not surveillance.

She could be a commit unit, and call your turn. Notice how just as your car approached her (from the north heading south, the way it was filmed), she walked behind the van so you could not get a good look at her face from the front. Could be coincidence, but if she was surveillance, it would not be. She would have been taught to use things like the van as concealment, so the target would not get a good look at her face, and maybe recognize her again if she was used in the future. Not dispositive, but could be consistent with surveillance.

As you cross the intersection, there are two cars driving away from it, equidistant, and a lawn mower, pointed right at you:[149]

It gets a bit tougher to tell who is who as it gets crowded. But clearly you were not alone at this intersection either.

Now we will return to where we began, the southern end of that street which abuts the property of interest. At the southern end of that street, there are two directions you can choose. Either you continue straight into the parking lot for a small beach, or you turn left to continue on the street there:

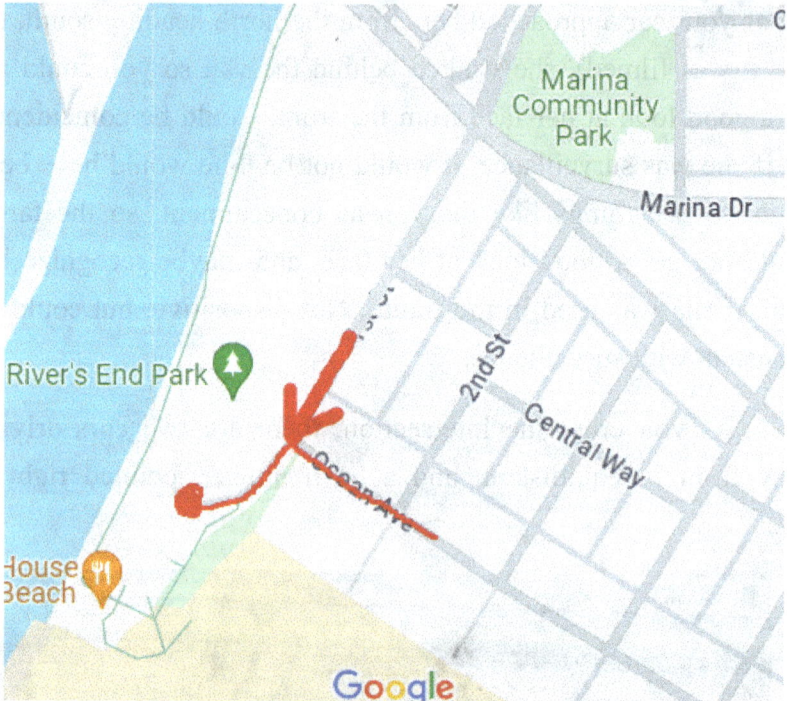

As you head south toward this intersection/decision point, and begin to continue straight south into the beach parking lot, two vehicles come from the left just as you enter the intersection. The nearest one has an open driver's side window, used by surveillance to observe and report auditory observations:[150]

Ahead is the parking lot for the beach. Go straight and enter the parking lot, and just as you drive in, a Jeep with an open driver's window is pulling out down the serpentine road from the lot. [151]

When a target of interest is in an area, I have found surveillance puts cars in each parking lot, and in each neighborhood, I assume so that a final head count of the target vehicle can be made on the target's entry, by the exiting vehicle. They will repeat that with an entering vehicle at 12 o'clock on your exit, to make sure there are no individuals who were dropped off and left behind, or picked up, without them knowing.

Again, surveillance detection is a game of probabilities. How many times per day does somebody drive out of that lot? A hundred times? Two hundred times? How long does it take them to drive that exit drive, to exit? Five seconds? Say there are 200 people on that little drive for 1000 seconds, or 16 minutes per day. From 7AM to 10 PM (park hours, displayed at the gate) is fifteen hours, or 900 minutes. What are the chances someone is on that street at any moment when you are, just as you enter? 1 in 56? Now what are the chances you drive on empty streets, but every time you hit an intersection, there is a car or a walker there? Every time, without fail. Those are the statistics of surveillance detection.

Again, it can be innocent here one time entering the beach midday, even though it is unlikely. But as you play probabilities, over and over again, you begin to tease out the likelihood. And it is beginning to look to me like the American Stasi was documenting exactly what the Google car did in this area.

I zoomed through the parking lot, and there were no other cars entering or leaving, furthering my impression there is not that much traffic this time of day.

There were a few pedestrians, and a few bicyclists, some of which I would expect, given my experiences, were surveillance. As a general rule, a park is a place where there can be a lot of operational activity from the perspective of surveillance, from sexual activity to drug exchanges, to even espionage dead drops. People who intend to engage in such activity, will tend to go to places unassociated with such activity, as a means of trying to hide it. As a result of the natural human tendency to try and hide illicit activity where it would not be expected to be found, domestic surveillance will often increase its presence in such places, as it

244

searches it out.[152]

It is very much like you feeling the safest place in the world to have a private conversation about some secret which could destroy you, would be in the interior-most room of your house. Meanwhile, at the very same time,. that is the place surveillance has devoted itself to penetrating most aggressively, for precisely the reason it is where your deepest secrets will lay.

There was an RV camper set up with a sightline to the entrance to the park, and drapes lifted at the lower corner of the rear window (highlighted by the yellow arrow), which could have allowed a camera to document those who entered. In 2018, these campers were not as common as they have become as things have headed downhill these last few years, and the conspiracy looks to bankrupt the nation:[153]

It was there in the June of 2017 timeline of photos a year earlier, and that drape is also lifted up there.

In that timeline, the entire time you drive the lot, midday in Southern California, this dude is sitting in his truck with the car door open, never gets in or gets out:[154]

The old tricks are the best tricks, and with surveillance, you will see them, all over, over and over again.

2007 timeline of photos, car door open:[155]

I know, car doors are open all the time in parking lots. It could be innocent. However, you have seen the same technique in both Russia and Bulgaria, and now here, as you are seeing other indices of surveillance activity. You have people sitting in cars, not getting out, or closing the door and driving off, and it is happening more than once. You just need to factor it in as one more little oddity when you are performing your statistical calculations to determine if there might be surveillance here.

And understand the magnitude of what you are concluding, if you begin to think it even possible they have recreated the East German Stasi's level of embedded domestic surveillance in America. Because suddenly there would be a lot more other nefarious intelligence activity which would be likely to be occurring alongside the surveillance – it would not travel alone.

Because if the Stasi exists in America, then our elections probably are rigged, and whoever has won, left or right, has been installed in the office, without us electing them - by a shadowy intelligence-agency conspiracy which would undoubtedly be telling them what to do.

It might make sense of why all our leaders treat all of us with such contempt lately. It would also mean the entire idea of a representative republic where we control the government, checks and balances, our Constitution, our legal system, probably our courts, even an honest news media, would likely all be fake. We would be living instead in a hidden dictatorship which was taking our money, and unilaterally killing people overseas, without the consent of the citizenry here at home.

It might also explain why everyone is working so hard, augmented by technology which should increase their productivity exponentially, and yet everyone has to work constantly just to maintain food on their plate and a roof over their head, when fifty years ago, a single husband, working without all the tech advantages of today, was productive enough to buy a new house at 20 years old, and have a large family they easily supported, while taking vacations all over the country and buying toys to play with like boats and motorcycles.

Surely each person's productivity should be exponentially greater today, and life should be an order of magnitude easier. And yet people are barely making ends meet, as just home ownership, not even considering forming a family, is entirely out of financial reach for most.

Lets move on. Go back to the last intersection where you entered this park, and make a turn right, to explore the turn which we just saw two cars come down before entering the beach.

When you exit, you have two cars waiting for you, one of which, a pickup truck, drives in front of you to lead your vehicle as you make a right turn:[156]

In front of you, taking a cheating command position:[157]

And in back, pointing into the beach parking lot, and looking in your windshield as you exited:[158]

So a pickup came down the empty street you just traveled

down before, and with perfect timing, turned in front of you as you exited. And an SUV that was following it ducked into the parking lot you just left, right behind you, as if replacing the Jeep which had to leave its station when you pulled in, to do a last headcount of your car. And they entered the beach lot exactly as you were exiting, and they are the only other cars around.[159]

Again, it appears the street was empty, except when you got to the intersection, and two cars popped up right by you, both precisely timed around your exit. The lot had no moving cars, except for right when you began to enter, and just after you left. The first intersection was covered, assuming at least one of the cars or pedestrians seen was a commit unit. Two walkers at the start, right at the intersection. Then two cars when you entered the beach, then two cars when you left.

Every intersection has somebody pointed at you right as you reach it. Those are things you look for, because sooner or later you'd expect one of them to not happen.

The fact this idea, of a covert undercover surveillance force, arrayed throughout your towns and neighborhoods, seems strange to you, is because you have been fooled. You were taught to think governments get power, and then the corrupt losers in power take no measures to see to it they will hold onto power. They told you the government is perfectly happy to be blind and totally helpless, and respect your privacy, and just leave itself prone to total replacement at any moment, by a whole new government you selected to serve you, just because you got piqued. Ha!

You believed it. Then again, that is how you would do it. That is how I would do it, too. But that is not how the psychopathic sharks of our corrupt and power-hungry intelligence agencies would do things. And there may be even more psychopathic sharks above them, who they serve.

At this point, after a decade going back and forth with this thing, I even use the word "government" loosely, as I do not think the US has a government as we think of it, fluid, and changing, and continually elected by the people to serve the people. I do not think any of the departments, or agencies, is anything more than a show, to make you think there is a government. I think the United States, only has rulers, who run this intel op from the shadows and make sure whoever gets into office is under their control.

As with so much, the changeable aspect of "government" in the US is just an illusion. And as this thing has grown, and the corruption expanded, and the crimes committed grown, and the money pilfered swelled, so too has the surveillance grown, because now they are all in too deep with the criminality.

Now they don't merely "want" to hold onto power. Now, they cannot possibly afford to lose power, or their crimes might come to light, and they could all end up in front of firing squads. What they have done is complete treason, pure and simple. It is all much different than they told you.

Now we'll go back to the first major intersection, but start at the bridge heading southeast toward the intersection. We will assume the Google car is under surveillance, given what we have seen.

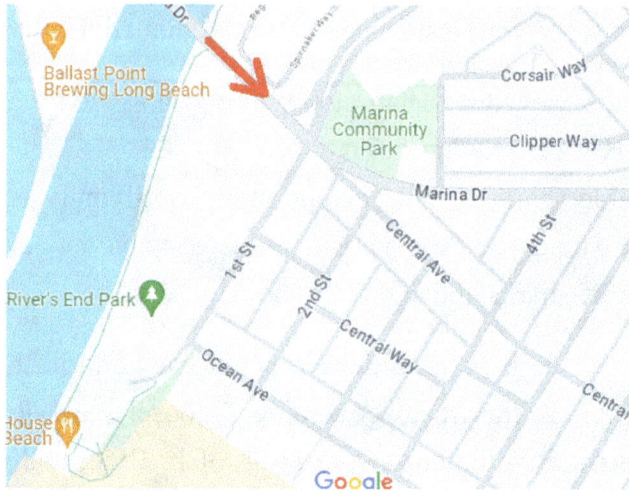

You will approach the intersection and turn left for continuity of the timeline, so you don't jump around.[160]

As you approach the intersection, you have two cars in front of you, stopped at a light which turns green just before you approach it. One black hatchback turns right, the other goes straight. Understand, surveillance controls the traffic lights with emergency services overrides, as well. I assume they didn't think you were going to turn left, so they popped the light green with the standard Emergency Services radio-remote light-control they carry, before you got too close to them, and they took the two directions they thought most likely.

There will still be a stationary commit unit at the intersection to call which way you went, but you'll have to look for it. It is a guy, on a hot sunny day, in long black pants mowing the lawn with his back to you:[161]

One car went straight to take a "cheating command" position, leading you if you went straight. One car went right, to lead you that way. But instead, you go left. I assume they did not want to send vehicles ahead of you in all three directions, since that might, in surveillance parlance, "spark" you, which can lead to you "smoking" as you notice something is odd, which culminates in the team getting "burned," when you realize you are under surveillance. Surveillance has a whole dictionary of radio codewords they use to obfuscate their communications.

So you do not see anyone in front of you, though there will doubtless be units arrayed in your path. Blocking your rear one way is the car which turned right, blocking you the other is the car which turned left.

Since you are now committed to turning left, the team decides to move one unit behind you up ahead of you, and have one of your rear blocking units take up that car's position sitting on this intersection.

If you look to the right, as you enter the intersection to turn left, there is a black SUV by the side of the road. He is pointed toward the intersection, likely acting as a redundant stationary commit unit. When you see him he is pointed so when he pulls out he will be following you.[162]

It has sun damage to the top and hood, probably from long stakeouts in the sun and his windows are cracked open. He flips his headlights on and pulls out to follow you the moment you hit the left turn lane:[163]

Note the hatchback pulling in behind the black SUV, to take up his position, as the black SUV pulls out to follow you:[164]

If you skim back, that is the car in the picture that just turned right as you first approached the intersection at the start of this, because if you look down the street, there is no other car.

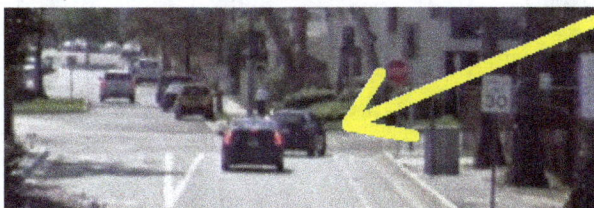

He was going to lead you on that street if you turned, until somebody called out that you were hitting the left turn lane, and he popped a quick U-turn before you could see down the street, and parked momentarily, taking up the position of the black SUV, where he will serve as a rear guard for the team following you, while black SUV moves up and joins your follow, racing to get ahead of you on the side street.

The SUV ducks right, and will parallel you, trying to speed ahead of you while out of your sight. He didn't want to follow you either, because one, his light is red, so all he can do is turn, and two, picking up like that and pulling right behind you might trigger your suspicion. He has already pushed his luck with this timing, At this point, you can begin to conclude they are doing the dance around you, and you are under coverage.

Once you begin to master the mathematical analysis of the probabilities around vehicle behavior at intersections, you will begin to see the surveillance innately. At that point, their behaviors and patterns of movement will begin to stand out. I drove this on Streetview, looking around, and knew instantly what this was. Soon you will, too, but most people are completely blind to this.

Everyone gets this type of coverage for short spurts each year to polish their files. And everyone, every single American, has a file with this thing, maintained by a local archivist who is assigned to know you specifically, like a best friend you have never met. They will live near you, in a house which looks like any other. They may have a regular job, and a wife and kids, and you may have even seen them in the yard once or twice as you drove by them. Meanwhile they have listened in your house, looked at all the internet pages you browsed, examined your

Google search terms, and tried to catch you doing things you would not want others to know you are doing. They know your extended family, your preferences, and even your most basic psychological nature - who you are inside.

If at some point, the local leadership in your area decides you are not contained, and could rise suddenly, they may assign to you the more persistent permanent 24/7 surveillance (and many more Americans have that in their area than you would think, sometimes just because there is so much surveillance, and it has to be assigned to somebody).

Once you see this surveillance, you will develop a second skill, the recognition of the timing surveillance uses when conducting follows. It will happen naturally, as you begin to constantly notice cars pull out like this one, just as you make a turn. It will happen as you notice people entering buildings just as you exit, people exiting buildings just as you enter, people turning corners to walk by you just as you just exit your car.

The timing is so precise, they will actually have people standing for minutes, just around corners, frozen in time, mid-stride, waiting for control to tell them the very second to move, to be turning the corner just as you exit a door.

One such case went viral. A guy saw a walker, stopped in mid-stride, frozen just before a corner for over a minute, waiting to turn it, before she snapped into motion. He shot video of it, leading others on Tik Tok to speculate the girl was trapped in a time warp, or he somehow was looking back in time. In reality she was just foot surveillance on Zersetsung duty, waiting to time her turn of the corner to some target's action to harass him. You can see that video here:

She was like that for a minute before

https://americanstasi.com/somebody-caught-a-surveillance-walker-on-pause-just-before-their-earpiece-said-go/

As you see your local surveillance, you will begin to feel cars driving out of neighborhoods just as you enter, and entering just as you leave. Cars driving past houses as you exit or arrive, and other instances where you either initiate momentum or cease momentum, and one of them is sent by to confirm the change.

You will note again, all of those things happen naturally without surveillance. But they should not happen every time you are in a position for it to happen, or the vast majority of times, with the precise timing surveillance procedures produce.

Eventually, you will combine the ability to notice timed movement with your statistical analysis capability, and an ability to ask where people are coming from, and where they are going, and you will immediately notice the timed movements, that they defy chance, and that they lack explanation. When they repeat over and over, you will feel the ballet going on around you.

Returning to California, if you continue on this path, you will notice you are not followed. However just as you get out of sight of the black hatchback posted at the side of the road behind you, you will notice that on the side of the road is an old friend from another timeline:[165]

That is our little tomato with the baby carriage, and again, we cannot catch a really clear look at her because she just happens to stay behind a car as we drive by. Again, she does not look over. It is almost like she is ignoring us, with our big camera ball.

At this point in the original piece, we took a moment to again jump timelines at the intersection behind us, and take a look at the first shot we would have seen if we crossed and had gone straight. It is a whole new timeline of photos from another time the Google car was here and crossed the intersection, going straight. Unfortunately, Google has deleted this entire timeline, due to what was caught in the photos, so you will have to accept my word these following pictures, which I saved when I did this piece, were from the April 2018 timeline after crossing the intersection.

Opposite you was a line of three cars going in the opposite

direction, waiting at the light at the intersection. The last car had an open driver's side window, common for surveillance to monitor any sounds of significance that would alert them to interesting things that qualify as operational intelligence:[166]

In the next photo, the driver of the first car in the line is taking covert video of you with his phone, which is being relayed wirelessly to central control.

I have seen this in my own life, while being followed. You can see it in this following news story, of a local affiliate news reporter who got busted doing exactly that to a civilian, while possibly being a part of harassment surveillance of him. At the very start of the video, while pointing his camera out the car window, at where the civilian was about to walk, the reporter mumbled, without moving his lips, *"You'll see him now."*

With surveillance, that would be a message to the central control center, which was looking through his camera, and listening in to his microphone. You can see the video here, and the news story is in the endnote:[167]

https://files.catbox.moe/nslnyt.mp4

Listen to the first second, where you can hear the reporter say, "You'll see him now..."

Here in our Streetview tour, this kid is allowing control to watch the Google car in real time, as it passes:[168]

Here is the full image, which would not be as obvious as you passed:

This is a common technique you will see the people around you performing regularly when you are under overt, hostile, harassment surveillance. Here are photos of Capitol protestor and according to some, alleged federal domestic intelligence asset Ray

Epps using his cell phone near a conservative influencer at a protest:

In this next photo, his phone is pointing directly at the influencer, as he holds it as if not using it. In the video of this at the endnote, you will notice how quickly he turns away and hides his phone when noticed:[169]

Conservative activist James O'Keefe captured a member of his surveillance detail performing the same trick. An associate of James videoed the phone, filming James.:[170]

James subsequently chased down and confronted the surveillance operator:

It is a common technique which I have seen so often in my own life, I could not tell you how many hundreds of times I have seen it. Here, the surveillance camera in front of my house captures a passing car, whose passenger is holding a smartphone to film my house as he passes:

Returning to our drive through Seal Beach, given the paucity of traffic, I suspect the car tailing you at a distance is one as well. Unfortunately, Google has deleted this entire timeline of photos so there will be no addresses to visit, but this vehicle was following far behind you when you crossed the intersection and the kid in the SUV pointed his camera at you:

Notice the one headlight out. Part of the package of modifications FBI has done to all of its surveillance vehicles is to run the wires powering both headlights to individual switches under the dashboard. This allows surveillance operators to do everything from communicating with other surveillance units by flashing one headlight or the other in prearranged signals, to killing one headlight to change the appearance of a vehicle (called its "silhouette"). If you later in the day saw a truck like this with both headlights on, you would assume it's a different truck, and not suspect it is the same truck you saw earlier, following you.

Notice the truck is a white pickup with a bedcover that rises just a little bit above the front cab. Also notice, the field next to you is empty:

Now the interesting part. Have you see that truck before? This truck, with the raised bed cover, had opened the locked gate to that field earlier:[171]

One inside the fence, he set up a stationary position, so he could watch you as you drove the perimeter of it, probably with a camera with a telephoto lens. As you drove that street with no traffic at the beginning of this chapter, he was watching you all along the way:[172]

It would imply surveillance was linked to that property, to

the point it would have access to it through the locked gate.

One final note – notice the incongruity in the covert surveillance you saw – namely that you saw it. This isn't law enforcement, or even intelligence. You will not see FBI surveillance holding a phone up, filming you blatantly as you drive by them at an intersection. Nor do I suspect they swarm intersections in obvious fashion in unpopulated areas for that matter.

Real surveillance hides. It restricts the "eye" which is exposed to the target to one surveillance operator, fully under a plausible cover, behaving as if totally uninterested in the target, which makes them blend in with every other normal person the target sees. Meanwhile everyone else on the surveillance team is kept out of sight and guided by radio calls made by the eye, which guides them to form a hidden bubble around the target, just outside of his sight.

Real surveillance doesn't always leave the windows down on its cars as it drives by, because people know what that means. And I will bet if you got the IDs of the people involved here, they would appear to be just average American citizens, with regular jobs, as well as a lot of immigrants who had citizenship issues smoothed over.

Some will have even grown up doing this as children, under parents in this secret society of surveillance people. As children they were operating in schools, building files on other children for an intelligence unit of adults which is assigned to every school, specifically to assess the children and find who are likely to grow up to be problems. I have seen that too, with my own eyes, and even met one of the adults running my school's operation when I was a kid.

And despite the conspiracy having a lot of kids like that, and tons of people in it, nobody has ever spilled the secret of the existence of this Secret Society, running strange surveillance procedures which I am sure the pros at the FBI cringe at the sight of.

Nobody talks. And note, this thing is global, and crosses national boundaries as well, according to the accounts of people who have fled overseas to escape it, only to find the local network where they land knows all about them, and continues their follow seamlessly in the new country.

This is a non-state, trans-national intelligence "agency," and by its size the entity which funds it is the real power which runs the Western world. All of these people, in the secret society of the American Stasi, work for a foreign power of some sort, against regular Americans, and against you – and against our real Constitutional government. I think it is the same organization which is presently crashing America.

Sadly, I can say there are a lot more Americans who desire living under a shadow dictatorship of a foreign, intelligence-based criminal-conspiracy than I would ever have believed possible, if only it will drop them a few extra crumbs more than the rest of us are allowed.

Chapter Seven

Surveillance Detection – The Professional Course Of Real Life Experience – The Alaskan Improvised Elevated Observation Post

Surveillance may not have houses in every neighborhood, everywhere. I could see the operation not being as heavily deployed as you get into regions of America like the more remote areas of Alaska, where Americans may be more believing in freedom, and less prone to join a treasonous intelligence operation seeking to overthrow the Constitutional Republic that is our government. In those areas, they may not even have enough vehicles to devote to your follow.

So how can they keep an eye on what you are doing, if you pull off into a little side village? It depends on the vehicles at their disposal, but here we will see one interesting solution to the problem of a shorthanded surveillance detail in rural Alaska. And in the process, we will show that even in the most remote parts of Alaska, there is no escaping the American domestic surveillance machine of the American Stasi.

We are going to look at a remote little town in coastal Alaska - Woodrow, Alaska, located here:[173]

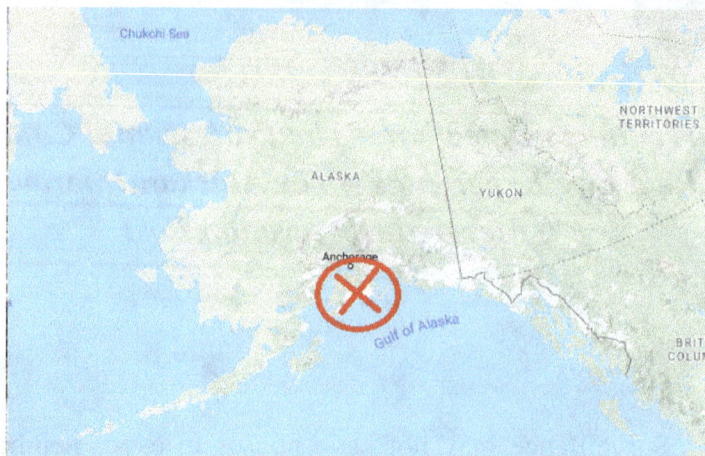

The population of the entire Census-designated-region, of which it is a small part, is 1,748 people. So not a major metropolis. I could not even find a population just for the town itself.

In the image below, we have a nice little bubbled-off neighborhood with one entrance. We will pull in there, and see if we can get alone, or if the shadows of the American Stasi begin to fall around us. The timeline of photos is September, 2011:[174]

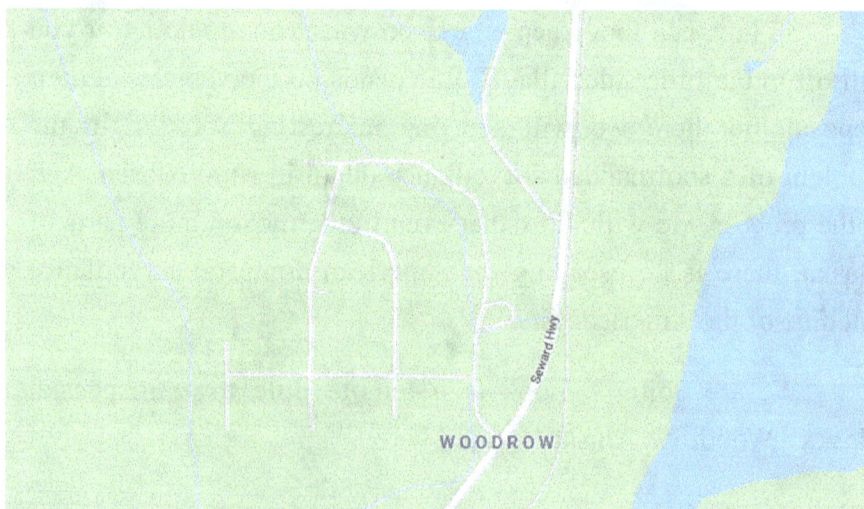

Procedure in the lower 48 would be to immediately call up the primary observation post hidden inside what appears to be a regular house, within the neighborhood (which all neighborhoods in more populous areas have). In many neighborhoods, such an observation post is wired into deployed telephone poll surveillance tech, or even surveillance cameras on other homes, allowing those inside to monitor your movements effectively without needing to expose vehicular or foot assets by moving them on you, unless something unusual happened and it needed a closer look.

A couple of vehicles might move in the neighborhood as backup, and a few pedestrians could be offloaded or exit houses to walk their dogs or ride bikes. If you don't know what is out there, they can get away with that, and nobody is the wiser.

But this is Alaska, so those resources are likely not available. Indeed, they may not even have an observation post in this little group of houses. Yet, they need to keep an eye on this Google car. So what will they do? Lets take a look.

Here is what is approaching the entrance from the north:[175]

So here we are, the middle of nowhere, Alaska, on a road connecting east nowhere and west nowhere, and we have two vehicles just hitting this crossroad, just as we approach. Purely by chance. Lets turn off and see what they do.

Here is a shot back at them just as we turn off, and you can see one is a utility line truck.[176]

Surveillance recruits heavily among the utilities, because it is utility workers who are routinely servicing the poles, and who as a result inevitably come to know a big secret – that the poles are wired with surveillance tech the American Stasi uses to monitor the entire population. I suspect you could not get a job as a line repairman if you tried, unless you were in the American Stasi first.

I am sorry, what were you saying? You thought you could grow up to work the telephone polls or fix power lines, or be anything you want? Not so much in America. Those positions are not for some people, even if they tell you it is entirely different.

Those positions are secured and kept away from the people

who do not know the big secret. Because an important part of the big secret is that there is extensive surveillance gear wired into those telephone poles. Utility workers will quickly discover that, if they notice it while working, so the conspiracy needs to know they will keep the secret. Anybody applying to work the lines is vetted, whether they know it or not, for whether they will keep the secret.

Everything in our free American society, especially relating to the occupations people end up in, has been subverted to some extent by the American Stasi, and thus tends to be controlled. If you are not in the club, you will be massaged into one of the positions where you cannot do any damage, probably without you even knowing. Because the big secret, if widely revealed, would destroy everything about the conspiracy, and probably get every one in it killed, or at least expelled from America. Once Americans know this exists, the spell will be broken, and a war-front will open between those citizens in the conspiracy, and everyone else.

The reasons for your occupational diversion will vary. After all, standardized tests have to be ignored, because they are biased, which is why your high scores on them didn't help you succeed where you wanted to, and racial disparities are why simple competence in a field is not enough for you to succeed in it, and "leftists" are everywhere promoting "leftist" allies for only political reasons, and white men are the enemy so they never get promoted, and minorities are discriminated against, so you, whether you are white or a minority, or have ability, or don't, you couldn't rightly expect to succeed anyway. Plus that is a union job, so you are not plugged into the union, and the excuses go on and on.

The important point, which they will imply in a million

different ways, is that none of your being shunted somewhere mundane, as idiots rise effortlessly to rule over you, is because there is a secret network assigning positions of importance to its brainlets and keeping those outside the network down. It is all due to other benign reasons you were told about, over and over again.

Returning to our Alaskan drive, turn in to the neighborhood, and look back over your shoulder:

In a shocking coincidence, they just happen to follow you in:[177]

Are you being followed? If you calculate the statistical probabilities, and you ask yourself how often vehicles pull into this little alcove with maybe twelve houses, in the middle of the day, in the middle of nowhere, and the fact this is the Google car, you'll realize the answer is yes. Note, they came from the opposite direction, which means somebody else was probably on the radio to them, while tracking you, to make the timing so perfect. It is possible they were following the uploaded photos from the Google car, or the GPS from the driver's phone, though that area looks rural enough I would think cell coverage spotty.

They can't follow behind you everywhere in the neighborhood. But they still want to get an idea of what you are doing in here. How could they possibly keep an eye on you, but not follow you around? It is quite clever. What they did was drive to the back of the neighborhood, and put the cherry-picker up in just the right spot. Google is deleting these images left and right, so some of the screenshots you may not be able to link into online, but you should still get the flavor:[178]

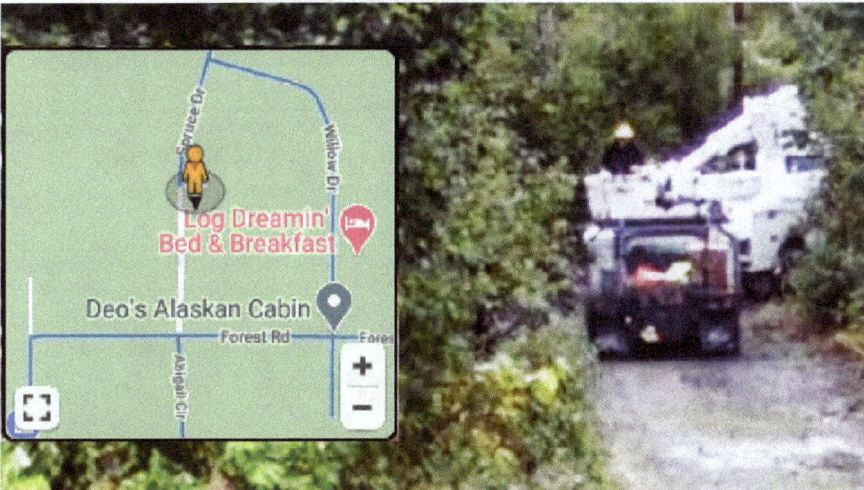

Here is the cherry picker going up:

This will allow him a bird's eye view of the entire neighborhood from a nice little adjustable perch, high above.

Note the location of the truck, and how he chose a spot with a good sightline to the entire neighborhood, in the center of all of its intersections, rather than a far corner which might have difficulty seeing the other opposite corner:

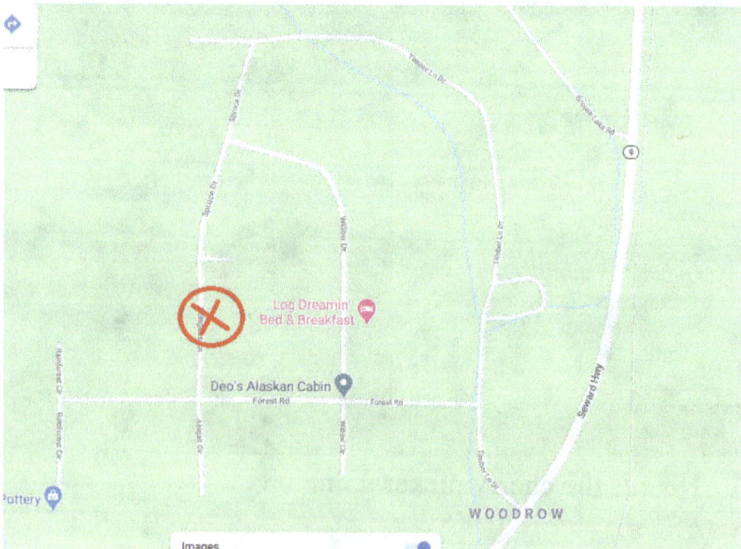

This position keeps him as close as possible to all

intersections, which as we have shown you, are the primary focus of a following surveillance team. From here he can either see or hear where you are at all times.

As a standalone piece of writing, this would sound crazy. He could have pulled into that neighborhood just as you pulled in by chance. Maybe he was just an innocent lineman doing some repairs. It is possible. But when you look at all these pieces, how often have there been coincidences like this? Is it a coincidence it looks just like Russia and Bulgaria?

Up here, in this rural, remote area, wouldn't it be more likely than not you would pull in here and be alone? Can you get alone somewhere else, like a single isolated street? Trying to get alone, and never being able to exactly manage it, is the essence of surveillance detection. Over time, it forces the statistical probabilities to the surface, where you cannot ignore them.

Lets go back, and pull out of the neighborhood. Then we'll run some more surveillance detection, and see if the probabilities continue to indicate there is surveillance, even in this remote, rural location with absolutely no national security interests:[179]

And just as you hit the intersection and are about to pull out to head south, this pickup is coming at you, and another white sedan just happens to be perfectly timed, pulling out of a street down the road:[180]

What does that white car look like when you get up to it?

The road is wet, because it is raining, but he is driving along with his window open. Kind of looks like nurse's scrubs, which would not be surprising. I am not sure why, but they do maintain a large roster of nurses, maybe to access medical info.

What about the street just north of this? It is just one road in. What are the chances a single dead end road would have an anomaly consistent with what a surveillance op might look like?

When you turn into the street, you don't see any other cars. So how might they have clocked whether you took the road or not? What if you had a pedestrian waiting deep back in the road, at the end of the straightaway, hiding at the curve, looking to see whether you took the road? Drive in, and take a look. Once you do, he runs as fast as he can from the curve as long as he can, until you are about to come into sight, and then he walks casually, just a dude out for a walk. To his van which he parked by the side of the road, because he doesn't actually live in that neighborhood.

Here is the turn, do you see him? He just happened to be in that position:

A closer look, at something a surveillance-aware operator would note is consistent with hastily deployed foot surveillance, watching the Google Car:[181]

Where was he going? What was he doing? There are no driveways there. Who drives in a long street like this, parks a vehicle deep inside it, and just walks for no reason back toward the entrance, to hang there watching who turns? If he was visiting someone, he would pull in the driveway. If he was interested in something on the side of the road, he would stop right there. It is illogical.

Here is his van, which he parked by the side of the road at the end, before jogging back to watch the intersection (remember this van, you will see it again):[182]

The main interesting thing about the vehicle is how it blends in, in this rural, poor area. I have done many of these routes in Russia, and in Russia, the Google car would still be followed. But that vehicle would be a brand new, latest model, freshly waxed sedan, which is unlike any vehicle in the area. In Russia, they do not recruit large numbers of locals to spy on their neighbors, I suppose because Russian citizens would think it unpatriotic to operate against their fellow Russians. Sadly that is not the case in America, where there are a lot of Americans happy to help this shadow dictatorship take over our republic, if only it will let them play junior spy, and harass some fellow Americans along the way.

So when Russia has to run coverage in a rural area like the south Caucasus, against a hostile actor like the American Google car, they bring in a team which was normally running coverage in central Moscow, and invariably it doesn't fit. The Russians don't have an extensive citizen-informant network being run against their own citizens. I have looked for it.

Lets go south to the next intersection. Here we are, at the intersection, in the middle of nowhere, looking back:[183]

And looking forward:[184]

One car on each side, roughly equidistant.

Pull off on the side street, and one of the residents appears to be coming back from getting their mail:[185]

It is possible she could just be a resident. But after a decade of being under hostile surveillance by the American Stasi, I have seen this often enough, that given this is the Google car and we know it is under surveillance, I would assume she was called up and told to wait at the mailboxes, maybe even dropped off by one of the surveillance vehicles with a handful of papers that looked like mail, to sit on the intersection and act as a commit unit.

Head back and pull out of this road, back onto the main road. You will need to bear left, to acquire the photos from the timeline when you were pulling out. If you do that, you will see that when the Google car was pulling out, on the right, you have cars in both directions, and on the left you will have cars in both directions, meaning whichever way you turn, you will have a car in front of you and a car behind you. Remember, the larger region this little town was a part of only has about 1,700 residents. This town has a fraction of that 1,700 people in it, and yet in the middle of the day, everywhere you go, the instant you hit an intersection, traffic is heading in all directions.

To the right:[186]

To the left:[187]

They are almost mirror images of each other.

And we have another car heading north which will pass us after we pull out:[188]

When we hit the next turnoff, and drive in a little ways we get a look at what was following us as it passes, and it was a van with tinted windows:[189]

Back out to the intersection to get on the main road again, and we have another vehicle oncoming just as we are about to pull out, but behind him the road is empty:[190]

If you look very closely, at that little dot, you will see he turns off onto the next road when you are quite far away:[191]

But when you get up to that street to turn off, he is fairly close, as if he was driving very slowly or pulled off right there, and you have another car pulling out:[192]

Once you pull off, he whips fast into a driveway. It could be an observation post for this neighborhood, and he is rushing to get the tech up and running while you are here:[193]

Go back and begin to pull out heading south to get the timeline right and you see three cars drove in front of the intersection just as you arrived at it, all heading south, and one is coming north, but no other cars are on the road:[194]

It's almost like this is normally an empty road, but every time you hit an intersection cars are pulling up to it just because of you. Pull out, and begin to drive for a while, and you will see no other cars in the oncoming lane after the one timed to your exit:[195]

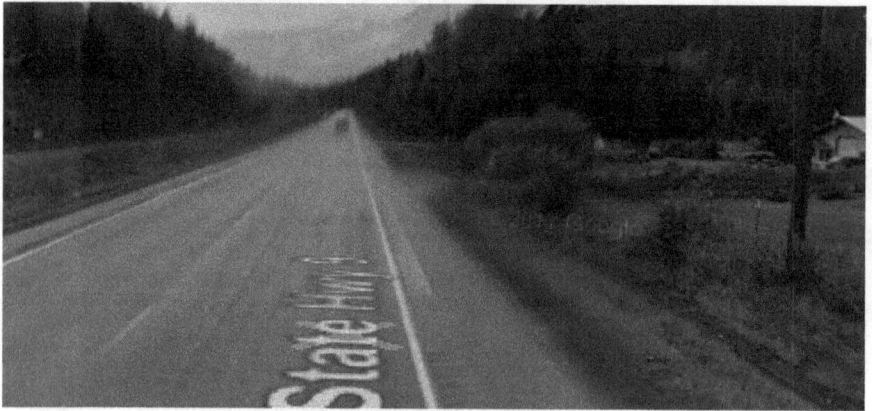

Look back, not another car on the road, save the one timed to your arrival at the intersection:[196]

This is why you do surveillance detection in an area without a lot of traffic. If there is a lot of traffic, the operators relax, because they have other vehicles that work as camouflage. They can make mistakes because your attention is distracted by a lot of other cars. But if you should be alone, each car can be focused on. Coincidences of timing begin to jump out. And stressed operators begin trying to give you as much space as possible, almost losing you, and then pulling in closer than they should only at critical moments.

It is easy to not make mistakes when mistakes might slip by unnoticed. It is not easy to avoid mistakes when you are stressed because every little mistake will be patently obvious.

Continue south, and you will go a very long way and see no oncoming cars, until here, when you hit another intersection (the car is blurry because it is raining and there is rain on the camera lens):[197]

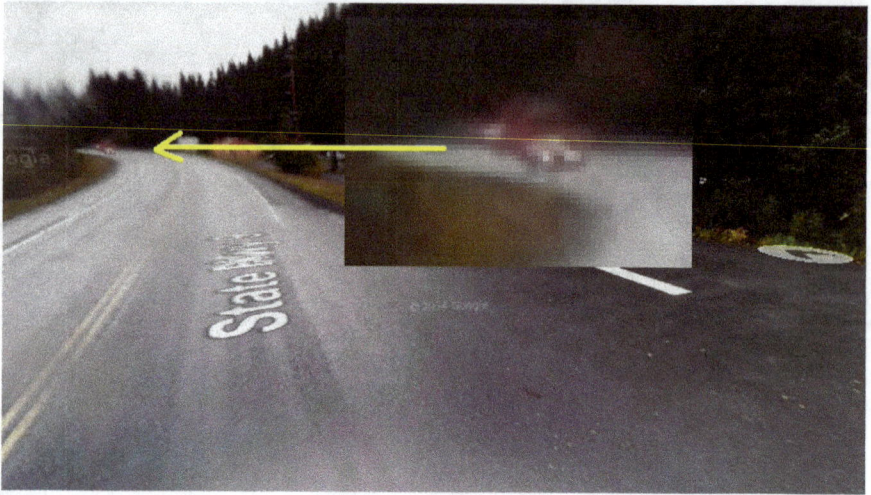

You'll then get a car passing when you come up on the Post Office (often a center of local Cabal operations for some reason), then another couple at the next intersection. Most likely, not all of the cars are surveillance. But most of them will be, and in America today, they all could be.

Go to the next street you can turn off on and make the turn and then look back:[198]

Probably means there is no established observation post in some part of this neighborhood, or his home is the observation post in that part and he needs to get it up and running. When the Google car turns off on the first little dead end side street he keeps going, rather than follow it in and then have to turn around and immediately follow it out and burn himself. Nice tint job:[199]

Periodically, you will hit areas where you don't see anyone. If you know how things work, you assume a surveillance op lives in a house nearby, and you are being watched there from within the observation post.

Here you will see a good example of the Principle of TEDD, or Time Environment Distance Demeanor, as you hit an area of the neighborhood with no visible coverage. The Principle of TEDD in surveillance asks, have you seen the same vehicle or individual around you at differing **T**imes, **E**nvironments, **D**istances from each other, or do the people exhibit unusual **D**emeanors.

Drive up farther. Where have you seen this van before?[200]

You saw this van earlier, when the walker was walking toward it after clocking you having entered the side street earlier in this chapter, as seen below:

Notice, there is no visible surveillance on the street here, right outside this house.

This is what is most insidious about the Secret Society. They live among us, look like us, and are on the clock even when and where you would never expect them to be.

Who would think an official surveillance operative, who

looks like a normal neighbor, could be on the clock in his own house in your neighborhood spying on you? But from within that house, he will have the technical ability to backdoor electronics like your Alexa or your cell phone, to listen in your house with remote eavesdropping equipment, and if you are more of a luddite, he will probably have devices he can point at your house to at least listen inside, and maybe even see in some form.

Moreover, he may have entered your house while you were out at work just to plant listening devices, and maybe even cameras, and maybe even in your bedroom, whether there is something going on in there of use to the operation, or if he is just curious, or a voyeur, as many who seek out this type of role may tend to be.

As you will see later, this conspiracy makes surreptitious entries into homes whenever the mood strikes them. The purpose of the main observation post in a neighborhood, is to establish monitoring operations capable of seeing in every house in the neighborhood, as part of this individual's responsibility to get to know everyone there.

Once they have that type of total situational awareness in a neighborhood, where they see everything from incoming traffic, to even inside houses, and what everyone is doing inside their homes, they can control who sees them breaking into houses, and they can organize any break-ins, in such a way, that there is zero risk of anyone seeing them, and zero risk of them being discovered or caught. And even if they were, many have the ability to intimidate local law enforcement, and exert control over any responding Police units.

It is very much modeled on the model of the monitoring apartment the East German Stasi would maintain in every apartment building. The monitoring apartment, manned by an undercover Stasi operative and their family, was wired into microphones that were installed in every other apartment while people were out during the day. Its job was to listen to the family conversations in homes, to build files on everyone showing who they were, especially behind closed doors, determine if they were a threat, and make sure they never rose to a position of wealth or power, where they could escape control, without the Stasi's explicit approval. Wealth and power are threats which are only allowed for those the conspiracy trusts.

Again, this seems unusual to you as an American, raised on the American myths of freedom and privacy. But from the perspective of intelligence officers, from the Gestapo to the Stasi, and even European intelligence agencies and the CIA, intel operations have long operated this way. And since this conspiracy taking over our nation is most likely based out of old Europe, their intelligence operation is modeled on that. This is how they operate – they play to win.

I have seen it firsthand for going on a decade. That you would not think it possible is a misconception they are only too happy to see fostered, as it makes you weaker, and makes their operations easier to conceal. The truth is, this is how intel operates, and how it it always has - ruthless, thorough, intrusive, and without any morals or scruples.

I am convinced that in America, the command actually tells individual civilian informants where to live, specifically so they can do most of their spying from their own house. It becomes even more impressive, given I would estimate that 4-10% of the populace has been recruited into this secret society of surveillance people spying on you. So spread out in an organized fashion, the coverage in neighborhoods, is unusually thorough.

I even suspect their jobs are often dictated, and in a not-insignificant number of cases their spouses and love life are also determined by the command. Those in the conspiracy are trusted because they assent to be controlled almost completely.

Their children even attend sleep away camps which school them on surveillance, and the operation then employs them in the schools to begin each American's file when they are just a child.

Shortly, we will even show that they have technology which basically lets them see your movement, and even use energetic beam weapons to assault and injure you through walls, while ensconced in their own homes with plausible deniability, without the target being able to produce 100% evidence of where it came from or who is responsible. And used on low power, over the entirety of a night, those weapons can degrade a target's health and performance, without the target even knowing a human being has done that to them. They'll assume it happened entirely organically. We will later show scientific studies indicating that may be going on much more widely than Americans would think possible.

You can see how the idea of a limited government that stops at your front door is a mere mirage. There is no limit to this thing's capability, and no threat of consequence to make it constrain itself. Again, I have seen all of this firsthand, and we will look at where it has all been documented in the official record shortly.

Until then, think about how far you have come. When

Russian deep-cover sleeper-spy Anna Chapman feared her role as a Russian deep cover operative in New York City had been discovered, she described exiting a building, and looking closely at everyone around her, wondering if any were surveillance. But she said she had no idea how to spot surveillance in America, and saw nothing.

Already you have the ability to stage and run a counter-surveillance detection route if you are feeling spooked. Already you are beginning to "feel" the strange coincidental timings and movements which will eventually trigger you when you see it in real life - and you will. Already you have made an impressive stride toward being far more functional at spotting the biggest threat in this world - to your safety and to our Republic. Already you are more of an operator than many of the militia members who think they could stand up to an oppressive dictatorship, but who have no idea how many of their "innocent" countrymen (and women) are arrayed around them, just waiting to stab them in the back for the powers that be – powers that be which at present are a full fledged foreign criminal conspiracy committed to destroying the nation.

The Secret Society is everywhere and it is embedded among us, always watching, always reporting back, from your church, to your gun club, to your child's second grade class. It is in suburban neighborhoods, and the remote wilds of Alaska. And these Stasi informants all know the secret - that we regular citizens are the targets, and the machine around us is our enemy, infiltrating our elected Republic, and replacing it with their shadow dictatorship.

Now in our next chapter, lets dispel any misconceptions you

may have about this surveillance machine possibly being somehow "government," and thus run legally, for your benefit as a citizen. Lets look at where it appeared to run overwatch for the murder of an innocent young woman.

Chapter Eight

Surveillance Detection – The Professional Course Of Real Life Experience – The Murder Of Irah Sok

Now we will do something a little different. We will show how this ability to detect surveillance using the Google car can be used to assess the nature of events which you see in the news.

On my news site, somebody posted a video about a case where the ATF seized a guy's guns wrongly.[201] The guy wanted some gun part, likely some kind of custom AR buffer tube. So he went to a local machinist, the machinist insisted on putting it in his trunk, he relented, and the moment he opened his trunk, he was swarmed, and ATF seized the guns in his trunk of his car.

Something didn't sit right with me about the ATF agent emphasizing over and over, that he had just been in the wrong place at the wrong time, and it was all bad luck. It had a "doth protest too much" quality. And the machinist insisting on putting the part in his trunk where his guns were, rather than just handing the small item to him, also felt off. They all knew what was in that guy's trunk. And the way they would know that was, he was under surveillance. And then ATF would not return his guns, even though he was cleared of all wrongdoing, and even the ATF agents said it was a big misunderstanding. It felt like a set up. And yet, if he was under surveillance, they knew he was innocent going in, and no crime would be found. It appeared surveillance set him up

299

specifically to take his guns. But why?

The piece mentioned that as he was undergoing what felt like a manufactured turmoil with ATF, his sister was murdered.[202] That felt off to me. Too coincidental. Knowing how US domestic intelligence and the American Stasi work, I wondered if it was possible the events had been orchestrated to disarm him and tie him up legally during the time when his sister was murdered for some reason. That would imply his sister was some sort of target.

If she was a target, she would have been under surveillance, so I decided to do an investigation and analysis of the surveillance infrastructure surrounding his sister, the beautiful wife and mother, Irah Sok, using the Google car in Google streetview. As you will see, the results were intriguing.

Irah Sok was, by all accounts, a well-loved pillar of the community. She was a devoted mother, with a thriving photography business, which did quite high quality work.[203]

A word on photography. As I have tracked down some of the surveillance assigned to me in my investigations, I have found a number have set up professional photography side-hustles.

The civilian component of the domestic surveillance in the United States exists almost as a secret society. Parents raise their children in it, and there is even a small sleep-away camp held at what appeared a hotel/dormitory in Florida, which you will find the kids often post photos of on social media, while they are attending it. In the background of the photos will be men in wraparound sunglasses with blue and white ID placards which appear to have FBI logos on them.

Most of the secret society members today are raised as domestic surveillance from the time they are children, even being utilized in genuine intelligence operations in the schools. There, they are run against other children as assets, as the adult domestic intelligence agents giving them orders use them to probe and assess the other kids - the next generation of citizen. At that age, children are too young to defend themselves, and too naive to hide who they are and what they are capable of. In some cases, where a student appears on course to one day be a problem for the conspiracy, the adults may try to intervene through the provision of pornography, or alcohol, or drugs, using their child spies to introduce the obstacle and derail the potentially problematic kids.

By the time they are adults, these domestic intel operators will have considerable training. One specialty they will eventually be trained up in is photography. As domestic surveillance, they will also tend to have first-rate photography equipment on hand, so

301

forming a side-hustle as a professional photographer is a natural fit for them. It is a cover identity, a source of additional income, and a way to perfect a skill the conspiracy needs.

However as a result, any regular, non-surveillance citizen who forms a successful photography business will be draining away business from other photography businesses which are very likely being run by domestic surveillance personnel. Those citizen spies will have at their disposal a considerable range of assets to deploy to get that business back. I have no idea if a jealous domestic spook took Irah out to increase their own photography business' success, but it would not surprise me. By the end of this chapter, you'll see she clearly angered someone in the conspiracy.

To begin, we will cruise by Irah Sok's photo studio. Here is the shopping center it is located in, circa February 2022:

Oddly enough in a series of photos taken in February of 2022 according to Google, in Washington State, months before Irah's murder on August 19th of 2024, where it is so cold there is salt on the cars due to icing, right in front of her photo studio is what looks like a surveillance vehicle with the driver's window open, despite the temperature:[204]

I have noted how keeping windows open to observe sound is a common procedure you will notice with surveillance vehicles. Out of about 75 cars, both parked and driving there, only one, parked right in front of her studio, has an open window.

You will notice his tailpipe producing copious condensate:

So the car was cold, on an overcast winter day, either early or late because her sign's lights are on, yet he has his window open to the outside, and he has been running the engine for a while, probably to power his heater. But he is not driving anywhere. I would have pulled out and taken off long before I dropped that much condensate on the ground.

Domestic surveillance appears to park different cars around in different parking lots, I assume for when they are shorthanded on drivers, so the drivers can swap cars mid-follow and increase and vary their number of vehicular "silhouettes." During my own early shock and awe phase, as they flooded cars by me one after another in an attempt to intimidate me, I saw the same driver go by in two different cars in a mall parking lot away from a residential area, during cold weather. The second car was blowing steam out of the exhaust pipe since it had just been started and was cold. I assumed they drove by in their car, then headed to a nearby lot in the mall where another car was parked, started it up, and cruised by me again to make me think there were all these cars, each with a different driver.

Also note in the photo below, as you drive past him, his other passenger side window is very open:[205]

So on the side which the Google car was coming from, where it would have a direct sightline into his car, the window was open, but less open, as if he closed it a bit as he saw the Google car approaching to be less obvious. On the far side, where he would be at the Google car's 7 or 8 o'clock after it passed, and the Google car would probably not be looking back, he opened it much more.

Notice also, it gives the driver a better sightline to the Google car when it is directly behind him, through that passenger-side, rear-view mirror. You can almost see the driver in the mirror in the picture above. All on an overcast winter day, in early morning or toward evening, in a cold car.

So if you continue driving, another pickup, driven by a woman, just happens to drive between you and Irah's studio, just as you pass it, perfectly timed:[206]

That could be a coincidence, but it is curious, as I have done these analyses in a lot of lots, and do not see cars often doing that, let alone, just as I pass a potential target business I am suspicious of. As I have said, they seem to pride themselves on timing things like that, as well.

Also curious, this yellow Chevy pickup truck picked up and pulled out of her parking spot and passed you as you entered the parking lot, and made her way to the exit, as you can see below, where first she is pulling out in front of you,[207] and then behind you she is driving to the exit, which is right to her left in the photo, as you continue to drive:[208]

Behind you:

Now the strange thing. You don't see that pickup again, until it came time to exit the parking lot, presumably several minutes later, when it showed back up to lead you out of the lot:[209]

So even though it picked up, left its parking spot, and headed to the exit, it did not leave, but instead waited until the Google car left, so it could assume a cheating command position and lead it out.

Plus, although people buy bright yellow cars, I think surveillance actually has some reason why they buy brightly colored cars, perhaps to be more noticeable during harassment operations.

Where I am, bright yellow, and a neon-puke-green are very common among their vehicles. And of course bright red is so noticed by those harassed, it was included in the famous meme by a 4Chan "Targeted Individual" who is under this. While 4Chan memes are an acquired taste, for informational purposes, the meme, featured on the next page, made fun of the surveillance people, which in the Targeted Individual community, are referred to as "Gangstalkers," while humorously portraying the extremely well endowed target of their operation as comically "cool":

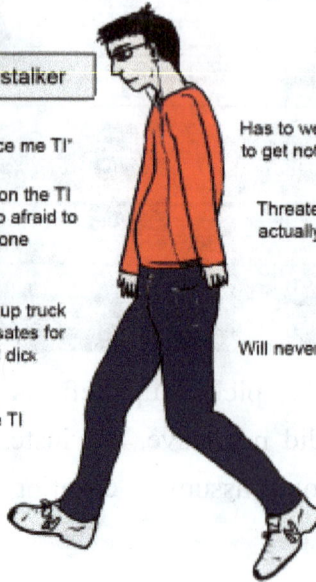

the virgin gangstalker

"P-please notice me TI"

Has to gang up on the TI
because he is too afraid to
face him alone

Red pickup truck
compensates for
small dick

Afraid of the TI

Has to wear bright colors
to get noticed by anyone

Threatens TI but never
actually does anything

Will never be as important as
the TI

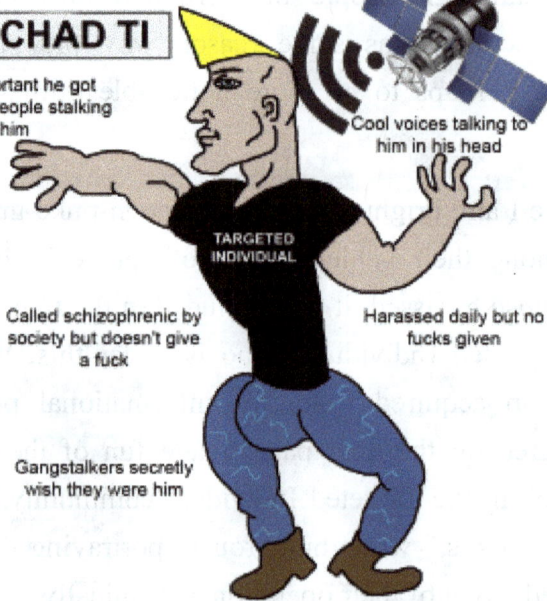

THE CHAD TI

So important he got
loads of people stalking
him

Cool voices talking to
him in his head

TARGETED
INDIVIDUAL

Called schizophrenic by
society but doesn't give
a fuck

Harassed daily but no
fucks given

Gangstalkers secretly
wish they were him

Regardless, continue around the back of the shopping center, just to see what you will see, and you happen on these guys:[210]

I classify them unremarkable, though I note, this guy has nothing in his hands:

As you continue to drive past them, you will note, he brings his hand up to cover his mouth:

It is always possible he is just a nail biter, or he coughed. However foot surveillance utilizes communications gear which features microphones taped to their chest. When they want to send out a communication, they will hit a microphone key, often in a pocket, and speak into their chest while covering their mouth, so it is not obvious they are talking. I have seen foot surveillance do everything from vape, to pick their nose, to fake-cough, to itch their nose, to hide the fact their lips are moving and they are sending a message through their chest mic. If his other hand were in his pants pocket, like on a button-key for the mic, I would say there was a 95% chance he was foot surveillance. Remember this photograph of this posture, as you will see this movement again.

As you continue around the back of the store, the other two pedestrians take the corner and continue to observe you:[211]

I know what the American Stasi looks like. I have been looking at it for decades. Even if only some of that were coverage, that is a lot of coverage around Irah Sok's shop.

As you will soon see, had Mrs Sok been surveillance aware, she might be alive today.

Next, we will travel to the murder scene, and see whether there is anything which could be consistent with surveillance activity around Irah Sok's house, here:[212]

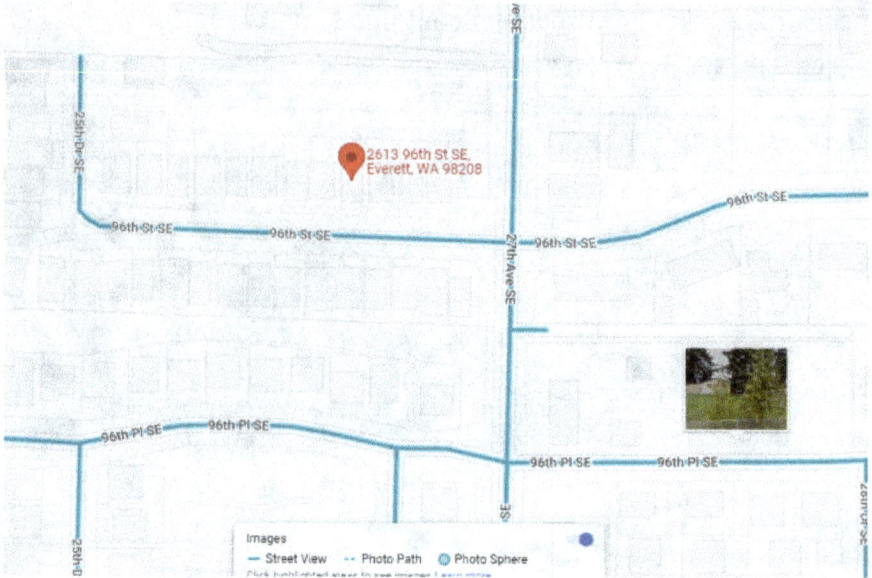

We will start near the back of the cul de sac, at the end of the dead end street Irah Sok lives on, shown by the arrow below. We will drive down, and then take the curve and continue to the right. The timeline of photos was taken as the Google car exited the cul de sac, and the photos were taken in August of 2018:

The Google car was exiting the street, traveling from left to right on the map above, heading to the main street.

Here is what you see. The arrow below is pointing at the back window of a car parked by the side of the road, which will pick up and lead the Google car out of the neighborhood, just as the Google car reaches the corner:[213]

His pickup was perfectly timed to the Google car approaching the corner and coming into sight. He is using a "cheating command" position, where instead of following a target, you drive in front of them.

It is possible it is a resident who just happened to start driving away the very moment the Google car happened to come into view, but again, the precise timing is highly coincidental. The way you spot surveillance (which tries to appear normal) is repeated statistically coincidental occurrences that correlate to your movement. You cannot look at surveillance and see it – it is designed to look normal. You can only see the repeated coincidences of unusual occurrences, which build as time goes on.

You would only see this kind of surveillance in a neighborhood of high importance to the surveillance. If there were not an active surveillance target in here, they would simply let you enter, post on the entrance, and pick you up when you left.

They do not like you seeing their cars, and little cul de sacs like this cannot have a mobile vehicular unit follow you or monitor you without you seeing it. They needed eyes on the Google car for this spot because one of these houses is under active surveillance. There is something in here they are interested in.

Here are a few shots of the car leading you as you exit. These photos were taken in August of 2018, according to Google, about four years before her murder, so surveillance was operative on this street back then, possibly indicating Irah was a long term targeted individual. As you are driving in these shots, Irah Sok's home, where she would be murdered, is up ahead, just to your left. So the surveillance car had parked by the side of the road before it, it picks you up, and maintains you, "sighted," using a cheating command position, as you pass her home on your way out:[214]

315

Now something serendipitous happens for our statistical analysis. We will change timelines again, mid-street, from August of 2018, to a newer timeline of photos which were taken in February of 2022, six months before the murder. When I do these pieces for my website, I frequently get these chance occurrences of good luck. Now we get to drive this street a second time, four years later, several months before Irah's murder, in the middle of the day, when everyone should be at work, and see if there was a car in here the second time too, which could have been watching us.

Seeing one set of eyes in an isolated cul de sac once, and having it move when you move is statistically unlikely, but not definitive. But if every time you are in this street, there is a car there, that is the kind of statistical anomaly which points to surveillance. Especially a small cul de sac, in the middle of the day, without many houses on it or many people living in it. So let's visit this street in 2022, six months before Mrs Sok's murder, and see if there will happen to be another set of eyes which just happen to be there as we are driving by:

Yes, we have a postal service truck, parked, in the middle of somebody's driveway, and not by a mailbox. For many first time readers of these pieces, the significance of the fact it is a postal truck will elude them. In several previous pieces, we have noted US Postal Service mail trucks in areas where people were apparently high-priority targets. We see them so often, we have come to call them the Postal Service Truck of Death[TM].

There were the people who were being harassed by their local surveillance, whose dog was skinned and left dead in their yard.[215] In an analysis of their neighborhood coverage, surveillance was noted all around their house, including a Postal Service truck parked right outside their driveway as the Google car passed, seen here:[216]

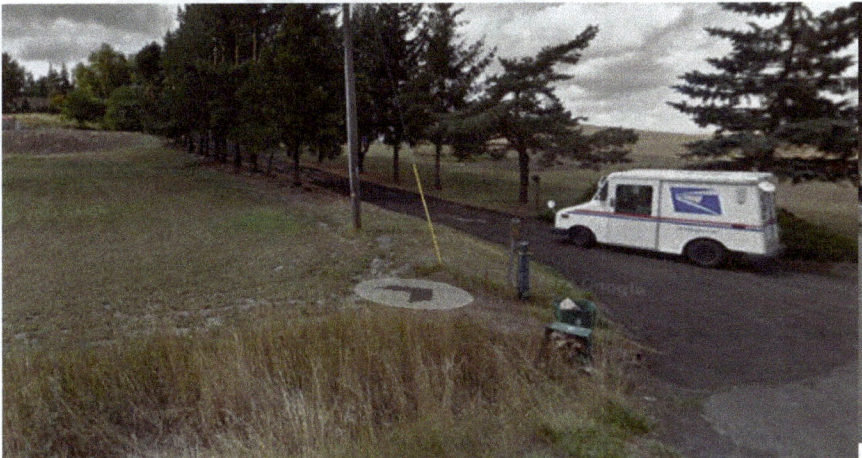

To show that what we call a Postal Service Truck of Death™ is in fact intelligence related activity, there was the case of a former NSA covert listening post which was listed on a real estate website after the government decommissioned it. It was a covert listening post established in a residential neighborhood to look like a home. But inside it was a warehouse for a data center, complete with lockers where agents would have to check their weapons. When a real estate youtube channel[217] did a Google driveby on Streetview, prominent in front of the building was, yet another example of the Postal Service Truck of Death™ running surveillance overwatch:[218]

And as in the previous case where we saw a US Postal Service Truck of Death™ staking out the entrance to the house of a (doggie) murder victim, The truck outside Irah Sok's house is parked exactly opposite the front door of the murder location.

Exactly across the street from this new Postal Service Truck of Death™ is the address listed for the husband of Irah Sok.[219] You can see the house number over the garage, in the next picture, and then pan 180 degrees to the opposite side of the street, where you will see the postal truck, perfectly across from the front door of the house. As you will see, the postal truck arrived here moments before you, and it will leave right after you. The driver never exits the truck. That's surveillance activity, 100%, set up on this house.

The reason he chose that particular spot precisely, is her front door was recessed, behind the front line of residences there. As a result, he had to be right there to have eyes on her front door. Any farther up the street and it would be blocked from view by the front of the house next door, any farther down the street, and it would be blocked by the garage next to the walkway. Go to this link,[220] and swing back and forth by dragging your mouse while holding down the left button, and look at how perfectly he is positioned to watch that door. It is creepy, knowing just a few months later, she was murdered in front of her family in the living room of that home.

So a few months before Irah Sok is murdered, you drive down her street, and they have a Postal Service Truck of Death™ posted exactly opposite her front door, sitting with its lights on, not near any mailbox, in the only spot with a sightline to her front door. And he will remain there as long as you are on the street. And if you drive past her wedding photography business, there is another surveillance vehicle posted directly in front of her wedding photography business, with the windows open, six months before her murder. And her brother is jammed up by ATF in a bogus intel op, which puts him on ice and takes his guns, just before she is murdered.

Had he not been jammed up by ATF and had his guns taken, is it possible she might have called him, saying she saw something which scared her, and asked him to stay with her? Might he have smoked the assailants right after they came through the front door? We will never know, because ATF put him on ice while she was killed.

After many years of observation, it is my opinion the USPS may actually be a covert domestic surveillance/intelligence agency. I strongly suspect the entire agency is an intel honeypot designed to trick you into handing them physical copies of interesting intelligence materials which you do not feel safe sending digitally or over the phone, with a promise your physical copy will never be opened, examined, or cataloged, because that would be against the law. I suspect within the organization is a cell of intelligence agents whose sole purpose is locating and reading those communications. And they probably, in loose fashion, utilize the closeness of the postal workers with their community to try and tease out additional intelligence about all of us, for our files.

Our valiant Postal Service employee will sit there the entire time you are driving the street in this timeline. You will see him arrive, and park, just seconds before you approach this spot, later in the piece.

Someone speculated these may not be real Postal Service vehicles, and surveillance has bought a bunch of these, and simply pulls them out of their storage facility whenever they want to sit outside a tier one target's house as the Google car passes.

While I can say I have seen a fake Fed Ex truck and a fake

Police SUV, I do not know if this is or is not fake, nor do I think you can tell. I do know my local surveillance operation has taken over the Post Office in my town, even setting up a perimeter of foot surveillance loitering all around the building, securing it. So it would not surprise me if it is a real employee in a real truck.

On the other hand there is a man named Richard Bruce who posts conspiracy videos on youtube based around Reptilian theory. Reptilian theory hypothesizes that a species of dinosaur evolved to be technologically sophisticated, and survived the meteor impact which killed the rest of the dinosaurs. It hypothesizes that today they are hundreds of millions of years more advanced than we are, they rule the world, and they are sort of farming humans for some reason, be it slave labor or an experiment. He uploaded videos to youtube to that effect, and immediately came under hostile harassment by the domestic Stasi in America in LA.[221]

He could have uncovered a non-human conspiracy, or he might have just been noticed by his neighborhood watchers, who thought him kooky and decided it would be fun to screw with him. Either way, his videos show he is clearly experiencing harassment.

He posted a video of an LA Police Department helicopter flying in circles over him. A helicopter buff in the comments linked out to the LA Police Department's aviation site which listed their aircraft inventory, identified the model circling him in the video, and showed the Department did not have that model of helicopter in their fleet. He wrote:[222]

L.A.P.D. operates a fleet of 17 helicopters, 12 are Eurocopter AS350's, 4 are Bell 206 Jet Rangers, and the 17th is a recently acquired Bell 412. The paint scheme has been recently

321

changed to a black and white motif that is consistent throughout the fleet. These choppers **[Ed note – The helicopters in the video]** *all have the basic shape of the classic Huey. Some of those things flying over you are ringers, in my opinion.*

If correct, the local Stasi bought a Huey-type helicopter and painted it in LA Police Department markings, and was flying it around LA harassing random people. I do not care which innocent fellow countryman is being harassed in my nation, nor do I care what he believes. Everyone of these is a crime which cries out for justice. Of all the nations in the world, the United States, most of all, should place a premium on protecting the weak, and not abusing them, simply because you can get away with it.

In my own life, my neighborhood crew bought a police light bar, and was running different cars back and forth in front of my house with the light bar running on top of them and a siren on the cars. They even ran it on a Tesla, before moving it to a white civilian Dodge Durango. A few days later, they added an undersized door decal for the local Police department to the Durango and Police markings on the fenders and back. Apparently they did not have an A3 sized printer to print a large door decal the same size as the local department, so they used a regular A4 printer to print the logo on 8x10 sticker paper.

Returning to the story of Irah Sok, the postal truck could certainly be fake. There is no way to tell.

Continuing down Irah Sok's street, we hit the intersection with the main drag.

As you look to your left, you have your cable/fiber truck and two people out on their front yard across the street. These photos were taken just months before her murder:[223]

As always, there is no knowing with certainty whether that is surveillance or not, though it is worth noting it is another corner house on the intersection of a high priority target's street. I put the chances of the mail truck being surveillance at 99.99999% based on my experience, given there is somebody in it just sitting there opposite the target residence for so long, in so many photos, with no mailbox nearby. I'd say the same for the fiber truck, if there were a guy sitting in it, not doing anything. Drive up and take a look:

Sitting in the driver's seat, there is a guy not doing anything, watching that intersection in his side rear-view mirror (a surveillance technique to minimize the exposure of the operative to the target, compared to parking facing the intersection, where the target sees the operator through the big open windshiel.).

Interestingly, as the Google car exited the street and began this turn, if you look back, the Postal Service Truck of Death[TM] decided to turn his wheels and begin to pull away from the curb:[224]

As you will see in a moment, he parked there, just before you entered the street. You drove in, to the end of the cul de sac, turned around, drove out, and the entire time he sat just in that spot, directly in front of Irah Sok's door, without leaving his truck, and now as you leave, he pulls away from the curb, and begins to drive off.

Surveillance detection depends on the observation of suspicious coincidences in timing that correlate with your movement. What are the chances of his movements correlating to your's that closely? What are the chances that you see all this activity on this street corner, and all of it is innocent, and coincidental? That Postal Service Truck of Death^{TM} is close surveillance, running overwatch on a future murder victim's house. These waters in the US are running deeper than you would think.

You also have a couple of walkers at your 6 o'clock, but it is much more difficult to tell if they are surveillance here. If they are, Mrs Sok was a high-priority target for some reason:

It turns out probably two to three minutes before the above photos in another timeline, we were approaching the target intersection behind us, going north, and just as we reached it, the walkers reached the corner, so based on the perfect timing, I would increase the likelihood they were surveillance:[225]

If at every intersection you come to, every corner you hit, somebody is there, timed perfectly to your arrival, you have surveillance. It is the most basic rule. Surveillance needs people at that decision point to call which way you go, and the corner where Irah Sok's street met the main drag, was a critical decision point.

They were timed to post on that corner just as we hit it, and then return to moving. It looks weird, but again, you see it often enough you begin to just accept, this is how it works in America, where somebody has recreated the East German Stasi, and an astonishing number of Americans turned out to have the same selfish mindset and lack of principles as the East Germans who spied for the communist government back then. There are a lot more of them out there than I would ever have thought possible.

I have the advantage of having undergone the shock and awe phase of an overt harassment campaign, during which both of these women would have glared at me as they held their wrists to their mouths, and talked into them while pinching their cuffs to try and look threatening. If you see that enough over a period of a year or two, at every corner you come to, it is a little clearer what this is. You see the astonishing magnitude of the size of the operation, and you are better able to accept something like this could exist.

In that timeline of photo-taking, the Google car turned right at this corner, heading east on this (technically still the target's) street away from the target's residence.

It is interesting to continue down this cul de sac on the other side of the intersection, because you have no eyes on you there, once you are out of view of the intersection. Similar street, technically the same street as the target's, but no cars on it. No residents in yards, no walkers, no Postal Service Truck of Death™, nobody. That should be normal for a cul de sac in the middle of the day. What you saw above is not normal, nor was it unrelated to Mrs Sok's murder.

The Google car then came out of this street, and crossed over to the target's street heading toward the target residence. Google combined these timelines, mixing and alternating the photos as you drive toward the intersection. So near the intersection, you will shift to your exit from this street, before crossing the intersection and heading to the target's house, generating the photos we saw in the beginning.

As a result, at the entrance to this cul de sac you get a few photos of the Postal Service Truck of Death™ you saw before, just before you crossed the intersection to pass in front of Irah's house. So when we turn on this street, we see what we would have seen right before we encountered the mail truck.[226] The mail truck was driving, and was about to pull over and stop, just seconds before we entered the street and passed the truck. Undoubtedly somebody radioed him at that moment that the target was coming, and he needed to post and wait outside the target house.

Here he is, driving toward his final posted position, in front of the house of Irah Sok, just as we are about to cross the main drag and then drive the street in front of her house:

All the time you drive there, and he never exits his truck, or does anything but just sit opposite that house. There may be cameras on the mail truck, and they are watching from the command center or the nearby neighborhood observation post as you drive by him. Or he was Facebook Live-ing you with his phone and command was watching. Or maybe he was just vocally relaying what you were doing. But that was close surveillance.

The corner is interesting in other ways. Across the street on the side of Irah Sok's house, there is a dark SUV pulling out of the driveway. He was not there when you entered this street. In the time it took you to drive to the end of this street and find your way back to this intersection, he has pulled quickly into the driveway, perhaps to drop someone off to man an observation post inside, and now he is about to pull out. Except he doesn't really pull out.

When you first see him across the street, the Postal Service Truck of Death is parking, and the dark SUV is pulled more into the driveway, but not fully in to park:[227]

Then he begins to pull out. You will notice the wheel has just begun to enter the drainage gutter as you pass him:[228]

But he does not pull out. You drive down Irah Sok's street and are well past the mail truck, and if you look back, he is still sitting behind the car parked on the street, and he is not continuing to exit:[229]

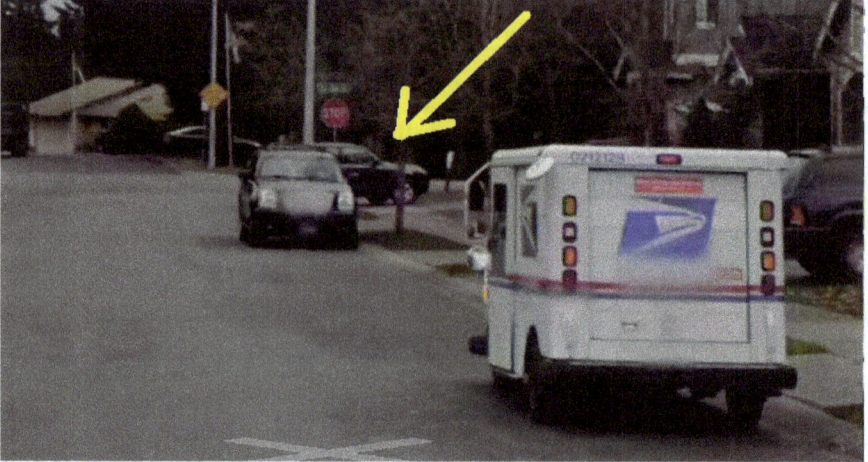

Once you get to the back of this street, he exits out of your sight, and you will not see him when you leave:[230]

As I have said, surveillance tends to preferentially purchase houses on street corners, and move its people into them to better cover those decision points. Given this car pulled in here for 30 seconds and would not finish leaving until you were out of sight, and this is a corner house on the street of a high priority target, I would judge it a decent probability this house is domestic surveillance, as is the owner, and it was being used as an observation and/or monitoring post as you drove the street.

Of course, as you approached the intersection, just as when you were exiting the dirt road in Bulgaria, you have two cars which passed each other exactly in front of your intersection, with no cars in front of them or behind them. Could be innocent, but it seems there was not much traffic, since those were the only two cars. So that which was there, was perfectly timed in a way surveillance will tend to do, so they can lead you in either direction should you go that way:[231]

Then to your right, the two homeowners of the house with a

sightline to the intersection there are outside doing gardening work, and you have the fiber guy who sits in his truck with his elbow propped up against the window not doing anything:[232]

It is a lot of potential surveillance activity for one corner, especially since you just came from a side street with nothing happening on it in the middle of the day while everyone is at work.

Again, you don't need to just look at the photos above. Click over to Google Streetview, and take the drive yourself, and look around, as if you are in the car yourself. It is better training for the apocalypse that's coming than the time you spend at the range. The most dangerous enemy you will face going forward in America is the American domestic surveillance machine. Here, you can see their operation prepping an intelligence package which would be given to a hitter they would bring in, and used to execute the murder of an innocent American citizen. Learn to see it. It could save your life in this nation America has now become.

If we continue east on the cul de sac across the intersection from the target, heading away from the target residence, but looking back toward it, we enter the earlier time frame. There, we have just turned on this street, and the walkers have just begun to cross the target's street after we turned. We see that in that timeline, they also had a truck that was driving out from the target location, just as we would have entered that street, had we turned left (west) to drive to the target residence when we were at the intersection.

Had we entered the street instead of turning away from it, that truck would probably have taken up the position of the Postal Service Truck of Death[TM], but now it sits at the intersection across from the walkers and watches us as we drive away from the target residence.

How often per day do you think that intersection has cars there? So far, you have never seen it without one watching her house or the approach to it:[233]

Exit this cul de sac and head north of Irah Sok's street, and you have a little stubby road off to the right. As you approach, a vehicle hits it, and you still have the cable truck behind you:

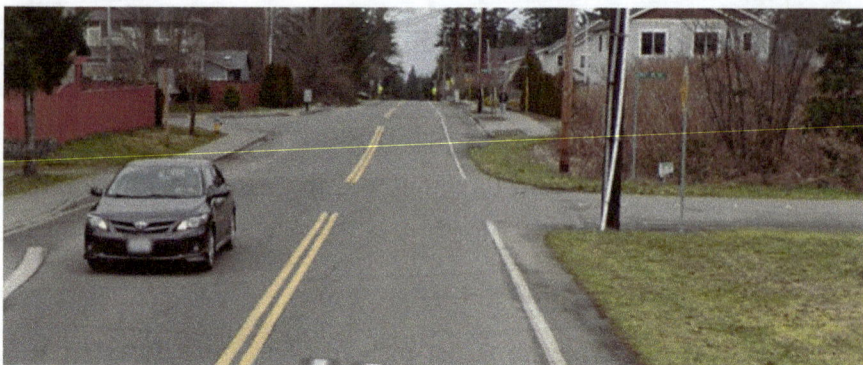

You also have this dogwalker coming around the corner of the next intersection ahead on the left,[234] but she is a bit hesitant to turn the corner I think, because she has been told to post across from the street, and she is hoping you won't notice her now, so when you see her later, it will be the first time.

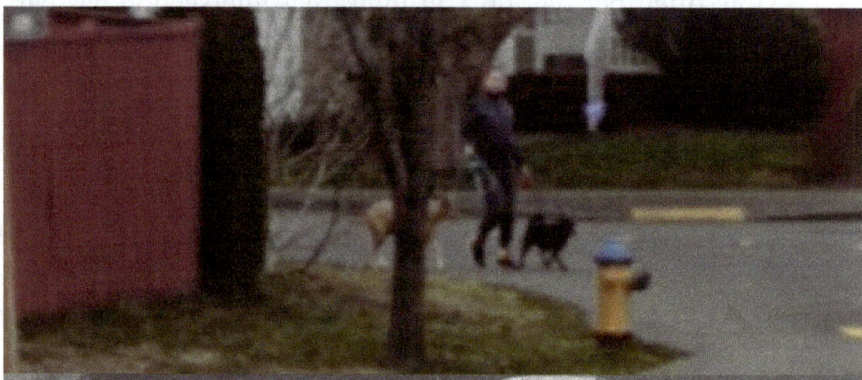

Notice her toe is next to her heel, which is not really a mid-gait position. It's more like you want to look like you are walking, but not really move. Even her light brown dog is barely walking:

When you exit, she is right across the street, seemingly picking up her dog's stool:

It is possible she is legit. Or she could be faking picking up stool just at this moment, so her face is obscured and the target would think she has a reason to be there that is not related to him. If she didn't seem to be pausing in the first shot, and she wasn't hitting the corner just as you hit this corner, I would be ambivalent.

The problem with surveillance is, it is taught to look like it belongs. *"Cover for status,"* and *"Cover for action."* In surveillance parlance, that is *"why would someone like you belong there?"* And belonging there, *"what are you actively doing which explains why you are there that moment, and does not involve watching someone?"* She is a resident of the neighborhood. But it is not enough to just be a resident standing there looking around for no reason. You want to be doing something like walking a dog, or gardening, or getting mail, so you blend in completely.

Interestingly, if you look behind you now as you head north, you will notice as you were driving the cul de sac street, a white sedan appears to have been paralleling you on the target street opposite you, and when you turned out of this cul de sac, it popped out of the empty street you drove opposite the target's residence, and continued straight across the intersection, back toward the original target residence. You can see it just over the rise in the road:[235]

Imagine how many cars Irah Sok had driving back and forth all around her house all the time on that little dead end street if there was this much traffic on the street just in the few minutes the Google car was here.

And now you have another car which will arrive at the next street up, just as you arrive at it, as well as a walker just about to walk up the street:[236]

Of course you turn up the next street, and in your last view of the dog walker, she hasn't really moved. She's still at the edge of that grass patch just standing there.[237] She could be letting her dogs sniff, although they are not really sniffing, and seem on pause too. None of this is 100%, but it is curious, especially since there's nothing where she's looking, but you're in the corner of her eye:

Now, as you turn left into this new side street ahead, and you lose the girl with the dogs behind that corner, you have another walker who will have a sightline to you as you drive, in this guy who just turned the corner:

What I am going to do here is post a picture of this walker with the Google car next to him, and splice in the overhead map

337

showing where the Google car and the walker are on the street when they are side by side.

Then we'll drive, and see how far the walker moves, compared to the Google car. Here he is next to the Google car, with the overhead map:[238]

Now we will drive, and look back, and see how far they each get. He will manage to walk to just past the nose of the pickup which you can just barely make out the rear of, on the upper left in the picture above. So in this next picture, under him, designated by the arrow, I will put the overhead map with a marker designating when the Google car was next to that truck, to mark his position, and on the left on the same map will be a marker designating the Google car's final position when the photo of him was taken by the Google car, looking back. Thus we will see how far each of them traveled over a set period of time, and from that we can deduce their relative speeds. Here, a final zoomed-in picture of the walker, way in the distance, taken by the Google car:[239]

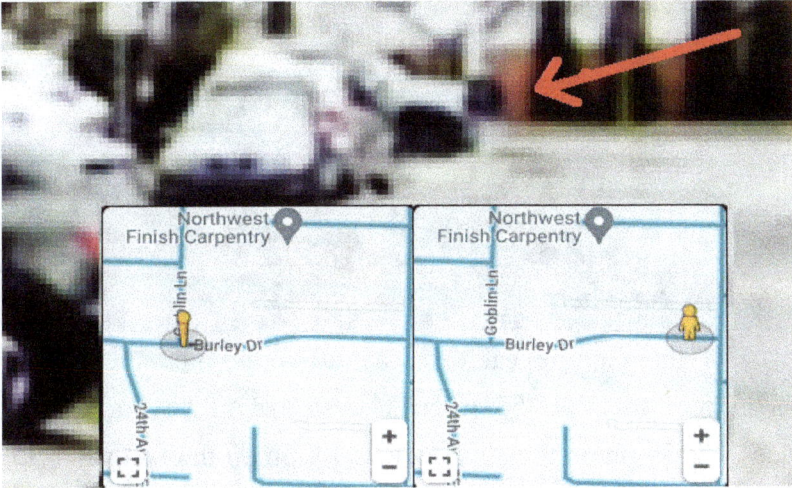

According to Google's map, the Google car traveled about 750 feet, starting from a slow turn speed. The walker has traveled 20 feet. I would say the Google car might have sped through here, but he could not because all along the street are these speed-bump speed limits,[240] which I would assume he nearly obeyed, since he has the camera ball on top of the car, and there is a bump and you cannot avoid it. Here, a picture of the Google car's camera ball, caught in a reflection in a passing car window on top:

And here, the street's speed limit sign:

If the Google car did, say 20 mph, then the walker did 1/37.5th of that, or .53 mph. The spread of "average walking" paces is 2.5mph on the slow side to 4 mph on the fast side. So your walker is walking 1/5th the lower bound of average speed and one eighth the higher bound of "average" speed – as he is trying to get somewhere. Or he is just surveillance, loitering near the corner.

I can continue to do these, showing that as you hit intersections, there will always be watchers at the corner to call your direction of travel. Here at the next intersection north, another cable/fiber truck has pulled off in front of an empty lot, and is again using the sideview mirror trick:

It is possible the extensive surveillance in the area is unrelated to the murder, though clearly Irah's house was a focal

340

point given the mail truck, as was her business. I have no doubt somebody was at least listening in her house, as she was killed, and they know exactly who did it. And I am sure the local PD at some level knows the surveillance is out there, and I will bet they whisper about the weird things they see on the Job among themselves, and wonder what was up with this. Her murder is still unsolved as of this going to press.

Why the surveillance is there is the mystery. A home invasion, in that neighborhood, resulting in a mother shot in the face in front of her young son, is not something which would be on my radar looking at the neighborhood. Clearly with all the walkers, people are not hiding in their homes in fear. The place looks delightful. It is hard to think it was entirely random.

And I should add, all this Google imagery predates the murder. So the surveillance did not show up after she was killed. It was there before she was murdered. And we will show this is not the only such case.

I tend to rule out the idea she was a criminal, this was law enforcement surveillance, and she was just killed by fellow criminals as surveillance stood by. She does not look the part, and if surveillance was unrelated to her murder, and she got hit by some fellow criminals, and the surveillance was normal law enforcement, how has the crime not been solved for years? A gang of men who murdered a beautiful young mother, in front of her child, by shooting her in the head? Even if she was a criminal, regular law enforcement would have parallel constructed a case by now, and wrapped these killers up. What you are looking at is not FBI, or local PD. It is the American Stasi, and I am pretty sure it is killing innocent people, even innocent mothers.

As I have long said, what I have seen has to have allowed 9/11 to happen, assuming 9/11 was not an actual operation run by the command of this thing to acquire increased surveillance powers – which is entirely possible. There is no way this massive an operation, watching everyone in the whole nation, sector by sector, with this level of granular detail, did not take a close look at all of the hijackers when they moved into somebody's sector, to figure out exactly what they were up to. And when they focus on you, you cannot keep secrets. Their penetration, in your house, in your phone calls and emails, in your technology, in your social circles, during your shopping, in your car - everywhere – it is complete.

Aristocrat and former girlfriend of Prince Andrew, Lady Victoria Hervey, said that Jeffrey Epstein and his friends not only knew the 9/11 attacks were going to happen in the months leading up to them, they purchased tickets on the doomed planes as mementos.[241] Of course Epstein was an arm of the pedophile blackmail wing of the American Stasi, and I have shown in other work it appeared at least one of the young girls he abused was guided to him by the American Stasi, working as operational support.

I am not exaggerating when I say this operation is a hostile, criminal, foreign-intelligence operation, which views the average patriotic American as the enemy. It is embedded like you see here, all throughout your neighborhood, and its children are operational as intelligence agents, working under adult intelligence officers, targeting your children in the schools, both building files on them, and intervening in their paths to prevent them from rising too high. I have spent the last decade, being overtaken by sobering

342

realization after sobering realization. I did not conclude all this easily or lightly.

It is interesting Irah Sok was physically beautiful. I assume in some areas, there are voyeurs in the local surveillance operation who would have nothing better to do with their time than set up on a girl like her, to watch her and her husband in intimate moments on video filmed on cameras planted in their bedroom while they were out at work. When your observation post next door can see and hear in all the houses nearby, and you have full vehicular surveillance overwatch, capable of tracking the residents while they are away from the house, to assure you only perform entry while they are far enough away they cannot return quickly and catch you, it is no big deal to enter a house and plant any devices you want. If they turn back to return, the vehicular team will alert you, and since you waited until they were far enough away to enter, you will have plenty of time to exit before they can return. You are not going to get caught. In that regard, this is exactly like the Stasi. They cannot be "caught," so there is zero risk and cost to them for any of this.

Nothing would surprise me with this thing. In fact I would be surprised if anyone has not had their privacy invaded by this operation, given it's scale, its embedding in every neighborhood, and the way things really work among the powerful. It is not like anyone would believe it possible if you told them. There is a near-zero risk of exposure or consequence, even if someone goes around telling people.

Even here, I am highly intelligent, I write cogently, I am showing you this using one of the most creative means possible so my cognition is not faulty, and you are seeing it with your own eyes. You know these coincidences are strange. You know, if you can see this thing just off Google Streetview, it must be ten times worse in real life, and yet I am sure your view is still tinged with disbelief. I am sure you are saying to yourself, it could not be this way in America. They did it in East Germany, but our intelligence agencies would respect our boundaries. Even if we give them more money than they know what to do with, they would not do this.

They would happily let others of greater intellect just rise freely, and unseat them and expose their crimes, before they would do this.

I am sorry, but that is not the case. I have spent the last decade learning that firsthand. Our societies are run by psychopaths and the sexually deviant, they are total sharks, and they will do anything to cling to power.

It is entirely possible a local surveillance operator with a side photog gig simply saw a petite Filipino girl, who had no power compared to them, in domestic intelligence, and she was in the way of their photography side-hustle, and they wanted to take her out to eliminate the competition. Then somebody looking things over pulled her brother's file, saw he was a veteran who rolled with an arsenal out of a John Wick movie in the trunk of his car "just in case," (which I would bet he got trained up on, with bucks like that invested in it). And then they saw he just retired from the military, and they worried he might just decide to come to town to do a little digging into who killed his little sister, and figure out what happened himself, since he has nothing else on his plate.

Having the local cell in his neighborhood set him up, and

then call ATF in (probably just telling them he was some sort of problem, without any further detail), to disarm him and keep him unbalanced, is not at all impossible in the rule-less, law-less world of the United States domestic intelligence service that is the American Stasi. In fact, it is exactly how intelligence would operate.

That the conspiracy disarmed and disabled him, and then took her out is ominous, if you stop for a moment and think about it. If they were related, and I suspect they were, that is a lot of planning and a lot of prep, and a lot of moving pieces, just to kill one pretty little Filipino girl. I keep wondering, what else she could have happened upon, in her life?

I know, this all sounds nuts. Fifteen years ago this would have all sounded like the ramblings of a schizophrenic to me, until I got into politics, "they" showed up in my life, they went out of their way for a few years to try and intimidate me with the scale of their domestic forces, and then I began getting vibrated in the middle of the night by one of their electronic harassment machines, waking me up in my bed.

Pretty quickly, I realized this thing is real, and it has simply hidden itself from us very well – and for very good reason. When America finds out about it, it will be a war which this thing will not survive.

All of this is coming out. It has gotten too big to remain concealed. You can see it right here on Streetview. You will see subsequently, this does not appear to be the only case where the American Stasi murdered innocent young women. And when it does break out into a broader awareness, there will be no containing the fallout.

346

Chapter Nine

Surveillance Detection – The Professional Course Of Real Life Experience – The Moscow Idaho College Murders

This will be a very subtle examination, and many of you may not see it without watching the video many times as we move through the piece. But I think I can guarantee, if you read this up to the startling part at the end, you will suddenly be able to go back and see what I see. This is another of those pieces God created for me to produce, complete with the unusual coincidences which highlight what I am saying. And for the amateur surveillance-awareness fan, this will be a masterclass in foot surveillance detection.

This analysis will assert there is a good chance at least two of the four students who were murdered at the University of Idaho[242] were under priority surveillance by the domestic surveillance machine I have written so much about, known as the American Stasi. I will explain a version of the events below consistent with surveillance activity, and leave it to the reader to decide if the explanation could fit the video evidence.

On the night of the Idaho murders, Kaylee Goncalves, and Madison Mogen, two of the students murdered, visited a food truck to pick up some food, and were captured on its internet livestream.

What this analysis will assert is a surveillance team made up of embedded college students was tracking the girls the night they were murdered. I have been under close harassment surveillance for a very long time now, and I can tell you this is exactly what close physical surveillance looks like.

It is worth noting here, one of the girls in this video, Kaylee Goncalves, reported she had been followed through a store by what she called a stalker.[243]

Surveillance shows extreme interest in what targets buy. If you have surveillance, it will be particularly aggressive when you are shopping. If she was under surveillance, it would have been prominent when she was shopping in stores.

We will begin at 9:25 in the video.[244]

This is several minutes before the girls arrive. If the girls were under surveillance, the operators would arrive and set up the scene before the girls arrived. That is procedure. Surveillance will always try to get there before you, so you will not see someone following you.

When you are under coverage, operators will always be lurking nearby, wherever you go, the control center will most likely have opened the mics on any cellphones you have, mobile units will have highly directional listening devices pointed at your car, and it is highly likely every word you utter is being listened to.

Wherever the girls were on campus before coming to the food truck, their coverage there would have heard them say they wanted to head to the food truck to grab a bite before going home. That would be radioed/texted to the central Control, and Control would look at who was in the area of the food truck.

Most likely I would assume that given it is a locus of activity, today's American Stasi would keep at least one operative present at the food truck, just monitoring it for anything of interest going on, regardless of whether a target was present or not.

Meanwhile control would look for a fresh team to deliver to the site, ahead of the girls, and message them to make their way to the food truck, so they would be there, fresh and ready, when the girls arrived. There is no way for the girls to think they are being followed, if their surveillance is already there waiting, when they arrive, and they walk into it. It is a basic surveillance technique.

You may read the descriptions of what happened below, look at the still shots from the video, and then go back and look at the video to see these things, in real time.

Seeing the close physical surveillance in real time, the way the people are looking at the girls without looking at them, the way they look to shield their faces when the girls draw near, the way they surround the girls and hold a conversation over them, so they can observe them without twisting their neck to deviate from their natural sightline, is crucial to your training. This type of surveillance activity is rife throughout American society.

Now to the videotape. Beginning at 9:25, you will notice this individual, who we will call Tank Top, while engaging in intermittent conversation, suddenly reach in his pocket, denoted by the red arrow:

He will extract a cell phone and look at it intently:

He will then rapidly snap his head and look to his left as he puts the phone away:

In the scenario of surveillance this could be consistent with, he would be the regular posted surveillance assigned to the food truck area to spy on everyone that night. One guy, just hanging out, watching a bunch of people, looking and listening for anything interesting to report to his superiors.

He received a text, which told him two priority targets were on their way, and Control was moving him out, to move four more-capable surveillance personnel into the area for this monitoring operation.

He says goodbye in a rush and he speed-walks in the opposite direction of the way he just looked. If surveillance, he seems less skilled at hiding his agitation. I would think a highly experienced member of surveillance would have left more calmly.

The first two people who look like his replacements (and they might not be surveillance, but they have the appearance you will see if you encounter surveillance) will arrive from the top of the screen, as seen below. We will call them Hippy Boy and Girl. You can make out Tank Top, on the left, has turned and is about to peel out of there, just as Hippy Boy and Girl arrive to take the scene. When Tank Top's head snapped after reading the text, he was looking at these two approaching:

Hippy Boy would be a pro, if he was surveillance. He is unremarkable and non-threatening, and would be very hard to spot. He has the perfect demeanor, and even clothes you would never remember. Which would make me think the girls would have been important targets for some reason to the command, if he is surveillance. If they were not important, Tank Top would just have been left in place and sent their pictures on his phone and told to watch them. If this is surveillance, those two girls were priority targets for some reason.

The two newcomers proceed to examine Hippy-Boy's phone intensely. If this were surveillance they were just roving a moment ago before getting tasked here. Now they would have been sent imagery of the targets, and they would have a minute or so to commit the faces, clothes, and data to memory, so they will recognize them when they arrive.

Notice, there is nobody ordering food on the right at the cashier who would be in their way of getting food, and they are not interested in food or socializing. They have a job to do:

At this point in the lower left camera, a rather large individual comes around the corner of the food truck in the left of the frame, and does not stop to survey the scene, or see who he knows, or look for anyone, but rather walks decisively through the crowd directly to the couple above, on the other side of the food truck and behind the crowd. We will call him Big Boy, and he knew where he was going before he arrived:

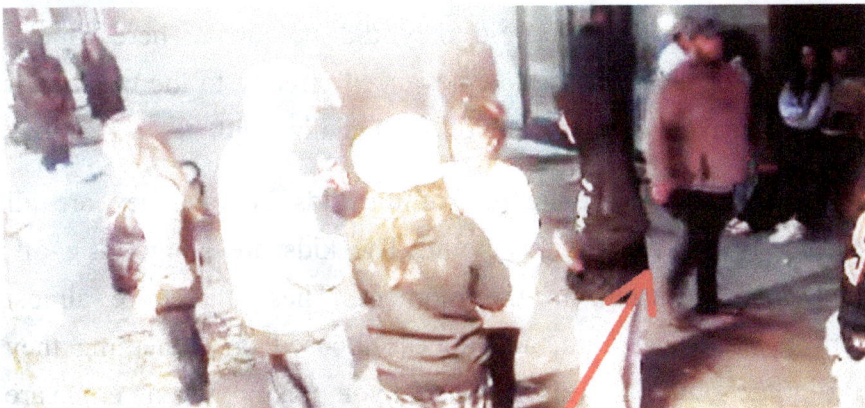

Hippy Boy and the girl do not seem to greet Big Boy. It is as if his arrival was expected, and he just joins them. At 11:19 below, Hippy Boy looks up from his phone and points in the direction the targets will come from, which would be consistent with saying to the others, "They will come from there":

At this point, surveillance will examine the scene and see if there are blind spots or blocked sightlines, and look at where they want to set up, so that wherever the targets go, they will not need to move around chasing after them to get a sightline, and risk the targets noticing. None of the three make any effort to get on the line and order food yet. So they did not arrive here to eat, primarily, or they would have advanced directly to the truck. Nor did they arrive looking for anyone to socialize with.

If you look at the rest of the kids in this, they are all noticeably different at this point. The kids are all goofing off, bantering, posturing, in the moment. These three are almost surrounded by an aura, and appear focused on something they have to get out of the way. It is a feel you pick up, when people are at work, doing something and controlling, vs on their own wavelength, and flowing with the circumstances.

Hippy boy dives back into his phone, and Big Boy turns and notices there is a food truck, and eating food would make an excellent cover for action:

12:33, and they are now ordering food, and doing so before the possible targets, and future murder victims, arrive:

They order, and Hippy Boy meets a girl he knows. At

355

14:49, targets arrive, and Hippy Boy just happens to break from his social group 7 seconds prior, to turn around and look behind himself casually, right at them the instant they round the corner:

Instantly after looking at them, Hippy Boy spins around, and waves his arm, making a big scene about how he was engaged in interaction with the girl he was talking to a minute ago, saying goodbye:

Either he is not surveillance, or he is a pro, constantly thinking about what the target is seeing, even as he is looking.

Immediately after the waving arm, he spins back around to look at the two targets, who as you expect go immediately to order their food. Notice the two targets are ordering their food after the three watchers. It will be significant later:

Again, they are cute, bubbly blondes, out for a good time, so it is not dispositive if men look at them.

Just as the targets arrived, another individual will arrive, almost walking between them, and he will never order food. He arrived with them at 14.50 and took up a rearward position alone.

He also likely notices the cameras on the truck which are livestreaming, and immediately takes off his hat which was backward, puts it on frontward and pulls the brim down, and then pulls up his hoodie as he turns away from the truck to move farther back. He will keep his hoodie up and his brim down while in the vicinity of the food truck's surveillance cameras.

Later, you will see he knows the cameras are there, when he points them out to Big Boy.

Remember him, he will shock you later, and make you realize I was not making this up:

One of the two targets is about to be hailed by a male who knows her off to the left in the picture above. As they indicate they know each other and are about to move to each other, Big Boy puts his hand to his mouth and holds it there. When surveillance communicates, they whisper into chest microphones, and cover their mouths so others will not see. Sometimes they will place a microphone in a shirt cuff, and talk into it. Regardless, the hand to the mouth is seen surprisingly often with surveillance:

03:43:23

You'll recall the man outide Irah Sok's photography studio in the last chapter:

As the target girl walks over, she passes Hippy Boy and Girl, who both noticeably try to shield their faces from her, something surveillance will reflexively try to do, to preserve their ability to not be recognized, if they surveil a target again later:

Here the target, marked with a red arrow, has walked over to say hi, made her greetings, and is now beginning to walk away. Hippy Boy appears to be looking at the guy she was talking to. A target contact is a significant event in surveillance. A surveillance operator would want to remember that face. Also look at the postures of the sureveillants, all upright, facing the same way:

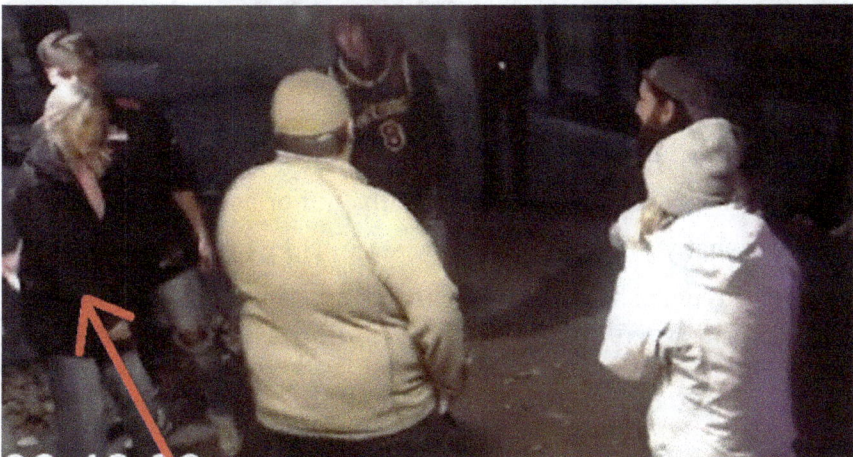

The target botches their plans, as targets are wont to do, and she decides to walk through their group. If they were surveillance, this would be bothersome to them, because surveillance does not want a target to get a good look at their face, or they are burned for future surveillance on the target. Look at how in a microsecond, she moves a foot and a half, to walk in between them, and all of their postures change, and they all try to shield their faces and turn them away from her:

Now Hippy Boy holds this position for six seconds, covering his mouth, a common move when surveillance wants to communicate, and not have people see their lips move. The girls are ordering, and that data is actually important to surveillance, just like what you buy in a grocery store. He will be relaying what they are buying. The records they keep are astonishingly complete:

He is sort of a smidge sheepish, and non-confrontational, but social, and easy-going. He is a perfect demeanor for the work.

Tank Top from Scene One returns, and Big Boy notices:

There is no reason to think Big Boy would know Tank Top. But obviously they know each other:

03:44:22

One of the things which would puzzle me in high school was finding out kids who assiduously ignored each other in school, would suddenly be revealed to have been together, like at a train station miles away. And it would be multiple kids from different grades and different neighborhoods, and different social groups, who in school ignored each other like they had never met. But suddenly it would pop out they were all at some train station miles away, and saw something notable which happened to one of them. I did not understand how they knew each other, but I do now. They literally were in the secret society, running surveillance together when not in school. And they could not let anyone know.

Here, Hippy Boy is looking directly at one of the targets:

03:46:53

But he turns sheepish when she looks at him. She noticed him looking and locks eyes on him for a bit. That can be natural with a pretty girl like that, or not.

She now has begun to expect her food a few times, as other people came up and got their food. So she is preparing to depart. He pulls out his cell phone again, and is showing Girl something on it. At least that is what he is pretending to do.

03:49:58

As the targets look like they might be about to get their food and depart, notice the position he immediately takes. He's

365

pointing his camera at them. Notice, his thumb is on the screen, not the edge of the phone.

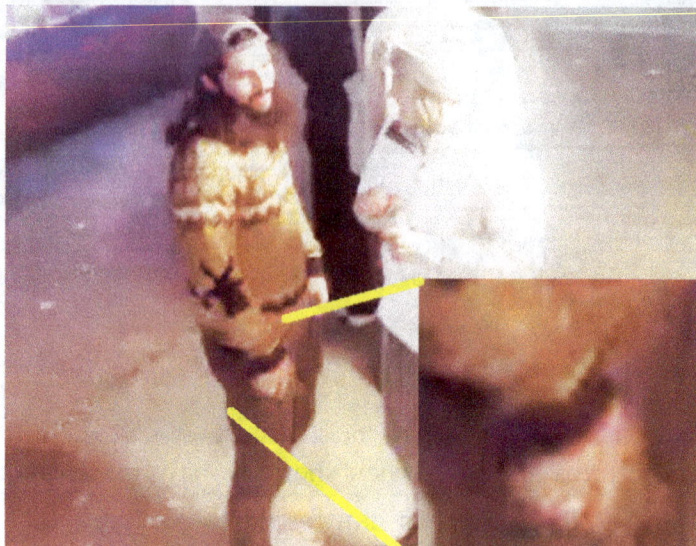

It is a slightly more subtle version of the posture struck by Rap Epps, holding his cell phone while positioned near conservative internet personality "Baked Alaska" while at a demonstration, before he quickly turned away:[245]

Again, thumb on the screen. That is a trained surveillance technique.

It turns out yet again it is someone else's food however, and the girl is forced to wait. He continues to hold that position, but pulls the phone up immediately as these two guys walk into his sightline and block his shot, seen below from two angles, the first of which you can see the targets departing.

Notice Big Boy is also focused:

If this was surveillance, it was very good surveillance. It would have been subtle, and you could have attributed many of the idiosyncrasies to innocent behavior.

What we will show now, is the part of this which would have been bad surveillance, if it was surveillance.

When we last left hoodie, he was lurking in the background, and had not ordered food, as the targeted girls were ordering. Look at these pictures, and then go and watch the video, from his arrival, at 11:11, to his departure at 21:49.

Here he is observing, as the targets/girls order their food. He is facing the camera:

One target-girl has begun to depart, and he brings his wrist to his mouth to communicate an update to Control. He actually looks like he may have placed the mic in his jacket cuff, which is unusual:

She departs, he continues to talk (his image enhanced):

He finishes communicating, and prepares for second target to depart the counter after placing her order:

Second Target begins moving:

Hoodie begins paralleling them, on the far side of the crowd:

Head down, he continues to move:

Moving in concert with the target, while remaining away from them:

From the other camera:

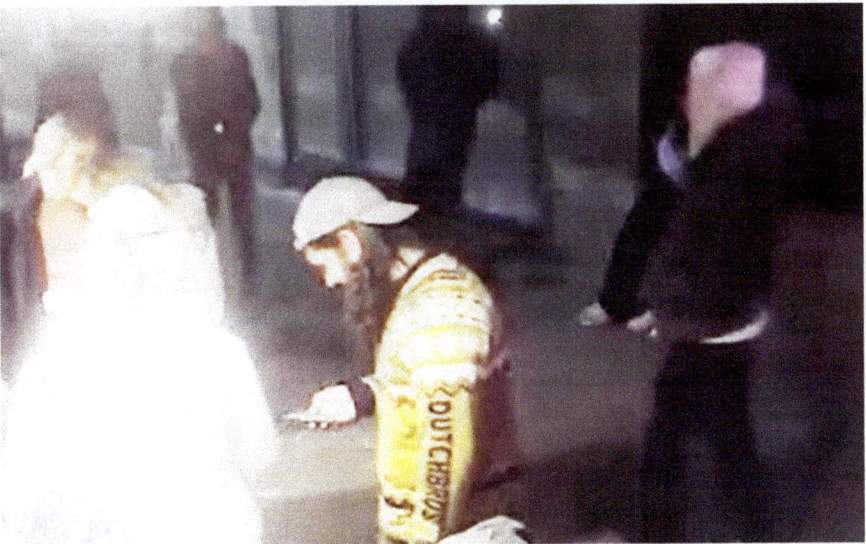

He sets up right behind the girls, who are waiting for their food, containing them with the other team. Why did he move exactly as the second girl moved, only to stop here? What is he doing? He isn't getting food. He isn't socializing. Here he notes the camera which is filming him, so he is surveillance aware:

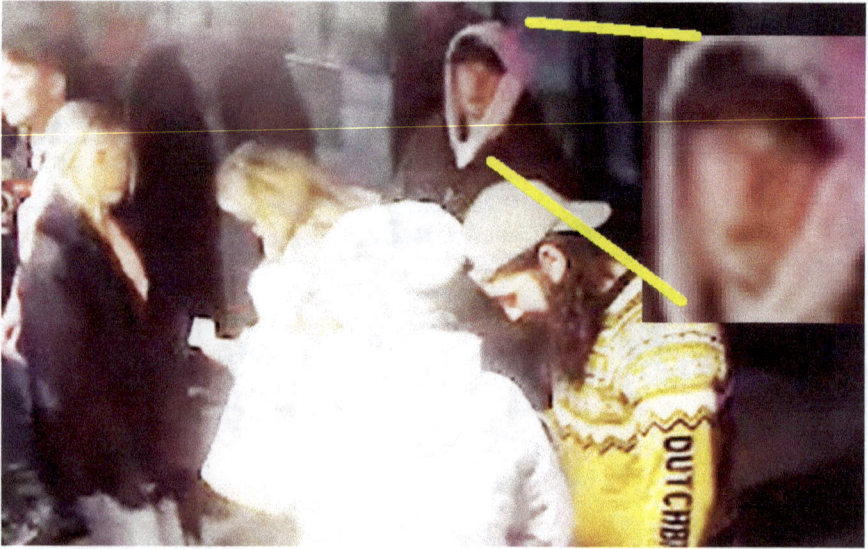

Big Boy shoots a knowing smile at Hoodie. These girls don't have a clue. They are so stupid:

Notice the girls are now surrounded by the surveillance team handling this phase of their phased coverage for the night. On one side is the food truck, Tank Top has a side, Hoodie has a side, and Hippie Boy and his crew square it off. If you are looking for surveillance hiding at a distance, peeking around a corner, that is not how it works. This is how it works. They can hear every word, see every detail, and the girls never had a clue. Watch Hoodie in the video. You will understand:

At 14:13, Tank Top and Hoodie have some words, and laugh. They know each other. Hoodie will later make a joking bowing motion to Tank Top, as if to say, "I am not worthy":

More talking, so Hoodie and Tank Top know each other:

Now a little round about conversation pops up, between Hoodie, Big Boy, Hippie Boy, and Tank Top is smiling as if he is in the group, and ironically the girls are in the center, wholly unaware their immediate death is approaching:

Big Boy moves over and chats it up with Hoodie, who still has not ordered any food. The targets are on the left:

That is Hoodie's left hand under his neck, pointing at the camera filming, as he tells Big Boy they are live on the internet.

Now Big Boy says, "You're telling me that is a camera and it is filming us? What kind of food truck has a camera?" Hoodie's crossed arms signify his discomfort and displeasure. Domestic surveillance does not like being watched, ironically:

The girls have gotten their food and are about to depart:

Big Boy goes up and gives the guy his ticket, likely saying

he never heard he was called (remember he ordered before the girls, by some time, but by doing this he had a cover to loiter). Hoodie meanwhile is back on the move after the girls, and gone, never having ordered any food. Big Boy does not wonder where he went:

Bear in mind, those girls were not just followed by those five operators. Those five operators were the phase of coverage assigned to that venue. All along their route, they were followed by differing groups of operators just like that who they walked into. Vehicles doing driveby's, walkers, bicyclists, dog walkers, people sitting on park benches, a group waiting for them at a bar, a married couple at a donut shop, a group of grade school kids waiting at a bus stop, some sorority sisters at a party, a bunch of male football fans buying beer at the liquor store.

Those two girls may have had as many as three hundred or four hundred followers involved in their follow that day and night, if they made enough stops, and traversed a wide enough distance. And those followers were probably mostly college students, children of the surveillance people, sent to those schools and assigned to run surveillance on all the other kids, gathering blackmail, identifying threats, and building files for the machine. You can see how big the machine is.

That is why when a spy wants to see if he is followed, he will do what is called "running errands," making a large number of stops in a short period of time, requiring many phases of coverage, to force his surveillance to use all its operatives to surveil him, and hopefully recycle some, allowing him to recognize faces at two or more venues, and confirm he is being watched.

And if these girls had that in-person physical coverage, and I would assume they did, their neighborhood was locked down tight, and surveillance would have tried to plant at least one of its people actually in their housing arrangement, living with them. You do not get mobile coverage while out, and not get the neighborhood observation post, and the tech, and the vehicular, and the infiltration, and the phone and internet monitoring, and even aviation when needed. Surveillance rolls out as a complete package.

So for that neighborhood the girls lived in, nobody would get in our out, even on foot, without being noted, tracked, and documented. I've done a Google car analysis and will put it down in a post one day. It is more or less what you would expect, except they pull the surveillance as you get back to their house, on that dead end. Of course these girls were not living there when the Google-car went by, so there was no need to station the Postal Service Truck of Death™ back there. Had Google done a more recent Streetview drive I would bet even that would have been included. Judging from this, these girls, for some reason, were high priority targets of the American Stasi.

There is probably pole tech listening for foot falls in the neighborhood, and a neighbor who is one of the watchers – and maybe two or three neighbors. I have six residences occupied by surveillance immediately around me, which appear to be devoted to me.

I would bet they had ears in the house too, as that is just procedure. Given the priority of the girls, they could have cameras in their house as well, even in their bathrooms and bedrooms. As you will see, there was something unusual about the house.

And later that night those girls were murdered. Did the surveillance kill them? Was it operating here, as operational support for the hitters? Did it offer overwatch of their neighborhood, to make sure there were no surprises, and the hit went off as planned? I have no idea. But it was there, watching and listening as they were killed.

Surveillance is somehow controlling the future, as well as the day to day conspiracy. It isn't law enforcement. Law enforcement would not follow the Google car everywhere, as a procedure. It isn't national security. It let 9/11 happen (at best – there is one other darker possibility), it probably killed Irah Sok, and it is out there, figuring out how to control some people, stifle others, remove still others, identify fellow travelers that they can recruit, and mold the human terrain that its conspiracy will build its future foundations on some day. It did not get this big, or operate this long, by just living in the moment.

It could have killed one of those girls. Or it could have gotten wind they were going to be killed, and it just wanted to watch, and maybe document it, so it could use the blackmail to turn the killer into an MK Ultra windup toy for their operation.

Or it could just have been following one of those girls for unrelated reasons, like they wanted to marry her to somebody in the conspiracy because she had impressive genes, and when the action started, they were not going to get involved. Whatever the circumstances, it was watching, or at least listening inside the house, as they were murdered, one by one.

Other disturbing aspects of this case have come to light. Some others noted Hoodie's proximity to the girls immediately prior to their murders. He was located and claimed that although he did not know the girls, he decided to walk with them from the bar they were coming from, to get them home safe, before the two girls ran from him and jumped in a car, "ditching" him at the food truck.[246]

However in another video filmed that night in which he is seen walking along side the girls, he is saying to one, *"They are going to get you for this Kaylee..."*[247]

It would imply he knew them better than he asserted, since he addressed one by her name. The girls did not know him as well as he knew them apparently though, as an enhancement of the food truck video showed Madison arguing with him, at one point saying, *"Fuck you mister!"* She did not know his name,[248] and viewed him as an older stranger who would not share his name.

Additionally, in one clip from the food truck video, available here,[249] Kaylee Goncalves can be seen absent-mindedly turning until she sees Hoodie, at which point she violently recoils and turns away. They were not friends, and she did not want to deal with him.

Also suspicious is that at the food truck, in the presence of a camera, he stayed back, and his immediate response was to turn his back to the camera and twist his ballcap forward and pull up his hood, to make himself less identifiable. That is not really the behavior of a guy just trying to see two girls get home safely.

Although a Police spokesperson said they had investigated and cleared him, in the world of the American Stasi, where ATF can be moved like a chess piece to tie up the brother of a woman it wants to murder, that may not mean anything at all with respect to what really happened. Many, many individuals who have gone to the Police to report their interactions with the American Stasi, report that local Police are unable to do anything to curtail the Stasi's harassment. In my own experience, officers evince a clear empathy, and sheepishness, as well as some fear, as they feign ignorance and confusion.

The most bothersome aspect of the case to me however is the fate of the residence where the murders occurred. In a rather inexplicable turn of events, the owner of the rental home decided to simply donate the home to the University, relieving himself of both a major source of his income, and a multi-hundred thousand dollar investment, for no recompense.

The university then asked the families of the victims what they wanted done with the house. The victim's families said they wanted it preserved until after the trial of the criminology student who has been arrested for the murders, Brian Kohberger.[250] The University then announced it would demolish the house as quickly as possible, before the legal proceedings of Mr Kohberger had begun. And until then, 24 hr/day security was placed on the boarded up house, to include a small portable guard shack wired into security cameras surrounding the house, to prevent anyone from getting inside.[251]

The house was subsequently demolished, and then the University took the additional step of having the materials the house was made from transported to a special processing facility, and buried deep underground, reportedly to stymie "souvenir hunters."[252]

It makes no sense the homeowner, who had a property next to the University, which was producing six rent checks every month, and which was worth $488,000 according to a Zillow Estimate at the time of its demolition, would just relieve himself of that property, when there was no pressure on him to do so, and insurance would not recompense him for the loss.

It makes no sense the University would destroy an asset worth almost half a million dollars, when the family asked them not to, and it might endanger future legal proceedings against the killer. And it is odd it would feel it needed to hire 24/7 security, and station a special guard shack and camera system on the property, when the house was empty, it had nothing to steal in it, and they were going to demolish it anyway. Of course burying the remains of the house, at even more cost, is also strange.

It almost feels like there might have been evidence in the house which might have pointed to the real killer, and the American Stasi put pressure where it needed it to, however it needed to, in order to make sure the real killers were never exposed.

Now, regardless of whether Mr Kohberger is convicted or acquitted, there will never be any further investigation of this case.

It should also be repeated that one of the girls, Kaylee Goncalves, reported that she was stalked at night, as well as at a store. From this news article at the Daily Mail:[253]

There have been several reports Goncalves was scared of a stalker in the weeks leading up to the quadruple homicide...

Goncalves reportedly told him that the stalker would follow her 'at night' when she was going to or from bars, either by the 'campus or down on Main Street.'

Another article noted:[254]

...the Moscow Police Department said.... "In mid-October, two males were seen inside a local business; they parted ways, and one male appeared to follow Kaylee inside the business and as she exited to walk toward her car. The male turned away, and it did not appear he made any contact with her."

Police said they investigated the incident, and believed the males were just trying to date women, however no member of the American Stasi, who was caught gangstalking someone, would admit to such if questioned by Police.

It is particularly disturbing if Kaylee was being gangstalked, or otherwise harassed by the American Stasi, as according to reports, her injuries were much more severe than those of the other victims, indicating she might have been the primary target in the killings.[255] If she had a hostile relationship with the American Stasi, that might be a natural place to suspect the attack came from.

If you have kids, it is important to understand, this is why the local high school did not extend their schooling three years, hire more teachers, and give your kids a Bachelors degree. College is about making your kids vulnerable. Getting them away from you, alone, in a place with alcohol, and drugs, and sex, and parties, as well as an organized operation manned by hundreds or thousands of college-aged Stasi agents posing as fellow college students who are getting their own degrees - and likely, a plethora of cameras and mics in the dorm rooms and frat houses of many kids, to get blackmail on them.

Because the future that this thing wants to control – it is your children. If you have a daughter, she needs to be aware, if she is not in the conspiracy, she is at risk, even in grade school, where the kids around her may not be what they seem. In college, from the accounts of people who have emailed me, if she is judged problematic, and has not been neutered, the risk of a violent sexual assault by a male acquaintance, or other event designed to derail her, will increase dramatically. And the more amazing she is, the more the risk.

America has a problem, and it is going to have to deal with it at some point. Until then, you need to educate your children on how intelligence-driven environments operate, and how they need to protect themselves, and take the game they are playing seriously.

The American Stasi certainly does.

Chapter Ten

The Long Island Serial Killer, The American Stasi, And The Police Chief Who Would Not Back Down

Now you are probably thinking, maybe this is surveillance I am showing you, but surveillance must be government, government has to obey the law, and it is not possible the surveillance would murder an innocent woman like Irah Sok, let alone rope other agencies, like ATF into their scheme. This operation could not have strayed that far, or exert control over the law enforcement agencies of government to that extent.

I understand. I was where you are, grappling with that conundrum ten years ago. The thing is, nothing works the way they told you. They lied to you, specifically to leave you confused, weak, and unable to resist them effectively, because you do not understand the world.

You think you live in this civilized world, which long ago left behind Darwinism and survival of the fittest and the most ruthless and immoral. But in reality you never escaped that Darwinian nature of the world. The fittest and most ruthless and immoral were so fit and so ruthless and immoral, they managed to trick you into making yourself defenseless - by feeding you that very lie at every turn - that the ruthless and immoral could never succeed in society, and thus you should never be ruthless and immoral yourself. Then, extrapolated from that, was the unspoken

387

assumption there were no ruthless and immoral enemies for you to oppose.

Blinded to our fundamental purpose of battling evil in this world, and seemingly with no enemy to do battle with, our lives became meaningless, and empty. Day after day, we went through the motions, surviving, but never living the lives we were meant for, and sensing we were designed for a different world.

Meanwhile, their criminal empire, fueled by ruthlessness and immorality, took over the very government you thought would protect you from their kind, without the slightest opposition from you. When you see it, even as you crave its total destruction, you cannot help but marvel at its brilliance and thoroughness. It defeated you without a single blow ever being thrown.

The problem is this thing, to exert the level of control it needed to, had to infiltrate everything, and it has been doing it since at least the nineteen sixties, when early victims like Pulitzer Prize winning author John Kennedy Toole complained of being harassed by it (to be discussed later), and probably earlier. My mother encountered it in the fifties.

I am trying to limit the scope of this book to the surveillance, because I feel once you see that, and how far it has gone, you will understand the rest of the operation must exist and be similarly ridiculous in scale and penetration of the United States government, its cultural apparatus, and its broader society. But as I only show you the surveillance here, do not lose sight of the fact the surveillance is but one small piece of the American Stasi, which is a full featured intelligence operation designed to gather intelligence and *act upon it throughout American society*

to cement its own control.

To that end, the operation has infiltrated everything. There will be surveillance infiltration operators in everything from the local chapter of the Bloods street gang, to the local Italian Mafia operations, to the local Chamber of Commerce. From the Town Council to the local Library Board, it will be in everything, in no small part because normal people like you are kept too busy to bother getting involved, so only its people will be serving there.

Indeed, because surveillance controls law enforcement at the top, and can selectively remove members of criminal organizations using those law enforcement agencies, I would assume whatever organized criminal empire you are looking at, from a drug Cartel to the local Mara Salvatrucha street gang chapter, it is in fact led by a leadership made up of covert members of the American Stasi, who report to the surveillance, and can be given orders.

The conspiracy will have protected them from any law enforcement action, like Jeffrey Epstein, as their compatriots who were not owned and controlled by the conspiracy were removed through selective prosecution. After enough time, the American Stasi will control those criminal empires through their covert assets, which were left in the leadership positions, unmolested by government action. Indeed it is probably more likely than not that any criminal organization of any stature now is led by a raft of Stasi informants/agents, and reports to the conspiracy.

It directly contradicts what you have been raised to believe. But if you look at how intelligence operations work, and if you see the scale of the surveillance operations, you will realize that how

389

you were told it worked, is highly improbable, compared with the reality you will see.

This operation had to infiltrate and seize control of any opposition groups which might have exposed the conspiracy to you, from the Mafia, to the American News Media. And it has had more than enough time, advancing wholly unopposed by the population, to do so.

What this necessity has done, however, is take a quasi-governmental intelligence operation, which began on shaky legal ground, since it appears to be ultimately foreign-controlled at the top, and it extended a culture of criminality down throughout the lower levels of it, as it took control of everything, leaving the regular American citizenry as its only remaining enemy.

In addition, between the harassment operations directed at innocent citizens, and the use of directed energy weapons to assault citizens in their homes, it has strayed quite far culturally from the ideals seen, in say, your local Police department, and our Constitutional Republic.

Here in this chapter, I will detail just how far I believe the culture of this operation has slipped away from the ideals of America. I will show where this operation has acted, not only in tacit support of a serial killer, but where it has overtly acted to remove a Police Chief who appeared to be trying to capture the serial killer, and set him up for a four-year federal prison term. This was originally published online, but here I will include quotes in italics following the endnotes, so you do not need look up the secondary sources. Rather you can just see what they said here.

By the time you finish this book, from the harassment of

Army veteran and Honor House founder Brian Mancini until he committed suicide, the directed energy attacks on NSA legend Bill Binney, the killings of Police Officers by shooters this thing wound up, the harassment of innocent citizens, the murder of Irah Sok, the killings of the college students in Moscow, Idaho, and this case I am about to describe, I believe you will understand, the American Stasi has transcended the regular levels of criminality you would normally associate with an intelligence agency, and become an outright menace to humanity within the United States.

I think you will also begin to gain a better understanding of what might have gone on in cases like the murder of JFK, where the evidence available, which points to a conspiracy, alternately points to the involvement of a diverse range of groups which you would not think would associate, from the CIA, to pro-Soviet communist-activism organizations in the US, to the mafia, all working in tandem to assassinate a President who sought to pull us out of Vietnam, and had promised to splinter the CIA into a thousand pieces and scatter it to the wind.

I never understood, why would the CIA, rife with the best trained assassins in the world, collude with the mafia, which you would think would be far beneath the CIA's stature and capabilities. What you will ultimately come to realize is the CIA and the Mafia were merely two divisions of the same organization, both run by assets of the American Stasi, pursuing that organization's mission objective – total control of the Western world.

If there is one overarching intelligence operation which sits above them all, has infiltrated everything, and has assets in all organizations, from the political, to the criminal, to the intelligence community, then the evidence in the JFK assassination would merely point to that organization utilizing all of the resources at its disposal in a coordinated operation.

In that light, I suspect the idea an organization today might be rigging our elections, or controlling our media as a propaganda outlet to push its narratives, or that it might be working for a foreign power to collapse our very government with a flood of third world migrants imported by the Cartels, so those foreign entities might profit from the collapse through investment-positioning, will seem much more plausible to you.

And you may get an idea of why later, I am so adamant that we must purge every element, and everyone associated with this treasonous, criminal operation, from our government and our nation, no matter the cost, and no matter what must be done. It will be unpleasant, but I am convinced, on the other side of such an action, lay a true utopia we can barely imagine, where real Americans, hand in hand, devote themselves to improving everyone's lives together.

Now, The Case of the Gilgo Beach Killer, and the Police Chief Who Would Not Back Down:

One of my ancillary interests is serial killers, mainly because I realize there is no way a serial killer can operate, and engage in the types of furtive activities serial killers would need to engage in, without triggering the awareness and interest of the American Stasi and bringing its ground surveillance in for a closer look.

As with 9/11, the American Stasi is designed and deployed specifically to notice where individuals seek to evade the awareness of the population, and avoid scrutiny, so it may focus on these more interesting cases. Just as there is no way the hijackers of 9/11 evaded the keen eye of the American Stasi, there is no way there are serial killers, driving the roads at night dumping bodies, and the local Stasi surveillance has not noticed them and placed their lives under a microscope.

Thus a few years back, I fond myself researching a then-active serial killer case with several interesting, American-Stasi-related aspects which appear apparent to me.

I have seen things which informed me of the way the world works - ways most people never recognize. As a result of these observations, this case appears much different to me than it will to most people. Much of this will be intelligent speculation, based on things I have observed about how the world works.

Most people will see this case and take it at face value, but all throughout it I see common themes I have come to associate with the criminal conspiracy which runs our government from behind the scenes, which many reference simply as the Cabal, and its domestic surveillance operations - the American Stasi.

The case is the Long Island Serial Killer case.[256] We will begin with where it began, or at least where it first took a turn which would bring it to the attention of the broader public.

Shannon Gilbert was an online sex-worker drifting through life quietly. On May 1st, 2010, she hired a car service to take her to a client by the name of Joseph Brewer, on the south shore of Long Island, New York. Something happened as she was standing in the entryway of that John's house. What she saw, if it is known, has not been revealed. But for some reason, Shannon began to think things were going sideways in some way, and the driver and the John were somehow colluding to harm her, so she called 911.

She panicked and escaped the house. It is reported that she told the operator that, *"They are trying to kill me."* Her call would ultimately last 22 minutes, before being disconnected, most people would assume by the loss of her phone's battery power.

She also approached a nearby resident in his home, and asked him to call 911, but in the time it took him to turn and grab his phone, she disappeared from his front doorway, and was gone.

The resident of the house went outside after calling 911. He saw her driver cruising slowly up the street, and approached his car as he drew near. The driver asked if he had seen a woman, to which he replied he had, and he had called 911. The driver made a comment to the effect that he should not have done that, and then fled.

Some time after these events had passed, an officer responded, conducted interviews, drove through the area, and left.

Shannon's family subsequently received a call from a doctor who lived in that neighborhood (who just happened to be the head of Suffolk County Emergency Medical Services when TWA Flight 800 burst into flames, killing all 230 passengers on board in 1996.). The doctor, Dr Peter Hackett, told them that he had taken Shannon into a home for wayward girls which he ran. From here:[257]

"He was sort of the local big shot in Oak Beach," Robert Kolker, the author of "Lost Girls: An Unsolved American Mystery" told Oxygen.com of Hackett. "He raised a family there,

was their emergency services guy, their security guy. Anytime there was anything going on he was helpful...”

"By all accounts, he really aggressively put himself in the center of things whenever anything was going on there," he said. "There are stories about him having a police radio and anytime there was any sort of emergency call within reach of where he lived, he would hop in and drive over to see if he could help out."

Hackett had served as head for the Suffolk County Emergency Medical Services when the TWA Flight 800 burst into flames, killing all 230 passengers on board in 1996.

And here:[258]

Dr. Peter Hackett, a local physician who called Mari Gilbert after Shannan's disappearance saying he runs a home for wayward girls and that he'd drugged Shannan against her will – and that's even before Mari knew that her daughter was missing. He then vehemently denied ever speaking to Mari until his telephone records showed he definitely did call her. Mari also began pursuing a legal case against Dr. Peter Hackett saying he offered to help Shannan Gilbert, drugged her and then tossed her out for her driver to find, who she then ran from – her position is that the Doctor's negligence led to Shannan's death. Mari Gilbert died before the case could be settled.

He subsequently called her family again, and when questioned by authorities, denied ever having called them. He was later forced to admit to the calls when phone company records showed he had in fact called the family.

Articles note it is a mystery how he acquired the phone

number of Shannan's family, as his first call to them occurred before she had even been declared missing, and he had no obvious way of having acquired her name, her family's name, or that sensitive phone number. Even stranger, cell phone triangulation data showed Dr Hackett had made the call after driving to a very close proximity to her family's home in New Jersey.[259] From here:

Two days after Shannan's disappearance, on May 3rd, her mother, Mari Gilbert, would receive a call from a stranger.

"Hello," said the voice on the other end. It was the voice of an older male, who gave his name freely. "My name is Dr. Peter Hackett. I'm calling to see if your daughter Shannan is there."

Mari is immediately alerted to... something. She's just not sure of what.

"No. Why? Who are you?" she asks.

The voice on the other end, Dr. Peter Hackett, explains that he runs a house for wayward girls. He further explains that Shannan had been with him two days beforehand, right when she went missing, and that he had taken her in off of the street after she began knocking on his door. He would also claim that he had given her something - by that I mean a drug - to calm down and collect herself. Apparently, at that point, she went missing, leaving with her driver and not returning.

Mari asks how this stranger got her number, to which Hackett explains that all of the people that stay with him - at his alleged halfway house - have to give an emergency contact.

This further confounds Mari, who knows that none of her family would give out her phone number to anyone. Also, she hasn't heard anything about Shannan going missing...

Roughly a week later, on Mother's Day - May 9th, 2010 - Mari Gilbert and the rest of Shannan's family would travel to Oak Beach to put up fliers and ask the neighborhood if they had seen anything.

Dr. Peter Hackett would later detail this as the first time he had ever spoken to the Gilbert family. He immediately denied ever calling Mari Gilbert, and claimed that he had never seen Shannan Gilbert before in his life...

... phone records show that Hackett DID call Mari Gilbert from his wife's cell phone, sometime in the early afternoon of May 3rd. How exactly he got Mari Gilbert's phone number is anyone's guess, because Shannan would not be reported missing until that day, and her phone number hadn't been released by anyone. In fact, police hadn't come to ask questions yet; and wouldn't, for over a month.

Both him and Alex Diaz, Shannan's boyfriend, recall meeting on May 4th, when Diaz made his second trip out to Oak Beach. But this would be a day after the phone call in question, and bring about the question of how Dr. Hackett knew what he did.

So, in someway and somehow, Peter Hackett learned of Shannan Gilbert's disappearance and also discovered a phone number to her mother.

Also, what's more concerning: records show that the phone call wasn't made from Oak Beach. The cell phone Hackett was using was close enough to Mari Gilbert's home in New Jersey to warrant suspicion. That's right: Hackett traveled to New Jersey to make that call to Mari Gilbert, and phone records show that he immediately lied about it.

He would also call Shannan Gilbert's boyfriend, Alex Diaz, on May 6th, along with another call to Mari Gilbert. Hackett would recall making these phone calls, claiming that he was wishing them well in the search for Shannan. However, this again goes against his prior statements; he claims to have met the Gilberts and their associates on May 9th, three days after this second batch of calls was placed.

So he actually drove to another state, near the family home of Shannan Gilbert (both a name and home address he should not have had access to), before calling a number for them which he should not have had.

From written accounts, it appears he has never explained how he discovered her name or acquired that phone number so soon after her disappearance, and before Police had even begun to question anyone or perform an investigation. Nor apparently has law enforcement probed that, despite its obvious relevance to the investigation. Nor can he explain why he would give her family such an outlandish story, or drive so close to their home, in another state, before doing so.

Note, one of the most definitive tells that one is a target of intelligence/surveillance activity is individuals possessing information that they have no explanation for possessing. Personally, I would suspect that Dr Hackett, at the least, has access to the confidential database of the American Stasi's domestic surveillance/intelligence operation.

(Interesting side note - Shannan's mother, who was the only

witness who could confirm Dr Hackett's calls and the content of them, was subsequently murdered by another daughter, who had suffered a breakdown after "hearing voices" in her head.[260]) Being an American Stasi operative could also explain why despite such strange behavior, Dr Hackett was obviously above being investigated, and could prevent law enforcement from asking such obviously important questions.

Months later, a K9 officer conducting training in the Gilgo Beach area coincidentally found what he thought was Shannon's body. It turned out to be an unrelated body of another female. Subsequent searches turned up additional unrelated bodies, and eventually Shannon's body was found in a marshy area nearby, partially unclothed.

At least that is the official story. I will postulate an alternate hypothesis and point out several pieces of evidence, which may point to another, more ominous storyline.

We will begin with the 911 call and the Police response, which was what first sparked my interest in the case. Authorities would not reveal much about what she said, beyond a report that she claimed *"they"* were *"trying to kill her."* The original copies of the 911 tapes it turns out, have been taken by the State Police and destroyed, without any technical analysis being performed, or even a transcript being made.

Copies of the call kept by the local Police Department have been released to a lawyer representing her family, and although the court forbid him from discussing the contents, he has said many of the public assertions about what the tape includes have been false, and that he is allowed to refute the falsehoods.[261] Using that legal framework, he has said,[262] Police said the call was 22 minutes long, however he says that is not true, though he implies that is approximate, and it may be 21 or 23 minutes. He says it is false that Shannon said she was near Jones Beach. He says it is false Gilbert was not about to be murdered, it was false she was calm on the call, he says it is false there are calm male voices in the background on the tape, it is false she was not desperate, and it is false she was not talking as if she was in danger.

So Shannon called 911, spoke for likely 21 or 23 minutes, the call ended, she approached one neighbor, hid while he called the Police, and then continued to hide while afterward he exited his house and interacted with the driver. She then fled to another house some distance away, interacted with another neighbor inside her house, producing another 911 call, and then fled again.

According to this site, Police response was about one hour,[263] on a call from a wealthy, low-crime area, less than 10 miles from two different highly-populated suburban areas with robust Police forces,[264] sporting some of the highest salaries in the world patrolling them. It was a 911 call, which involved a young girl telling a 911 operator that she was being actively pursued by multiple men who were trying to kill her.

Personally, if someone is on the opposite side of a car, with a knife, trying to stab me, I call 911 and tell them I am about to be killed, and we begin running around the car with my assailant trying to kill me, I am thinking that after about five minutes of running around the car, Police are going to show up. Ten minutes might be reasonable. Fifteen minutes later I would have begun getting impatient. By twenty minutes, I would consider letting

400

myself get killed, just to end the exhaustion. And if it is a half hour later, I might as well be on my own.

And I am not even a young girl, which I would assume should expect an even faster response given her helplessness facing multiple men, and a Police officer's natural inclination to protect the helpless.

Add to that you had an officer who responded to two 911 calls, and spoke to a resident who saw a girl fleeing, as well as an ominous male seeking her who told him he shouldn't have called 911. Yet still the call was cleared, after just a short drive-through, without any resolution as to what happened to the caller, and with no real effort to locate her. For Police, protecting a young girl would be paramount. Why would that scene have been abandoned so quickly that they never discovered Shannon's body, laying in the open a few hundred yards away?

There are several aspects of this which struck me as being consistent with surveillance activity. First was the slow Police response. When surveillance operates in an area of operations, it will place the area "under a flag" in surveillance parlance. That "flag" boots the local Police department out of the sector, and will often even require that uniformed units get permission before entering the area, even in exigent emergency circumstances.

In a normal surveillance operation, this will be done to keep the targets from curtailing any interesting operational activity which surveillance wants to document, due to fear of a law enforcement presence. However in modern American Stasi harassment surveillance it has the additional benefit of allowing surveillance to operate freely against the target without fear of any law enforcement interference.

One of the first things I noticed when my surveillance arrived, was that the local Police, which I had seen for years conducting regular patrols in my neighborhood, disappeared completely.

If surveillance were operating in this area, or had declared it a no-go zone for local Police, then when Shannon called 911 the 911 operator would have immediately seen that the area was under a flag. From there, the operator would have had to send word up the chain of command to request permission for a uniformed unit to enter the area. This site does mention the initial call was shunted from the local department, to the State Police department, rather than the local Police who would normally respond to such a call.[265] That might have been done to shunt the call toward whatever agency needed to approve of local Police entering the area.

If the area was under surveillance, first word would have had to travel up the chain of command to a supervisor who was high enough in the hierarchy to know what was going on (the existence of flags is need to know among Police and local utilities, and usually involves being forced to sign a non-disclosure agreement), and only that supervisor would know who to contact to request permission to enter the area.

That supervisor would then have had to make contact with the surveillance leadership, and then that word would have to travel far enough through the surveillance infrastructure for local teams in the area of interest to redistribute exposed assets and get everyone out of the way for incoming Police. The local operatives would have to signal they were ready, and then word would have had to travel back to the surveillance leadership, then to the local Police supervisor and back down the chain of command to allow the officer in.

And even then the responding Officer's ability to operate would have been at the discretion of surveillance, and he would likely be told there was something about that area that meant he could not linger any longer than absolutely necessary.

Another aspect I notice is that the area is quite isolated. American Stasi surveillance operators sometimes will group their homes together in isolated areas where they can hide unusual aspects of their activities. Numerous cars filling the driveways of flop houses which transient operatives filter through as they rotate around the nation, frequent comings and goings at all hours, changing faces, vehicles, and license plates as the rotating elements pass through, bringing out of state plates with them, changing fake plates, or using constantly changing rental cars are all facets best kept hidden.

These are all things which could attract attention in a normal neighborhood. Grouping together also allows a smaller, more focused counter-surveillance operation to track the environment around operatives and their residences, to see if anyone else is following operators home, entering their neighborhood, and perhaps trying to get a leg up on their operations.

Also, I notice they are by the water. There is a robust presence of surveillance wherever there is an ocean or ocean-accessible waterway nearby. I have wondered if one justification for the massive surveillance state has been a need to secure

403

shorelines after the war on terror. The houses in that area offer the ability to keep "pleasure crafts" (which could operate as surveillance crafts for water-borne operations). At the same time they allow the installation of tech to monitor parts of the shore with observation posts right there on the properties, to house the monitors, as well as boats to perform water-borne follows.

In short, the location has some indices of surveillance which first attracted my attention as I began to read about the case, and as I looked closer, more aspects began to draw my attention.

Another thing which caught my eye was, Shannon was an online prostitute, who visited a client at that location, and then went missing, at a location where numerous other such girls would subsequently be found after going missing themselves. It feels as if it would likely be related.

American Stasi intelligence operations are focused around gathering blackmail. Even New York State Governor David Paterson said a surveillance operation threatened to blackmail him, as we'll cover shortly. Given that, it is highly likely a Craigslist prostitute could be a target of such an operation. Cabal's blackmail operation might take measures to try and gain penetration around such activities, or they might even take measures to assure that women they ran as assets would be predominant among the girls offering their services on that platform, to better control john-prostitute interactions, and facilitate documenting them more completely for purposes of blackmail.

In short, I could see domestic intelligence taking measures to remove regular prostitutes from the platform who were not its agents. Whether they would kill them or not to remove them, I do not know, but anything is possible with this operation.

Then we have the driver, who Shannon reportedly implied was colluding with her client in some way, at the least offering her no security, and possibly even also trying to kill her. It would seem unlikely a random driver and a random serial killer would be linked in any way.

What I notice there however, is her driver is a driver, and surveillance will often recruit professional drivers, be it taxi drivers, towncars, bus drivers, limo drivers, delivery drivers, Access-A-Ride and other medical transport drivers, etc. If you want someone to operate as your eyes and ears on the street, it helps if that person works all day long on the street, driving around, and even transporting targets who might be unusually prone to need such transportation due to being fresh arrivals in new cities as they travel.

In addition, suppose you are following a target who calls a cab, and you can get one of your cabs to quickly pull up and pick him up before his cab arrives, and he never knows the difference.

Now you don't have to follow him with a train of cars, each one handing him off to another in a complicated ballet designed to keep him from seeing the same car behind him following him. He is actually riding in the car which is following him, and he cannot lose the tail. He even tells your driver the destination where he is heading at the outset, so your team can speed there, arriving ahead of him, allowing them to be all set up when he arrives, so he doesn't see them hustling to catch up to him right after he arrives.

And all along the drive, your operator is quizzing him and getting as much intel as he can get, under the guise of a mere chatty taxi driver. Think the chatty taxi driver with all his questions is just a meme? The chatty taxi driver is a domestic intelligence agent, performing an interrogation. The meme is a cover story. It works that way throughout the world. For domestic intelligence operations, infiltrating transportation businesses in cities is practically a procedure.

So now you have a guy who lives in an area that may be high in surveillance activity, and a driver who is in an occupation commonly filled with surveillance personnel, and stifled Police activity consistent with a surveillance operation blanketing an area. You have multiple people who have no obvious relationship to each other linked by this event, and at least one individual with multiple pieces of information he should have been unable to access. This was beginning to peak my interest, even before the word "surveillance" popped up in the news coverage to follow.

As victims were identified, it was revealed one victim's family had received phone calls from the killer after her disappearance, using the victim's cell phone. The phone had made numerous calls, however it was reported that the identity of the caller was never ascertained.

News reports said this led Police to suspect someone in law enforcement, and law enforcement surveillance specifically, because when calling, the individual had used specific countermeasures to cloak the location they were calling from, which would only have been known to an individual who was familiar with how high-level law enforcement surveillance tracked cell phone calls, and specific countermeasures which would thwart those methods. From here:[266]

406

Whoever killed four prostitutes, and possibly four other
people, and then dumped their bodies in heavy underbrush along a
beachfront causeway on Long Island appears to have a
sophisticated understanding of police investigative techniques,
according to people briefed on the case.

A series of taunting phone calls made to the teenage sister
of one of the victims — calls that the police suspect came from the
killer — were made from in or around some of the most crowded
locations in New York City, including Madison Square Garden and
Times Square, according to the people briefed on the case and to
the mother of Melissa Barthelemy, that victim.

The locations, detectives say, were probably chosen because
they allowed the caller to blend into crowds, so that if
investigators pinpointed his location from the cellphone's signal,
they would be unable to pick him out of the crowd using any
nearby surveillance cameras, one of the people said.

This fact, as well as the killer's use of disposable cellphones
to contact the four victims who have been identified — women in
their 20s who advertised their services on Craigslist — suggested
to some investigators that the killer was well versed in criminal
investigative techniques, gleaned either through personal
experience or in some other way, and could even be in law
enforcement himself.

"He is a guy who is aware of how we utilize technology,"
one investigator said. "Frankly, people are thinking maybe he
could be a cop" — either one still in law enforcement or one who
has moved on.

I do not see law enforcement surveillance (which is vetted

even more highly than regular law enforcement due to the material you learn being, in essence, law enforcement's most important and sensitive crown jewels (and probably to some degree, in some cases, illegal)), being involved in the murder of an innocent girl.

The American Stasi however, could easily be involved, and due to the conspiracy's control of the government, it is essentially indistinguishable these days. They have the same toys as government, enjoy the same protections government agencies do, and even appear to pretend to be government law enforcement.

Of course the fact many of these victims were Craigslist prostitutes also would point to Cabal and its American Stasi in two ways. One, computer records never disappear. If the killer met the girls on Craigslist, or another escort site, those interactions are almost certainly recorded and housed in the master surveillance database of the intelligence infrastructure, and yet no advance in the case has been forthcoming until years later, and computer records supposedly played no role in identifying the alleged suspect.

Either the killer is brilliant in covering his tracks with computers, just as he was brilliant in covering his tracks with the phone calls, or again, Police were ordered to drop a line of inquiry, and they complied. Both are consistent with the involvement of the American Stasi's domestic intelligence machine.

Second, as I have pointed out, Craigslist prostitution would be an area of extreme interest to the American Stasi. For that reason, I could see it wanting to create the meme that dealing on Craigslist is dangerous and seedy, so only its agents would be operative in it. A Craigslist prostitute serial killer is an excellent meme for this, as it simultaneously gives Craigslist an air of the seedy, due to the involvement of prostitution, and it makes it appear dangerous, as if those girls who deal on it are actively being stalked by hidden killers who can't be caught.

I am sure some girls, not in the conspiracy, who thought about putting up profiles would be dissuaded by that. Meanwhile, the prostitutes which were being run by the intel operation which sought to blackmail Governor Patterson, would know they were under protection, and it was perfectly safe for them.

Whether Cabal would go so far as to actively kill several girls advertising on the platform I can not say, but given that whoever this killer is, they have intimate knowledge of cell phone tracking technology and computer tracking capabilities and how to thwart both, it would not surprise me, nor would it be inconsistent with my observations to date of this surveillance/intelligence blackmail machine.

As you delve deeper, you see other indices of Cabal and its American Stasi Intelligence operation. The 23 minute 911 call of Shannan Gilbert, the prostitute who set off the entire investigation, was not released by Police during the investigation, and was only recently made public. In it, she is known to have said, "They're trying to kill me."

When Ms Gilbert's estate sued for it, the judge agreed it should be released and ordered first a transcript be made available and then that the tape be released. The judge was informed there was no transcript, and it appears the date he mandated the tape be publicly released by, came and went with no tape released.

When a copy of the tape was finally made available to the

lawyer for the family, he was only allowed to listen to it, and he was not allowed to reveal anything about the tape publicly. Similarly, he requested any technical analysis of the tape, including any copies produced with enhanced audio, and was told the tapes had never been submitted to any audio specialists for any sort of further analysis.

The biggest serial killer case in the country, this is a key piece of evidence, and the originals are gone, there is no technical analysis of the tape or attempt to enhance it, and nobody ever even made a transcript.

Moreover, the media says nothing. This type of media silence is not what one would expect if a regular citizen has been murdered by a serial killer who is still at large. This type of media silence is what you see in cases, such as the blackmailing of a New York Governor, where Cabal's surveillance is operative, and the media runs cover for the intel operation.

Then we come to the mysterious case of Natasha Jugo, who some suspect of being one of the victims of the Long Island Serial Killer. Natasha was a young girl who walked out of her apartment one day and disappeared. Her clothes and ID were found on the beach right where the other bodies of the killer were found, and a few days later her body was found at that exact spot where bodies were being dumped.

Authorities say they assume her body had washed up there, carried by ocean currents. Her car was later found parked in a parking lot about a mile away.

Some say she must have committed suicide, because her family told people she had some sort of mental problems - namely in recent months she had become convinced that a large number of people in society were following her around everywhere she went, as part of a massive surveillance operation. From here[267]

Jugo's mother told police her daughter had a history of problems in which she thought people were following her, the source said.

If she was under surveillance, even if it was innocent and unrelated to her being selected as a victim and killed, nothing happened to her that was not documented in detail. Yet again, you have a young girl, her dead body turning up at this specific site, far from her home and her normal haunts, and a connection to the domestic surveillance of the American Stasi.

One other thing here reeks of the American Stasi when I looked at the case. One of the first things I do when I think the American Stasi is operative in an area is look at the Police Chief, because the American Stasi will first look to either corrupt him or replace him, to gain control over his department. When the American Stasi is operating, the biggest threat is local law enforcement. As we have seen with the Trump campaign surveillance, the federal agencies will always be compromised at the top, allowing orders to be sent down to constrain any rogue agents at the ground level.

However local law enforcement is like an army, headed by a local official who can create enough headaches to make operating difficult for any outside-the-law operations. In the LISK case, the Police Chief appears to have been an interesting example of this.

James Burke was the Police Chief at the outset of the

investigation. If you have viewed the Wikipedia page on the Long Island Serial Killer case prior to the arrest of the current suspect, you will be familiar with the name, as James Burke was the first suspect listed in the case before the current suspect was arrested.

From Wikipedia here:[268]

Suspects and persons of interest

James Burke

On December 15, 2016, the attorney for Gilbert's family said that an escort who had conducted business with former Suffolk County Police Chief James Burke claimed he was connected to the Long Island murders.[32] In November 2016, Burke had been sentenced to 46 months in federal prison, along with three years of supervised release, for beating a man who stole a duffel bag filled with sex toys and pornography from his vehicle. Burke had pleaded guilty in February 2016 to charges of a civil rights violation and conspiracy to obstruct justice.[33] Gilbert's attorney said in December that one escort claimed that she had had "rough sex" with Burke during an Oak Beach party.[32] The escort identified herself as "Laenne". She specifically stated that at the first party she attended in April 2011 in Oak Beach she saw Burke drag an Asian looking woman by the hair to the ground. She stated that the woman did, however, think that this was playful rather than violent. Laenne said that when she saw him for the second time, she decided to hook up with him, as she was told that he was a high ranking official and that was intriguing to her. She described that he violently yanked her head during oral sex to the point where she started tearing up. Burke was unable to reach orgasm and proceeded to throw 300-400 UD Dollars at her afterward. This was in August 2011. At this time she was not a professional prostitute and she states that this was the first time she was paid for sex.[34] Burke was reported to have blocked an FBI probe of the LISK case during his time as police chief.[35]

Yes, you read that right - the Police Chief was listed in Wikipedia as the prime Long Island Serial Killer suspect, despite that allegation being made nowhere else, and the idea of it being preposterous.

As most should assume by now, Wikipedia is merely the source you go to when you want to see the narrative that the intelligence operation running our government wants people to believe. So what did Commissioner Burke do to gain such ire of Cabal, as to be labeled the number one suspect in a serial killer case he tried to investigate?

My impression, based on my examining other cases across the nation, and seeing the American Stasi operate up close, is that Burke, who was a long time uniformed patrol officer before working his way up to Chief, was probably a more or less honest cop who was displeased to begin with, having a girl report being attacked in a sector his officers had been banned from operating in, and to have her lost on his watch due to American Stasi operations.

I disregard stories of him having a "relationship" with a prostitute on his beat as something all officers who cultivate informants can be accused of, if Cabal wants to sully their name and cannot cite an actual crime they committed. You will see he is accused later in the story of drug charges, which appear entirely fake, so the machine is clearly falsely accusing him of crimes in an effort to rein him in.

413

My impression on reading the articles on the LISK case is the local Stasi neighborhood surveillance crew had constrained further investigation within that sector after Shannon Gilbert disappeared. That is why rather than officially running cadaver dogs through the area on an official investigation after her disappearance, complete with grid searches, the first set of remains was discovered by a K9 officer conducting innocent "training" exercises of his dog, when he "accidentally" discovered the body.

From there, we see that Burke's relationship with the FBI rapidly deteriorated. Burke ordered his detectives to cut all FBI agents out of the LISK investigation, and when he found out a detective had been contacting the FBI, he removed him from the case, presumably demoting him for disobeying orders. Searches on Burke also revealed this gulf widened when he pulled his officers from a gang taskforce which involved federal agents.[269]

Note that Long Island had a long period under Obama where MS-13 was essentially rolling fully above the law, planting bodies in dumping grounds all over the Island,[270] some even just innocent teenaged girls[271] - something which was only brought to heel once Donald Trump came to office (Note the politically active mother of one of those girls, who lobbied over the murder of her daughter and appeared with President Trump, was herself killed by some "random" person who drove over her after destroying a memorial to her daughter).[272]

So Burke may have been seeing his ability to enforce the law being thwarted by the American Stasi in other places as well, especially in combating MS-13. I can see no reason for a police officer, seeking to close a case, to shut out the resources of a federal agency like the FBI, unless he thought that the federal government was somehow trying to thwart his case.

Of course it is natural to assume the American Stasi is the FBI when you first encounter it, as it is so far outside our paradigm to think there would be any other organization with such power, with any other agenda beyond law enforcement. I assumed it was federal law enforcement when I first saw its massive size.

I assume the Stasi ground surveillance claims some sort of federal jurisdiction, just as a matter of trying to keep quiet the existence of the conspiracy itself and to make it easier for local law enforcement to abide by their wishes.

If they simply rolled in and said they were the new power in the area and local law enforcement had to submit, I suspect local law enforcement would fight back in many cases. If they claim FBI, or DEA, or maybe even CIA jurisdiction, local law enforcement is probably more likely to follow their orders, even if they know they are engaging in, or promoting illegalities. There is probably even some established jurisdictional mechanism which they can exploit to seize power from local agencies lawfully.

I presume Burke also realized his officers were barred from the area due to an active surveillance op. That meant he would have assumed there would probably be detailed records of what happened to Gilbert, perhaps gathered by trained surveillance operators with advanced tech, both tech in houses and mounted on the telephone poles in the neighborhood where she disappeared, and those records were not being shared.

To this day, a subpoena to local utilities to see what agencies had put the area under a flag during the active years of the killer, and what poles had surveillance tech on them, could

415

reveal a whole new tranche of data which would resolve the case once and for all. However the American Stasi's surveillance product is not for use by law enforcement.

And then there were all the bodies, some of which could have been dropped at a time when surveillance was tracking everything in the area, which means the killer would have immediately been picked up by an extraordinarily well funded and well manned ground surveillance operation.

And yet, Burke had to know, surveillance would not help. I am sure when you added a girl who disappeared there and turned up dead, who had complained of surveillance targeting her, and the use of a technique to prevent the tracking of the phone calls to victim's relatives, Burke had to wonder if the surveillance itself was involved in the actual killings. Indeed, he may have even spotted his own surveillance tracking him, which I'm sure it was.

Burke subsequently was the victim of a car break-in. According to reports, the perpetrator did not break into any other cars in the area, and told an improbable tale of being almost psychically drawn to the residence.[273] It would seem unusual that an individual would break into a Police Chief's car specifically, of all the cars on the block. Nevertheless, that is what happened.

On arriving at the precinct after the suspect's apprehension, Burke confronted the perpetrator, who promptly insulted him over pornography which was reportedly in a briefcase he stole from Burke's car.

According to the most detailed report, when the perpetrator purposely escalated his taunts and insults, Burke slapped him in the back of the head, and told him that as the Police Chief he could

416

do anything to him he wanted.

That is inappropriate. However if, as I suspect, this is an American Stasi intelligence operation, such a move would be preceded by priming the target (Burke) emotionally, and in that context, it might be more understandable. His mailbox could have been vandalized repeatedly in the weeks prior, he could have been subjected to threatening and harassing actions by his surveillance teams which he could not stop, his wife could have been subjected to it as well, and there could have been other stressors applied based upon an in-depth psychological and surveillance file they were probably maintaining on Burke going back to when he was a child.

Reportedly there are even thru-wall infrasound weapons which can alter a target's amygdala/irritation levels through physical damage to the brain structure, without the target knowing it, actually making them more prone to anger. There is no doubt multiple neighbors of Burke would have been operating observation posts for the American Stasi, complete with directed energy technologies, likely both for through-wall observation and as weapons.

All together, if it was a Cabal operation to set him up, it would be within Cabal's technical and operational capabilities to assure that when the perp accosted him, and tried to escalate it, Burke would feel an uncontrollable urge to vent his frustrations on the perp.

Strangely enough, this immediately became a federal investigation. Burke was arrested and denied any bail, despite being a veteran Police Officer with deep ties to the community.[274]

417

He was held incarcerated until and through his trial, through the holiday season. He was ultimately sentenced to four years in federal prison for slapping a burglar on the back of the head.

While in prison, Burke was subjected to a spot check of his locked footlocker, which found a large stash of the illegal drug Oxycodone in it.[275] However authorities appeared to just seize the drugs, and then released Burke. Of course, in prison, two entities have access to foot lockers, the inmate, and the prison officials who issued him his combination lock. And it would seem coincidental a search was conducted by jail leadership, right after Burke says the drugs were planted. That he was not punished in any way, would make it seem the American Stasi was simply threatening him.

Another interesting aspect of the case is that even as the Police profile states the killer may be associated with law enforcement, it also notes that he would have access to burlap.

There is one area of law enforcement which would use burlap, and that is surveillance, which uses it to construct Ghillie suits used in long term surveillance postings in wooded areas to camouflage the surveillance operators and their equipment. From this link,[276]

While you may think that only the military snipers use ghillie suits, law enforcement agencies use ghillie suits on a daily basis during undercover work, surveillance and training.

Interesting as well is that one victim's boyfriend received 30 threatening phone calls in eight months from the killer, who knew he had tattoos, and while inside the privacy of his home "was usually drunk."[277]

That type of detailed information, of specific personal data like a phone number of a boyfriend, as well as details regarding his appearance and daily habits while inside his home and not visible to the public, by an individual who he ostensibly had never met, would not be uncommon for someone who ran physical surveillance, and had access to The American Stasi's detailed files on everyone.

I am not sure some architect, like the current suspect, Rex Heuermann, would be able to acquire access to that kind of information. My own feeling would be it is most likely the phone caller was high-level surveillance, and pulled this guy's file. If the girl was targeted by the operation, it is even likely they would conduct a surreptitious entry and plant cameras to watch her inside the house in the run-up to killing her, as part of their preparation.

The vast majority of us have files like that, compiled by the neighbors assigned to amass the files on residents in our neighborhood, from what I have seen of domestic surveillance. Everyone, at least for short periods every year or two, are treated as priority targets to polish up our files, and that includes at least monitoring via audio while inside our homes.

Interestingly the killer also called the half-sister of another of his victims, and knew she was mixed race, as well as other private details of her life which he would not have ordinarily known. From here:[278]

"He said that he knew where she lived, he called her a "half-breed," in reference to the dark skin given to her by her father. He seemed to know details about her own life, details he wouldn't have known unless he had been after Melissa for quite

some time. "

I should pause here to highlight, there is an alternate theory that could fit some of the evidence. It is possible the killer was a regular serial killer, operating alone, perhaps even Rex Heuermann, but that the American Stasi's surveillance was on top of him, and trying to get control of him, and turn him into an asset, or maybe even just playing with him for fun.

I could envision a scenario where surveillance observed him killing, and when he went to dump the victims' belongings in a dumpster, or otherwise dispose of them, Stasi-agents ran in after him and grabbed up the belongings, including the girls' cell phones. Then, to amuse themselves, or send the killer a message, they made these phone calls to the victims using the phones, while pretending to be him, and employing countermeasures to avoid implicating themselves.

Imagine the killer, thinking he had gotten away clean and disposed of all the evidence. He is sitting, watching the news, and suddenly it says the victim's cell phones were making calls to the families of the victims, telling them details of the killings, and telling the victims' families what they were doing inside the privacy of their own houses.

What would the killer think then a few days later, when a surveillance machine exposed itself to him through overt harassment surveillance? He would realize all the evidence tying him to the crime had been picked up by this surveillance operation. He would also realize they could redeposit the evidence in his custody without his knowledge, and arrange for him to be arrested with it in his possession.

I would tend to discount that theory, however, at least with respect to Heuermann, given the spontaneity of the case of Shannon Gilbert. That case indicates that either the American Stasi was, for some reason, running an operation in Gilgo Beach which was targeting online sex-workers for murder, or the surveillance of the American Stasi had set up in Gilgo Beach to document someone who was targeting online sex-workers for murder there, and it would seem unlikely that was Rex Heuermann.

Shannon was almost certainly associated with the other victims due to her being a sex-worker who advertised online, her body being found in the same area as the other online sex-workers, and all of them being killed through violence inflicted upon their throats/strangulation. And then there is the fact that in Shannon's case, as with some of the other victims, there were individuals who spontaneously involved themselves in the case, by calling the family and friends, and they knew information which they should not have known – an indicator of domestic surveillance activity.

That would point to someone other than Rex Heuermann as the killer, as it is unclear how he would have had access to Shannon that night, he appears unrelated to the American Stasi's ground surveillance network, and he had no linkage to that location. For Rex Heuermann to be the Gilgo Beach Killer would have required him to have been present, by chance, in Gilgo Beach that night, at that exact time, just as an online sex-worker mistakenly thought she was about to be killed by her John and her driver, and ran off.

It seems unlikely that an online sex-worker, by chance, right after mistakenly thinking one group of people was about to kill her and calling 911, ran into a separate real serial killer who focused on online sex-workers, right in that area, if the killer did not live there or frequent the area. It is not impossible, but it seems unlikely.

It would appear more likely either she was delivered to the real killer of all the girls, or by chance she ran into the real killer who opportunistically killed her that night, because the real killer lives in the area.

It would also explain yet another neighbor, the doctor, calling Shannon Gilbert's family out of the blue and trying to reassure them that their daughter was fine. Normally, such a neighbor would have no relation to the John or the driver, and no interest in whether her family pursued the involvement of the authorities in searching for her.

But if the killer were under surveillance, suddenly neighbors would have common interests in what happened to the killer, and operational interests in his activities, and the course of any official investigation of them.

It is not impossible the doctor was local surveillance and was seeking to prevent involvement of the authorities in the case, while the American Stasi conducted its surveillance of the killer, for whatever purposes it was pursuing. It would make sense of how he knew who Shannon was, and how to contact her family, and that she was missing and that they would otherwise be looking for her, all before she was even reported missing, or identified by authorities. It would also explain his constant monitoring of the Police scanner, and showing up unsolicited, whenever anything happened in the neighborhood of any note – he was on duty.

Another interesting aspect is that Police reportedly have

audio recordings made by a victim's relative, which feature the killer taunting them, on a call made from the victim's phone, giving them his voice. From that they have reportedly deduced he did not grow up in that area, but rather was a transplant from another area, based on his accent. One victim stated he clearly enunciated his S's and T's, and spoke "very proper." From here:[279]

Karnes, who passed her information on to the police, says the man she spoke to didn't have an accent.

"He definitely isn't from New York, Boston or Maine, because those are the strongest places the accent comes out of," she says. "But he accentuated his S's and his T's. He spoke properly."

The currently arrested suspect, Rex Heuermann, reportedly was born in New York City and lived most of his life on Long Island.[280] If they have a recording of his voice, and it is distinctive, why would they not have released it during the pursuit of the suspect, to see if it might be recognized? It is very difficult to control cops who want to solve a case, and make them suppress evidence and follow investigative paths less likely to solve cases - especially serial killer cases. And yet no cop has ever leaked those calls. Only the American Stasi is capable of leaning on local Police Departments that hard.

In the case of another victim, she disappeared while working the streets near the Port Authority Bus terminal - an area which would be rife with surveillance of all forms, looking for everything from criminals fleeing the city, to couriers running drugs and money using the buses as cover, to gun-runners, to terrorists looking to inflict a mass casualty event. And yet, law enforcement cannot find a way to identify who picked her up, despite multiple agencies likely having that terminal under 24/7 surveillance coverage, and recording everything which passes through there.

That is yet another law enforcement jurisdiction. Suppressing this investigation in so many jurisdictions, and among so many agencies, would lean against the theory of this being merely the Police Chief of the local department on Long Island covering up the perpetrators of the case.

As with the case of Jeffrey Epstein, who was protected for years from investigation by the FBI,[281] and who later could not be touched by US Attorney Alex Acosta, because he was told Epstein *"belonged to intelligence,"* private investigators who have examined the case have been baffled Police were not able to immediately figure out who the killer was, and felt there must have been some force suppressing the investigation.

From here, an interview with a private investigator regarding a belt found at the dump-site, with initials on it, which investigators had asked for the public to provide additional leads on:[282]

<<Manuel Gomez, private investigator, your thoughts about the police department out there, there's been a lot of skepticism about them, they've gotten, some of the folks have gotten into a lot of trouble out there, what happened here, what happened, why why can't this thing be solved, why has the investigation gone the way it's gone?

>> Well it could have been solved if they wouldn't have dropped one major ball in this case, and one of that was, all five of

these women had online aliases, and they were being sex trafficked online. For example, Babylon escorts, where they sell women and they advertise prices. All of them were doing this. All of them had the same John Doe initiating contact with them, trying to hook up with them. The Police Department failed to subpoena these Internet services, these escort sex-trafficking services, that would have shown the connection, that all these women had the same guy reaching out to them, or the same men. They unfortunately dropped the ball on this and I know this personally because like I said, I've done numerous cases in Long Island for sex trafficking, and these sites are still up. And one of them you can go on now, Babylon Escorts, they not only sell the women, but they star rate them. It is insanity. And it is a shame, because you know, this girl was on the call for 22 minutes with 911. She was asking for help. Now listen, anybody knows Gilgo Beach and Long Island, that area, a cop car could've responded within that time frame. And the fact that the ball was dropped on so many levels and fact that they did not subpoena, and to this day still have not subpoenaed, the Internet sites that five of these women were on. And the sad thing is that the records stay on the sites between six and eight years, the ghost image stays on the hard drive up to ten years, that evidence is still there and it is not being researched. And it is a shame...

[Regarding a belt found at the murder scene, which Police believe did not belong to the victims, and was somehow related to the murderer, and was embossed with the initials "HM," or "WH" depnding on how it was examined.]

...And we've identified at least 2 people who who share those initials to the police, they have not interviewed the persons who have those initials. And they have been high profile suspects

in this case before and the police have refused to interview them. Instead, they they held press conferences, two of them so far in which they announced that they have all these other people like the FBI and so on actively working on this. That's not true. Nobody has been interviewed in the Oak Beach community since they claim that they were having this investigation. They rolled off Shannon Gilbert as a tragic accident with no evidence whatsoever and you'll notice that at both press conferences the key person was missing, and that was the district attorney of Suffolk County. He did not participate in that. I don't think we're being treated in good faith here. I do think there's a serious cover up and I never used to say that until recently when I see some of the developments. There is a police cover up here and it needs to be broken....

... I believe as Mr John Ray said, this has been a police cover-up It's not being taken seriously because of the victims, who they are. And I disagree with this gentleman. The police were obligated to investigate everybody within that area and no one did. And the fact that they didn't shows the egregious behavior that has been conducted and continues to be conducted in this case And again I believe it's a cover up and this lawyer is correct. These people have not done the job. The Police Department has failed these families on so many levels. And it's because unfortunately, because they were ladies of the evening and that is my professional opinion in this case. "

Slightly more disturbing would be this comment from Reddit here:[283]

"I live pretty close to Gilgo Beach and the most popular theory around here is that there are numerous individuals involved..one or a few of which are in (or have extensive

knowledge of) law enforcement-and that they may have had "sex/kill" parties. Sick fucks getting together, doing sick things to people they feel won't be missed. Very disturbing."

I've seen this theory a few times on various boards, so I assume the writer is being truthful about those living there believing that. Combined with the girl who reported being followed by surveillance at her home some 40 miles away before her disappearance, the idea of it being a large group of people, operating outside the law, who are intimately familiar with law enforcement procedures and surveillance capabilities, and who have the ability to suppress multiple investigations among many agencies, federal, state, and local, raises the uncomfortable question of just how involved US domestic surveillance might be, and just how organized this whole affair could have been.

As we will highlight later in this book, there is a domestic surveillance cell operative in Texas which uses their quasi-governmental powers to break into the homes of women while they work during the day, drug their food, and return to gang rape them at night after the drugs take effect.[284]

You have to understand, when you mix the omniscience of US domestic surveillance's surveillance operations (which can see any attempt to penetrate or thwart their activities before it even begins), the jurisdictional authority which seemingly places them entirely above any local, state, or federal law enforcement agency, and the types of personalities willing to so completely subvert and corrupt the Constitutional liberties and basic human rights of neighbors and community members, anything is possible.

Returning to Police Chief Burke, if you continue digging,

you will uncover an interesting series of incidents,[285] in which he and the local DA seemingly stumbled upon a political corruption ring which has eerie similarities to what many today refer to as the Cabal taking over our nation, which uses as its frontline shock-troops in the US, the US domestic surveillance network.

You need to read the article to understand the full scale of what occurred. It is an interesting story of intrigue, spying and surveillance, which began with an assistant district attorney taking bribes from a central lawyer who it was discovered ran a practice which functioned as a central node in a bribery network. As the investigation expanded to everyone involved in the network, it brought together everyone from politicians at the state Capitol, to local functionaries, to drug dealers, to mortgage fraudsters, to armed robbers and local prosecutors.

One investigator said he was shocked when the investigation inexplicably shut down despite it amassing considerable evidence of corruption and criminal activity that was ongoing throughout the government.

It is worth a read as long as we are alleging a potential massive criminal intelligence operation, operative in the area, which had corrupted/suppressed various agencies, and which was at odds with the local Police Chief.

My guess would be, as the operation the article describes began to close in on the corrupt actors in New York government, the American Stasi stepped in, and made everything go away, and Burke and the DA had no choice in the matter.

But it did not go away before Burke fell on their radar, and saw his file archived under the heading of troublesome individual.

And from other articles you will find if you Google the local DA, you will see he fell on Cabal's radar, and was ultimately dealt with as Burke was, though he apparently escaped office without prison time.[286] But just barely.

New York Governor David Paterson almost single handedly broke open the story of the American Stasi's domestic surveillance operations when he alleged a political blackmail operation was ongoing in the State PD surveillance division. You will recall, at the time Governor Paterson decided to not seek reelection, he was the target of a criminal probe begun by none other than then NY Attorney General Andrew Cuomo, who then went on to take Paterson's office, once he abandoned it.[287]

Burke has since been released from federal custody, with the issue of the oxycodone pills supposedly discovered in his footlocker having just gone away, with apparently no culpability assigned to him. The incident with the pills appears a veiled threat to him, that at any time, he can be framed and reincarcerated.

In what appears as another veiled threat, the local legislature began, but ultimately abandoned an attempt to sue him, to try and not only end his pension, but to claw back as much as $1.5 million in funds which were already paid, something which seems strangely gratuitous for merely slapping a junkie who robbed him in the back of the head when the junkie purposely provoked him.[288] Obviously, somebody was trying to keep Burke on a short leash.

Recently, authorities have arrested an architect for the Gilgo Beach killings, Rex Heuermann.[289] His case is preparing to go to trial. It is possible he is somehow involved. However, notice just as he hired a lawyer and his legal defense began, coincidentally, Police Chief Burke went for a walk in the park and was arrested by an officer who claimed Burke walked up to him, dropped his pants, exposed himself, and reportedly said, *"I like to suck dick."*[290] Burke has no prior history of homosexuality, having exclusively been tied to relationships with females, and he had no history of sexual crimes or indecent exposure.

The only individuals who know what really transpired there, and whether that account is correct, or whether Burke was merely on a walk when he was approached, handcuffed, arrested and that was alleged, are the arresting officer and Burke. What is undisputed, however, is that just as the new arrest was made in the Gilgo Beach case, Burke was immediately, preemptively discredited, and will not be able to be called as a witness to testify to any aspects of the Gilgo Beach case which were unusual in the course of the investigation. The timing was incredibly precise, if the goal was to prevent any questioning of him.

Burke had initially been charged with soliciting a male prostitute and offering a sex act, as well as indecent exposure and public lewdness, however the first two charges were immediately dropped by prosecutors.[291]

We also got a look at Police Chief Burke, who had been staying out of the spotlight, and who I have no doubt has spent the last few years targeted by domestic surveillance, potentially even with thru-wall directed energy weapons such as I have encountered. Below is Chief Burke in 2015, before Gilgo Beach. and in 2023, after:

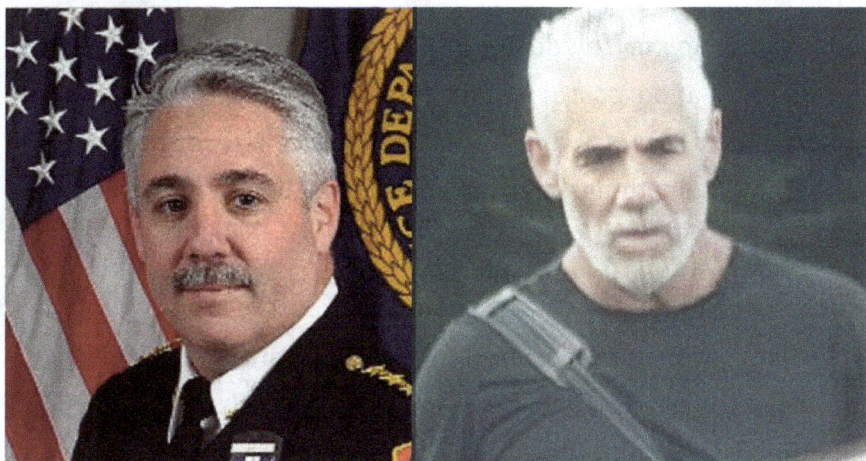

Facing the American Stasi, and especially the continual wear of its physically degrading directed energy weapons, changes you. I notice similar changes in my own face and expression.

You can see what just a casual look at one case with interesting facets will show. This thing is all over, and involved in a lot more criminality than anyone would believe. And our society is under much more control than most would think possible.

My guess is the American Stasi's intel operations will be thick in the areas around New York City. And given the mix of omnipotence, the preferential recruitment of psychopathy, and the willingness to subvert the normal mores of society, it will not surprise me if we find cliques here and there which have spun horribly out of control, and become criminal empires, even sadistic criminal empires, wholly unto themselves.

The reality is that the meme of ten or twenty serial killers out in the US right now, operational, and nobody having any idea who they are, strikes me as highly unlikely. Serial killing involves a raft of the types of unusual behaviors, performed while trying to evade prying eyes, which US domestic surveillance is designed to detect and pick up on. You do not pull into an area at 2:30 AM that the local observation post does not immediately notice a vehicle has entered their sector at an unusual time, as if someone may be trying to hide something, and they set about unraveling exactly what is going on using their available pole technology, foot surveillance, available aviation assets, and vehicular units.

To my eye, it is just as unlikely there are any unknown serial killers, as it is the American Stasi's sectorized, neighborhood-ized domestic surveillance op, which assigns agents in the cell responsible for a local sector/neighborhood to know everyone in that sector/neighborhood, missed the September 11th hijackers, and had no idea that the attacks of that day were coming.

So the question would arise, why aren't all serial killers picked up, or at least forced to stop their activities? Oddly enough there have been accounts of serial killers who were recruited into an organization which has all the hallmarks of an intelligence operation. There they were used to perform operations for that covert intelligence-like organization, while allowing the agency which ran it to maintain plausible deniability. In returnm, it allowed them to remain free in society. From here:[292]

"Henry Lee Lucas and his partner Otis Toole have admitted to killing over 30 people. Most of which they claim was to do with the secret satanic cult they belonged to, called The Hand of Death.

It was this satanic cult that had trained Lucas and Toole to be killers. Lucas said he was taken to the Florida Everglades in a camp-like environment where he and the others were trained by The Hand of Death. There he was taught skills in killing, rape, car theft, drug trafficking, and other forms of organized criminal

432

activity.

Lucas said this cult was part of a nationwide ring, that had people killed, and children abducted and taken to a ranch in Juarez, Mexico. At the ranch, they would make child pornography and carry out ritual sacrifices.

The Hand of Death has connections to killers such as Son of Sam David Berkowitz and the Manson's Family leader, Charles Manson.

The name *Hand of Death Cult* was mentioned independently by both Henry Lee Lucas, and David Berkowitz, It arose in the Manson investigation, and it was not publicized enough at the time for one to have heard of the other's usage of it when it emerged in each case.

The deeper you go into it, the more you will hear of the nexus of the American Stasi's domestic intelligence operation, and the Cabal of Elites which run it, being the meeting point of government agents and criminal enterprises, all of which appear to be under some level of unified control.

CIA was alleged to have operated in concert with the mafia to kill JFK, the Mexican drug cartels used a CIA interrogator to interrogate captured DEA agent Kiki Camarena[293] before they killed him, and there is even an allegation MS-13 was used by a DEA agent, hired out of the Department of Justice which had been operating for the Democrat Party, in the murder of a Bernie Sanders campaign operative named Seth Rich, who was believed to have provided files to Wikileaks showing the Democrat primary had been rigged against Sanders.[294] It would be unsurprising to find out that serial killers also pass through that nexus.

As for the Gilgo Beach case, what is the truth? I have no idea. It is possible the current suspect killed some of the girls, and the American Stasi planted a few of its own victims in his dumping ground and now wants him to take the blame for all of them. Or it is possible the Stasi was responsible for all of them. I do not know why they would be killing young girls, but it is possible somebody in this conspiracy had their reasons.

Nothing today is necessarily as it seems.

Chapter Eleven

Who Can You Trust?

What this book alleges is too far outside of what the average American is taught as normal, for me to just lay out to you what I have seen with my own eyes, or even to show it to you.

But you will need to understand, the surveillance you have just seen, which is undoubtedly tracking you and your children, making sure you are all limited in your ability to rise, is one small part of this massive machine, designed to control everything. In addition, you may doubt your own eyes, as the idea of the East German Stasi existing in America is so far outside what you have been raised to believe would be possible in our nation.

So to support our assertions further, and give you a better idea of the scale of this conspiracy, we will now begin citing instances of people who you will respect and believe, asserting the premise of this book is correct.

Hopefully we will begin to establish in your mind, that in a nation of good trusting people who let psychopaths run their intelligence agencies unobserved, it was inevitable such a system as described in this book would arise.

You are also going to have to confront that even as I show you rock-solid substantiation for the shocking accounts to come, the media will not have shared any of these shocking revelations with you. That is because the American Stasi is an intelligence operation, and as such, it ruthlessly wargames against itself, looking for how an enemy could defeat it, or how it could come to ruin. When it identifies such a mechanism, it will take proactive measures to defuse the threat it perceives, long before the danger can manifest.

To that end, it would appear it long ago realized that the biggest risk it would face would be individuals in the news media, or even the online social media sphere, one day presenting this material to you. To defuse that threat, it began infiltrating its people into the news media, until it had a robust enough network that in order to ever hope to work in the media, you would need the approval of one of its agents, and by extension it.

It then controlled hiring, and now, after decades of control, at a minimum, things are at the point that, as you will see, there are astonishing stories out there, of real luminaries running into this machine and experiencing unimaginable things, and yet the media will never even broach the stories, because their masters in the American Stasi control them, and will not allow it. The fact you will never have seen some of the more shocking stories we are about to present, anywhere, should give you an idea of just how total the control the American Stasi wields over the news media is.

It is one lesson I hope you will take from this work. You cannot trust any talking mouthpiece they present to you, unless they will tell you about the surveillance. All of them, like me, have had it show up to intimidate them as they were starting out. Those who caved, and agreed to keep the secret from you, and lie to you while reciting its daily narratives, are the famous faces you see, from big names in radio and TV, to minor online personalities.

436

They all work for the conspiracy you see here, and they are hiding it from you to keep you weak and vulnerable - and under control.

Those who, like me, told the surveillance to get lost, are the names you do not see promoted all over, and who you have likely not heard of. We are suppressed and kept isolated online, because in the machine's wargaming, we were the threat. It is the isolated voices who will tell you the truth. We want to make all of our kind strong, because all of us strong, will foster freedom. In contrast, the conspiracy needs you to be weak and helpless, and it does that by having its agents misinform you, misdirect you, and keep you in the dark about how things really work.

If you ever find yourself wondering if somebody is in the conspiracy, and cannot be trusted, just ask them about this work, and the surveillance. It is the one thing conspiracy members are not allowed to even broach.

We will move quickly here, as I want the bulk of this book to be training for you in detecting the surveillance in your neighborhood, as well as documenting the dangerous nature of this program's ruthlessness. I intend to simply give you a name, and link to where you can see it online yourself, and a relevant quote showing that someone respectable, who you know and trust, said there is a massive surveillance operation illegally targeting American citizens within the borders of the United States.

I will try to include a couple of links to access the relevant material, as it has been my experience the US domestic surveillance apparatus has extraordinary technical control over the internet, and it is possible, and maybe even likely, that if this work becomes popular, they will seek to disconnect the links on the internet to prevent you from accessing the pages.

I have actually seen tinyurls which pointed to one site changed inside tinyrurl's server to point to another site, entire websites have been made unavailable to some IP addresses and not others, while the website BiggerThanSnowden.com, where a raft of prominent US intelligence officers detailed a program to target innocent Americans with directed energy weapons within America, was mysteriously taken offline entirely somehow, and nobody knows what happened to it, or why everyone associated with it has suddenly gone silent about it.

At my other website, I have been told repeatedly people who visit it get a 404 page, telling them the site does not exist. After persevering, the site shows up, and the source of the 404 is a mystery. But if they were potential new readers who just accepted there was no site there and left, they would be gone for good, as would my ability to find new readers.

We will try to correct any such changes at the website AmericanStasi.com, so if these links cease working, please visit the site and see if we have found a workaround to access the pages for you.

Many of these people we document will have assumed the surveillance is unique to them, it is a single unique incident, or it is some small, local law enforcement thing. As you see the number of cases however, you should realize these are people all over the country, all describing the same national organization, and the program is bigger than just them.

The first account in America I can find of this operation would be the Pulitzer Prize-winning author John Kennedy Toole, who won his prize posthumously for his novel *A Confederacy of Dunes.*

From here:[295]

"In the following years [Editor's note: the late 1960's], *Toole developed symptoms typical of paranoid schizophrenia. Initially, he started worrying about his students stalking him and people driving past his house at night. In his graduate class, he stood up and declared 'There's a plot against me here'. Finally, while discussing his concerns about stalkers with one of his colleagues, he raised the possibility that the government had implanted a device in his brain."*

It is tempting to conclude he must have been crazy from the last part. However having seen this operation firsthand, I know not to trust any account I am provided with about a surveillance target.

The operation will move its agents into close proximity to targets at the outset of targeting them, befriending them even before designating them overt targets. All of us know American Stasi citizen-agents - they are that prolific. Those real Americans who believe in freedom, or who are prone to high levels of success, who are deemed potentially problematic, will not only meet agents, but have close "friends" who are actually American Stasi agents, sent in by the conspiracy to befriend them. The operation can also seek to drive away real friends from a target, leaving them entirely within a bubble of Stasi-agent "friends."

When I was 18, "Danny" showed up at my martial arts club. When I first saw him, it was his first night and we were rotating through ground work. When the call came to rotate partners, he came off another guy I knew, to me. As we briefly shook hands and exchanged names before rolling, I noticed what I thought was a hunk of bloody flesh hanging out of his nose. My first impression was respect, as he wasn't blinking, and though I wasn't sure exactly how that would happen, it looked pretty nasty.

I motioned to my nose, and said, *"You have a little thing going on there..."* He said, *"Oh, I got a bloody nose and had to jam some tissue in there,"* and he pushed it back up in. Soaked in blood, the tissue had looked like flesh. Though I had not in fact been looking at his sinus flesh hanging out of his nostril, that first impression stuck, and we ended up friends.

Unfortunately he was American Stasi, sent in by his command to get close, and he ended up asking for help when I was short of time, and it now appears his purpose was just to saddle me with extra work and tie me up as he reported back to his superiors everything he could learn about me. I was happy to help a friend, and probably burned more of my scarce time back then than his command had hoped would be possible.

It is what it is, but if someone had wanted to get an insight about me from one of my best friends at the time, they would have been asking him to explain to everyone else who I was, and he could have said anything. I had bestowed upon him the imprimatur of authority in defining me to everyone else, just by being close friends with him.

It is tough to not be friends with these characters when they have read your file, they know how to have all the same interests as you, they know what traits you value or respect in friends, and they show up actively using all that intelligence, soliciting friendship. There will be a lot of freedom-loving Americans with friends like that. If you are a freedom-loving American, I think it almost certain you will have at least one such friend, as that is how it works. The conspiracy does this, specifically so should the need arise, they can define the target to observers, using the imprimatur of their agent's friendship with the target.

The American Stasi wants to do this because once you become a target, you also become a threat of exposure. You could tell others about this criminal surveillance/intelligence operation targeting regular Americans. So the operation will take measures to be able to discredit you later on, if the need arises.

The best friend infiltrator, just like the neighbor they plant next door, is an excellent method by which to do this, since nobody is thinking your best friend, who you approved of, was sent in by the conspiracy to gain that friend-status, or that your neighbor was actually planted next door by a Stasi-like intel operation specifically to exert this type of control, and they did not just come to be your neighbor by chance.

This is not a group of amateurs in the execution of intelligence operations, nor do they shy away from taking active steps to gain control over the flow of information. These are trained intelligence professionals, drawing on possibly centuries of experience in the field of intelligence operations, who constantly wargame against their own positions, and develop techniques and measures to address any weaknesses in their positions based on what they find.

Given no other source claiming Toole complained of a brain implant is apparent, I would question if Toole ever said that, just based on my own experience, and the fact that my family has "family friends" who we believe were sent in to befriend us long before I became an overt target.

Were you to one day see a description of me, given by "old family friends" who had known me for years, or any of my neighbors for that matter, that description would very likely have been written by this operation, and delivered through the agents it infiltrated into my social world. It would likely have been designed to make you see me as however the operation would have wanted me to be seen, such as irrational, or untrustworthy, or even mentally ill. The intelligence world is the hall of mirrors.

From here, Toole had an experience common to targets of the American Stasi:[296]

"Toole told Byrne that people were passing his home late in the night and honking their car horns at him, that students whispered about him behind his back, and that people were plotting against him. Byrne had a talk with him, which he felt, for the time being, calmed him down."

The car-horn thing was actually profiled on ABC News more recently:[297]

"Long-time Hubbard, Ohio, residents Rick and Cindy Krlich told ABC News' "20/20? that everyone in their town has turned against them.

Over the past seven years, they said, horns have been honked 5,000 times by people driving past their house."

I have had the car horn thing, as well as the revving of engines as cars pass, and the extra-loud reverberating bass of an enhanced sound system. Those are all procedures today. Anything to get the target's attention, and remind them they are always being watched and controlled, even while in the privacy of their home - and the world outside their door is entirely against them.

Toole's account however shows, this thing has been infiltrating America for some time now. It is not surprising it is this big, or is looking to overtly take over the nation now.

The next instance of support I would like to cite is difficult to cite, and that itself is noteworthy. On September 11th, when the planes hit the towers, William "Bill" Binney was the fourth in command of the National Security Agency. It was the Director, the Deputy Director, the Director of Operations, and the Director of Technology, who was Bill.

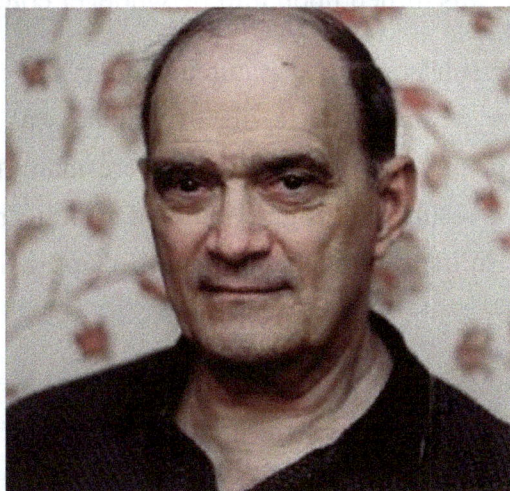

William "Bill" Binney

From that position, Bill oversaw all of the technology development at the NSA. That means Bill had been found by the NSA to be trustworthy enough that he was given full access to all of the most sensitive technologies and secrets at the most technologically sophisticated intelligence agency in the world.

Bill subsequently approached the ICIG, the Intelligence Community Inspector General, which is the oversight agency responsible for making the intelligence community obey the law.

He was concerned about the adoption of a program at the agency which he felt would be used against American citizens illegally. You can see him describe this to the New York Times in an interview here.[298] He was even played by the actor Nicholas Cage in the movie *Snowden,* who related his story to the protagonist, to communicate to the audience how seminal Bill's experience was to Edward Snowden's decision-making. Though beloved and respected by the rank and file in the intelligence community, he was ultimately removed from NSA, and the secret American Stasi was turned upon him by whoever controls it.

Bill was subsequently assaulted regularly in his home by directed energy weapons.[299] He discovered he was not the first person that happened to, and that there were many more victims nationally. As a result, this rogue abuse of American intelligence resources to criminally assault civilians became a life-cause for him.

Now, with that background out of the way, we will present the support for this book's premise which we would like to cite - For a brief time Bill helmed the website, BiggerThanSnowden.com, which featured a raft of highly decorated intelligence officers from the NSA, the CIA, Military Intelligence, private intelligence companies, and prominent citizens who all asserted there was a program in the United States government which was using directed energy weapons to assault Americans in their homes for falling afoul of *something* operating in the US government.

Although Bill was featured on the TV show 60 Minutes[300], and he was renowned and beloved throughout the intelligence community and the media, not one media outlet ever covered this blockbuster story. You have the fourth in command of the National Security Agency saying there was a covert American intelligence community operation, which was not only operating domestically within the United States, and not only operating against American citizens within the United States, but that it was assaulting American citizens with covert directed energy weapons, sometimes even burning them with microwave beams, in their own homes. He went on to allege this entity was doing this arbitrarily and without any form of due process, absent any legal authority, and absent any oversight by any other governmental structure. Notice, that is a blockbuster story, and the media ignored him, and to this day most Americans have no idea this website ever existed.

From the website archive of BiggerThanSnowden.com:[301]

"William Binney's career with the NSA spanned more than 30 years, and in that time, he acquired the title of Technical Leader for intelligence. After September 11, 2001, he was astounded that the agency didn't stop the attacks. He started exposing waste and corruption, through proper legal channels, and faced illegal retaliation as a result. However, he maintained his integrity and was vindicated. Now many refer to him as the original Snowden. In recent years, Binney has engaged in activism in support of the countless victims being tortured with electromagnetic weapons. He began supporting these targeted individuals when he gave a speech at the 2015 Covert Harassment Conference. More recently, in late-2016, Binney along with his

former NSA colleague J. Kirk Wiebe, announced on the Triumph Over Targeting webcast that they were launching scientific surveys to supplement the overwhelming evidence related to these crimes against humanity. He helps targeted individuals understand the bigger picture behind the subjugation of at least tens of thousands of Americans with electromagnetic weapons. He states that it's about subverting democracy to expand the budgets & power of criminal cliques within the military-industrial complex a.k.a. the Deep State."

From here, things went downhill for Bill. The American Stasi amped up its harassment and has been assaulting him with directed energy weapons in his house, forcing him to retreat into his basement, under steel shielding he installed over his living quarters, to try and attenuate the intensity of the beams hitting him. Then one night, Bill awakened to the sounds of explosions, as the operation turned up the power on their weapon, and blew two holes through the steel shielding he had installed to try and diminish the weapon's energy levels. From X, formerly known as Twitter, Bill confirms the attack to another poster:[302]

← **Post**

Bill Binney, Constitutional Patriot
@Bill_Binney   **Follow**   ...

(46) This is true. @realDonaldTrump @GenFlynn

Joint Investigation @Stop007now · Dec 27, 2020
Meanwhile, please help to stop the live running GENOCIDE being conducted by the @usairforce. They are droning the house of @Bill_Binney. He just survived an assassination attempt where Directed Energy Weapons shot holes into the shielding above him!

We will discuss Bill's case in greater detail later in a chapter touching on directed energy attacks by the American Stasi. For now, our first piece of evidence that others of respectable reputations have supported the assertions of this work, would be found at the archive of BiggerthanSnowden.com at the url in the previous endnote, where Bill leads a who's who of highly respected intelligence officers from the NSA, CIA, and military intelligence, as well as doctors, lawyers, and others who have met this machine, who will tell you it not only exists, it is operating against regular Americans, and wielding lethal weaponry in doing so.

In another global story which supports the assertions of this book, it would appear that the directed energy weapons aspect of the American Stasi's operations, is most likely related to the widely publicized Havana Syndrome. (Based upon the anecdotal reports of victims, the "Havana Syndrome" may actually consist of several different types of directed energy weapons, which have all been lumped together by the oddity of any directed energy weapon being fielded against American government officials.)

The Havana episode would appear to show there is some conflict between official segments of the United States government, (such as the State Department, CIA, and Secret Service), and the American Stasi, which is wielding such highly advanced technology that they were able to assault White House staffers, on White House grounds, and Secret Service was helpless to stop them, or even punish them following the attacks.[303]

If there were no conflict, the conspiracy as I see it would simply have exerted influence over both the agencies involved, as well as the news media, and never have allowed the reporting of the attacks to the people.

Regardless, William Binney, as well as the intelligence officers on BiggerThanSnowden.com, all will testify there is some sort of highly matured, criminal conspiracy afoot in the intelligence community in America. While the covert use, by a hidden hand, of thru-wall directed energy to attack and degrade Americans is an incredibly important issue, and we will touch on it to demonstrate the incredibly criminal, and evil nature of what this nation faces, we will not focus on it here. Our purpose here is simply to show you we are not the only voices asserting there is a criminal intelligence operation operative in the United States.

In the 1970's, sci-fi author of such classics as Blade Runner, Total Recall, and Minority Report, Phillip K. Dick found out the FBI and CIA had been spying on him, even installing agents as neighbors to record license plates of all his visitors, despite him not being associated with any criminal activity. Here, he says:[304]

"It was march of '74 that CIA's operation chaos, which was to harass, disrupt, and keep surveillance on American dissidents, was officially abandoned. So the kind of paranoia which Michael Demuth noted, was based on the fact we were harassed, we were under surveillance, we really were. There was no doubt about it whatsoever. I have seen my CIA file, I have seen my FBI file. The CIA opened my mail, the FBI had a file on me. I've seen both... My house was being watched, the license plate numbers of every car which stopped in front of my house were taken... Anyone who visited me, their license plate number was written down by the people next door... I was told the house was being watched, and that eventually the house would be hit, my files would be opened, my papers would be taken, and so it came to pass... When I came

home and found my house consisting of nothing but rubble, ruined, chaos, broken windows, smashed door knobs, blown open files, I said, thank God I am not crazy, I have real enemies."

As we will explain, after extensive study, it would appear the CIA and FBI are partitioned, into two divisions. I have referred to the first division of each agency, which fulfills the agency's stated purpose, (in the case of the FBI, official federal law enforcement activities, and in the case of CIA, actual national security (NatSec) intelligence gathering), as either law enforcement fantasy camp, or national security fantasy camp.

Those fantasy camps, are where they send idealistic patriots, who might otherwise be problematic, to keep them occupied fighting some form of dragon which is not related to the greater conspiracy behind the American Stasi.

Meanwhile, the other, non-fantasy-camp side of the agencies, do the real intelligence work, domestic and foreign, to protect the hold on power of the conspiracy, as described above by Phillip Dick.

It creates the amusing circumstance where, as fantasy camp agents in the law enforcement or national security agencies are often trying to unravel some criminal conspiracy, or stop some terrorist attack, there will be, right down the hall, the real, non-fantasy-camp agents in the very same agency who are actually perpetrating the criminal conspiracies and terrorist attacks, for the benefit of the conspiracy.

Ted Gunderson was a legendary FBI Agent whose nearly 30 year career took him through everything from the investigation into the murder of JFK, to overseeing the organized crime

449

investigations of 26 field offices out of DC, to leading the entire Los Angeles field office.

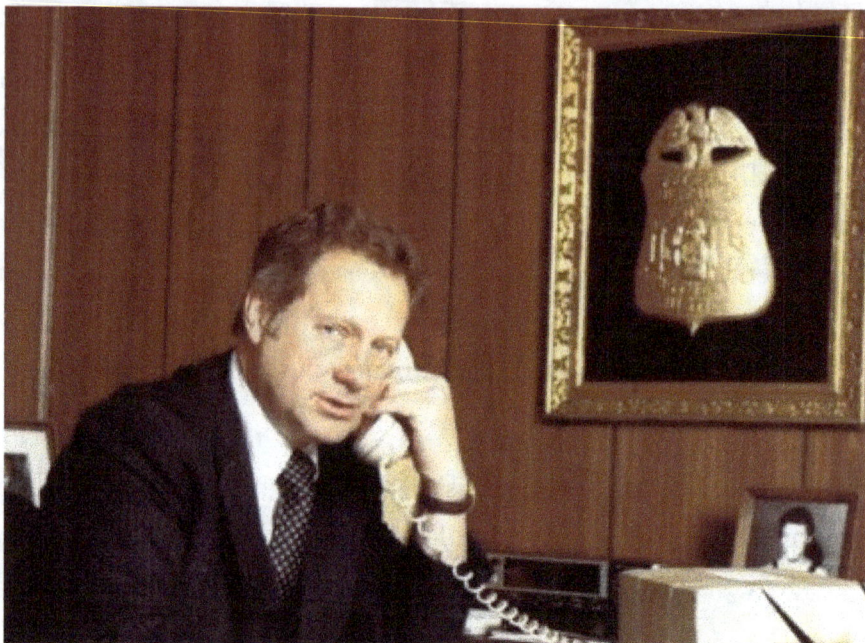

Ted Gunderson, Legendary FBI Law Enforcement Fantasy Camp Attendee

Approached for a supporting affidavit by a litigant named Keith Labella, who was suing the FBI over its failure to produce any files in response to a Freedom of Information Act request (FOIA) for documents related to a massive illegal spying operation he referred to as gangstalking, the retired FBI legend wrote the following in his sworn affidavit:[305]

I have read the complaint in the current action of Mr. Keith Labella against F.B.I. and D.O.J. It is my professional opinion, based on information, knowledge and belief, that the information sought by Mr. Labella in this F.O.I.A. suit regarding "gang stalking," "gang stalking groups," and "gang stalking methods," reasonably describes an ongoing, active, covert nationwide program that is in effect today, and, based on my investigations and experience, has been operational since at least the early 1980's. Since the 1980's gang stalking has increased in scope, intensity and sophistication by adapting to new communications and surveillance technology... These programs are negatively impacting thousands of Americans and severely abusing their civil rights on a daily basis.

Based on my investigative work, which includes intelligence from sources such as active and former members of the Intelligence Services (including the F.B.I., the C.I.A., the N.S.A. and Military Intelligence), information from informants active in criminal enterprises, and, victim testimonies, I have come to the conclusion that thousands of victims have been targeted by an illegal government rogue criminal enterprise that is active 24 hours a day within the U.S. This conspiracy is far too active to be controlled or operated by private enterprise, whose goals are achieving financial gain. These operations require extensive financing with no return on the investment. This program's operations are financed by illegal black operations, i.e., narcotics, prostitution, child kidnapping (children sell at covert auctions for up to $50,000 per child), human trafficking, gambling and other rackets.

I have documentation and know that throughout the U.S., operating 24 hours-a-day and 7 days-a-week, there is a Central Command, located within the U.S., with multiple satellite offices, whose administrators can instantly initiate surveillance, phone taps, and harassment against any individual in the country. They have the technology, financing and manpower to dispense illegal

451

surveillance and harassment against anyone at any time, day or night, I have files on numerous cases of active, programmatic, illegal government harassment currently being conducted against thousands of Americans. This makes the F.B.I.'s former COINTELPRO program, which I worked on, including in a supervisory capacity, look like a Sunday school program by comparison.

I firmly believe that most individuals working in the F.B.I, other intelligence agencies, and the government overall are honest, law-abiding public servants. However, a sophisticated network of rogue operatives has secretly infiltrated the F.B.I., other intelligence agencies, including the C.I.A., and other key government positions. This rogue element seeks personal power and wealth and considers themselves above the law and the Constitution. They are carrying out the aforementioned surveillance and harassment activities in conjunction with organized crime, the cult movement in America, including Satanic cults, other commercial and political interests, and even misguided civic organizations and neighborhood groups. This illegal surveillance and harassment program is being called gang stalking and organized stalking by the victims targeted by it. The victims are targeted for a variety of reasons including government and corporate whistleblowers, parties to financial and employment disputes, parties to marital disputes (usually divorced women), and even jilted paramours. Journalists covering controversial issues, and, even attorneys and private investigators representing unpopular clients or interests, have been targeted by this program.

Individuals targeted by this program have been subjected to illegal and unconstitutional phone taps, illegal re-routing of business and private phone calls for purposes of harassment, illegal audio "bugging," surreptitious entry into home, office, and vehicle, visual surveillance in the home conducted by illegal placement of miniature remote, wireless cameras (often accessible via internet), illegal internet spyware, illegal GPS tracking (often through their own mobile phones), regular fixed and mobile surveillance, mail misdirection, mail theft and tampering, financial and employment sabotage, slander campaigns and community ostracizing, internet disinformation and smear campaigns, poisoning, assaults and murder, illegal set-ups on drug charges and other felony charges, amongst many other civil rights abuses.

In addition to high-ranking members of the F.B.I., other intelligence services, and the government overall, wealthy, powerful members of criminal syndicates, multi-millionaires and the corporate elite are using the government gang stalking program to harass enemies. They can get a targeted individual harassed for the rest of that individual's life (individual cases of gang stalking lasting for over a decade are common). The higher status members of the gang stalking conspiracy initiate the gang stalking and coordinate logistics and funding. Lower echelon government rogue operatives, lower ranking members of the military (in violation of Posse Comitatus), petty criminals and street thugs perform the actual grunt work of daily monitoring and harassment of individuals targeted by the program.

Based on my professional experience, extensive intelligence information and belief, it is my professional opinion that the F.B.I. is involved in, and has investigative files on, the subject of gang stalking, related gang stalking methods, and gang stalking groups

453

in the F.B.I.'s vast intelligence files, that are responsive to Mr. Labella's F.O.I.A. Complaint. Furthermore, I have personally referred numerous victims of gang stalking to the appropriate agents at the F.B.I. for investigation of their cases. I have also furnished the F.B.I. with documentation of an active, international child kidnapping ring probably operated by rogue C.I.A. agents. The F.B.I. has ignored my requests to investigate even though it is their responsibility to investigate kidnappings. I have a contact in Germany who advises me that the C.I.A. has set up secret operations on U.S. military bases for the kidnapping, sale and trafficking of children worldwide. The FBI may be using a unique codename and nomenclature for the gang stalking phenomenon in its records. However, this is a semantic difference, and, in no way changes my professional opinion that the F.B.I. has investigative files on the nationwide phenomenon of gang stalking described in reasonable and specific detail in Mr. Labella's F.O.I.A. Complaint. These F.B.I. files contain information responsive to Mr. Labella's F.O.I.A. Complaint regarding the subject of gang stalking. The F.B.I. and other intelligence agencies are administering and covering up the rogue, covert, government criminal enterprise of gang stalking. The gang stalking phenomenon appears in the records of both the F.B.I. and the N.S.A. in their records pertaining to the Echelon Program, Carnivore System, and Tempest Systems. In addition, the gang stalking phenomenon appears in the records of both the F.B.I. and the N.S.A. in their records pertaining to information collected by Narus systems. Narus is a wholly owned subsidiary of defense contractor Boeing that produces sophisticated, mass surveillance computer systems currently being used by both the F.B.I. and the N.S.A.

Ted was among the most respected legends of the FBI. You

454

can view his curriculum vitae, and see all the cases he was at the center of during his career, at the link for the affidavit.

His assertions are quite extraordinary, and many, such as his reference to the CIA-related Finder's Cult, are beyond the scope of this text. The Finder's Cult was briefly uncovered by a local law enforcement agency, before being covered back up by the CIA.

Before it was covered up, it appeared the CIA and intelligence community were running a private sector cult in the US. The leader of the cult was the husband of a former CIA Officer, and himself a veteran of military intelligence who still maintained some connection to the community.

The CIA had reportedly intervened in the investigation to kill it as "a CIA internal matter," according to official government documents. It was reminiscent of US Attorney Alex Acosta being told Jeffrey Epstein "belonged to intelligence," before quelling his objections and signing off on Epstein's sweetheart plea deal.

The cult was attempting to procure children which were never registered in any government files, so they could presumably "disappear" without attracting attention.[306] It is believed by many observers, myself included, they were procuring children to present to pedophiles in an Epstein-esque blackmail operation, before the conspiracy would promote the pedophiles to high positions in government, where they would then be fully controlled by the blackmail.

Those running the operation appeared to not expect the children to reliably survive the operations, and were looking for ways to minimize any operational exposure from that, by procuring "paperless" children the system would not miss. Though

455

cases such as that are undoubtedly this intelligence operation, in this text we are focusing solely on the ground surveillance operation which you will be able to see with your own eyes. We need you to see this thing yourself, and know it is targeting you, and your children, before delving into the massive scale the operation has grown to, over the decades, and maybe centuries, that the operation has been growing, expanding, and infiltrating everything, from government agencies, to criminal operations, such as street gangs and the drug cartels.

Once you see the surveillance, you will realize such a massive surveillance operation must support a similarly massive intelligence operation in other areas, and that will make the unbelievable aspects of the conspiracy easier to process and understand.

Regardless, Ted Gunderson is one more respected leader in law enforcement who is on record having asserted that he had seen evidence of an American Stasi surveillance operation, extending back at least to the 1980s.

Here in this next link, former New York Governor David Paterson says he was approached by ten New York Legislators, and they all said they felt they were under illegal surveillance by an intelligence type-organization - an organization which he himself feared enough, that he held a press conference to air all the dirty laundry he could possibly be blackmailed over, based upon its threat.

Here, Paterson says,[307]

"There was obviously an element in the police force — and it wasn't Republican or Democrat — it was just out-of-control

456

people who had power that were clearly monitoring a lot of the elected officials. And I was kind of afraid of leaks of inaccurate information about myself." So, besides the pre-emptive admissions of infidelity and youthful indiscretions, he asked Attorney General Andrew Cuomo to investigate the state police.

After the radio interview, Paterson gave a press conference and later told the NY Post, "I just thought it was unusual that over 10 legislators would approach a new governor asking him to take action on the situation, and the individuals were Republicans and Democrats from upstate and downstate."

At the time, there was a story which circulated, which said that he held the press conference where he discussed his affairs, after being threatened by two men, following his swearing-in ceremony. They walked into his office, told him they were government surveillance agents, he had been under illegal surveillance for decades, and they had documented compromising material, and he would work for them or they would reveal it.

Although Paterson was adamant he would run for reelection, in the run-up to the next election he suddenly and inexplicably dropped out of the race.

Another New York politician spoke of the surveillance from another angle. New York Attorney General Eric Schneiderman reportedly told the woman he was beating and raping, as he forced her to perform slave fantasies, that he would ruin her life with surveillance, and then kill her if she resisted.[308]

"Selvaratnam says that Schneiderman warned her he could have her followed and her phones tapped, and both say that he threatened to kill them if they broke up with him."

Judge Andrew Napolitano said Chief Justice Antonin Scalia told him he believed the entire Supreme Court was under illegal surveillance by some organization, and Senator Rand Paul said he felt he and another Senator were being illegally surveilled:[309]

"Judge Andrew Napolitano said on Fox Business Monday that the late Justice Antonin Scalia told him "that he often thought that the court was being surveilled" roughly four or five years ago.

Napolitano appeared on the program to discuss the claim made by Sen. Rand Paul, R-Ky., accusing the Obama administration of spying on him and another senator.

"It's about your own government spying on the opposition party," Paul said on "America's News HQ" last week. "That would be enormous if it's true.""

Rolling Stone Reporter Michael Hastings died in a mysterious car crash, and afterward an investigation of the days preceding his death showed he felt he was being targeted for surveillance by an operation which was following him with aviation and had tampered with his car:[310]

"By the middle of June, though, Hastings, then 33, had become openly afraid. Helicopters are a common sight in the Hollywood Hills, but he had told Jordanna Thigpen, a neighbor he'd become close to, that there were more of them in the sky than usual, and he was certain they were tracking him. On Saturday the 15th, he called Matt Farwell, his writing partner, and said Farwell might be interviewed by the FBI. Farwell was unsettled. "He was being really cagey over the phone, which was odd, very odd," Farwell says. On the 17th, Hastings e-mailed colleagues at BuzzFeed to warn them that "the Feds are interviewing my 'close

friends and associates," he was, "onto a big story," and needed to go, "off the rada[r] for a bit ... hope to see you all soon."

"He was deeply agitated," says The Young Turks host Cenk Uygur...

He had told his neighbor Thigpen that he thought his car had been tampered with, and back at the apartment, he asked his brother to look under it with him. That night, shortly after midnight, he asked Thigpen if he could borrow her Volvo; he needed to "get away.""

He was last seen racing through the streets on a security camera at a restaurant before his car hit a palm tree and exploded, possibly not in that order:[311]

"His Mercedes reportedly hit a tree at high speed, causing the car to burst into flames. But there are some eyewitness accounts which suggest his car exploded before impact."

Also strange was the ejection of the engine from the vehicle, causing it to travel 150 to 180 feet in the opposite direction to his direction of travel. Some have implied that could be consistent with an explosive charge under the engine detonating:[312]

"Witnesses described the car's engine being ejected 50 to 60 yards from the scene."

One national security official said the crash had hallmarks of a vehicular cyberattack, where someone had remotely taken over the vehicle's computer control system and accelerated it to a high rate of speed before crashing it:[313]

"Former U.S. National Coordinator for Security, Infrastructure Protection, and Counter-terrorism Richard Clarke told The Huffington Post that what is known about the single-vehicle crash is "consistent with a car cyber attack."

Clarke said, "There is reason to believe that intelligence agencies for major powers" -- including the United States -- know how to remotely seize control of a car.

"What has been revealed as a result of some research at universities is that it's relatively easy to hack your way into the control system of a car, and to do such things as cause acceleration when the driver doesn't want acceleration, to throw on the brakes when the driver doesn't want the brakes on, to launch an air bag," Clarke told The Huffington Post. "You can do some really highly destructive things now, through hacking a car, and it's not that hard."

"So if there were a cyber attack on the car -- and I'm not saying there was," Clarke added, "I think whoever did it would probably get away with it.""

Clinton mistress Sally Miller describes what every target of the American Stasi sees, famous or not:[314]

"The signs are evident - I'm being followed. I'm being inundated with facebook requests from young, handsome men in search of an older woman, and my phone rings with numbers listed as "unknown." No messages, only more "unknown" phone calls. For no reason, a writer and neighbor who never so much as waved in the 8 years I've lived here wants to be my friend, visit me, come into my house and share her writing tips. Now on my early morning visits to the doggie park, men driving trucks with dark

windows stop to ask directions. Recently I watched two men videotaping the area and they laughingly pointed the camera in my direction. Today, looking out my window, I noted two cars driving slowly by my house. In a few minutes they returned to drive past again. The drivers were hidden behind dark windows... In my neighborhood, two cars driving past my house at the same time constitutes a traffic jam."

More aggressively, she describes being threatened and almost run over in the parking lot of the FBI field office:[315]

"Miller later found the back window of her jeep shot out from the inside with a handful of shot gun cartridges left strewn across the back seat.

When she reported it to the FBI she says she was nearly knocked down outside their office by a car with no plates."

The talk radio industry website "Talkers," rated Radio Host Tom Bauerle as one of the top 100 Radio Talk Show hosts in America. He ran into the American Stasi here:[316]

"The kind of surveillance straight shooter WBEN Buffalo radio talk show host Tom Bauerle was under right in his own backyard would, in the telling, make anyone, even the CIA sound crazy....

In Fall 2013, the observant Bauerle noticed a marked increase in vehicular and pedestrian traffic in his quiet neighborhood in Williamsville, NY.

"I purchased my home in 2003, and you get to know the patterns of neighborhood ebb and flow, and the faces of those who walk, exercise their dogs or jog regularly. But in October 2013, I

461

started thinking 'something is out of the ordinary' here. My home was equipped with a basic security camera system, and I began to track and note the vehicles regularly circling the block or an adjacent side street, and what I noticed was somewhat disconcerting. The same vehicles would not just make frequent 'passes' by my home, they would slow down in front of it and people inside the vehicles would all be looking at my place. I'm a logical guy. So my first thought was that someone was trying to gather 'dirt'' on my personal life. I also saw pedestrians I did not recognize walking past my home at intervals, but changing clothes between "walk byes." That is just classic surveillance 101 stuff."

"In mid-October, I saw and recorded an event that really raised my eyebrows. As I entered my home in broad daylight with a lady friend, someone emerged from an across the street neighbor's side entrance and walked down the driveway to take a photo of us entering my home. When we were leaving, a couple of guys darted behind a tree to photograph the two of us driving away. When I later showed my neighbor the video, he turned ashen and said 'My wife would have been alone in the shower then.' He immediately called Amherst Police and filed a trespass report....

"I figured the surveillance would be short-term, and passing, but it continued and even intensified. On my video, I saw that when I left my home for work, there was a flurry of traffic in my ordinarily docile neighborhood. When I left my home to see friends, the same pattern. There'd be no traffic for an extended period, but when I drove off, suddenly 10 vehicles would be in motion. Repeatedly. Freaky.""

The article ends with Bauerle scoring a legal settlement with who he thought were the perpetrators, however later articles

462

gave the impression he was allowed to gain the evidence he had, so that he would enter into the settlement, and sign non-disclosure agreements as part of it. At that point other parties resumed his surveillance and harassment, and the non-disclosures he had signed constrained his legal options, leaving him forced to endure the harassment in silence.

Brian Mancini was an Army Veteran grievously injured in a roadside bombing in Iraq. He was featured on the TV Show 60 Minutes for his work through his charity Honor House, which he founded after his recovery. It was devoted to helping wounded veterans recover from traumatic injuries.

Brain Mancini, US Army, Ret.

Brian encountered the American Stasi, which proceeded to harass him until he supposedly committed suicide.

Since nobody could believe America would ever have such a domestic intelligence/surveillance operation, or that it could build a civilian informant network which would be willing to harass a selfless and purely good hero-veteran like Brian, none of his family believed him when he tried to explain what was going on.

When 60 Minutes revisited his suicide, they acted as if he must have been crazy:

But as he reached his peak in 2015, Mancini suddenly began to suffer delusions. He imagined the government was spying on him, that members of the Honor House board were with the

CIA. And he thought he was being tracked with cell phones.

Michael Mancini: It was delusional, it was irrational, it was like, a progression.

Nichole Mancini: He wouldn't let us have our cell phones around him.

Michael Mancini: Very paranoid.

Nichole Mancini: His mind had started to almost turn against him. And people that—

Scott Pelley: His mind had turned against him?

Nichole Mancini: Yeah. Brian would often say, "I don't know if this is real or if I had if I dreampt it."

The Honor House board took control of the charity from Mancini. He had been depressed before, but not insane. Last year, Mancini donated his life savings to his church, drove to this remote canal, and shot himself in the head. The betrayal of his mind had been so sudden, so shocking, that his family was certain there must be a cause that no one understood.

There was some speculation online at the time, that the operation targeting Brian might have focused on him as a result of covert research being done on wounded veterans with Traumatic Brain Injuries (TBI) to see how different forms of TBI might affect the ability to influence or even control them mentally.

The speculation was Brian had found himself near an outgrowth of the infamous CIA MK-Ultra mind-control research program, this one targeting wounded vets. Some think Brian just got too close to something they could not have a regular person

465

aware of, and his harassment was designed to remove him from Honor House.

From what I have seen with my own eyes, it is not impossible. However all it would really require to receive that level of targeting would be to become highly successful in a field, and especially highly successful in a way such as Brian did, where you would threaten to become famous, or maybe even be able to run for political office.

People do not know that following such a course in life is not allowed, since most never even try to explore such a path. If you did, and threatened to be successful, you would quickly be introduced to the American Stasi, who would look to put you in your place.

At this point, I want you to think about the story of Brian, a wounded vet who served his country, who fought his way back from horrific injuries, back into a life in society where he was devoted to helping other wounded vets. Imagine him suddenly one day noticing that everywhere he went, groups of people were following him, targeting him, harassing him. He tells his family, and they tell him he is crazy, and in America such a thing is unimaginable. Yet, he knows what he sees.

A man who was devoted to serving others, from his military service defending the nation, to helping wounded vets, was out there, all alone, told he was crazy, as it seemed the entire community turned on him, until he gave up and committed suicide.

Understand, Brian was loyal to us, and we failed him. Every American reading this has a responsibility to make up for that by examining this material, and if you find it credible, helping to spread it, in the ways we will detail later. Do not allow his killers to win. As an American, you have a duty to not let evil win.

To get a flavor for what Brian experienced, go to the video at one of the following addresses, where a random young woman, who encountered the same thing, recorded her own local surveillance as she left her house to go out.[317]

I have been under this my whole life, with overt harassment for over ten years now. That was five minutes of what that young lady experiences 24 hours per day. She never steps out of her house they are not ready to harass her, because they are somehow monitoring her inside her house, most likely from a house right on her street. Don't ask me where they get all the weirdos who get off on doing it, but they do.

24 hours per day, they are watching, to see when she is about to leave, so they can set up outside and be ready for her. I know, it seems impossible. And yet I see it with my own eyes, in my own life, as do others.

Brian Mancini was certainly seeing the exact same thing. He rose too high, could have ended up a Congressman or Senator, and was marked as a potential threat, at which point hordes of evil people came out of the woodwork to drive him mad, exploiting the very brain injury and weakness he endured due to his service to us.

And when he, the man who served everyone else selflessly, needed us the most, none of us were there for him because none of us could imagine this would be in America. But I can tell you firsthand it is, and it is bigger than the Stasi ever was, and just as evil. We need to all, as Americans - Republican, Democrat,

467

Independent, all ideologies, all races, all religions, all ethnicities, unite together as one and destroy this, for Brian. We all failed him before. We will not fail him this time.

I could go on, and cover the use of the CIA and FBI to spy on the Trump campaign. That is a documented use of the full weight of our intelligence machinery in the United States to control an election outcome for the benefit of those in power, and then, having failed, to neutralize a duly elected President of the United States.

They have attempted through the media to make that interlude ideological, to further the divide in the nation and prevent any unification of the population against them, but it would have occurred were Trump a conservative Republican or a progressive Democrat. What mattered to them was, he was not under their control. This thing, and everyone in it, are the enemy of every real American, regardless of race, religion, ideology, or social status.

The Trump campaign-spying operation featured every intelligence technique, from infiltrators sent in to perform human intelligence gathering and manipulation of everyone from Carter Page to George Papadapoulos, to honeypots, to surveillance teams wiring super-sensitive vibration sensors into the superstructure of Trump tower, so they could triangulate waveform arrival times to eavesdrop on the Trump campaign's headquarters, as well as Donald Trump's residence itself.

We could go back in time to discuss the FBI's attempt to use blackmail it gathered to coerce Dr. Martin Luther King Jr. to commit suicide. We could cover the assassinations of JFK or RFK, or the fact "billionaire" Jeffrey Epstein appears to have been merely an actor, with little or no financial acumen or intellect,[318] hired by an intelligence operation and used to lure any influential person he could into a recorded sexual encounter with an underaged girl or a child.[319] We could look at how the FBI was forced to abandon any investigation of him early on, and it was only the dogged detective work of a lone local Police detective which brought him down. We could look at how all it took was someone telling US Attorney Alex Acosta that Epstein *"belonged to intelligence,"* after he began to say Epstein should get a more severe punishment, and Acosta immediately shut up and signed off on a sweetheart plea deal which involved no prison time for Epstein.

But instead I will just tell you that fifteen years ago, I could not have believed something like an American Stasi could exist. Then it entered into my own life, and after five or six years, I was forced to acknowledge, it exists.

It is monitoring every American and maintaining incredibly detailed files on them, with cells embedded in every neighborhood. It is bigger than I would ever have imagined possible, and all of these people had been telling the truth all along, but nobody would believe them.

The goal of this work is to make everyone believe it, by showing you how to see the ground surveillance portion of it in your own neighborhood. From what I see, this thing has matured to the point it is looking to perform an overt takeover of the United States government in the near future, most likely after collapsing the present government. Which means it is coming for all of us, openly, soon, and we do not have much time.

470

Chapter Twelve

A Hidden Conspiracy In The Public Eye

Now we will examine where this operation has bubbled up into people's awareness, to give you an idea of its scale and nature.

Here I will go through various places online where you can see this covert surveillance machine briefly emerging from the shadows, from news stories, to youtube videos posted by its victims. Where feasible, I will put the website link in an endnote, and then quote the relevant portion of the page here in italics, so you do not have to seek out the link. If you wish to research further, you can follow the link, and see the source material.

Where there are videos, I will quote the dialog, however some videos will need to be watched, usually to see the operation in action with your own eyes. I will make note of those.

We will begin with a video you have likely already seen, as we mentioned it earlier. However if you did not watch it earlier, you must watch it now, as it is one of the best representations of this operation in action against an innocent American citizen.

This video, which we showed earlier, shot by an innocent young woman leaving her house, shows exactly how the surveillance will operate as you leave your residence, and how obvious it is once you see it. It will leave no doubt in your mind that at least in some spots, there is a hostile surveillance operation in America targeting random, innocent people. I will guarantee you, unless you live in the most remote, rural area, you have similar operatives in your neighborhood, right now, and they are periodically watching you. You may find the video at: https://www.bitchute.com/video/t2Z2f1SEqAlU/ [320]

If it has been deleted from those locations, visit AmericanStasi.com, where we will locate the most recent upload.

Notice at 18:21, the guy pushing the baby carriage, holding his phone in a position with the camera pointing at her:

You have seen Ray Epps do it, you have seen Hippie Boy do it, and you have seen a driver in a car do it, in southern California. You have even seen a picture of a guy in a car, doing it to my house. Again, I see that type of surveillance, even a much more aggressive form of it, everywhere I go. We will link to more of these types of videos at AmericanStasi.com.

This is just a massive domestic intelligence/informant network, created in the model of the East German Stasi - which was noted for similar "Zersetzung" harassment operations on regular citizens. It is probably run in the nation under the guise of training operations, I assume under auspices of CIA. You thought CIA isn't allowed to operate domestically? Overstock CEO Patrick Bryne's friends at the FBI said to him, things have changed:[321]

"They explained that in 2008 a law was passed that gave authority to the Director of the CIA to sign a piece of paper and, in a sense, "take the steering wheel" of the FBI...")

Although from an evidentiary perspective this next video is not overly impressive, it is a must-watch to see the way these domestic surveillance teams perform the tactic of "mobbing" in a store, to try and intimidate a targeted individual.[322]

That is what the young girl in the first video would have seen at the store she was driving to – a completely new set of people, different from those who sent her off from her home, surrounding her. I have seen this myself personally. These people are swarming this guy in the store in an effort to intimidate him:

That corner was empty when he walked into it, in a mostly empty store. Those people flooded into the corner, glaring at him, he left, looking back over his shoulder in that pic, he came back quickly just to see how many people were there, and the corner was empty again, with nobody there, after just a few seconds:

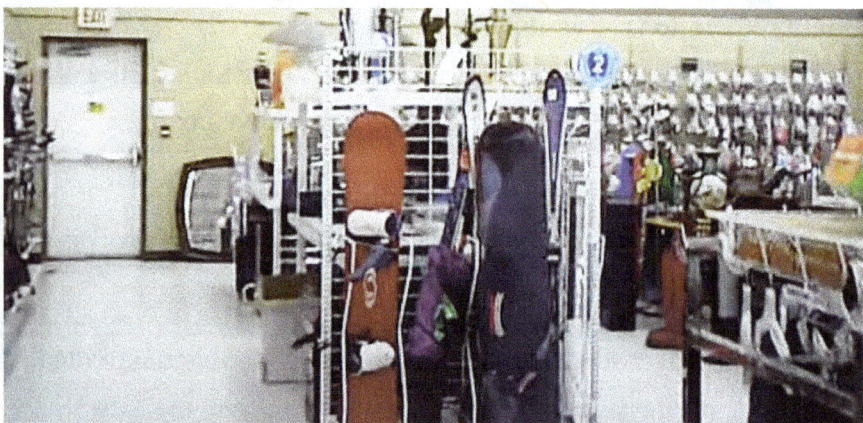

I actually have a relative, also under surveillance, who walked into a BJ's, and lost their followers. They were in an aisle, when a BJ's stock boy came to the end of the aisle, saw them, and turned and yelled at the rest of the store, "They're over here!," and walked off. Within moments, the mob materialized around them as followers rushed to the aisle.

These people are the people in your neighborhood who follow people around, spy on their neighbors, and run their children as assets against your's in the schools. East Germany had them, and so do we. Much like Jan 6th rioter Ray Epps, they have regular jobs, regular homes, regular families, and to all outward appearances, are just regular citizens. You cannot connect them to this thing. But clearly they're a part of something, we just cannot pin down yet exactly what it is. They have doubtless amassed a mind-blowing file on you, just as we all have mind-blowing files, even though you have never laid eyes on them.

I would estimate it is presently between 4 and 10% of the population nationally, with that percentage being higher in some places and lower in others. Their informants may have befriended you, and gathered data on you for your local neighborhood archivist. You will know at least a couple of them, as they want their people to have first degree connections to everyone. Had you not known any, your local archivist would have noted that, and some would have drifted into your circles and befriended you.

The most common surveillance they will perform is shopping surveillance, ie following members of their community through stores to catalog what they buy. Most towns, for this reason will have operatives arrayed through parking lots of shopping centers, waiting for orders to follow targets. They most often perform their shopping surveillance in a low-key fashion, following you through stores covertly, handing you off from one to another, aisle to aisle, cataloging what you purchase by standing behind you on the checkout line, often covertly photographing your haul on the conveyor belt with their cell phone as it is being rung up, while pretending to text someone, or check messages.

Everyone gets such a follow at least every few years, to polish their file. Mobbing is fairly rare, and reserved for recalcitrant targets, and people who have made the wrong surveillance person angry somehow.

Here, for whatever reason, their operation is attempting to intimidate this guy, and so they all flooded around him in an overt display. Note, they were toning it down because they knew he was filming. Had he not been filming, they would have been much more overt and openly hostile. Sometimes they will even loudly comment to each other disparagingly about the target. If confronted about that, they will deny it, and allege the target is crazy or paranoid. They are impressively good gaslighters, and the tactic is meant to irritate and frustrate.

Next up, John Lang was a small business owner who fell afoul of this machine when he complained to the local newspaper about license plate readers deployed in his town. The machine began flooding cars and pedestrians by his house, and he began videotaping. He stored his videos on his youtube channel, at the following address: https://www.youtube.com/@langmarine1910 .

Here is an enhanced still from one video which he filmed, of somebody pointing some piece of high technology at his house from across the street, as the driver talks on his cell phone:[323]

John was convinced it was the Fresno PD harassing him, however I am not so sure, since I would assume Fresno PD cannot operate across the nation, and what we see is country-wide. What John documents here parading in front of his house, I have seen over a thousand miles away, and other targets have documented it across the country.

Elements of Fresno PD would have been told by this conspiracy to show up in some places, and act intimidating. However it is unclear how much local Police know about the criminal nature of this operation. Whether they knew it was a criminal harassment operation by a criminal conspiracy, or whether they were told FBI Agents needed help with a show of force at a domestic terrorist's house, is unknown. It may prove locality-dependent, with some departments taken over by the conspiracy and filled with dirty cops, and others entirely clueless.

Regardless, I would assume what really targeted him was this national conspiracy, which is not law enforcement, though it seems to have acquired some sort of federal law enforcement authority. Whether it is based out of an official federal agency or organization, or not, is yet to be determined.

John's story ended with him Tweeting to a reporter:

John Lang ▸ **Corin Hoggard ABC30 Action News**
January 15 at 6:41pm

Corin, you want some news? Corrupt Fresno Cops are going to try and kill me this weekend, possibly tonight. This is no joke. Please follow up on my story regardless of what happens or what version the cops and the fresnobee come up with. Please check out www.jodymurray.com and my youtube site: https://www.youtube.com/cha.../UCTMI9Ncxd-jhZ81s4z3XA6w/videos

Thank you..

He said the van pictured below had delivered some men to the empty house next door, and he felt he was about to be killed:

Shortly thereafter his house was seen on fire, and a Police Lieutenant which surveyed the immediate aftermath once the fire was put out, told the media John had been stabbed in the back and was dead on his kitchen floor. Later authorities said the autopsy found John had stabbed himself to death, and set his own house on fire:[324]

"The Fresno County coroner has ruled the death of a man found in a burning central Fresno home in January as a suicide. Fresno police originally reported that John Lang, 51, had been stabbed in his abdomen and upper back on Jan. 20... Tony Botti, a spokesman for the Fresno County sheriff and coroner, said Thursday that Lang had "three superficial, self-inflicted stab wounds" to his chest and no cuts on his back, despite initial reports by law enforcement... Botti said investigators believed Lang started the fire himself. Fresno police Lt. Burke Farrah, head of the department's homicide unit, said the confusion about the wounds was the result of incorrect information released at the scene by Lt. Joe Gomez, the department's public information officer... "Joe made a mistake," Farrah said. "This is an

aberration. Typically, we are very careful."... Five days before he died, Lang left ABC30 reporter Corin Hoggard a Facebook comment saying: "Corrupt Fresno cops are going to try and kill me this weekend, possibly tonight. This is no joke."

The next video is a local Texas TV news station segment which documents the experiences of a young Texas woman, who was one of several young women who are apparently being drugged and raped by their local domestic surveillance unit.

https://www.youtube.com/watch?v=V46U-hiu5Yc

From the segment:

" Cynthia Verbeth is moving. Her home, she says has become a house of horrors. She says, "I feel that I've lost my mind. I've lost my life."

Incident reports from law enforcement tell the tale numerous break-ins at the address, vandalism to her car, her motorcycle, her computer.

Verbeth believes she's being targeted "Everything, they just went through everything!" But sheriff's detectives had little to go on because the vandals though often destructive, stole nothing, even from her portable safe, drilled into and torn apart, the contents, the jewelry, remained untouched.

Verbeth... suffered months of oddness, "...coming into the front door and I touched the doorknob and it just falls into pieces." Lights left on, doors open, furniture moved, her clothes dryer disassembled, her friends say they noticed the strange happenings. They tell the I-team they even witnessed a gas oven left turned on, "As soon as you walk in the house you'd smell gas in the house so the whole house smelled from gas so I immediately turned it off and opened up the doors but I mean I think it doesn't just turn on by itself they'd been running for a good length of time..."

Verbeth says all these happenings culminated in an assault. The 39 year old believes someone drugged the food in her home and returned later to rape her. "I know something happened to me because a woman knows." She filed a Police report and was briefly hospitalized with signs of sexual assault....

Verbeth is not alone. Others in San Antonio have contacted the I-team and described similar types of occurrences. Linda Johnson says somebody poisoned her water supply with heavy metals in Northwest San Antonio. Then there is her story about the bracelet which went missing and then reappeared. Police, she says have stopped listening to her, and like Verbeth, she too believes she has been sexually assaulted, though she never filed a Police report. "I've gone to doctors many times, and I have been to the rape crisis center for counseling."

The report briefly touches on other rapes in the area which appear related to Verbeth's, but which local Police have been completely unable to stop.

It also notes, her troubles began when she began dating a high profile target of the domestic surveillance machine, Dr John Hall, a practicing physician who was actually one of the members of Bill Binney's website, mentioned earlier, BiggerThanSnowden.com. He himself became a target after dating, and attempting to help a local woman who was being assaulted with directed energy weapons by the local surveillance team. They took offense, and now he is targeted too.

In a normal nation, these types of things would be front page news across the nation, however in America, the American Stasi has heavily penetrated and subverted the national news media, and it suppresses any mention of these cases, leaving the victims to suffer alone, without the support of either the local law enforcement machinery, or the national news media.

In this case, the local surveillance operation in San Antonio appears to be using their overwatch capabilities in the neighborhood to facilitate their entry into the houses of young women they pick, while the women are out at work. Once inside the houses, they drug the women's food.

They most likely then observe the women in their houses, either on cameras left behind or using thru-wall tech, to confirm they eat the food. When they observe the women go unconscious, they re-enter the houses and rape them. The women discover this the next morning, after the drugs wear off. With the backing of the local surveillance infrastructure, it is a zero-risk crime which will never catch up with them. Local Police claim to be unable to solve the crimes, but even if they could, the Stasi would pull rank, as with Epstein, and shut any case down. Meanwhile, the surveillance operators continue to break into the women's houses, and leave indications they were there, as a form of intimidation and continuing torture.

Unfortunately this is the power the American Stasi holds. It appears to have secured some sort of authority within the law enforcement community which allows it to simply order local law enforcement to abandon criminal investigations. You have seen what happened to Police Chief James Burke, who refused to back down in the face of this operation as he attempted to unravel a serial killer case, which may have been some sort of local surveillance commander killing prostitutes.

Burke ended up serving four years on trumped-up federal charges, was nearly charged with possessing narcotics inside the prison, almost lost his pension, and then nearly had to repay $1.5 million to the county. In addition, he cannot even walk in a park without being arrested, and charged with soliciting sex and indecent exposure, and he, a former Chief of Police, is powerless.

Another case where the local surveillance was devoted to harassment would have been the case of Bryce LaLiberte.

Bryce was a well-known young writer looking to break into online political and cultural commentary. He disappeared for a while, and then re-emerged to publish a piece in an online publication called The American Sun, explaining his absence. He subsequently asked them to pull the article, however an archived file of the article exists.[325] In it, he writes:

I am aware of the likelihood organizations such as Masons were conscripted into my torture, employing tactics of paranoia-inducing sabotage and surveillance originally founded in regimes such as East Germany.

For the past five years, probably longer, I have been stalked and surveilled by numerous organizations at various times, I have been made to feel perpetually unsafe even in my own home, without respite to the law or law enforcement for actions that perpetually bordered on the illegal but which are, or precisely because they were enforced by law enforcement officials under various "official" guises, impossible for a poor individual such as myself to fight against. How is an ordinary American citizen to fight against forces called down upon him by the highest office in the land?

My encounters with various facets of the rulers that be, particularly with what might be popularly called "The Illuminati," have involved Masons, homegrown internet hackers acting (unwittingly, I believe) on behalf of higher ups, Anonymous, "Industry," FBI, Thelemites, encounters with UFOlogists, demonologists, various zealots of innumerable doctrines produces a strange tale that is mostly unbelievable and designed, for the most part, to be unbelievable.

Whenever you encounter those who have been exposed to this machine, understand they will sound deranged to you. You have been lied to your entire life, told conspiracies are bunk, and those who peddle them deranged and to be shunned. Powerful groups never work in concert to advance their position, everyone abides by Marquis de Queensbury rules, there is no surveillance in your neighborhood right now watching you, you could produce a hot idea and turn it into a multi-billion dollar fortune, and run for President and then expose the corruption in DC.

You are told nobody in power is actively, right now, taking any active measure to protect their hold on power, and keep you contained, such as by deploying surveillance, neighborhood by neighborhood, to watch everyone. Nobody is assessing, and on occasion intervening in the lives of children to derail them, as they develop into the next generation of adult who could pose a threat to their control, even though to do so would be easy, and nobody would believe such an organization could exist in America.

So you begin, really, with no firm grasp of reality. Then you have these targets, who themselves had no firm grasp of reality. Out of the blue, they are exposed to an unimaginable, horrifying reality, and then they are subject to the professional psychological headgames, gaslighting, and psyops of a domestic intelligence machine which is well practiced in gaslighting its victims, so if they speak out, they will sound crazy and nobody will believe them. I have no doubt Bryce ran into the American Stasi, and they did a job on him.

Bryce began to intrude into that world, where power is apportioned, and he saw the machines you have been told do not exist. You see him say they dosed his food with LSD, and think

484

him crazy. But they know you will think him crazy if he asserts that, and they dose his food specifically to make his story unbelievable, while knowing they are shouldering no risk, since nobody will believe him.

He mentions the Masons. When I am followed, there will often be Mason stickers on cars. Are they Masons? Or do they just want me to tell people I am followed by Masons, because it will degrade by credibility? He mentions demons. As you will see at AmericanStasi.com, they have a technology, which they have deployed on me, which can mimic the paranormal. How better to discredit someone truthful, than to make the story they tell sound unhinged? I recorded my encounter with their tech, so you can actually hear what transpired, but even so, it's nearly unbelievable.

In short these stories will tend to be unbelievable, because the people inflicting the stories on the targets will make them unbelievable as part of a procedure to make the target unbelievable, should they ever try to tell anyone. This entire operation is very sophisticated. It's been doing this a long time.

All of which ignores the psychological effects of living 24/7, even in your own home, in some combination of the movies Enemy of the State, 1984, Brave New World, The Exorcist, and The Twilight Zone - and doing it for years, or even decades. I have done it, it is a definite stress on your neurological structures, and it never abates. There is a reason the East Germans called it "Zersetzung," which is German for, "decomposition." It is designed to break down normal individuals quite effectively.

Be understanding and empathetic when encountering the people who have labored under this machine. Their path has not

485

been easy, they have acclimated to things you could not even imagine encountering, and they will inevitably endure damage along the way. Remember, they are still, deep inside, your countrymen, and they have been wronged, horribly.

Bryce died of a heart malady at 30 years of age, however given the stress he was under, and the potential technologies deployed on him, I would assume it was not unrelated to his targeting.

Another tragic case was already described - Army soldier and IED blast survivor Brian Mancini, who encountered this machine and ended up committing suicide due to the stress.

There are many well-documented cases of people who were targeted due to rising to positions of power or fame which they were not allowed to occupy, but with these units deployed throughout the nation, invariably bad apples will rise to positions of power, and they will begin harassing random people as well, just to enjoy the feelings of omnipotence. Here, a young woman is being followed by lookouts for other people who break into her house to frighten her, by moving furniture and opening windows, so she will know someone was in her house while she was out.

San Diego mom thinks she's the victim of "community stalking"

From the news piece:[326]

Facika Tafara thinks she may be the victim of a bizarre practice called gangstalking or community stalking.

"It's like an alternate reality, really," Tafara said. "It's spooky, and it's my understanding that if this is actually what it is, it can go on for years."

Community or gang stalking is an eerie practice that takes aim at your psyche to make you almost feel like you're going crazy.

In Tafara's case, she said she would notice strange things out of place in her house when she would get home from work, such as her windows being opened, dresser drawers opened, and she said she even found a camera inside the bedroom of her 11-year-old son.

"It's so creepy, I had a bolt put on the door and I'm having my son sleep in here with me," she said.

"Are people following me? And then I started to wonder also well how do they know when I'm here and when I'm not here then?" - Farah found this small camera in her 11 year old son's bedroom...

Community stalking is not some group of random people in the community just joining together and working together that seamlessly, as a unit, and employing advanced surveillance technologies and techniques. That is a recruited and trained neighborhood unit of the American domestic surveillance machine, the Amerian Stasi, outfitted with all the advanced domestic surveillance equipment such an agency would be issued.

487

In another case, anti-vaccine activist and former pharmaceutical executive Brandy Vaughan ran up against this when she challenged vaccine requirements for children. She made the following video, and ended up being "found unresponsive"[327] at age 44, by her son, before being declared dead.

Brandy Vaughan

From the video:[328]

The first one happened when I was coming back from the capital rally in Sacramento against SB 277 and I came home with a friend to my Hide-A-Key being on my doorstep open to the key. And the story behind this was a year ago when I bought my house I hid that deep in the bushes and six months ago I had looked for it because I thought well it's probably not a good idea to have a key to my house outside mine, right outside my door. I couldn't find it.

But when I came back from Sacramento that one time, it was about two months ago, that key was on my doorstep open to the key. That day I had my locks changed and I called an alarm service and I installed a $3,000 alarm system.

Two days later, so what happened apparently, is someone

opened the door, the front door, went through the front door, picked the lock, and my alarm went off and they immediately disarmed it with the master code, which nobody had but me. I made sure nobody else had that code, and they disarmed it at the panel and with that code, according to the alarm company.

At 3:45 in the morning somebody entered in through the front door, the alarm went off, they disabled the alarm by putting in the master code right away into the panel, and then at 3:46 in the morning my hallway monitor sensor went off, so someone went down the hall. And then at 3:48 someone opened my dining room window and then closed it right away. And then if you notice the dining room window actually faces out towards the backyard which is much more private than the front door which they used to enter that time, and then they went over to the keypad, entered the code again, and then left through the front door at 3:49.

After the incident I talked to some security experts who have actually done intimidation for corporations and they explained a few things. They said, well, they were probably tapping your place so everything I say and do in here is listened to if not watched. And then opening of the back window because it's a much more private way to get in for future reference for future visits.

There is more at the video. I do not think Brandi was dealing with a special "Big Pharma" intimidation unit brought in from out of town. I think she encountered the regular neighborhood domestic surveillance operation, which was told to frighten her, to dissuade her from entering the political arena.

She was a beautiful woman, intelligent, headstrong, with

beliefs and principles. People liked her. I saw the video, and I liked her. She was already getting to be a moral, principled, natural leader who people followed. Domestic intelligence, which runs the domestic surveillance, is under strict orders to keep people like that, who are uncontrolled, out of politics.

They tell you the great thing about our nation is anyone can be anything, even run for political office. But that lie only persists because nobody ever tries. I wrote a political book, and I have experienced everything from harassment surveillance, to honeypot operations, to being hit in the night by Directed Energy Weaponry, as I will detail later.

My guess is Brandi's neighborhood archivist, after assigning coverage for tracking her to rallies, and analyzing her speeches, and looking at the decades of surveillance they already had on her just as a regular citizen, predicted she might one day run for office. I think what she encountered was designed to ease her out of the political realm, before she would need to be killed.

Her death is a mystery. According to the coroner,[329] she suffered bilateral pulmonary thrombosis, meaning at least two massive blood clots blocked off blood flow through her lungs and suffocated her. At age 44, in the physical condition she appeared to be in, it seems quite unusual.

On the other hand, you have a woman who is a top-level target of the American Stasi, a group which, according to Bill Binney, is fielding directed energy weapons, which it fires through walls at people in their homes. You have to ask, given that, would it be a higher probability a thin, healthy 44 year old female, heading for political stardom, dies from a random bilateral

490

pulmonary thrombosis, or would it be more likely domestic intelligence accidentally turned up The Beam™ too high and triggered a clotting effect in her blood with the microwaves?

You see the problem, and why I am willing to risk death or being crippled to resist this and inform the nation. This is not America. American men do not do this to young women. Young mothers. Young single mothers. This is pure evil, and worth fighting, at any cost. I hope to find my fellow American patriots feel the same and will join me in this call to arms.

In this section we are only describing the act of stalking, so we will not have an inordinately large number of such cases to characterize, since the vast majority of these cases do not make the news. To be noteworthy, targets will usually need to die or engage in a shooting themselves, and leave behind evidence of the targeting.

As an example, were I not web savvy, and unusually aggressive, nobody would ever have heard of my own case. There are at least tens of thousands of innocent Americans, perhaps hundreds of thousands, who endure such harassment operations every day.

I am convinced that just about every American is actively affected by the surveillance covertly, through such varied means as hidden interventions to derail life-opportunities, or the use of directed energy weapons to subtly degrade an individual's health.

Much of this operation's mission objective at the neighborhood level, seems to be keeping everyone in the neighborhood occupationally constrained, running on the treadmill of life while still falling behind, almost in an enslaved fashion, so nobody can rise to a level where they might be able to break free of the system and live their own life freely, without the need to slave away every day of their lives for a subsistence living.

I believe they do this, even to the extent of assigning a handful of vehicular units to create traffic jams on the highways every day, to waste the free time of commuters on their way to and from work, so they will have less free time to be "problematic."

I myself have been trapped in an engineered traffic jam, which I caused to disappear entirely within moments, merely by pulling to the side of the road and sitting for a few minutes. The rest of my trip was driven at 75 mph non-stop once I picked up and resumed moving. My vehicular units, not knowing if I intended to sit by the side of the road for five minutes or five hours, did not have the vehicular assets to maintain the traffic jam around me indefinitely, and within minutes my surveillance, which had been obstructing traffic ahead of me, exited the highway and cars began moving.

When I wrote about this on my website, one of my readers immediately pointed me to the video here,[330] which shows a vehicle creating a traffic jam during a morning commute, by driving at ten miles per hour on the freeway. In the still below, where a vehicle is pulling out from behind him, you will notice, he has shut off one headlight, the signal surveillance vehicles use, to notify law enforcement who are aware of the illegal surveillance operation, that they are operational, and should be left alone:

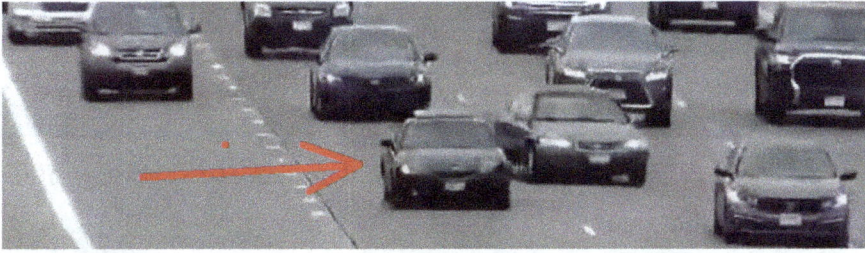

Ask yourself how prolifically surveillance must be creating traffic jams, that not only has it been caught on video, and published online, but on top of that, one of my readers immediately can point me to the video to document it.

Regardless, he apparently encountered a highway patrol officer who was not aware of the secret society of surveillance people, or who did not notice his far side headlight was out, who immediately pulled him over and forced him to wait for a tow.

Much of what I say will sound crazy, because you have not seen the American Stasi firsthand yet, and do not know how badly those in power do not want to lose power to you. But once you see this machine, you will realize it has nothing to do with law enforcement, or national security. Its entire purpose is making sure you can never rise to a point in life that you can compete with those who hold power.

To that end, assigning a handful of its vehicular surveillance units each day to the highways, to drive slow during rush hour and jam it up, is an effective use of resources to make sure thousands of people, and you, cannot create a side-hustle which would allow an escape from the system's treadmill. To the surveillance, it's not insane, it's merely an effective use of resources to make sure everyone stays busy and under control. Because if everyone stops being under control, their little secret club will cease being able to pay them their benefits for surveilling you.

493

Those who refuse to be kept under control, or who appear as a threat for some reason, will get the overt harassment operations, as I have. This will sound improbable to the newcomer, who will say surely America cannot be that bad. However, I would urge you to contemplate what you have seen so far.

Just the covert surveillance is an affront to the very spirit of America. We real Americans do not want to live in a surveillance state, which charts our movements when we leave our house. Once that Rubicon is crossed - making something real Americans would not want - things begin to snowball rapidly.

Now you need to control who is allowed to know this thing exists. That means you need to control who works the poles for the utilities. That means you need control over the union.

Now you are an intelligence agency controlling a domestic union, which has effects on elections. Now you really can't let anyone honest know, or attain any status or political power to oppose you. So you take over more things, to protect your operational security. Now a citizen finds out and opposes you. If you let them expose your operation, your life, and the lives of all your people are ruined, so you have to harass and intimidate them.

Now you are a domestic intelligence agency, exerting control over your nation's elections, controlling who rises in society, and harassing innocent citizens over free speech. Now you have to take over the media, so it will not hear of this and report it. And it will keep snowballing, as you try to control more and more, getting in deeper and deeper, until you have to control even more.

And as it progresses, you start monitoring everyone, listening in houses, corrupting law enforcement, even controlling elections. Now you've hit a point where you have so transgressed, that real Americans will want to kill you if they find out. That kind of motivation will easily produce even more extreme behaviors, as well as a need to abolish every last vestige of liberty which might threaten you, all while keeping the secret, assiduously. I have seen this thing, and that is where we are right now.

The scale of the operation I have seen is so large, they could not allow random people to even accumulate large amounts of money, or have businesses which are too successful. If they allowed that, somebody might then run for office, and from there exposure is never more than one press conference away. They need total control, and for you to absolutely have no clue.

So now the control needs to go granular, it has to be neighborhood-ized into local cells, which get assigned a specific raft of people, and everyone gets watched, and suppressed if they look like they are about to rise too high. And now you really can't let anyone know. You need to get control of the news media, and the law enforcement apparatus, and the Inspector Generals. You need to get in the schools, and make sure you are on top of the kids from the very beginning. And to do that, you need to get your own kids operational.

The secret is so big now, they need to do whatever it takes, because when the nation finds out, everyone will want blood. And with 150 million gunowners, that could end up being the result.

Once you see just the surveillance, and how extensive it is, you will realize that is the path this thing inevitably took. And suddenly them having their kids report intelligence to them on the other local school children, and build files on them - it is not so unusual. Suddenly you will say, of course our elections are rigged. Suddenly, you realize there is no way this extensive a machine missed 9/11 – it had to see it coming – and it let it happen.

However, by the fact something that criminal, and that antithetical to the most basic American values exists, you can extrapolate out what else it must be doing, from rigging elections, to controlling the media. Chief among its other activities, however, must be making sure anyone honorable, such as yourself, can never rise to a high position in society, from which you could pose a threat to it. You must be kept a peasant, by this hidden hand.

Moreover, it will need to make sure that if your children seem decent and honorable, the surveillance in the schools will be extensive enough to find them, so that their wings may be clipped too, and their academic development sabotaged.

If you think the American Stasi is real, that will, by simple inference mean, you and your children will have been consigned by that operation to boring, mundane lives as peasants, and any chance either you or your children have for true success in life, will need to be picked up by the conspiracy's surveillance, and sabotaged by the operation, outside of your direct observation.

I know, it's unimaginable any fellow American would stoop to this level, but stoop to this level they have. I will tell you now, we can expose and destroy the surveillance – its biggest advantage – and we can take back our freedom. I just need your help.

Chapter Thirteen

Technical Harassment – Beware of "The Beam^{TM}"

Once the American Stasi's machine focuses on you, it will begin with intimidation operations, using its vast civilian network of volunteer spies/harassers. The message is clear – you need to acquiesce and recognize their control of the country, or else. That was essentially their entire message to me.

It is possible if you bend the knee in some fashion, they will officially pretend to ignore you while simply keeping covert surveillance on you, or maybe even recruit you to harass others. Some report their surveillance is continuous no matter what they do. In my case, I rebelled and resisted, and my conflict with them seems to only escalate day in and day out.

From following and intimidation, the operation will progress to electronic harassment, or technical harassment – the use of weapons which direct energetic emissions at you which strike you after they pass through the walls of your house. This allows them to physically assault you in your home, while leaving no trace.

Here we will detail a few of the most credible cases of electronic harassment, to establish in the public eye this is a real phenomenon. I should add, I have seen some of these technologies in my own harassment, and can attest they are real, and cannot be

497

mistaken for something benign. I deem it most likely these individuals described here are all giving accurate accounts of their experiences, and I can attest beyond all shadow of a doubt that the American Stasi has put an inordinate amount of effort and resources into developing a rather extensive tool kit of energetic weapon technologies to attempt to both silence, and constrain the advancement of, regular Americans within our supposedly capitalist system. Meanwhile, they have implemented a covert dictatorial government, just below the surface of American society, with outright fascist control over the business environment and the economy.

Before we begin, we should reiterate that for a brief period, many of the most respected names in the American intelligence community, led by William Binney the former fourth in command at the National Security Agency, opened up a website, asserting that the intelligence community had begun operating domestically, and was fielding directed energy weapons against regular American civilians.

Together with a who's who of former US intel community officials, Bill's website said that it had come to their attention the United States intelligence community was fielding directed energy, electromagnetic weapons (DEWs), such as microwave weapons, operationally, on US soil, against innocent American civilians, without any judicial imprimatur or government oversight of their operations. It went on to note this rogue operation was unacceptable, and it called on Americans to act.

The website was located at the web address https://BiggerThanSnowden.com . [331]

You would think a legend as big as Bill Binney, combined with a who's who of intelligence community personnel, all saying that Americans were being tortured, in America, by the intelligence agencies of the nation, would provoke some mention in the media, but no. The media is apparently infiltrated and controlled by the American Stasi, which forbade all mention of it.

The site disappeared sometime in 2019. All that remains of it are the screenshots on the Wayback Machine, reproduced here to show how many illustrious names supported the project. To read the archived site, visit the link in the note. I will blow up Bill's biography, as in a moment we will delve deeper into his case. The other individuals are a melange of CIA officers, Military Intelligence Officers, a British MI-5 Intelligence Officer, private investigators, doctors, lawyers, a DARPA scientist, and others, all with similarly illustrious curriculum vitaes.

Here is the website:

Electromagnetic Weapons are Being Used to Torture and Subjugate Countless American Citizens...

The Whistleblowers:
(updated February, 2017)

William Binney
NSA Veteran, Technical Director
William Binney's career with the NSA spanned more than 30 years, and in that time, he acquired the title of Technical Leader for intelligence. After September 11, 2001, he was astounded that the agency didn't stop the attacks. He started exposing waste and corruption, through proper legal channels, and faced illegal retaliation as a result.

John DeCamp, U.S. Army Capt. (Ret).
Army Intelligence Officer; Lawyer; Senator
John DeCamp first learned about the machinations of the Deep State while serving as an Army intelligence officer in Vietnam, under former CIA director William Colby. Upon retirement from the army, DeCamp served as a Nebraska State Senator, and also established a successful legal practice. However, he didn't rest on his laurels. In the early 1990s,

Dr. Corkin Cherubini
Educator; Superintendent

Dr. Cherubini is a retired educator that spent much of his career championing the cause of civil rights and equality for all. His noble efforts earned him the John F. Kennedy Profile in Courage Award. In 2014, he wrote about the use of electromagnetic weapons, and other stealth warfare tactics, on an exponentially increasing number of civilians. He especially focuses on organized stalking, or "gang-stalking," which is a psychological warfare tactic - derived from COINTELPRO and Zersetzung - that is commonly used in conjunction with electromagnetic weapon assaults in order to further terrorize, isolate, and breakdown victims. Dr. Cherubini, himself, became targeted by these stealth weapons and sly repression tactics. He believes that he was targeted due to his dedication to human rights activism. Learn More.

Cheryl Welsh, J.D.
Investigative Journalist; Lawyer

Cheryl Welsh is a respected journalist in the field of research related to the Deep State's illegal use of electromagnetic weapons on American citizens. She became aware of these "experiments" - that have now transformed into treasonous crimes - in 1987 when she was targeted & assaulted with electromagnetic weapons for purposes of sadistic torture, subjugation, and behavioral control. Welsh took a stand in 1996, by launching her human rights website, Mind Justice. Since then, she has made numerous appearances on large television networks, and has delivered many excellent interviews. Her writing is prolific and highly praised, as well. Welsh's articles serve as a great resource for the growing number of victims being deceived; attacked; exploited; and enslaved by electromagnetic weapon assaults. Read more.

Mark Phillips
CIA Veteran

Mark Phillips is a veteran of the Central Intelligence Agency, and he has witnessed firsthand the mind & behavioral control programs that are being used to torture; exploit; and subjugate innocent U.S. citizens. Phillips was outraged by what he saw, and he began to expose these crimes. He has adamantly pursued the goal of revealing that MK-ULTRA, and behavioral / mind control programs in general, never ended - they just became more concealed. Phillips has revealed that the torture and conditioning methods, studied in laboratories in the past, are now being applied remotely with electromagnetic weapons. Government officials have thus far denied or ignored the facts that Phillips has exposed regarding these embarrassing and illegal programs, but at the same time, when he took the matter to trial they swept in and used the National Security Act to stop his case from proceeding. Learn More.

Carl Clark
CIA & MI5 Operative

Carl Clark worked as an operative for numerous intelligence services, including the C.I.A. and the MI5, from 1980 until 2003. Upon retirement, he began exposing the massively illegal operations he was involved with. Clark openly speaks about his clandestine duties of performing organized stalking on victims, and the deployment of Microwave [electromagnetic] Weapons to anonymously inflict pain and terror. In a 2010 interview he reveals that: "People can be tracked anywhere by radar, satellite, a base station and complimentary computer programs. For example, three radar devices would sometimes be positioned in the vicinity of the target. The radar emits electromagnetic waves, some of which pick up the target and the result is then evaluated.... This form of localising the target made it easy to deploy the weapons accurately. My colleagues could see exactly where to aim and also observe how the target reacted." Carl grew repulsed by the operations, and he described the individuals targeted in the 2000's as "not political, quite normal, nice people, not criminal or economically dangerous." Learn More.

Karen Stewart
NSA veteran, 28 years of service

In 2006, Karen Stewart voiced complaints to her superiors at the NSA about credit for her work being stolen, through the proper channels. The agency responded with a harassment campaign that involved organized stalking and intimidation. Eventually she filed a lawsuit against the Agency, and instead of addressing her valid complaints, they retaliated by starting an illegal campaign of torture with Directed Energy Weaponry a.k.a Electromagnetic

David Voigts
Naval Academy Graduate, Former Officer

While at the Naval Academy, David Voigts, gained a solid education and grounding in ethics. So when he was in the service, he was disturbed to find out about classified government programs that were illegally using Directed Energy Weapons (DEW) on US citizens for various purposes, including, subjugation, entrainment, experimentation, and retaliation. As a result of his investigations, Mr. Voigts, became a target of these weapon systems.

Weapons. Read more.

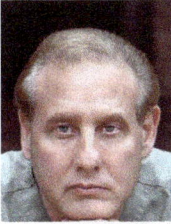

Read more.

Dr. John Hall
Practicing Physician

John Hall is board certified physician with a medical clinic in San Antonio, TX. He became aware of these covert human rights abuses in 2006, when his girlfriend was targeted with a campaign of gang-stalking, intimidation, and directed energy weapon torture, for the purposes of sexual harassment and abuse. Dr. Hall, himself, became targeted when he began assisting her and reaching out to his contacts in the government to help him engage in counter-surveillance. Since beginning his activism, Dr. Hall has uncovered widespread, nation-wide abuse of electromagnetic weapons on innocent Americans. Learn More.

Renee Pittman
Human Rights Advocate, Author

Like many victims, Renee Pittman was a normal woman from a good family before she became targeted with a campaign of organized stalking and harassment, combined with constant assaults with electromagnetic weaponry. Renee did not take the torture, and nonconsensual experimentation, lying down. She became a vocal activist who regularly shines the spotlight on these crimes directed against ordinary citizens. She has also published numerous books on the subject. Learn More.

Doug Rokke, Maj. (Ret.), PhD
Retired US Army Officer, PhD in Physics

A military veteran whose career spans four decades, Doug Rokke, has been a tireless whistleblower against negligent and illegal practices of the military that have harmed soldiers and civilians. Dr. Rokke warns that electromagnetic weapons are 100% real, and in use. He has personally witnessed the use of these devices through multiple platforms: automobile-mounted, plane-mounted, and handheld. Rokke further states that civilians are being targeted with these "exotic weapons." Learn More.

Dr. Daniel Lebowitz
Former FFCHS Board Member, Practicing Physician

Dr. Lebowitz, became a targeted individual in 2010 when he became victimized by a continuous campaign of organized stalking and electromagnetic harassment for subjugation purposes. In response, he engaged in steadfast activism to expose these crimes, and even took a leadership role on the board of the victims' advocacy group FFCHS. Dan Lebowitz's speeches, letters, and outreach campaigns have helped numerous victims and their family members gain a better understanding of these human rights violations. Learn More.

Paul Batcho, PhD
Whistleblower, Former DARPA Scientist

Paul Batcho is a former DARPA scientist who worked at Los Alamos and held a top secret security clearance. He holds numerous engineering degrees and a PhD in Computational and Applied Mathematics from Princeton. In the spring of 2016, Dr. Batcho became targeted with a campaign of electromagnetic torture and harassment for purposes of subjugation. He reports that these technologies are illegally being used on civilians, on a widespread basis, with harmful intentions. Learn More.

Dr. Nicholas Begich
Researcher, Author

Nick Begich began his research on electromagnetic weapons in the early 1990s. Since then he has given numerous speeches on the topic, and has written several books on the science that allows these devices to control the biological systems of humans. He has appeared on many radio and television programs and has served as an expert witness in front the European Parliament. His message is simple: these technologies have been in use for decades, and they should be used to benefit mankind, instead of subjugating it to advance the agendas of the deep state and the deep-pocketed. Learn More.

Dr. Terence Robertson
Activist, Practicing Physician

A past Chairman of the Medical Committee for Freedom From Covert Harassment and Surveillance. Dr. Robertson has championed the cause of victims that are being subjugated with electromagnetic weapons and organized

Barrie Trower
Physicist, Royal Navy Veteran

Barrie Trower specialized in Microwave Warfare systems while in the Navy. He calls these devices "stealth weapons" that enable the perfect crime. As an activist, he has gained great respect for revealing how

501

stalking, often called "Targeted Individuals." In his leadership role, he launched numerous research programs, and statistics gathering efforts to shed light on these emerging crimes that are harming an increasing number of innocent civilians every year. He further reveals that, in addition to torture, these weapons can cause heart attacks, cancer, and even drive someone to suicide. Learn More.

criminal elements within many governments have, and continue to, illegally target their citizens with these weapons. Trower warns that the technology and infrastructure now exists to target "anybody, anywhere" with electromagnetic weapons. He reveals that these weapons are often used in sly ways, to create symptoms in victims that mimic psychiatric diagnoses, in order to discredit them. He further states that such tactics are a favorite modus operandi of the perpetrators, and have been used to illegally subjugate hundreds of thousands of people. Learn More.

Here is the page, resized and clipped just to show Bill Binney's biography. The "Learn More" link at the end links to Bill's Wikipedia page.[332]

Electromagnetic Weapons are Being Used to Torture and Subjugate Countless American Citizens...

The Whistleblowers:
(updated February, 2017)

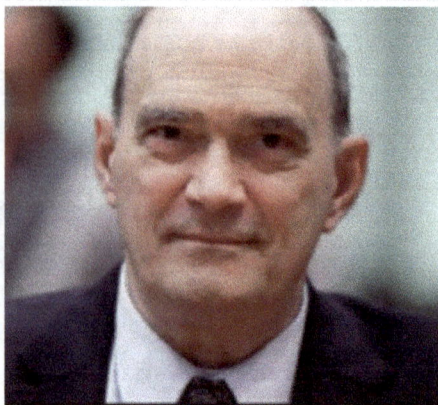

William Binney

NSA Veteran, Technical Director

William Binney's career with the NSA spanned more than 30 years, and in that time, he acquired the title of Technical Leader for intelligence. After September 11, 2001, he was astounded that the agency didn't stop the attacks. He started exposing waste and corruption, through proper legal channels, and faced illegal retaliation as a result. However, he maintained his integrity and was vindicated. Now many refer to him as the original Snowden. In recent years, Binney has engaged in activism in support of the countless victims being tortured with electromagnetic weapons. He began supporting these targeted individuals when he gave a speech at the 2015 Covert Harassment Conference. More recently, in late-2016, Binney along with his former NSA colleague J. Kirk Wiebe, announced on the *Triumph Over Targeting* webcast that they were launching scientific surveys to supplement the overwhelming evidence related to these crimes against humanity. He helps targeted individuals understand the bigger picture behind the subjugation of at least tens of thousands of Americans with electromagnetic weapons. He states that it's about subverting democracy to expand the budgets & power of criminal cliques within the military-industrial complex a.k.a. the Deep State. Learn More.

Bear in mind, that as the former head of all technology development at the National Security Agency, and the fourth in line in the chain of command of the entire agency on 9/11, Bill was trusted by the government, not only with the most elite operational technology used by all of our intelligence agencies, but also with all of the developing technologies which were so cutting edge they had not even been fielded yet.

Here, in a later interview done with his wife, Dr Katherine Horton, Bill and Katherine describe the attacks being launched against them in their own home, using directed energy weapons, after his falling afoul of the machine.[333] Some choice quotes by Bill about the radio-frequency energy beamed into his home:

"From my field, I wanted to see it in a spectrum, I wanted to try to detect where it was, so I could say, "Hey, here it is!" Well, if you know, the spectrum is allocated to different services by the federal communications commission, and they post their allocation, it goes up through 275 Gigahertz. So they had the entire spectrum allocated to different functions there. And a lot of it is military. and when you go through they define the certain frequency ranges which belong to the military. Now we only had spectrum analyzers which could give us all the frequencies up to 4 gigahertz. It is too expensive after that. Up to 4 Ghz we could see, there were two major signals which were ten to a hundred times stronger than anything else in the environment. And they were in the 1.7-1.8 Ghz and 2-9-3.1 Ghz range, and that turned out to be military allocated signals, line of site.

According to the FCC, this was in their notes, and we have that captured to post for everybody to look at, it says it is used in electronic warfare. Now we had these signals from our spectrum analyzer hitting us in Maryland, when we were up there, and we could see that it dropped off about 200 yards away. We drove away from our house and the signal went away at that point, so we are talking about a beam signal, or focused signal, that is fairly confined, not like it was blasting down on the earth from a satellite.

Also it is not a satellite because the FCC also defines what space to earth transmission frequency spectrum are permissible and at what power range. And this is far beyond that and not within the range assigned for space to earth by the FCC.

When we moved down here, we put our spectrum analyzers up and found the same signals down here. Now these are line of sight signals. And we sent notes into the Inspector General of the Department of Defense, and asked, why are you irradiating us with this line of sight energy as we move around in the United States? They never answered us. They never did. We don't know the exact function of it because we cannot "diarize" the signal, break it down, and then start to analyze what is being transmitted in the signals. That takes a lot more money to do, and we simply do not have that resource to make that happen...

We are also discovering, we used Faraday cages to see what we could reduce in terms of the energy. Some of this stuff, through the bug detector, which goes up to 8 Ghz, some of that energy goes right through that, without being degraded, so there is something else going on. I just don't know what is going on there.
[Ed note – A Faraday cage is a conductive surface which completely encloses an observer, and shields them from an electromagnetic field, guiding rf energy around the observer. It is commonly used in the intelligence field in the construction of Secure Compartmentalized Intelligence Facilities, or SCIFs, where it is supposed to prevent all electronic transmissions into and out of the cage, maintaining all discussions and materials

inside the SCIF secure. What Bill is saying is, he built a Faraday cage to try and shield himself from the EMF/rf radiation assailing his house, got inside, and found that somehow the radiation was penetrating right through the walls of the Faraday cage - something classical physics would say should be impossible. Bill continues:]

What you really need to do is have signals analysis go in and look at the signals, and break them down, see what their structure is, see what kind of information if any is being transmitted, or is it like a radar kind of transmission, looking for a return pulse, or some image, like thru-wall radar or is it some kind of other machine to machine transmission.

In Maryland, when I was living in Maryland, I didn't know about all this radiation at the time. My particular cul-de-sac - court area where I lived, had a particularly high cancer rate. My first wife died of cancer, every other house at least, as well my son had cancer, the next door neighbors, at least four or five others in this culdesac, at least every other house had someone with cancer... They were in The Beam, was all I was saying.

Bill's second wife, Dr Katherine Horton, who is an Oxford-trained PhD in particle physics who worked at CERN, and whom he married following the death of his first wife from a cancer which may have been induced by surveillance technology deployed at his home, picks up the story:

This is the second part of this which everyone needs to understand, in addition to this being everywhere. As far as I can tell, based on my PhD in particle physics and high energy physics, directed energy weapons appear to use a novel type of physics, as

506

far as I can tell, and I can explain why I believe that. When you build any type of energy weapon, there are only really three different types of weapons you can use. You can use electromagnetic waves. You can use acoustic waves, so a shockwave for example - an explosion is a big old shock wave which blows you across the yard. And then the third thing is particle beams. Out of these, acoustic weapons and particle beams, have a longitudinal impact, so they can achieve longitudinally, both of them can shoot a hole into any object. But electromagnetic waves are such that the electric and magnetic field components of the electromagnetic waves are transverse, so if the photon is going that way, the electric field and the magnetic field are pointing transverse to the direction of travel. What that means in plain english is that no matter how powerful your laser beam, you can never, ever push something or kick something. And that is extremely important to keep in mind, because what we are being attacked with, these directed energy weapons - so typically we just hear a knock, so something is impacting, on the roof, on the ceiling, on the wall next to us.

And I had also a situation where by the drone actually shot a lamp and shattered glass. The attacks on us were so bad in Maryland, that we actually moved our bedroom into the basement and put a sheet metal on the ground floor, on the first floor. And there was an attack whereby the drone shot two holes, like "Bam, bam," into the sheet metal. And these two holes were not there before. The shots made an awful impact sound, that we heard in the basement, even though the door was closed and locked. And then we found those holes. So how the hell can that be? Because there was no hole on the roof, there was no hole in the ceiling of the top floor, or the ground floor, yet there were two holes in the

507

sheet metal. How can that be?... It didn't burn, it was punched, punched through, so the metal was bent through where the shot went through... It was not evaporation, it was not heating, it was not melting. The holes were punched. And when these shots are impacting, at low level, it can be just a dull impact, and at high intensity, it can shoot holes through sheet metal, or break glass.

Because of these observations, that there was no hole in the ceiling, or in the roof, as a physicist, I do not think that can be particle beams, or acoustic beams, because they would have to deposit the same amount of energy, on the other surfaces as well.

And...I have done other experiments, where at my home in Switzerland, where to protect myself from the nightly gunning, I kept buying more and more pieces of large sheet metal, so one meter, by one and a-half meters, and I built a little bulk around my bed, and in the end, around my head area, I had 25 pieces of sheet metal... It even came through 25 layers of sheet metal, I could still measure these impact sounds, with an electromagnetic measuring device. Particle beams at high intensity can cause ionizing radiation, you can pick them up with a Geiger counter, acoustic devices can be picked up another way, But neither particles, nor acoustic weapons, should be depositing any signal on an electromagnetic measuring device.

So the bottom line of our research is that these new gizmos, which they are now selling around the world for close to $13 billion per year, they are not good old microwave weapons, they are this novel technology, which which you can just shoot holes through sheet metal, which means you can literally shoot a hole through somebody's head or shoot a hole through their heart, or make one of the veins in their head explode, and make it look like

508

a stroke, and not leave any traces, which I can detect anywhere else, in the wall.

Before Dr Horton and Bill Binney met and married, she, an Oxford-trained PhD particle physicist, who worked at CERN, recorded her own assault with the impulse/particle beam here.[334]

I have personally experienced that weapon, and recorded its use on me. The page at American Stasi which documents the recordings is at this note.[335]

In my experience, there are several different types of energy weapons developed and employed by this machine. I can personally vouch, I have felt myself bathed in a sensation of tingling electricity, while in bed in my home. I have awoken as I have felt my body vibrated aggressively in the middle of the night, by what feels like a beam of energy which sets up some kind of resonant vibrations in the body. I have experienced the impulse beam Dr Horton describes, which feels kind of like being shot by an invisible energy impulse in the head, and which seems to produce a much more powerful, loud impact when striking metal.

The impulse/impact beam Dr Horton describes, seems to me to involve two facets. The first is the generation of a sort of static charge in the room, which charges the materials around the target area with a static electric charge. I have actually heard and recorded static discharges from the materials in the room, as the charges on their surfaces exceeded what they could hold. The second facet of that weapon appears to be the skimming of some sort of beam off the targeted material, which applies an electric field which confers a force upon the now-charged particles, causing them to "jump" within the field, on an axis transverse to

509

the direction of "The Beam." I have recorded a thermal video of this beam hitting me, by placing a sheet of aluminum foil over me in a cool room, with paper towels beneath it to keep it cool, so the heat from the beam would become plainly visible on it in the thermal video. That video is also available at the previous link.

I have felt the degrading cognitive effects of a high-pitched sound-sensation, which is difficult to tell the degree to which it is a high pitched sound, or an ear-piercing sensation. I have been hit with what I would call, an irritation/electrical-tingling beam in the chest, which accelerates your heart-rate to ridiculously high levels. I have even walked, on several occasions, into rooms, and watched fluorescent light bulbs flash brightly, even though their switches were turned off, and there was no electricity going to them – a clear sign of radio-frequency energy.

A few times, my local surveillance crew used the impulse beam to simulate me being tapped, awakening me with taps by invisible fingers in my bed. This is likely the same effect which punched through Bill's steel shielding.

In another instance, when I ignored the taps attempting to awake me, the impulse beam was dialed up to a higher power, and applied a force of about ten to twenty pounds downward to the thick shielding covering my face, driving my head into the pillow, an event I recorded the audio of, with a cellphone.[336] The microphone appeared to catch unusual electromagnetic effects prior to this, similar to an MRI warming up, which were not able to be heard with the ear.

There have actually been numerous mass shooters who said they were driven to the shootings they engaged in by these types of attacks. Many researchers believe that in a subset of cases, the operation seeks to drive targeted individuals to become mass shooters through the use of technology like this, possibly in an attempt to institute gun control to disarm the population, and further weaken it, rendering the average citizen more helpless when confronted with its intimidation.

Aaron Alexis was a Navy veteran who served his country before becoming an electronics contractor in the defense industry. He finally broke down after he was not allowed to sleep for three months, due to the vibration beam being applied to him every time he laid down, which prevented him from sleeping. From here[337]:

"Washington Navy Yard gunman Aaron Alexis left a note saying he was driven to kill by months of bombardment with extremely low-frequency radio waves, the FBI said Wednesday in a disclosure that explains the phrase he etched on his shotgun: "My ELF Weapon!"...

"Ultra-low frequency attack is what I've been subject to for the last 3 months, and to be perfectly honest that is what has driven me to this," read an electronic document agents recovered after the shooting.

The attack came one month after Alexis had complained to police in Rhode Island that people were talking to him through the walls and ceilings of his hotel room and sending microwave vibrations into his body to deprive him of sleep."

I myself have felt the vibration beam, many, many times after my surveillance went overt and began harassing me. In its focused form, it creates a ball of vibration within the body, which moves, clearly under intelligent control, and can travel up your leg, to your abdomen, and even enter your head. Where it slips out of the body, it will redirect itself back in, before continuing its travel. It also comes in a more diffuse form, which can encompass the entire body. It produces a physical agitation, which raises the heart rate, and makes sleep impossible for hours after its application. It was during one such post-Beam period of sleeplessness I came up with the idea of using Google Streetview to reveal the surveillance to people.

The vibrations can range from a soft, subtle buzz, to quite strong reverberations. Imagine reaching into your abdomen, and shaking a sphere of your viscera one quarter inch, back and forth, at a rate of four times per second, and that is what you will feel from this weapon. Oddly enough, you will not feel the vibrations physically if you place your hand on the vibrating area.

When they moved up to my head a few times, they were clearly dulling to the brain, but I was also stuck by another feature. In striking arts, the first punch you are hit with in the face in a training session will create a specific sensation in the sinuses. Subsequent strikes that night will not produce the sensation for some reason. When the vibrations moved up to my head, I was struck by how that sensation, normally a sharp clear sensation which occurs suddenly, built up slowly in the sinuses over a period of twenty or thirty seconds.

I was reclining within sight of my surveillance camera system once when the vibrations began, and I was able to count the vibrations as they happened, and time out exactly one minute, using the timestamp on the surveillance camera image on the TV. I counted exactly 240 vibration pulses per minute, for an exact measurement of 4 cycles per second, or hertz. If the vibrations were a random neurological effect, or a hallucination, it seems unlikely they would precisely structure their timing to an arbitrary human measurement of time, such as a second. I would think it more likely I would have found they produced some random number, not divisible by 60 when counted for one minute. That they occur at a precise 4 Hertz would indicate to me they are being produced by some form of human technology.

There are numerous other accounts which were published online of targeted individuals describing being attacked with some sort of energetic weapon which caused them to feel vibrations. Several people describe feeling vibrations here, in the comments below the article, including Darren M:[338]

"My name is Darren M. and I believe I am being targeted with concentrated infrasonic sound waves while I attempt to sleep at night. I believe I am being targeted for D.E.W. (directed energy weapon) experimentation/harassment purposes by an entity within the U.S. government employing private contractors to carry out this experimentation/harassment.

I am awakened many times throughout my sleep periods to a feeling of vibrations traveling through my body in a straight line. The vibrations are focused in a narrow beam. It is impossible for me to stay asleep when I am targeted with these inaudible concentrated sound waves which increase my pulse rate as they travel through me. Different parts of my body are targeted at different times. When my head is targeted I will awake with moderate to severe headaches. I have also experienced head spins to the point that I had to lift my head up out of a lying down position to make them stop. When my chest area is targeted, I will awake with rapid or irregular heartbeats. In addition, I experience

513

sleep deprivation on a nightly basis due to the repeated forced awakenings. The private contractors that target me hit me every 1-2 hours on average during the first part of my sleep period, and they increase the frequency of their targeting to every 15-30 minutes during the 2nd part of my sleep period. I fear that I will lose my job and become homeless due to the sleep deprivation that this experimentation/harassment has caused me. I also fear that my health will deteriorate.

I want to make sure that my story is told in the event this experimentation causes my premature death. I also want to make sure that potential future victims do not suffer the way I have from these silent sound wave weapons. I don't believe anyone can help me because of my failed attempts to provide proof of this experimentation and the apparent disbelief and disinterest of the authorities in the U.S.

Darren M.

Email: dewtarget05 AT yahoo DOT com"

It is worth noting, from Aaron Alexis' account, to Darren's account above, to my own writings on my website at the time, about the vibrations I experienced, to still other accounts, those writings all preceded the public description of the Havana Syndrome as manifesting as vibrations. This is a vital point to make note of, since it reveals who is likely behind the Havana attacks.

Since I and other targets of the US domestic surveillance of the American Stasi have described our own targeting with a directed energy weapon which produced vibration sensations, the government has come forward and said that the directed energy

514

attacks on our nation's diplomats and intelligence personnel, first seen in Cuba, featured as one of its hallmarks, the onset of "vibrations."[339] From this piece which was released in 2022:

Scott Pelley: *You must have thought that when you were home in America that you were safe?*

Robyn Garfield: [Ed note: A Commerce Department official, hit by Havana Syndrome in China]*: I'll tell you, when I landed from China, I literally was kissing the ground.*

Scott Pelley, voiceover: *We met Robyn Garfield in 2019. He's a Commerce Department official who told us that he, his wife and two children were repeatedly hit in China.*

Scott Pelley: *Your daughter was literally falling down?*

Robyn Garfield: *Yes, she fell down multiple times a day.*

Scott Pelley, voiceover: *They were evacuated and enrolled in a State Department treatment program at the University of Pennsylvania. Recently, Garfield told us his family was hit again during their year of treatment in Philadelphia.*

Robyn Garfield: *My wife catapulted out of bed and sprinted down the hallway to check the children without any word. And she came back, and she told me that an extremely loud, painful, sound had woken her up.*

Scott Pelley, voiceover: *So, they moved to a hotel where Garfield says it happened again.*

Robyn Garfield: *And we woke up around I believe 2:00 a.m. with strange vibrations in our bodies, and a sound.*

Here is something I wrote in May of 2018, after a prominent blogger shut down his blog, saying he had been threatened with violence, and hit with an energy beam:[340]

For the past several years...I would wake up in the night to an unusual sensation. Imagine yourself when you are really cold shivering. You look down at your arms, and they are visibly moving with the shiver. Now slow the shivering down, by about 30%. Imagine how that would feel, as you look down and your arms vibrated, almost seizure like, at that half-speed. Now take away the cold sensation, and imagine you felt that vibration, but when you looked at your arms they were not moving. There was no movement of the flesh, and not even any muscle contractions in response to the sensations. Now imagine that all over your body, and throughout your core.

It is possible all of these cases of American citizens who were being gangstalked and describing directed energy vibrations, instead of burnings, or electrical sensations, did so coincidentally. But I think it more likely these domestic cases, my own included, were the first beta-testing of the weapon which was ultimately rolled out against select CIA and State Department personnel, as well as White House staffers - the Havana Syndrome weapon.

That is highly significant, as it would indicate a decent likelihood that the individuals wielding the Havana weapon against our intelligence personnel, are in fact the same individuals performing the domestic surveillance - the American Stasi. It would indicate the deployment of that weapon on our government personnel may be a final purge of honest Americans from our intelligence and governmental structures, in a sort of covert, technology-based coup of our government by the American Stasi.

This conclusion would also be bolstered by the fact that individuals have been struck by the Havana weapon while on White House grounds.[341] From the 60 Minutes piece at the link, which details the cases of multiple people struck at the White House, which sits within Washington DC, one of the most heavily surveilled and monitored pieces of real estate in the world:

"Since 2016, U.S. government officials overseas and their families have reported sudden, unexplained, brain injuries with symptoms of vertigo, confusion and memory loss. The CIA, FBI and State Department are investigating a theory that some of these officials were injured by an unseen weapon. Who might be targeting Americans and why are unknown. Incidents have been reported in Europe, Asia, and Latin America, but, as we first told you in February, our reporting has found senior national security officials who say they were stricken in Washington and on the grounds of the White House. The former officials you are about to meet are revealing their experiences for the first time. They were responsible for helping to manage threats to national security."

That news piece included the fact that a Cabinet-level official in the Trump administration was hit with Havana syndrome in his home, in DC:

Taylor says he became alarmed by that threat in 2018 after he heard of another case like his in the Washington area.

Miles Taylor: I became aware of a U.S. government official more senior than me who'd experienced similar episodes at their place of residence.

Scott Pelley: You say more senior than you. Are you talking about a cabinet level secretary?

Miles Taylor: *This was an individual that, yes, was roughly at the cabinet level in the Trump administration who had similar episodes occur. That to me, as a homeland security professional, was a big blinking red light. I mean, to me this said, "five-alarm fire." We may have ongoing activity targeting U.S. government officials here in our country.*

Others have been struck very close to White House grounds, and elsewhere on US soil.[342] From the article:

"Several US officials have reportedly been targeted by sonic attacks on American soil over the last three years...

The symptoms became known as Havana Syndrome, due to where they were first reported, but in the years since several more US officials have claimed to have experienced the mysterious illness on US soil.

An unnamed American diplomat and his family said that they heard mysterious sounds and fell ill while working in Philadelphia in 2018, according to the Daily Mail.

The diplomat and his wife both claimed that they felt a pressure in their heads and found their children moving "in unison" in their sleep.

In November 2019, an unnamed White House employee said that she experienced similar symptoms when she was allegedly targeted by a man while walking her dog in Arlington, Virginia.

She said she felt a tingling in her face and experienced an intense headache, while her dog seized up.

A third incident has not been described in detail as of yet, but the Mail reported that it took place on US soil, and that the American official experienced similar symptoms."

As we have shown you, domestic surveillance in the United States by the American Stasi is far too thorough to allow a foreign actor to enter a sector and operate in any form, especially in the Capitol region. This would imply this intelligence/surveillance operation is in the midst of some sort of shadow coup of our government – a coup launched against the official, elected US government using violent directed energy weapons which are leaving victims with crippling injuries.

I can personally attest to the criminality of the American Stasi, and the fact it is entirely capable of attempting such an act. The question is, is it an operation being deployed by a foreign actor, which is attempting to take over the United States? I suspect so, given how freely it operates on foreign soil.

In addition, wounded State Department and CIA officials who were struck by the Havana Syndrome overseas have reported that on returning to the United States, they observed hostile surveillance activity targeting them, breaking into their houses and rearranging furniture, as well as following them overtly as they traveled in their home neighborhoods. From the article above:

"Even in the United States, not all evacuated from Cuba and China are convinced they're safe.

At least six of the evacuated Americans have reported suspected harassment or surveillance in the U.S. to the FBI, four U.S. officials and others familiar with the investigation said. They include evacuees from both China and Cuba, including some who have never met...

Some reported suspected break-ins at their homes or temporary housing, after finding items moved or tampered with, or lights and televisions turned on that had been left off. Some handed over potential evidence to the FBI, including surveillance footage and a laptop suspected to have been tampered with.

Others reported being conspicuously followed — including from their doctors' offices in Philadelphia — and suspicious activity on cellphones. At one point, patients whose treatment was transferred from Penn to Washington's MedStar National Rehabilitation Network were told all of their MedStar appointments were canceled indefinitely due to safety concerns, four people familiar with the cancellations said."

As with civilian targets of the American Stasi, these officials have reported that the FBI has proven powerless to help them, or identify and arrest the perpetrators. That is the American Stasi that you just saw all over Google Steetview, and which you have seen perform the exact same harassment in the United States against innocent Americans. Here it is harassing Americans who were wounded while serving their nation overseas. It is consistent with the hypothesis it was the foreign conspiracy behind the American Stasi which injured them in the first place while they were overseas.

Take a moment to contemplate the facts, if that is correct. An intelligence operation, acting to injure American officials, did so overseas, even in China (which itself has extensive, neighborhood by neighborhood surveillance), and it continued the harassment in the United States. There are three possibilities.

Chinese government intelligence assaulted the officials in China, and then continued the harassment in the US, and the US government was helpless to stop them, even on White House grounds. Or, US government intelligence assaulted its own nation's officials in China, and continued the harassment in the US. Or the most likely possibility – there is some kind of a non-state intelligence operation, separate from both the Chinese and United States government, which has infiltrated and penetrated both nations enough that it can operate freely within them, injuring who it wishes to, and it is in the process of removing certain people from the US government through both the use of technological weaponry, and harassment using its physical surveillance network.

It is also worth noting, among the potential victims of Havana Syndrome is US Senator Ron Johnson, who now has no hearing in one ear and has balance troubles, after being struck.[343] From the article:

"CIA employees around the world, including in Wisconsin and U.S. Sen. Ron Johnson, are among the latest possible targets of Havana Syndrome.

"I don't publicize this much, but I have certainly been evaluated for possible exposure myself," Johnson said during an interview with the Wisconsin Law Journal on Wednesday.

"I lost my hearing and my balance simultaneously," Johnson said, noting that the 2018 hearing loss has been permanent.

Johnson said he experienced significant neurological symptoms consistent with Havana Syndrome following a 2018 trip to Moscow, which resulted in permanent hearing loss in one ear, balance issues and evaluation at the National Institutes of Health (NIH) and Walter Reed Hospital for Havana Syndrome.

"I had blood loss to my cranial nerve ... I am basically deaf in my right ear. My balance has come back to a certain extent, but it's still impaired," Johnson said, noting he wasn't given a definitive Havana Syndrome diagnosis, but that was what was being evaluated."

Returning to Aaron Alexis, deprived of the ability to sleep for months, one day he took a shotgun to the Washington DC Navy Yard, where he felt some of the people who had developed the tech worked, and he was shot by responding officers while committing a mass shooting there.

Myron Mays was, by all accounts, a young, very nice, peaceful, gifted Assistant District Attorney, when for some reason, this machine decided to target him, to prevent his rise in society. In videos he left behind,[344] you see a polite, kind man, unable to fathom why he is being tortured by directed energy weapons. He ultimately went on a mass shooting at Florida State University, after leaving behind a video explaining in a calm, rational tone, what had been happening to him, and his hope that his death would help others by drawing attention to the American Stasi. Watch the video here,[345] and understand, I have seen what he is describing, and he is not crazy. That heartbreaking video is a gifted young man with honor and decency, who should have risen effortlessly in society, who was wantonly broken by this machine for no reason other than to make sure their criminal conspiracy maintains full control of the government.

I could go on further. When the truth comes out you will find there were tens of thousands, and maybe hundreds of thousands of your fellow Americans, being assailed this way. It will include the victims of the Havana Syndrome, who were all assaulted by this tech, as well as a plethora of people who never even knew they were assaulted, but who simply endured poor health and perpetual exhaustion, as they struggled to get ahead in life, to no avail.

I am convinced these weapons are being used against broad swaths of the population, in levels not high enough to trigger full awareness of what is happening, but at levels high enough to negatively impact health and vitality, to prevent people in the population more generally, from attaining their full potential. I will discuss the evidence for this later.

What people need to understand is, individuals like Bill, and Myron, and myself, we are the pilot program for this thing.

This civilian network, of supposed Americans who are so eager to betray their fellow countrymen, as well as everything their nation stands for, for personal advantage - it is here now. The tech they are deploying to assault people in their homes and weaken them absent any cost or consequence, is now a thing. It exists. There are multiple different devices, which work different ways. There are blueprints, and probably tooled factories, and assembly lines hidden in the shadows, turning these machines out.

They are making the devices and distributing them to the local surveillance crews for testing on guys like Bill, and Myron, and me. Worst of all, these machines are now advanced enough, and proven enough, the conspiracy of the American Stasi feels confident it can roll them out against active, operational members of the CIA and FBI, even at locations secured by the executive protection detail of the Secret Service, and there will not be enough evidence left behind to generate any consequences.

Our intelligence agencies, and the people above who have seized control of them for the American Stasi, are not made up of fiercely libertarian Constitutional individualists. They do not believe in everyone being free and happy. They do not want you free to do whatever you want to do. They want to turn you into a peasant, living a limited life of forced servitude you can never escape. They want the same for your children.

Understand the magnitude of what you just read. Throughout the West, some sort of private sector, non-state intelligence service has penetrated our government, seized control of federal agencies, subverted our elections on all sides of the political spectrum, infiltrated the schools with its children, and recruited between 4 and 10 percent of the civilian population into organized, distributed, surveillance/intelligence units, modeled on the East German Stasi secret police, embedded in and tasked to learn everything about everyone in their neighborhoods. They are assigned to know and control everyone, including the children, who are not to rise too high or develop too much potential.

This thing is now assaulting the remaining elements of government it does not control, as well as regular citizens - with energy weapons - forcing them into some form of submission. And that treatment is working its way down to you. More beam weapons are coming off an assembly line somewhere, every day.

I know that sounds incredible. Ten years ago, I was just like you. There are things you will see as you grow surveillance-aware, which will show you it is out there. Keep your eyes open, and understand, in a Darwinian world, where the citizens sleep, it is inevitable the craven and corrupted, and most especially the most evil, will rise and seize control.

If I am correct, now these units, embedded in every neighborhood, and increasingly being told to wrangle ever-greater control of the individualists and iconoclasts in their communities, as well as the high-flying children, have access to a myriad of directed energy weapons, which can degrade health, exhaust energy, trigger heart attacks, inflict physical pain, and even launch physical-impact assaults on innocent citizens. And those citizens, once attacked, cannot appeal to the law, or seek any form of redress from any authority, because the weapons leave no evidence. They are completely helpless to resist within the "law."

Bill was fourth in command at the NSA when the planes hit the towers. He has been featured on TV Shows from 60 Minutes to Frontline,[346] and NSA Executive Thomas Drake called him one of the best crypto-mathmatician code-breakers the NSA ever had.[347] He had the highest security clearance in the nation as one of the highest ranking national security officials, and he is now forced to hide in his basement under steel sheeting as impacts from some directed energy weapon rain down on him and his wife, even blowing holes in the steel sheeting. And there is nobody he can turn to. No law enforcement agency which will even take his calls or acknowledge he exists. The media refuses to even mention his name now. Nobody is willing to pitch in to a GoFundMe.

30 years of committed service to the national defense, he sacrificed his career because he felt Americans were being

victimized illegally by the intelligence community, and now in his senior years, he is all alone, facing a Goliath which assaults him at will. And on this path, one day you may find yourself in that predicament too. I already am there, and I am far less notable than Bill.

The Beam weapons have exited the beta-testing on no-name victims like Aaron Alexis. They survived the more rigorous testing in Havana, Cuba. They were successful in Washington DC, even targeting victims on White House grounds, and they proved unable to be detected or countered, even by Secret Service. Now they are in production. There is an assembly line somewhere, and as they come off it, they're being handed to local units, where Bill Binney and I are seeing them. The Beam is working its way down to you - and your children. Soon, everyone will know of it, and how frustrating it is to be unable to tell who is doing it, where they are, and how to deal with them. Most will have no choice, and comply.

America has big problems. And they will only increase until such time as a unified mass of real average Americans step up to rid the nation of this Stasi menace. Sadly, I doubt that will happen at the voting booth. Things have gone on too long, and the enemy has developed too much control over those mundane processes.

Unfortunately it is going to be hard, and average Americans will have to decide soon, before it is too late, to do things which they presently would view as extreme.

However, soon it will be clear, it will be those extreme measures, or it will be America as a slave state, with every citizen cowering in their basements like Bill, living in perpetual fear of The Beam™. You are going to have to choose, and do so, soon.

Chapter Fourteen

Your Child Is A Target - Surveillance In The Schools

Even the children of the people in this operation are running surveillance on fellow students in their elementary schools, and reporting their observations back to their parents, beginning every American's file before they are even into their teens. You can see one such video here, where a child, roughly ten years old, while speaking to another child of the surveillance machine on a public street, mentions casually that they had followed the resident of the house they are passing that day.[348]

Those are two children of the secret society of surveillance people, in their natural environment, just casually discussing the fact they are operational in a massive domestic surveillance machine which is following ordinary Americans, through grocery stores and all around town.

Where I lived, it appeared in the early nineties there were roughly twenty to thirty children out of 400 students total in the school, all embedded in the student body, all apparently taking orders from some group of adults which were responsible for school monitoring operations.

Since I lived in a remote area as an adult, the surveillance parents of children in the local grade school would send all of their kids to socialize with each other privately at my neighbor's house,

527

before they realized my family member was running such extensive counter-surveillance on them that it granted a window into that world.

It was fascinating. My assumption is surveillance parents worry about the socialization of their children. These are kids, at eight, nine, ten years old, who all know the big secret. They know that the American Stasi exists, and is waging a shadow intelligence war on every regular American from within our communities and neighborhoods, designed to keep their criminal conspiracy operational. They know the "real government" is compromising politicians, and business and society leaders with pedophile blackmail networks, looting the treasury, starting fake wars which kill and maim millions, and suppressing every honest, loyal American before they could rise to a position where they could oppose them.

Furthermore, not only do they know the secret, adult agents of the American Stasi appear to be running these children against the other kids in their schools as infiltrators/informants/agents/provocateurs. These kids spend their whole childhood, knowing they are guilty of all of these crimes themselves, and their peers would turn upon them mercilessly if they knew.

Every moment spent among other normal children, these kids have been taught to have their guards up, and never share these unimaginable truths with the other children, who they must be taught are sworn enemies who will destroy them, if they ever learn the truth. They are probably also imbued with a fear of the conspiracy itself, which as Bill Binney can attest to, you do not want to end up crosswise with.

I think the conspiracy recognizes that is unhealthy, and these kids need time alone with their kind, where they can emotionally bond, and freely interact, without having to maintain their guard up constantly. So they sent them to the house next door to gather and socialize, and they would wander down the street, where my relative's counter surveillance would capture them, talking about their lives in the conspiracy, where it was periodically sending them for usage or training, operations on other children, even about being used running surveillance on regular American citizens.

I was blown away. Even the children of this thing, exist in their own secret society, where they are deep cover secret agents, and where regular American children are a hostile, oppositional force which they need to gather intelligence on and compromise, even sabotage, for the good of their secret conspiracy.

We have this whole secret enemy nation in our country, which hates America proper, fears the freedom so many of us assumed everyone would crave, is devoted to the destruction of every Constitutional provision, and which works, every day, devoting their entire lives, and even using their children, to sabotage everything the rest of us feel is beautiful about America, as well as sabotaging us, even though we are loyal to them as "fellow Americans." I am still blown away.

Once realizing the operation worked this way, however, I flashed back to odd situations in my own childhood. Although it is beyond the scope of this work, my family has a rather long history with this operation going back generations, the full nature of which we still do not fully understand.

I attended a grade school which for some reason appeared to contain a hive of surveillance-kid activity, however I am unsure whether that is normal for every school (it is entirely possible, given how the American Stasi works, in my opinion), or whether their numbers were somehow increased due to my presence, or perhaps even some other, unknown factor.

As a result though, once I grew aware of the operation as an adult, I realized I had often seen things with the kids around me growing up which did not make sense at the time, because I did not understand they were being run as surveillance/informant operators.

Stories would come out that two kids, from different grades, and different types of kids, (ie, goth, preppie, jock, rebel, nerd, druggie) saw something while together at some far away location, such as a train station, often involving still other kids who it would seem they should not have been socializing with, and who they assiduously avoided in school.

When I would hear that a senior rebel who smoked and got a tattoo was hanging out with a sophomore Advanced Placement honors math genius geek, at a train station 50 miles away, watching another freshman jock do something which resulted in him being beaten up, I can remember wondering, first, how were they all at the same place so far away? And second, why, if they are socializing together out of the school, would they assiduously pretend to not know each other when crossing paths in the school?

It was decades ago, but I can still see the videos in my mind, and tell you exactly where I was standing in the school, when a fourth kid, who should also not have been socializing with those kids, related the story to me, because he was there too. Now I realize, those kids were all in the secret society of surveillance people, and were drawn together at the train station, helping to track targets.

Now, looking back, it is even possible their statuses as rebels, or jocks, or theater kids were roles they were assigned in the school, to give them proximity to the children who the machine decided it wanted more closely surveilled and controlled.

Numerous other incidents came to mind. A few days into sixth grade, I was sitting in an English class. The teacher had given us a writing assignment the first day, and he began the class insisting he read one of them to us. It was an amazing piece of writing. I cannot even remember the words, but the video it conjured in my head, of night enveloping the earth like a cloak wrapped around it, was so vivid I still remember the image it conjured.

Halfway through his reading of it, one girl blurted out, *"Tara, that's your's!"* The whole class turned and looked at Tara. She was diminutive little waif of a girl, with shoulder-length wavy red hair and freckles, dressed very neatly and conservatively, albeit not in anything you would say had fashion. She was by far, the quietest girl in the class. She had never spoke that I saw, and once fingered as the author, she just smiled sheepishly, clearly embarrassed.

Over the next few months, it would become clear she was a genius, and a polymath, as I observed her in a few of my honors classes. Her math scores were always perfect, over 100, with the bonus questions. Science, she was the top of the class, perfect

531

scores across the board. Every homework assignment done perfectly. Obviously she was a brilliant writer, so her English scores were perfect. And as I recall, for the first half of the year, she was the first chair oboe or clarinet in the band class, and must have regularly practiced the instrument on top of everything.

I can remember wondering, how could she had all that time? I was a testosterone-filled cement-head who liked shooting, martial arts, and goofing off, and I was impressed by her academic perfection, unsure how she could be perfect constantly.

Yet, she never talked. And though I, in passing, thought it odd another girl had read her homework and could recognize her assignment, given her lack of socializing with anyone, it quickly receded from my mind.

Tara made it several months into sixth grade as an academic force, one of those flawless students who was just a machine, and you wondered where she was getting all her time and energy. She may have been small and helpless looking, but you had to respect her. Every single thing she did, her grade was perfect. She was going places. Her parents must have been ecstatic.

I was in the cafeteria, when I first noticed she had been approached by some of the kids I would classify as goth/dirtbags. The group of kids was lower IQ, most were in the special education programs for kids who were borderline-retarded and needed more remedial instruction, and a few even smoked at that age.

I can see the image in my mind, where they were standing when I first saw it, the image was so incongruous. Tara was dressed like a Mormon, long skirt down to her ankles, sweater, her hair perfectly combed, holding her books against her chest, and her manner clearly high-IQ and aware, surrounded by dullards and slackers, dressed as if they got ripped and torn hand-me-downs from the local homeless, which they had dyed all black.

It puzzled me for a moment, as I thought Tara was all honors classes, while the goths were special ed, or "Speds" as many derisively referred to them. How did they become friends? How did they even meet? I told myself they must have met in gym class, and put it out of my mind. But in that school, neither would have approached the other, even in gym class, and certainly neither would have extended an invitation to create a relationship. Even had they, there was something strange in the welcoming, ingratiating nature of the entire group of goth-dirtbags, when dealing with an obviously much higher IQ nerd. They all were clearly charming her. The scene stuck in my mind for all these years because it was wrong. Something was off, you could feel it.

The goth dirtbags were making her smile and laugh however, saying all the right things, and Tara looked delighted to have friends and not be eating alone, doing schoolwork. Despite the incongruity, at the time, I thought it nice Tara had friends and seemed happy, and dismissed the scene from my mind.

By the end of the year, Tara's hair was filled with some kind of hair product which made it look kind of wet and stick to her head, and she was wearing the typical goth excess of eye shadow makeup. He clothes were all black, and quasi-slutty, with ripped stockings and shorter skirts. The transformation was total, and by high school, I did not see her in any honors classes.

Looking back, I remember now seeing indices of the secret

society in one of her closest friends in the goth group, a girl named Amy. I now think what happened to Tara was an intervention, organized by adults who were monitoring the school. Those kids were sent in to befriend her, and derail her academics.

Which brings me to the interesting indices of my own story. This was farther into sixth grade. Rob was a nice kid who lived a little deeper in the remote part of the town where I lived. He seemed like one of those harmless kids who never got mad, and although we really only knew each other in passing, when we interacted we got along well, though in retrospect, he was almost certainly told to get along with me.

I was in the hall outside the science classrooms, when Rob came hustling up, all amped up. He pulled out a dark brown manila-type folder over an inch thick, with something filling it to overflowing, from his backpack.

He jammed it in my chest, and said, *"I broke into my neighbor's house, and he has a whole chest full of Playboy magazines. I ripped out all the pictures, and I want you to have them."*

As quickly as he materialized, he was off running down the hall, as I was standing there trying to picture him in some stranger's house, every moment at threat of being caught, and him taking the time to open up a chest, and go through Playboys, one by one, ripping out the pictures, probably a neat pile of pictures on one side, and a discarded mess of ripped up magazines on the other – all for me. I wondered what the neighbor thought when they came home to their playboy collection, raided, strewn about, ransacked and cleaned out of all the naked lady pictures, but nothing else in the house taken or disturbed. It immediately struck me as beyond weird.

And although I liked him, I really did not know Rob that well. He must have had ten other friends he was closer to than me. Did they all get packages like this? How many Playboys did this neighbor have? How big was the pile of discarded magazines left behind? And why was he giving this to me?

I was quickly jarred back to reality with the realization I was now in the hall, openly holding a ridiculously sized bundle of embarrassing contraband I did not want to be caught with and have to explain to the principal or my parents.

I saw Rob, years later in my travels, and I now assume at the time he was not passing through where I was by random chance. I suspect he was there, as part of a team following me. He was a surveillance kid. It is weird, but they are out there.

What had just happened, in that middle-school hallway, though I had no idea at the time, was I had actually met the *"Porn Fairy,"* face to face - or at least one of the Porn Fairy's emissaries.

Since about the year 2000 on the internet, the term *"Porn Fairy"* was coined for a nationwide phenomenon, whereby some person would leave pornography where children would play.

I suspect the Porn Fairy was not individuals, all by pure random chance, acting independently across the country in the exact same way, leaving pornography laying around where kids might find it. I believe, based on my own experiences, that what was happening in each of those cases, was the neighborhood surveillance would note where a child of unusual nature, who

535

could one day pose a threat to the machine, and thus was marked by the operation to be targeted for control, played and when they would do so.

Then, as part of an established procedure, one of the neighborhood agents of the surveillance could arrange to place pornography there, at an appropriate time for the targeted child to find it. The goal was probably to addict a child to sex during a critical developmental period, when such was most effective.

The phenomenon has been widely discussed online since then. Some choice posts from a discussion of it at the message board 4Chan here:[349]

"Another phenomena that united both rural and urban kids of our age was the porn fairy. In my neighborhood, the porn fairy bestowed porn mags on us beneath a bridge on the way to school. There were porn mags stuffed in the rafters and we'd check them out and scan them into the spank bank. But I heard of rural kids that would find porn mags magically placed in the woods by the porn fairy."

"I remember hearing about that, and thought that some pervert left them there and would watch off at some distance. I mean, why the fuck would you look at porn mags in hidden areas? To jerk off. Some pervert was watching from a distance and would record or jerk off to you jerking off."

"The Porn Fairy. That phenomenon was real."

Here on Reddit, an American waxes nostalgic about how finding porn from the Porn Fairy was a rite of passage growing up in his time:[350]

I found it in a garbage bag like the rest of us old people here on reddit. I was just exploring things like old abandoned houses and ditches around the neighborhood, then BAM black hefty bag full of porn, on top of porn. No name porn like "open butts" or " blacks banging other blacks". I know for fact that this will not happen anymore and it makes me sad, because I feel like there was this "porn fairy" that went around dumping black garbage bags full-o-porn around the US. I think that is one thing people will forget about in this new age of ours, that and telephone booths.

Another Reddit discussion notes it was happening in Japan:[351]

Amazing. This must have been a world wide phenomenon as I too have stumbled upon discarded porn in parks and wooded area in Japan where I spent my childhood.

Here on Reddit, it is noted as a feature of the UK as well:[352]

Why was there always porn in the woods? Magazines, torn out Page 3, random photos printed off the internet. Why were the woods of the UK overflowing with such adult bounty? Who was putting it there?

There are too many comments from others with the same experiences there at those links, as well as all over the internet, to quote them all here. You may peruse the conversations there yourself, or search "porn fairy" on Google to see how common this was in many parts of the world.

I have no doubt, all of that was the child-monitoring division of the American Stasi. In domestic intelligence, targeting children is just be seen as a common sense measure you take, to make sure you hold onto power once you have it in your grasp. You watch the kids, and catch the problematic ones early, so they cannot surprise you, and you always have an advantage over them.

Having seen things from the perspective of the American Stasi, and the elites who set it up, I now view it as comically retarded to think there is a government-controlled school system, ultimately funded and controlled by the criminals raiding our treasury, which is designed to take random genius kids with morals and decency, and hand them the levers of power by educating them to the greatest degree possible. It's laughable to think domestic intelligence, which has the power in this moment, would not infiltrate in there to get control over which kids rose, so they could make sure it would only be corruptible kids they would control.

From there, it should be obvious they would devote considerable resources to making sure high flying kids who were psychologically likely to be problems were taken down a few notches, so they could not take over the control of society exerted by the American Stasi. Intelligence people are psychopathic sharks, so evil, so controlling, you are probably not equipped to predict their behavior, as a regular, moral, patriotic citizen.

For me, the Porn Fairy experience was different. Since I lived in a rural area, with no kids around, on a fairly large piece of property, I did not spend time exploring other people's properties. I hung around and explored pretty much exclusively on my family's land, wandering the woods alone.

Finding a stash of porn there would have been viewed as an intrusion into private property by some sort of perverted deviant, and that would have been noted as a potential threat. So the American Stasi did not have the ability to deliver this contraband to me and weaken me the normal way it would, with other kids in whom it might want to engender an addiction to sex. They could find it in a park or alleyway, but not me.

So I was high functioning, cognitively, but there was no opportunity for me to "find" porn. And yet still, it found its way to me. I do not think it was by chance. I am sure had I ended up becoming addicted, like Bill Clinton, you might very well be looking at me right now on TV, as a governor or even a Presidential candidate. However, that was just not how my neurological system worked.

I now understand, this was the American Stasi's childhood control division, attempting to create moral weaknesses in children, to weaken them neurologically, so that could be exploited when they became adults, and those weaknesses could be used as a psychological lever.

That is not unheard of in intelligence and psychological operations. From here:[353]

When Palestinian residents of the besieged West Bank town of Ramallah turned on their TVs over the weekend, what they encountered was neither news nor any of the usual Palestinian Authority programming; they encountered pornographic movie clips.

Three of the four TV stations in Ramallah, headquarters of Yasser Arafat, had been occupied by Israeli troops. The town's remaining TV station was meanwhile running a crawl at the bottom of the screen explaining that the porn clips were the work of the occupying forces. "We urge parents to take precautions," it read.

An Israeli army spokesman told Agence France-Press that their forces had nothing to do with such clips, and even blamed Arafat for the footage. "Arafat is willing to go low in order to make himself look better in this uncomfortable situation," said the spokesman. However, an Israeli foreign ministry spokesman, taking into account that the porn-playing stations were after all occupied, was less sweeping in his denial, saying "I cannot believe that Israeli soldiers would engage in such despicable behavior." He called it "shameful."

That was psychological operations, not the regular combat infantry. Sexual stimuli actually activate the same dopaminergic neurological systems responsible for pleasure as drugs like cocaine, methamphetamine and heroin. Exposing a target to hardcore pornography is similar to giving them cocaine or methamphetamine or heroin. It does not strengthen them.

But whereas the drugs would require continually resupplying the target with the drugs, the pornography can supply a similar, albeit weaker stimulus indefinitely using endogenously produced neurotransmitters, which the body will naturally replenish. If you can engender addiction, the target will begin seeking out the stimuli themselves, to trigger the release of their own neurotransmitters, both weakening their fortitude and their tolerance for spartan conditions, as well as wasting their time. It will weaken the mind through addicting the target to sexual stimuli – a weakness we see routinely exploited by intelligence in cases such as the Jeffrey Epstein operation.

I believe the porn fairy is a domestic intelligence procedure for that reason. It is domestic intelligence attempting to mold a child to be more controllable and weaker at adulthood, in ways the operation can exploit. Note, the provision of pornography by an intelligence operation is only a procedure which is executed on what the intelligence operation perceives as a hostile enemy. No intelligence agency provisions pornography to any allied group it wants to strengthen and make powerful, nor would it do so to any group it was tasked with protecting. Intelligence only gives pornography to enemies - and the American Stasi is giving pornography to your children.

It is astonishingly bold, to imagine a parent trying to raise their child right, to be moral, and for the parent to make a conscious decision to not let their child have access to pornography. Meanwhile, down the street, some other adult, fearing the parent was doing too good a job - and looking to weaken the child mentally so they could be exploited later in life, is provisioning them with a stash of pornography behind their parents' backs. It is even more egregious when you realize the parent is paying for the salaries of the intelligence operators in that intelligence operation working against their interests, every time they pay their taxes.

It is even stranger to imagine an intelligence unit, made up of trained adults, poring over a child's file, concluding they might grow up to be a problem, and then going to a store-room down the hall, with piles of pornographic magazines in storage, and as a procedure, ripping out all the pictures and creating a stash to be delivered to the child, to activate their dopaminergic pathways, and seed a potential future addiction.

I believe it is exactly what happened in America, and the UK, and probably elsewhere. The Porn Fairy was in reality, an operation by the global intelligence operation which is in command of the American Stasi. And that command structure was made up of absolute sharks, doing whatever would help them control the world, no matter how extreme or morally out of bounds.

You can say it seems unlikely, but what do we see in schools today, with the overt sexualization of children by teachers and administrators, who do so in spite of parental wishes? In some cases, they are exposing children to sexually explicit depictions of homosexuality, or even trying to sexually transition children to different genders, behind their parents' backs.

It is not natural for a teacher, or an administrator, to work their whole life to reach a lucrative employment position, with a job which secures their future and provides for their family, and then to endanger it all wantonly by doing things to children which parents object to, especially sexually transitioning children. Why would they not just teach math and science, take home their paycheck, and be debauched themselves in their private lives? Why create the risk to their entire lifestyle, for no reason? I would propose you do not do that of your own volition, unless you have been given orders by a command structure.

It is very much like the political world today. If we elected our leaders, they would not waste our money, prioritize criminals over us, attack the Police who we want to see making our community safe, seek to import foreigners who cannot vote for them, and give those foreigners our tax dollars. If we elected our leaders, they would seek to curry our favor by doing what we want, since they would need our votes. But they do not, and as the politicians turn on the very people they supposedly need to elect them, so too, do our school officials turn on the very parents they are supposed to be serving.

It is not the way things should work - unless there is a coordinated intelligence operation in control of government, issuing commands to all of them, and capable of securing their employment, in spite of the public sentiment toward them.

I continued on in school, and in my freshman year of high school, the operation rolled out the bullies to attempt to wrangle me. Not one other freshman in my class had a conflict with an upper-classman. Meanwhile, I had more fistfights than I could remember for the first several weeks of school.

There was the 180lb junior on the bus with 50lbs on me, who was supposed to slap me around in the morning before we got to school, and then again in the afternoon, after school ended. There was another junior in my gym class, and another junior who would post up and wait just for me with his buddy outside the cafeteria. There were still more, who would be waiting in the halls, along routes I took to get from class to class.

Almost all of them started our interactions the exact same way, claiming I was looking at them, and telling me to avert my eyes.

My parents had put me in a pretty rough martial arts club

starting years back. It was so rough there were only a few kids in it. Even fewer after I accidentally put too much mustard on something and broke the leg of the kid I was always paired off with.

Eventually there were so few kids the club threw us in with the adults. By the time I was a 130lb 13year old, it was completely normal for grown men who weighed 200 lbs and knew what they were doing to be tossing me around like a rag doll. I learned you just stepped up and ignored whatever was going on, to attack regardless. Sometimes you were the bug, but sometimes you got lucky and got to be the windshield too. I caught national champions sleeping when they got lackadaisical around me, and most of all, I learned not to think about what I faced, to just get in it and attack, and that every opponent, no matter how big or skilled, can fall if you can hang in long enough to catch them at the right moment.

As a result, the bullies, who had no idea what they were doing, did not really impress me, and we went at it - and I liked it. The kid on the bus ended up fleeing and taking another bus to a nearby area and walking the rest of the way to his house for the rest of the year. Cafeteria kid ended up having to avert his eyes, one blackened, whenever I passed.

After a few weeks, I had a whole list of bullies I was planning to work through, and I looked forward to each of the spots where we would encounter each other every day, hoping that would be the day I could escalate things to blows.

Then just as I grew exhilarated, it all stopped overnight. All the bullies, every one, cut off all interaction with me on the same day. I would lock eyes on them and glare as I passed, and they all would ignore me, or avert their eyes. I could not even get anything verbal going, let alone get it to progress to blows.

At the time, it made no sense. But now I realize I was enjoying what I assume the operation had hoped would wear me down. I was supposed to get smacked around on the bus to school, pushed around between classes, punched down during lunch, beaten up in gym, and slapped around again on the bus on the way home. I was supposed to dread every day I had to go to school. And that dread would affect my academic performance.

Instead I was walking in on cloud nine, jubilant to face each day, and invigorated when I walked into classes. It had not gone as planned, so the adults, one of whom I actually met, had called off the bullies and told them all to ignore me. And they all did, overnight.

I realize now the American Stasi adults who ran the kids at my school were a group of men who many there may not even remember. They were grown men, about four or five of them. If you asked about them, you were told they were "security aides." Supposedly they were there in case some fight happened which was too violent for a teacher or hall aide to break it up, although the school was all well-behaved suburban kids, and outside of my situation, rarely was there any fight.

All I ever saw in terms of work by them was one who periodically stood by the area where the kids who smoked were allowed to smoke, and a couple of others once or twice, walking through the halls, but never doing anything. There were rumors some were ex-cops, but I never caught how anyone knew that.

545

They never really dealt with anyone, and I paid them little mind.

After I had it out with cafeteria kid, he ran off with his black eye, shouting over his shoulder I was crazy to mess with him. I think the adults who ran the kid agents at the school were afraid I might start torturing the kid, so the next day a teacher came up to me in the cafeteria and told me to go the entry office.

This was odd, as the entry office was just a small room with a counter at the front of the school for visitors. If you got in trouble, you went to administration on the third floor to deal with a vice principal. I had already been there a few times for fights.

I walked into the entry office, said my name, and one of the women behind the counter motioned for me to come around the counter, and go in the back. An older Irish man, heavy and out of shape, with short graying hair, who I believe now was the senior "security aide," and thus commander of the American Stasi unit assigned to this school, met me, and motioned to follow him down a small hallway. I had never seen him before, but would later see him interacting with one of the other security aides, and he was clearly the boss.

We entered what looked like a dirty storage room. He had moved some boxes to the side and brought in a regular school desk unit which he sat at, facing the wall, and next to it, pointing in the opposite direction, he had positioned a chair for me, back to the wall. It was set up kind of like police detectives would have a chair for someone to sit in relative to a desk, positioned in a police TV show, but the use of a common school desk-chair combo unit which he had to slide into made it seem kind of silly.

He proceeded to say someone reported I was in a fight with

someone the day before. I said "Yeah, the kid hit me and I defended myself." He looked very earnest, and asked if the conflict with the kid was continuing, to which I replied it appeared he was going to leave me alone, so I was done with it.

It was all very puzzling. This guy was not a teacher or administrator. I viewed him as like a janitor, only with less workload. He had all the authority to discipline me of the old ladies who stood in the hall between classes, asking you if you had a hall pass, which is to say, he had no official authority in the school administration hierarchy. Vice principals were the only ones with authority, and even teachers would send you to them to be dealt with for punishments.

Yet, a teacher sent me to him, and the ladies at the desk were deferring to him, as if he had authority. It was kind of like teachers sending you to meet a UPS messenger passing through the school, and he tells you he has read your file, and you had detention for something. Only vice-principals handled discipline. And yet everyone else was acting like this was normal.

He then proceeded to tell me that with my intellect and the classes I was taking, I should be above getting into these scuffles, and he didn't want to see me fighting anymore. Again, as far as we were told this guy was some low-IQ muscle the school kept around to break up a fight if the kids were too big for a teacher to handle - something I never saw any of them do. How does he know my course load, or whether or not I am smart? Why is he so concerned with my fighting or not fighting? How would he have access even to my records? I doubt even teachers had free access to the full files of students. I certainly did not look smart, so the only reason he would say that was, he saw my full file.

I also briefly wondered how he would have handled it if I wasn't as compliant. Suppose I told him I kind of liked pushing the other kid around, and I was thinking of making him my own personal punching bag, who I would torture to blow off steam. He wasn't about to give me detention, he had no authority. What would he have done?

I now realize he was one of the adults who ran the surveillance kids in the school, and probably oversaw the intelligence gathering, and life-interventions, on all the normal, non-Stasi kids in the school. From what I saw those "security aides" were actually some sort of domestic intelligence unit assigned to the school to handle watching all the kids there, filling out their files, and in some cases, controlling where they would be able to go in life, with an eye to the larger operation's control of the government, entertainment, news, and broader nation. I now think every school has such a unit. This thing has gotten so big, and come so far, it has to control everything, including where people go in life. If it failed, even once, someone might one day get somewhere higher up and notice it, and be able to reveal it to everyone, and then all of the conspirators in it would be executed for treason. Once you see how big this operation has grown over the decades, and you realize they have no choice but to be this thorough, it all will appear as merely prudent organization, rather than bizarre, conspiratorial theory.

Given the criminality in our government, from pedophile blackmail networks like the Jeffrey Epstein operation, to the pilfering of the treasury, to the phony forever wars they use to keep patriots busy fighting as they pad the stock prices of defense contractors, to the criminal surveillance operation intruding in every citizen's life, they have to keep you as far away from government, and the levers of power as possible. There is no better time to begin than when you are a naive child, unaware of the way the world works, and the ever-presence of surveillance and intelligence operations targeting the citizenry.

They tell you that you can be anything, and then work feverishly behind the scenes to see you never get the opportunity to try to be anything. Because if you tried, you would find out the truth – that you are not allowed to do anything, except for what the American Stasi dictates. Everything is much more controlled than you would think possible. If you have not found out, you have just never tested the boundaries - and you cannot imagine the extent of the criminal activity up there, or how the conspiracy needs to stop you from rising to a position where you notice it.

As a result, having never tested the boundaries, and having been stifled covertly if you did without it being perceptible, you will be complacent and compliant. You will feel that any failure to attain your potential, in this free, opportunity-filled environment, was simply due to your own personal failure. After all, you grew up in the most free, opportunity-filled nation, where we do not allow things like the CIA to operate domestically. Indeed, nobody even knows you exist, because nobody is allowed to spy on you.

Don't feel stupid, I believed all this too. We believe it, because it is how we would run it. We believe it, because we are good, and nothing like the psychopathic sharks of our intelligence community, or the people above them who have taken them over. Best of all, NOBODY, would believe any of this is possible. I have just told you I have seen it with my own eyes. If you look at it logically, it would be the most effective way to hold on to power.

Yet how many would dismiss even the possibility, out of hand, assuming it would not be possible? What an amazing shield - to do something so bad that nobody would believe it even possible. Of course the psychopathic sharks of intelligence would do that. There is almost no risk, as even if people find out and try to alert others, nobody would entertain the possibility, or believe them – unless they see it too. Were I to just have alleged this in this book, without showing you the surveillance on Google Streetview, I am sure you would have thought me insane. Even so, I am sure you have doubt.

So returning to my meet with the Cabal boss in the broom closet, this guy was afraid I liked hurting his kid-operative, and would be doing it more for fun in the future. This was some sort of intervention to try and head that off, done below the radar of the school administration.

About seven years later, after a martial arts class, we all went out for beers in a bar, and I saw cafeteria kid, all grown up, looking sketchy, following me. There was no doubt by his demeanor, he was surveillance, and years later he was still assigned to me.

The next year, the unit apparently felt I could be better controlled through girls, and so it began trying to hook me up with girls, whose interest at the time seemed strangely obsessive and weird, but who I now realize were surveillance, and were being sent in by the command. Amazingly, the American Stasi makes full use of its children intelligence agents, even using their daughters as honeypots in the schools. I have seen it. I also saw the use of a male "bad-boy" to try and derail another female honors student. They were quite active back then.

When the honeypots failed to derail me, the next year, my junior year, my health collapsed exactly two weeks before the SATs for reasons which remain unclear, despite more doctor visits than I can remember, including a nationally recognized specialist who confessed his befuddlement.

However in the course of my health issues, I did one morning wake up to find my legs were vibrating softly. They continued to do so as I lay motionless and in awe, afraid if I moved, the spell would be broken. So for a few full minutes, I laid there frozen, trying to figure out if the bed was vibrating, if I was having a neurological event of some sort, or if something else was going on. Whatever it was appeared so interesting I was riveted.

I even entertained the possibility of some kind of constructive interference node which had cropped up entirely by chance, due to various vibrations from car engines and other things in my neighborhood, all coinciding in that one spot around my legs, producing a node of constructive interference that was vibrating my legs. It felt like seeing a UFO, as the coincidences necessary would have seemed so unlikely, and the event so rare.

It is now my strong suspicion my health issues were just a third attempt to bring my future under some kind of control of this operation. That morning, an application of the vibration beam which had been being done nightly at low levels had been applied just a little too strongly, and awoken me, and the operator had neglected to notice I awoke, and turn it off fast enough to evade my notice. My staying motionless may have convinced them I was still asleep.

I suspect done nightly at low levels, it causes a non-specific

551

inflammation and degradation of health, and degrades sleep quality to reduce your functioning. I assume there are many children throughout the nation as you read this, with incredible potential, who are getting that treatment each night, to prevent them from rising to areas which would allow them to see how the elite levels of society function.

They will not be deathly ill, but they will be degraded, and periodically suffering from a variety of seemingly random infections and maladies. They will awake in the morning exhausted, they will get frequent colds and infections, and they may have autoimmune issues. A life they once bounded through, will suddenly seem a struggle.

They may also notice their health inexplicably waxes and wanes, as the beam is adjusted by whatever house nearby is administering it, and they may notice it does so in conjunction with any pets which sleep near them. In my case, my health status was perfectly correlated to that of the German Shepherd who never left my side during this period, even though we ate different food, and were different species. I was always puzzled by that, as I grew ill, and his toe infections grew, his ears became infected, requiring medication, and a skin issue he suffered from would suddenly flare up.

Again, it sounds incredible, even though if I am right about the surveillance, and the American Stasi has gone that far, it is not much farther to begin intervening like that with kids, using some surveillance imaging device on a high setting to degrade them. But I do not expect you to believe me. File away in your mind I alleged it, and it is possible, even if incredibly unlikely, and see if anything you see in the future will bear upon the question, and help you to determine its veracity conclusively.

Obviously if you are a parent of a moral, decent, empathetic child with high potential, I would urge you to keep the possibility in mind, if any nonspecific health complaints come up in your child's life. They will purchase homes next door to children of incredible potential, and install agents in them, expressly for purposes of monitoring the child, and potentially intervening in their life. I have seen it, and I wish someone had warned me.

Again, I do not think this is unusual, now that I have seen it personally. In fact, I think it would be unusual if you looked at the elites running a government somewhere, and found they did not have people looking over the children in the schools, with a wary eye, looking for who had the ability to rise to the top of society effortlessly - and moreover, who might try to take power when they grew up - and be moral, operating for the good of the citizenry. They literally can't allow that, given what they've done.

I would even think it bizarre, if somewhere such elites freely allowed children of incredible potential to rise effortlessly and take high positions in society without trying to stop them by any means possible. Because the people in power, the real people in power with the money and the influence, do not want to give that up. Moreover, they cannot give that up, due to the nature of how the intelligence operations who run all of that, control it through blackmail and criminality. Not only would they lose money, power, and influence, they would be imprisoned, and maybe even executed.

In fact, having seen this, I now think there is nothing more preposterous than the idea we have a government ruled by the corrupt, which is clearly pilfering the treasury and rigging elections, with numerous pedophile blackmail networks like Jeffrey Epstein's operative, and the people behind all of that would let anyone come up with a killer idea and become a billionaire, and then run for President, and maybe expose all of these things going on in our government. It is preposterous. That we believed it at all, even as kids, is a testament to the power of psyops - psychological operations. All of that was brainwashing to leave us naked and helpless, while cloaking us in a mirage of power and enablement.

I suspect that although it is not public knowledge, you will find that from the Hilter Youth of Nazi Germany's Gestapo, to the Stasi, to MI-6 today in Britain, to the secret services of Germany, Italy, France, Australia, New Zealand, and beyond, the intelligence agencies of nations are all throughout the schools everywhere, because that is where the greatest advantages, and the greatest threats, lie.

And how better to spy on children, than to use the children of your domestic intelligence/surveillance operatives in the schools. It bled out somewhat with the Gestapo and the Hitler Youth. But somehow they have kept that ubiquitous technique a secret since then, in the West, but have no illusions, it is being used today.

I have seen the reality, and with time, so will you. One day, not only will you see it clearly, it will make perfect sense, and the idea intelligence would not do that, will seem ridiculous in retrospect. I suspect, of all the areas in which the America Stasi gathers intelligence on Americans and operates to control the course of their lives, we will find that the schools, where Americans are at their most naive and helpless as children, were one of the most focused upon areas.

It will also be the most shocking aspect of this operation to come to light. Between the use of operative's kids as child-spies, and trained adults assigned to the schools making decisions on what children are allowed to succeed, even them punishing the more moral and empathetic due to the risks they present to the corrupt and criminal system, and then actually moving to undo decades of good parenting, just to make sure some child or other did not get to actually grow up free, moral, well developed, and able to do what they wanted, it will be shocking.

When it comes out, I see it as one more factor, making a civil war, of regular people vs the surveillance people, inevitable.

Clearly, even if you only view my assertions here as mere allegations, it behooves every parent to investigate this, and get to the bottom of it, for the good of their children. I know you will be shocked at what you find. I have seen it myself, already, firsthand.

To begin your journey, stop by AmericanStasi.com, and view the video of a surveillance kid talking about running a follow.[354] From there, your only question should be, not whether or not the American Stasi is running children as assets against the rest of the nation, but rather, just to what extent they are being run, and whether they are being run against other children in the schools.

You are going to realize that they are, and that this is how intelligence operates.

Chapter Fifteen
The Stasi Fears Your Gifted Child
The GATE Program

Before we move forward, I must touch on one program being run by the American Stasi, which targets gifted children, as a warning to parents of children with unusual academic abilities.

My mom carried genes for both high functioning in mathematics and, we will say, strong-headedness, which she passed to me. Although she did not know it at the time, she had recounted to me instances which were indicative of surveillance activity, and more puzzlingly, street theater, stretching back to her days as a child, over a decade prior to the time of John Kennedy Toole's targeting.

She would get on a bus as a young girl, back when children could roam freely, and a group of adults would all come on, move to sit around her, and then conduct an overly loud conversation around her, about things going on in her social circles with her friends. She told herself they must have friends with the same names, undergoing the same travails, or maybe they somehow knew her friends, but you could see it didn't sit right with her. When I was a teenager, and she recounted one such instance, she finished, furrowed her brow, and asked me if I ever felt like strangers around me were having a loud conversation, specifically so I would hear it.

In fact, I had that happen numerous times growing up in school, as the child-Stasi-agents were trying to get me to see some girl or other they were throwing at me as attractive, or to get me to see some behavior as desirable. I could tell the speech of the kids was even rehearsed when this happened. I could even predict when these events would occur, simply through a minute or so of tension which would precede them, as you would see the conversers furtively looking back and forth at each other, as if to get the timing straight, and make sure everyone was ready to begin their pre-rehearsed skit.

At the time these were bizarre events I dismissed as having been mis-observed somehow. Surely there could not be any conspiracy, I told myself. However later, as my surveillance became evident, it became clear, my coverage had begun much earlier than you would think possible in the United States.

My mom was not from a wealthy or powerful family, and one would have thought there was little chance she would have grown up to be of any unusual noteworthiness, save for her intellect and hardheadedness.

I assume it was her targeting which led to mine, as I can distinctly remember being six or seven years old, going out a back door of my house, and seeing several cars suddenly appear and drive both ways on the street behind it, and being puzzled. Cars were rarely on that street. It led nowhere, and there were few houses on it. Yet whenever I went out that door, cars drove in both directions. Even as a small child, I marveled at the bizarre statistical anomaly, before dismissing it as having to be randomly generated, albeit strangely improbable.

The point being, surveillance targeting of special children begins quite early, before they even enter school, and given the American Stasi has been at this for some time, I think it likely they have probably identified that certain people carry genes for the types of things they are concerned about. The American Stasi knows who you are, who your parents were, and who your children are likely to grow up to be.

This means, if a child is gifted, I think it likely the surveillance will have foreseen that child could be gifted, through its genetic ancestry, and they will probably have begun surveillance on the child, and possibly even the parents, going back to before such gifted qualities had begun to manifest, or become evident.

When I entered school, I was placed in the Gifted And Talented Enrichment (GATE) program in elementary school. This was a national program that went by many names across the nation, including the Special Talented Enrichment Program (STEP program), Talented And Gifted (TAG program), and others.

It sounded good at the time - a special program to help gifted children reach their full potential. Of course the school's job is to make your child as successful as possible, so helping the most gifted reach their potential so they could one day run the nation simply made sense. However, after comparing notes online with others who went through it, it now appears it was just a means by which domestic surveillance could separate out the gifted kids and perform detailed intelligence gathering, on children whom it now clearly appears to view as potential adversaries.

All of the kids in the program who have compared notes online have noted the rooms in which the classes were held either had no windows, or the windows would be papered over so nobody could see into or out of the room. Many have seeming gaps in their memories, and are not able to recall much of what went on in the classes. Some have described taking "talking naps" which were pitched as tools to focus thought and creativity, but which sound suspiciously like hypnosis sessions. Others describe what sound like pharmacological experiments, and many describe seeing indices of surveillance coverage persisting into their adulthood, which seem related to their involvement in the program.

In my school, we were given batteries of tests, which at the time our teacher told us were for some friend at a local research college who needed the data for some thesis or other. Most were measuring physical and neurological capability. Eye range of motion, hearing ranges, hand-eye reaction times, hand-ear reaction times, peripheral vision range, and so on.

All were given with special equipment attached to a computer (which was not nearly as common in academic settings back then, given this was before the age of the PC), all of which came in special customized, foam-lined hard cases. I was surprised the school had such extensive specialized testing equipment which had been so carefully produced and packaged, when there were only ten or so of us in the program. Obviously now, that equipment was probably provided free of charge by domestic intelligence, probably under the cover of some benign organization.

Some of the testing was strange. My class was told by the teacher that his friend at the local university was doing a paper on

560

psychic phenomenon, and he needed data, so we were going to do a test of our psychic abilities to help him out, but it was kind of unofficial. However he emphasized everyone knew all psychic phenomenon were fake and not real.

Regardless, for the good of his friend, he implored us to take the testing seriously, and do the best we could as if it were all real, and we had psychic abilities to test. As each of us began the test, he would walk us through a procedure, clearing our mind, relaxing, breathing, focusing, seeing the image he was seeing, and so on.

The test was the classic Zenner card test, where the tester looks at a card with one of five or six images on it, with the back of the card facing the student, and the tested student clears their mind and then tries to read his mind and see what card he is looking at, as he is projecting his thoughts at us.

We were not told how we did, which seemed strange given it was all fake. I expected jokes and prodding over our random scores, but we did the test, and never spoke of it again.

Of course now, having stumbled on forums where other GATE students were discussing their experiences, I find out that the Zenner card test was not being done for the teacher's friend at the local university. Rather, it was a standardized test which was part of the national program, which all students who were in it, took. None of us were ever told our scores.

Why the teacher felt the need to lie is perhaps the most interesting aspect. He had to test the psychic ability of the students in the class, but he did not want the students to know that was being tested. It implies those running the program at least held out the possibility such phenomenon were real, and as part of a thorough assessment of potential adversaries, they felt they needed to test that.

I now view such gifted programs as just another intelligence-gathering exercise, though a strange one, as it implies the powers that be appear to have some belief in psychic phenomenon, and a concern about any student potentially possessing a psychic ability.

There were other strange aspects to the class. Most kids who were in it seem to remember at some point drinking a pink liquid they were given, in a small paper medication-sized cup with little explanation as to what it was, or why they were drinking this strange concoction.

I do not know if whatever was in the pink liquid was given to my class, or if we were some type of control in an experiment, but I do remember distinctly a hot day we came in from recess, and the teacher had laid out, on a platter with paper on it, the little paper medication cups you see, about half the size of a shot glass, each with a small portion of Welsh's grape juice in it, which he said we should drink.

We assumed he was serving it as a refreshment, though I remember thinking at the time it was odd all he had were these little cups, as they are so rare compared to regular-sized paper cups. I thought to myself, I would not even know where to go to buy cups like these. It felt like he had to go out of his way to procure an inferior paper cup, and had things been as I was assuming, and he just wanted to offer us a refreshment, it was vastly more likely statistically, that those would have been regular paper cups. The amount of grape juice was also not enough for any sort of refreshment, which seemed strange, but I assumed he had not had enough to offer people real amounts. You do not really ask questions at that age. Now, of course, I wonder whether something was in the grape juice, or if we were some kind of control group for the kids with the pink liquid.

The work we did was really not of any academic use either. We spent almost the entire two years of fourth and fifth grade just reading Greek mythology, with maybe a week-long divergence into Rube Goldbergs, or making popsicle stick bridges here and there.

I place this here as a warning to parents, to not trust their children's schools, or to blindly accept any program their gifted child is offered is really for their benefit.

The powers that be do not really want your gifted child to become so amazing they can take power themselves one day. They want them limited, and they want to make sure, above all else, they will not pose a threat to the criminals and degenerates which intelligence has installed as controlled assets, running our governmental, private sector, and social power structures. In fact, they need to do so, for at this point, to lose power to principled, moral leaders would be to consign themselves to death for treason.

There is a good link compiling information on the mysteries of the GATE program at: https://rentry.co/gate-general

Archive.ph - https://archive.ph/dREBM

Wayback Machine - https://web.archive.org/web/20230725 174117/https://rentry.co/gate-general

Chapter Sixteen

Guess Who Has A FISA Surveillance Warrant - (You!)

But how can this be fellow patriot, you ask? It could not be legal to spy on all Americans in such a detailed fashion without some kind of warrant?

Au contraire. First, the American Stasi already controls all the law enforcement agencies which would normally enforce such laws. It has penetrated them and subverted their leadership so none will investigate any illegal spying. The lore of gangstalking is littered with the stories of victims, from Aaron Alexis to Bill Binney, who approached law enforcement agencies, and were entirely ignored. Fall under the harassment of the American Stasi and you will find there is no law or justice in the United States, just the illusion of justice.

However even if you could trigger an investigation, in all likelihood, it would make no difference. Any reasonable examination of the mathematics of surveillance would indicate it is legal because just about everyone has a FISA warrant authority which allows the government to spy on them now. That will be another big reveal that is coming. We already know for a fact that as of 2017, there had been 40,668 FISA warrants issued.[355] However a single FISA warrant allows primary surveillance authority for more than one person.

As an example, if a mosque is known to be organizing a terror attack with the help of a foreign entity, under the law, the government can submit an application for a single FISA warrant to put all of the members of the mosque under primary surveillance, and the single warrant will justify making each of the two hundred or three hundred mosque-members a primary target. So there may technically be far more primary FISA surveillance targets than 40,668. However for the purposes of this elucidation, we will assume each warrant is for a single person. That means the coming estimate will be conservative, and maybe very conservative. The real numbers could be much larger.

Once you have a primary target, a FISA warrant allows two "hops."[356] That is, the warrant allows surveillance of the primary target. It then allows investigators to also unleash surveillance on every single one of the primary target's direct contacts and relations, as identified in their databases, no matter how brief the contact or how vague the relationship. Expanding surveillance to this first associated contact is called the first "hop."

So your FISA warrant also opens up all of your family members, friends, and people you make contact with, however brief, to full, Osama bin Ladin level, terrorist-level surveillance and eavesdropping, as well as all your work and business contacts - your plumber, your mechanic, everyone you exchange mail with all your phone contacts, perhaps going back ten to twenty years, and anyone else you cross paths with in any way. Remember the guy who you called accidentally, when you mis-dialed a number? He is a hop, and now the domestic surveillance neighbor next door is listening in his house, entirely legally.

However the FISA law then allows "investigators" to take

566

each of those secondary targets the primary target contacted or had a relationship with at some point, and perform a second "hop" to all of their contacts and relations, who become tertiary targets. One analysis found that a single FISA warrant on one person would justify surveillance of 25,000 additional people on average, after factoring in all of the hops, and hops from hops, which would be justified off of it.[357]

Now the interesting part. If there are 40,668 FISA warrants as of 2017, and we assume each FISA warrant only targeted a single person conservatively, and that one primary target would allow surveillance of 25,000 additional people off of all the hops, and hops off hops, then the government presently has a raft of official FISA surveillance warrants, already issued by the judicial system as of 2017, (almost seven years ago), which gives it the right to roll out terrorist-level surveillance, right out of the movie *Enemy of the State,* on over 1 billion American citizen-surveillance-warrant targets - 1,016,700,000 warrants, to be exact. And that was only as of 2017, and assuming only one person per FISA warrant.

Some of those FISA warrants may be for fifty or five hundred people in some groups, and given the extent of the data stored in government/intelligence databases, and the ability of intelligence to stretch laws far beyond their original intent, it is possible the estimate of 25,000 hops per target is also far smaller than it works out in reality. There could be two billion surveillance authorities off those warrants, or ten billion, since it is probably the goal of intelligence to create as many targets as possible.

Of course, there are only 300 million Americans. So all of us probably have several FISA warrants coming at us from several different directions, allowing the government to legally listen in our homes, tap our phones, and even make entry to our houses to poke around, while we are out at work, or at a child's dance recital. All of us are Osama bin Ladin-level targets, who might as well be smuggling a bioweapon into DC which would kill everyone there.

Those warrants give the government multiple justifications to build our file. And that probably extends to our children as well, given if you look close enough, you can probably find a hop or two to any of them from you or someone your family knows. Even Donald Trump and Barack Obama each would have multiple FISA warrants, as will everyone who has ever been in contact with them in some capacity, including Trump's toddler grandchildren. And if there is no hop? The government need only send in a confidential informant who happens to be a primary or secondary target to make contact with your family, and now every family member is a tertiary-level target, and can be spied upon.

Basically, through some clever legal wrangling and some logarithmic mathematics, the government has essentially given itself the ability to treat every American like a James Bond villain armed with a nuclear weapon, bent on raising a mushroom cloud over Washington DC.

It should not be surprising. You have seen the surveillance, from a port city in California, to the remote wilds of Alaska. It is out there, and when the Google car is not rolling through town, the surveillance vehicles are still there, gathering information, and the command center is still operating, actively following targets. It is just that those targets are you and your children, and the information it is gathering is on you – and your children.

Of course we were told the CIA would never roll out on American soil targeting Americans. While I have no idea who exactly has rolled out like the CIA on American citizens, I can assure you somebody has established a surveillance state right out of the East German Stasi, complete with extensive numbers of civilian informants and elite spook technology, all hiding as regular fellow citizens, living right down the street, as they build detailed files on every American, including our children.

Even worse, although this machine may have the authority of the US government behind it, there are indications it is run by some foreign, non-state intelligence operation, which has come in and infiltrated our government for some foreign interests. That would explain how such a fundamentally un-American operation could come to be so ever-present throughout our nation, even as every real American would oppose it with every fiber of their being, were they made aware of it - and as everyone in the military, law enforcement, and intelligence community are supposed to swear an oath to the Constitution of the United States of America.

Sadly, it also explains why this operation now appears to be trying to collapse the nation, through the importation of savage third world migrants, the freeing of criminals onto our streets, the attacks on Police to erode the security of our communities, and the wasting of our national treasury on foreign adventures in which we have no national interest.

We have been infiltrated and taken over, we are no longer electing our leaders, they no longer represent our best interests, and those who are in control are working to destroy us.

Our time grows shorter by the minute. Making matters worse, there is somewhere between 4% and 10% of the nation which has actively pledged its loyalty to our enemy, which we will have to deal with first and foremost, before we can get our Constitutional Republic back. We will not be able to have a United States of America, organized around an elected, Constitutional government, so long as they remain within the nation. For whatever reason, they seem dedicated to destroying it for our enemies.

We must work quickly. At the end of this, when I ask for your help, I hope you will join me, and follow the small steps I lay out. I will not ask you to sacrifice much, but I need your help to destroy this thing very badly, and we do not have much time.

Chapter Seventeen
End of Watch, Rest In Peace

Here we will detail the cases of Police Officers who were struck down by individuals this operation seemed to gaslight and spin up into a murderous frenzy, before allowing, or arranging for them, to encounter and kill the officers.

It is unknown why they do this. It may fulfill specific mission objectives, or it's possible some of these officers discovered the conspiracy, and needed to be eliminated. We record their cases here for posterity, and in the hopes their families will see justice.

NYPD Detective Miosotis Familia.

From here, about her killer:[358]

In new surveillance video, the man who police say is 34-year-old Alexander John Bonds can be seen going up to the passenger side of the vehicle before firing a single shot at Officer Familia, then ducking out and running across 183rd Street, CBS2's Janelle Burrell reported...

"We believe that he fired once killing the officer, and then fired again on Morris Avenue at police officers. We have a witness who says he fired at the two officers who stopped him, who then returned fire," NYPD Chief of Detectives Robert Boyce said...

"He was paranoid the police were following him and he felt EMS was also following [him]," Boyce said.

LA Sheriff's Dept Deputy Ryan Clinkunbroomer

From here, about the killer:[359]

Salazar said her son was diagnosed as paranoid schizophrenic about five years ago. He'd say he was hearing voices in his head, she said, and sometimes came home telling his parents or siblings that cars or people were following him in the streets.

At times, she said, he'd grow so upset that he would cover his ears with his hands, yell or stick his head in a trash can to try to drown out the voices.

One of the technologies some targets report encountering from the American Stasi is a microwave-based, focused sound weapon, which projects voices inside their head utilizing the microwave auditory effect, also known as the microwave hearing effect or the Frey-effect. Oddly enough, a metal garbage can would function as a rudimentary Faraday cage, offering some relief from such a weapon by blocking the rf emissions it uses.

Davis, California Police Officer Natalie Corona

From here, regarding her killer:[360]

The gunman who killed an officer in Northern California left behind a letter accusing the Davis police department of hitting him with "ultra sonic waves."Limbaugh left behind a letter, according to Davis police spokesman Lt. Paul Doroshov, who read the letter on camera to CNN affiliate KMAX.

"The Davis police department has been hitting me with ultrasonic waves meant to keep dogs from barking. I notified the press, internal affairs, and even the FBI about it. I am highly sensitive to its affect [sic] on my inner ear," the letter reads. *"I did my best to appease them, but they have continued for years and I can't live this way anymore."*

The letter is signed "Citizen Kevin Limbaugh."

Capitol Police Officer Billy Evans

From here, about his killer:[361]

In online posts since removed, Green described being under government thought control and said he was being watched.

Some have speculated these people may have been subjects in some kind of social experimentation, designed to develop techniques to break people's wills, or make them subservient, or even manipulate them to kill. It is thought the techniques being tested may be an outgrowth of the CIA's old MK Ultra program, which examined how to brainwash people to change their personality, beliefs, behaviors, and thought patterns. The MK Ultra program is a good topic of research to understand the type of inhumanity intelligence operations, even those run by the American government, can exhibit.

Of one researcher's experiments, which he conducted for the CIA, covertly, on innocent, non-consenting patients who were seeking established treatments for such disorders as minor depression, it was documented:[362]

His experiments were typically carried out on patients who had entered the institute for minor problems such as anxiety disorders and postpartum depression, many of whom suffered permanently from his actions. His treatments resulted in victims' incontinence, amnesia, forgetting how to talk, forgetting their parents, and thinking their interrogators were their parents.

Lafayette Police Corporal Michael Paul Middlebrook

From an article on his killer:[363]

Howard told officers the FBI wanted to kill him, and that white vans had been following him.

Police Officers Brad Garafola, Matthew Gerald, and Montrell Jackson

From a New York Times article about the killer:[364]

Many labels for Gavin Long have emerged from the rich digital footprint that he left behind — former Marine, antigovernment radical, alpha male, life coach. But one has stood out for its peculiarity, that of "targeted individual."

Louisiana investigators have yet to describe a motive for Mr. Long's carefully planned ambush that left three law enforcement officers dead and three others injured on Sunday in Baton Rouge, La.

But Mr. Long, who was killed in the shootout, said in online posts and videos that he was a victim of a vast government conspiracy that watches and harasses everyday Americans.

Numbering in the thousands, the self-described targeted individuals, or T.I.s, say that they are being tortured with mind-control weapons and put under surveillance by armies of covert agents known as gang stalkers.

Colorado Police Officer Eric Talley

From here, about his killer:[365]

A lawyer for Mr. Alissa said in court that Mr. Alissa had an unspecified mental illness, echoing public statements his older brother Ali had made asserting that Mr. Alissa was paranoid and had delusions of being watched and followed.

Police Officer Talley was a staunch, pro-gun, Second Amendment activist, who believed in individual liberty and freedom.[366] Whatever your political leanings, he supported other citizens having freedoms a despotic government would not want them to have, despite those freedoms making his job potentially more difficult, and even personally dangerous. He was clearly a man who believed in the freedom of others to do what they wanted, even if it endangered his own life, and I cannot help but think it is not a coincidence he was one of our kind, and he was killed.

Officer Talley's case is interesting in another way. A bystander happened upon the scene in progress, and recorded video of the shooter's initial takeover of the supermarket where

Officer Talley would be shot. The video, to the nuanced eye, shows surveillance operatives very clearly setting up a "static box" perimeter around the building, curiously with very little worry that the shooter might shoot them. I have met these people, and they are not courageous if they think they are going to die. For some reason, they felt this shooter would not shoot them.

The video[367] shows the following scenes pictured here. After each scene I will offer analysis. If you watch the video, despite everyone's knowledge a man is inside the supermarket with an AR-15, and occasional audible gunshots, you will see very out-of-shape, apparently non-combat capable individuals show no fear as they loiter in positions which I think you or I would flee from, in search of cover, or at least concealment, if we were not pushing forward with weapons to engage. But they do nothing, other than observe and text message.

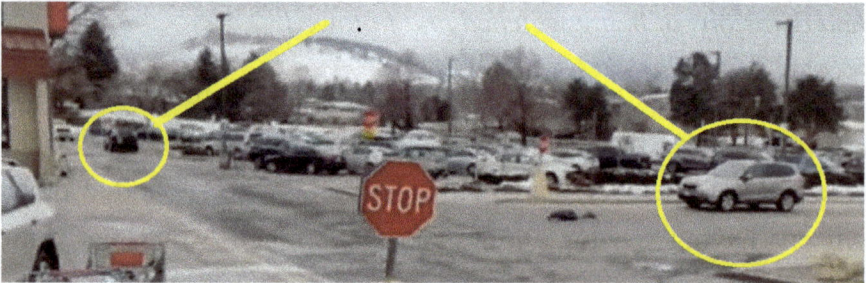

Despite there being obvious bodies laying in the streets, these two vehicles drive up and stop at 90 degree angles to each other, simultaneously. The drivers do not get out of their cars to check on the bodies, as you would if you thought someone had innocently suffered a cardiac event and needed aid, but they do not flee the scene as if they think there is a shooting ongoing.

Both cars pause, at 90 degree angles, which, if they have

cameras out the front and back of their vehicles will offer a central control center excellent live video coverage of what is going on.

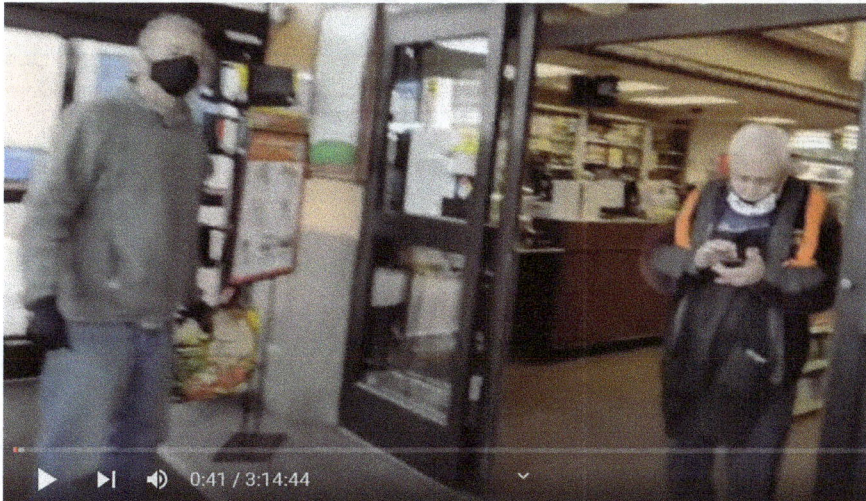

The videographer says, "Oh my God, is there a shooter? Does anyone know where he went?" Chubby, on the right, above, nonchalantly pauses his texting and says, "Oh, yeah, he is right in there," motioning behind him, inside the doorway, before he resumes text-messaging away.

It is a guy with an AR-15, mind you, and he saw him run in there after leaving a trail of bodies outside. But Chubby just holds his station, updating central control, as Numnuts on the left stands there, a carbuncle on the ass of heroism.

Those people are not behaving as you or I would. This is what they do, when Americans, who are not of their own, are in peril. They set up a perimeter, and begin updating central command.

Chubby is still going. He is not bold enough to go inside and begin filling up a shopping cart, but he isn't heading back out to his car either.

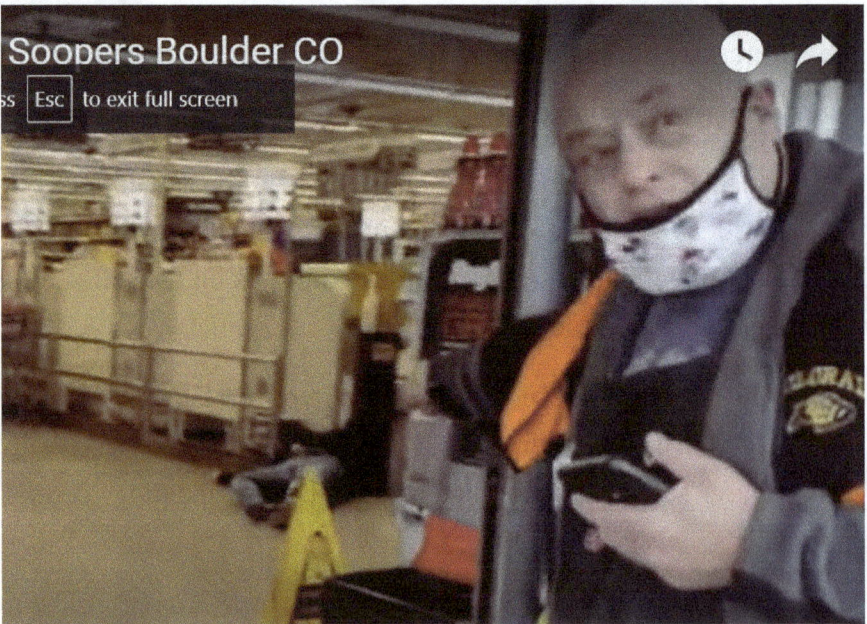

Soopers Boulder CO

Esc to exit full screen

That is a dead body he is pointing at in the picture on the last page, as he says, "Yeah he's right in there!" But he is still not running, and his texting app is still at the ready. Who is he texting, do you think? Officer Talley has not yet arrived on scene. But you can see, more is going on here than meets the eye.

Gunshots have just gone off, from a 5.56 NATO rifle, which is not known as a quiet round, and you have two cars holding position outside, at 90 degrees, as somebody checks on one body, which has been shot to death, but again, nobody is fleeing. Now the videographer will run around the outside of the building.

The videographer sees these people standing right outside, after they have clearly all heard gunshots. He says, "Guys, there is an active shooter!" Their response as they stand there? "Yeah we know, we were just inside the store." Then they continue to stand there, even though the shooter could come out and begin clearing the parking lot any moment now.

581

The videographer runs around the back of the store, and these two people are just standing there at one corner, one literally with their hands in their pockets, watching the back door. Notice, two people posted on the other rear corner, looking this way

The videographer asks, "Are you guys OK?" Their response? "Yeah, we are OK." And they keep standing there, hands in their pockets, even though the shooter could exit the back

of the building, and kill anyone there, at any moment.

As the videographer approaches the other corner, these two begin walking away. They must be camera-shy.

Wild Afro is standing watching the front corner, as if covering the 3-O'clock of the two who had been watching the back.

As the videographer approaches, wild Afro turns and follow the wall of the building to the back corner, where the two who just left had been posting. There are no vehicles which might belong to this character back there, however.

Two vehicular units, most likely. When something like this happens, central control will flood vehicular units to the scene. I suspect most have cameras pointing front and back, and maybe out the sides, broadcasting wirelessly to central control, which is watching all of it up on the big screen in a control room.

The videographer has made a full circuit, walking all the way around the building, stopping periodically to warn people and offer assistance, after hearing a barrage of 5.56 NATO going off at the start of the video. As he has been doing that outside, Chubby here has just been standing in the front doorway like a tool, gleefully texting away, not ten feet from a dead body, and just around the corner from the active shooter who killed it, who is still popping off rounds. Just now at this moment, he has begun to meander away from the sounds of active gunshots.

The man is a text messaging machine. I stop and stand, and

my sausage finger still hits a wrong letter every other tap and I have to go back and delete it, but Gramps here, he isn't even a poker. He is double-thumbing it rapid-fire, while he's walking, no less. Could he be debating with his granddaughter over who is hotter, Justin Bieber or Usher?

It is also worth noting, Chubby cleared the scene moments before Police officers, presumably including Officer Talley, arrived on scene. You will see chubby nonchalantly walk down the ramp, the videographer walks forward, and there Officers are, running up frantic, as the stockboy yells to them he (the shooter) is in the back.

Most likely, whoever Chubby was texting with was monitoring the location of responding officers in real time, and texted him that the officers were arriving, and he should clear the scene. Imagine a control center, with all of this information and video up on a big screen, overseeing the event. Who are these people, and how did all of that expenditure of resources and effort help?

These idiots around the store look like the exact same boobs, in the same numbers, who follow me on every grocery store outing. Just here they are standing outside, and in my case, they follow me through the store. Probably if I popped and began shooting, this is what they would do – move to a perimeter, and update control on the bodycount in real time.

Understand, all of these shooters would have been under the type of surveillance I am under. The cars you saw following the Google car? When they were not following the Google car, they were tasked to these characters, because those cars are rarely idle.

And when these shooters went home, the surveillance observation/monitoring post in their neighborhood would know they were a priority target, and would pile the surveillance on there, watching all internet activity, reading all emails, even listening to conversations in their homes.

That would mean these shooters were watched, to a degree most people would not think possible, every moment. Their Facebook posts, their internet search histories, their purchases, their phone calls, their private conversations in their homes would all have been monitored by an operation which is designed to catch everything and predict target behavior.

In the vast majority of cases, the surveillance would have seen weapons, ammunition, and body armor purchases, seen inflammatory posts online, followed specific search histories, grasped the fact the target blamed local officers, and understood what was coming when they began to make an atypical trip with their weapons and body armor.

In every case, after spinning up their wind-up toy, they let him go and then sat back and passively observed, allowing a Police Officer to approach, or otherwise end up in contact with the shooter while offering them no warning of what was happening, or the danger they faced.

Even worse, in some cases, it has appeared the target was guided to the officer, while they were unawares and vulnerable, as in the case of Detective Miosotis Familia.

This is a dangerous intelligence operation, which it will be shown thinks in ways we would never think, and does things we would never have thought possible.

Chapter Eighteen

Where Do We Go From Here?

First, take a moment to reflect on some of the more shocking touchstones of truth - immutable, undeniable facts - which this book has revealed to you, and which, if you followed our links, you will see were reported independently by reputable, responsible news agencies.

The fourth in command at the National Security Agency on 9/11, the head of its technology division, has publicly stated there is a criminal, off-the-books intelligence operation that has taken over the United States government and is operating on American soil, utilizing directed energy weapons on innocent civilians. He has said publicly that because of directed energy attacks on himself, in his home, he cannot leave his own basement, and this operation blasted two holes through steel shielding he installed to try and blunt the effect of its directed energy weapons. He has said he has tried to turn to official government agencies, through official channels, and they have refused to help, despite knowing what is going on.

This operation is hostile to your elected government. It has hit high ranking White House officials, with directed energy weapons, both in their homes, and on White House grounds, where the Secret Service, our nation's premier protective service agency, with unlimited access to the most advanced technologies we have, is helpless to secure its protectees from injury. It has hit CIA Officers, and then entered their homes in the US to rearrange their furniture after following them on the streets to harass them, and CIA can do nothing, nor can FBI or local Police. Nobody is coming to protect them, just as nobody is coming to protect you. We are all on our own with this thing. Nobody else will be coming to save us.

FBI Agents in Miami have this operation set up on their homes, hitting them with directed energy weapons, and doubtless hitting their loved ones with splash back from those weapons. FBI is helpless to stop it, because the infiltration of our government agencies is so deep, and everything's so compromised. Each night, FBI Agents retire to their beds knowing they and their families are about to be assaulted, and they can do nothing but take it.

This operation's agents are so prolific, you can see the surveillance, even in areas as remote as Montana and Alaska, following the Google Streetview car. There, you see no traffic, except at every intersection when you hit it. And I will guarantee you, the American Stasi was expansive enough on 9/11 that there is no way it failed to foresee those attacks. In the most innocent scenario, this operation knew those attacks were coming and allowed them. And there are less innocent possibilities, especially given intelligence operations like this tend to take measures to see that they know for certain what will happen before it happens, and chance cannot derail events accidentally, leaving them unprepared.

Given how intelligence agencies operate, between the fact the American Stasi had to have known, and the fact the attacks were not stopped, I tend to think they took measures to see that the hijackers would succeed, rather than sit back, and not know what was going to happen. I suspect this surveillance operation functioned more as support for the 9/11 hijackings, than opposition, because the attacks succeeded. When in control, intelligence controls what happens, and this thing is in control, and 9/11 happened. I think it helped do it, and I think everyone in it, even the grandmother following you through the grocery store, knew.

In my own opinion, this operation wanted 9/11, to allow for a legal expansion of surveillance powers it would be able to exploit. I suspect this operation took measures to make sure the attacks of 9/11 could not be stopped, and even had the 9/11 hijackers failed, it had backup plans to make sure the attacks happened and could be blamed on them. That is how intelligence operates, where a common phrase it uses is, "The best way to predict the future, is to make it happen." It is why you do not want it in your nation, operating against the citizenry. It is evil to the core.

And I think deep down, every soccer mom and grandma following me through grocery stores knows the operation it serves allowed 9/11, and that their command is that big of an enemy of "Real America" proper. As bad as Al Qaida was, this is an even worse enemy of America, because this adds a dimension of betrayal to the equation. And its secrecy makes it far more dangerous a threat.

Notice, neither the media, nor the "influencers" online are highlighting any of this, even as our nation is being attacked, and the enemy is well within our gates, in control of our elections, and throughout our government. Its intelligence apparatus is even in the first phases of setting the stage for a full civil war and national collapse, but nobody will say a word.

I will guarantee you all of them – influencers, reporters, commentators, media personalities, ideological figures – they have all seen the surveillance I have shown you. I am in that world, it is rife throughout it. As you rise, it shows itself to you, to make sure you will bow in subservience. All of those people are being allowed to continue, even seeing their careers advanced, because they are hiding the conspiracy from you. They are all enemies, as well.

The media has been infiltrated and subverted, and will be of no use. If you rely on the media, or the "influencers" online with the big names, who everybody knows and follows, you are giving the enemy the power to dictate what you see and pay attention to. You are giving them the power to deceive you and misdirect you.

To all that, I will add a Tweet, posted on the site X, formerly known as Twitter, by former US Army Special Forces operator and journalist Michael Yon, who has devoted himself to covering the migrant crisis:[368]

Pigeon Forge, Tennessee - 03 March, 2024 - Mind-dump, sans edit.

The drone footage below has never been seen and was made yesterday. This is a United Nations Camp in Darien, Panama, after "migrant" attack two days ago.

This is China Camp in Darien, Panama. Locally called San Vicente. Notice this camp is the header on my X page. Same camp. I have been here dozens of times including two weeks ago.

Secretary @SecMayorkas came here on 18 April 2022 to

expand the camp. I was there that day. @ganaha_masako, and @rangerholton, and I first went together shortly after Biden was installed several years ago. Chuck Holton had been to Darien many times over the years. We watched the United States grow this terrorist camp.

Realizing Darien Gap likely would become a main invasion route to USA, I have spent about six months in and around this area since Biden was installed.

Over the past three years I have taken only a small number of select people to this camp and into Darien. These include @annvandersteel, @EpochTimes, @LauraLoomer, @Matt_Bracken48, @RepTiffany, @BenBergquam, @Oscarelblue, @realmuckraker, @MaraMacie, @BretWeinstein, @chrismartenson and a few more.

There is no doubt in my mind that people who pass through this camp will become responsible for the deaths of countless Americans. You have never seen a more serious terrorist camp in your life.

This camp is funded by @DHSgov and others through front organizations such as @UNmigration, and @HIASrefugees.

@HIASrefugees has an office about 50 yards from this fire damage.

The Government of Panama wants to close this camp but @wef, Chinese Communist Party, and @USEmbPAN and others work to keep this open. This is a war camp. Panama could shut the camp with snap of a finger but do not. This camp and others will be instrumental in the coming revolution in Panama. At this *rate, Panama will be taken from Panamanians due to allowing this to grow within their bellies.*

Again, @HIASrefugees has an office about 50 yards from the fire damage that destroyed the "migrant" records two days ago.

@SecMayorkas was a board-member at @HIASrefugees before being installed as an operative at @DHSgov.

Two days ago, a riot occurred in this camp. Several courageous @senafrontpanama men [Panamaniam Border Guards] were seriously hurt trying to save the camp and stop the attack.

Arson was committed including an attack on vital records of invaders who pass through this camp. According to @senafrontpanama, computers and vital records were burned and destroyed.

The attack is said to have started from an internal dispute between "migrants". The records were attacked during the violence. 44 "migrants" reportedly have been arrested so far. Others vanished into the night. Vanished with what? The records?

Records that include CCP operatives, Hamas, Hezbollah, and others who have passed through were said to have been burned. It is unknown if backups are intact. It is unknown to me if the records were actually burned or maybe just vanished into the night.

Powerful forces are at play. This is a multiplayer game.

This drone footage was made yesterday afternoon on 02

March 2024. On the right side of the camp notice the fire damage to @senafrontpanama offices. This is exactly were @LauraLoomer interviewed the Somali, the Iranian, the the Chinaman about two weeks ago. I was there beside her with @ganaha_masako, @annvandersteel, @MaraMacie and others. We know this camp.

China Camp is a terrorist bus station to United States funded by United States.

The surveillance we highlight here is the most visible part of a multifaceted, full-featured non-state intelligence agency/organization, funded by unknown foreign interests, which now is seeking to destroy the United States.

Everything you see, from George Soros installing District Attorneys who will release criminals to continue to prey on citizens, to legislatures and state governments enacting no-bail laws to see criminals released to maximize the chaos and carnage, to attacks on local policing to dissuade local law enforcement from opposing it, to the wasting of the economic resources of the United States on overseas adventures and causes in which we have no interests, to the migrant crisis – this is a covert attack on our nation, waged by an enemy embedded in our society and government, and modeled on the former East German Stasi.

Worst of all, because it controls our media on both the left and right, the vast, vast majority of the nation, on both sides of the political divide, will be blind to this battle, and none of us are resisting it. Do not get bogged down in ideology, left or right, Republican or Democrat. This war pits citizen-agents of the

American Stasi on both the left and right, who are serving foreign, enemy interests, vs regular citizens on both the left and right. Seeing this battle may be the one force which could reunite our ideologically fractured nation, against a common enemy.

There are Americans, both Republicans and Democrats, who have sold us out, and are helping this thing, destroying our nation for handfuls of trinkets and a promise The Beam will pass them over while it is being meted out to us. There numbers are not at all insignificant, and they will have to be dealt with first.

I strongly suspect many, and maybe most of the migrants being brought here were ground surveillance in their own countries working at the behest of this trans-national, foreign intelligence organization, and they are being brought here to serve as operational assets, in events yet to be initiated.

What will happen is going to be far more controlled than you would believe. This should terrify you, and make you understand, these times are unlike any other in our history. You and I have never known such times, nor has our history ever involved such an evil enemy. Our psychologies, our expectations of how we should act, they will all be malformed.

What is to come will be men's work, and it will require the brutality and ruthlessness men have shown in the past. We will all need to become those men of old, who carelessly rendered dangerous species entirely extinct, and viewed it as a good day's work, because it protected our own. From here on out, protecting our own will need to be paramount. If it is not, you might as well enslave your own children yourself and hand them to the conspiracy, for that will certainly be their fate.

I am highlighting the surveillance because it is the most exposed part of this operation. You can see it yourself, in your own neighborhood, and it highlights that fellow Americans, who live right down the street from you, are a part of an enemy organization trying to destroy the country for their own personal gain. The coming war will be a civil war, pitting neighbor against neighbor.

You are going to have to deal with those neighbors, most likely violently, either on your timetable, or on their's. What is coming is a tsunami which cannot be avoided, in my estimation, and for all their mealy mouthed smiles, and protestations of horror at events like 9/11, they intend to see you ground under the boot of their operation, so their operation can take what you have, and throw them some scraps from it. They prefer you not resist in the process.

This is the point where American patriots are going to have to begin to stand up, and understand what it is to commit to something so entirely you will die for it, let alone endure privations. This is a period which will make the heroes which Americans a hundred years from now, will read about with reverence and awe.

Now, here is the plan. It begins most gently, and requires almost no sacrifice from you. But you must commit to it. If this war is to succeed, it is going to need you leading the charge.

If you wish to be one of the chosen few fighting for this nation, the very first step is, you are going to have to look for the surveillance in your neighborhood. Watch your own approach to intersections. Travel to isolated parks to go for a walk and get away from everyone and see if you have trouble getting alone, without walkers happening by, or park maintenance showing up to clean garbage cans out, or planes or helicopters flying overhead.

Go out early one morning to your telephone pole, outside your house with a ladder and a tool belt on, and climb up to inspect the lower level of non-electrified communications wires. Bang on the wood of the pole below them with a hammer a few times loudly, and see if your neighborhood monitor panics, and dog-walkers pop up out of nowhere, a bicyclist just happens by, or cars begin driving by out of the blue to see what you are doing, because the people watching the neighborhood 24/7 began to get antsy and sent coverage by for a closer look at what you are doing near their pole-tech monitoring the neighborhood.

I guarantee you the surveillance is in your neighborhood to some degree, no matter where you are in the United States, and probably throughout the Western world.

Once you see it, the second step you must follow is, spread this work. To do that, we are going to employ two phases of action. You are going to begin spreading this work at first covertly, and anonymously, seeking to create a vector of spread which the conspiracy cannot track. Then, once that phase is completed, you are going to tell friends and family to read this material, and lend social proof to it, even if only by saying it was curious. We need them to read this.

To begin, I am supplying a chain letter[369] which I am asking you to copy, and send anonymously to as many people as possible, both friends, and random individuals, using the delivery service of your choice, be it USPS, UPS, FedEx, DHL or private courier. The letter is here, and I would ask you to go there now, and save the photographs of it, whether you intend to take part in this or not. If you never send the letter, just by saving the file, you will confuse the enemy and give cover to those patriots who do begin sending it.

I will supply detailed instructions in the addendum at the end of the book.

The first stage of this coming civil war is not a violent uprising. You will not have to die for the cause here, or even risk imprisonment. What is needed is a marshaling of our troops in the information warfare space, by informing them of this work. You need to spread this information, and help me to get everyone to see the surveillance. And you cannot do it online.

The online environment is controlled, and I cannot explain to you in this work how bad it is, but as with the surveillance, it is worse than you think. I have worked that space for the last ten years. They have identified and seized control of all of the nodes where information could have spread freely. The censorship mechanisms on the internet are mind-boggling.

However I think there is still a window for us to operate within in the real world. If we can get people to send enough chain letters that each sent chain letter averages just two fellow compatriots, who will in turn send enough letters to find two more people like themselves, who will themselves send enough to find two more compatriots, we can send this book viral exponentially.

If you can print 50 copies of this letter, or even 100 copies of this letter, and send it according to my instructions, and we can find just two of those people in that group of letters to continue the process, in a few months, the whole nation will know about the surveillance, and the political force driving the government to do something to reduce or eliminate it will be immense.

To send the letter, print the letter by taking a picture of it with your phone, and print it from the picture. Or photocopy it at the library. Alternatively you can download it from here, however you will be more trackable that way.[370] Do not type the text, or enter the text into your computer. Print off the images, remove them while wearing gloves, place them in unmarked, stamped envelopes, each with a different fake return address, and mail them to people you know who will be receptive to the information, as well as random addresses you pick online by dropping a pointer on a random house on Google maps, not near an intersection (and thus likely to be surveillance), and pulling up the address.

Do not mail them all at once, or from your mailbox. Take two or three with you when you go shopping, and drop them in a Postal Service drop box while you are out, or send them UPS or FedEx, even in boxes so they look like packages, paid in cash.

Do not discuss this work anywhere out loud, even with trusted loved ones. Not in your home, or your car, both of which are listened to at least periodically, and maybe more if you are a known independent thinker and patriot who cares about the nation. You may be able to write notes in your home to communicate with loved ones, though if you are deemed an important enough target, even that is a risk which they have adapted measures to deal with.

I would recommend, you do not write about it online, post any urls to Twitter, or send any messages with the name American Stasi on Facebook, at least at the start, until you have mailed the letters. These online comments will be detected by AI, the comments will be shadow-banned, and you will immediately go on a list for more aggressive surveillance and suppression.

Do not tell anyone you sent the letter to, that you sent it to them. Some of them, even decades-long friends, will be assets of the operation, and will report you to their command as a problem. Do not let anyone know where the letters are coming from. We want the conspiracy to identify as few of the sources of letters as possible. This attack is best launched from within a thick fog, which obscures everything from our enemy.

The more letters you can send during this covert phase, the better. I have no idea how many Americans still care about this country enough to actually spend money on stamps and send letters to try and save it. We need to find those who do, and it may take a lot of letters to find them and continue the chain, let alone to get it to expand.

At that point, having sent the letters, you will begin the overt phase of spreading this information. In this phase, you may hand out chain letters and place stickers around town, or even promote the work overtly at your social gatherings, bars, churches, gun clubs, and so on, but be aware you may get some additional overt attention from your local surveillance. That will be the conspiracy, telling you to stop. You are now facing the East German Stasi in America. Things are not like you were raised to believe.

If you do not care, and are willing to take some slings and arrows, as I am, drop chain letters on front lawns, put bumper stickers on your car, wear some of our T-shirts and branded clothing, tape chain letters to front doors, hand them out at political rallies, raise the issue at school board meetings, post chain letters on bulletin boards at universities. We need all the help we can get.

Most of all, however, tell friends and family they must read this site. It would be best to say you have seen what it is talking about, you think there is a problem in the nation, and you would like them to read the site and maybe participate in exposing it.

As you spread this information, you will need to process that you are a target, and begin adapting to that reality. You have always been a target, but before you were weak, and ignorant, and the conspiracy liked that, and felt safe. Now you know and are dangerous, and what we are doing here will lead to the destruction of the conspiracy.

That means you are being listened to in your home. Friends who you have known for some time may be sent in to pull information out of you. You will have at least one "friend" reporting to the surveillance, and maybe more. Workers you bring in your house may be assets of the conspiracy, waiting for you to leave them alone so they can poke around in your house, and maybe even plant something. You may want to leave things like threads on door knobs around your house to see if anyone entered while you were out and disturbed them. This thing does that. This is the real deal, and not a game. I live it now, every day.

Begin molding your brain to make yourself an effective operator in an intelligence-driven environment in which you are a dissident target of a mature intelligence operation. Recognize what comprises sensitive intelligence in your life and protect it. Do not send it by email, don't talk about it on the phone, and do not ever mention it out loud in your home or your car. You are a target by virtue of being a patriot who knows how things work, and is capable. Act like it now and begin developing that tradecraft.

This operation will ultimately get most, if not all of your secrets. Your goal is not to necessarily keep them in the dark, at least not now. I am not sure you can keep secrets with their tech.

Your goal is to make them work, and drain their resources, as you condition yourself to be an operator against the less capable operation we will face, once we expose the domestic network and degrade it through political action. Don't let them just have intelligence or get on top of you easily, and do not condition yourself to give up, and not hide your secrets from them.

Also recognize your victories. Whenever I get Beamed now, I take solace in the fact this operation has wasted that Beam on me, and I have not broken. In addition, they are then likely short one Beaming device elsewhere, and unable to break someone else who might otherwise have broken. Our side is then two up against the enemy, and the true civil war has not even begun.

In addition, I have developed a constant awareness of the surveillance procedures around me, and conditioned behaviors to counter them which, though of limited effect now, will make me a genuinely dangerous operator in what is to come, after we get surveillance weakened through exposure, and get the ground network disassembled. If you get used to operating against the current ever-present sectorized phase-coverage surveillance, the simple small-team surveillance the conspiracy should be forced to use after its exposure will appear as a joke to you.

I would also begin to mold my brain to understand, your

reads of people in the intelligence-driven environment are meaningless. As harmless as the grandmother following you through the grocery store appears, as nice and loyal as the parents of your son's friend seem at a soccer game, if they are intelligence operators serving this thing, and I estimate as many as one in ten Americans could be now, you do not know them, and they have shown, by their choice, they are as deadly an enemy as any street gang member who breaks into your house in the dark of night to do you harm. Their operation is destroying America, and they apparently will get something out of that, and they are fine with that deal. You do not know them.

By their fruits ye shall know them. I have been dealing with these people for decades. They are not what they seem and the nation will not miss them when they are gone. Grow accustomed to the idea they are enemies, and you will have to deal with them as such on a battlefield to come. I assure you, in the civil war to come, they will deal with you that way.

They know they are in deep, and they have no intention of suffering the consequences which will come if the nation is not destroyed. They have crossed their Rubicon, and burned the bridge behind them. In their perfect world, everything you know of freedom in America will be gone and you and your children will simply spend your life cowering in fear of The Beam, as they are given stuff taken from you by the conspiracy. In that perfect world, you dare not complain.

In searching for allies, there is only one reliable litmus test I have found – that is, who will talk about the surveillance to everyone they know. The ground network is under absolute orders to never discuss operations. Mention surveillance around one, and they will go wide-eyed, and mute. The more committed will try to cow you with ridicule for thinking it possible, usually by denigrating you as "paranoid." Those who read this book, and pooh-pooh the premise, will be revealing themselves as the enemy.

You have read this book, and seen the evidence. It is at the very least, intriguing, if not concerning, and should be approached by all real Americans as such, with at least cautious curiosity, if not outright concern. No real American should shy from the discussion of it.

The former fourth in command of NSA, a respected and beloved legend in the intelligence community, saying a covert intelligence operation is beaming him in his house, and the government is complicit, is a problem. An out of hand dismissal - an ardent refusal to consider the premise, or even broach the issue, and especially an attack on you, will be abnormal, and indicative of an ulterior motive by everyone who displays such, from public commentator, to neighbor, to leader of your congregation.

Those in the public eye who hold themselves out as authorities, or influencers, who will not discuss the ground surveillance, or this book, will reveal themselves as the conspiracy's propagandists, and enemies of the people.

Every public face you see on the news, on Twitter, or the Sunday shows, has seen the surveillance. It shows itself to them at the outsets of their careers as a test, and demands their fealty – and silence. Many will have taken part in surveillance of fellow Americans for the conspiracy in their own lives, before being handed their fame as a reward for being a loyal agent willing to betray America. Every blogger, every news-site, every voice on

605

Twitter who refuses to extol the dangers we face, or acknowledge the evidence in this work – they will all be revealing themselves as traitors, enemies, and agents of the conspiracy. Look for those who highlight the threat, and only entertain the possibility of trusting people who first will warn you, that you are being watched.

To that end, I hope one day to see our political scene dominated by the Targeted Individuals of this age, who labored under the surveillance, and who know firsthand it does not belong in our nation. They were targeted specifically because they would be loyal to you and the nation. President William Binney has an unusually nice ring to it. The American Stasi would tremble at the thought, and that alone would be reason enough, even if Bill had not suffered mightily, holding loyalty with you.

Aside from the coming civil war, just in living your normal life, with the degree to which the American Stasi has been diffused throughout communities, in a directed, planned fashion, you have to assume there is penetration into your personal life now, even if only to passively monitor you, to make sure you are not about to make some big, unforeseen move which could rocket you up the social ladder.

In your regular life, recognize that in any business environment, you are in direct competition with those at the top, even when just starting out. Recognize they are aware of this, and recognize their position is so precarious up there, they have taken extreme measures to make sure you can never get near them. Know this machine is watching you, and will be used against you.

As they say, strive to keep your plans as dark as night, and when you move, fall like a thunderbolt. Strive to keep your plans from them until you execute, whether forming a business, or planning to hit your local neighborhood observation post, to neutralize it and seize its intelligence, in whatever it is which is coming.

If you are truly committed to American freedom, and do not want to live under a totalitarian dictatorship, I would also pick up a battle rifle and handgun, as well as spare magazines, ammo, and a holster and sling, and perhaps body armor, ideally Level IV plates and a carrier, for what it appears to me, inevitably, is to come now.

Go to Palmetto State Armory and pick up a cheap AR-15 in 5.56 NATO with a flat top upper, have it shipped to your local gun store, pick it up, then get a Holosun 510C, and back up iron sights, maybe at Optics Planet online. Get a streamlight rail-mount flashlight and mount, and mount it on the side. Get ten to twenty 30 round mags, and a large black dufflebag capable of concealing the rifle and holding your spare magazines and plate armor, and as much ammo for it as you can afford, and then go online to youtube, look up basic AR-15 handling drills for the rifle, and follow the videos to gain basic proficiency with it, practicing as often as possible, until handling it safely is second nature. Gain a grasp of the use of cover and concealment, and various shooting positions to exploit them, as well as surprise.

Then take it to the range, sight it in, and practice hitting targets at various ranges. I would try to make sure everyone in my household was armed up and ready - unless any of them seemed likely to be surveillance, in which case I would not arm them, and would actually try to lull them into complacency.

For a handgun, Smith and Wesson M&P 2.0 compact is a

cheap option, and probably the best 9mm out there to boot, though even striker fired Berettas can be found now for as little as $250 in this oversaturated environment. You can get the Smith with a safety. Get a holster for concealed carry, and spare magazines and mag carriers for concealed carry. You will want to be able to carry everything, while looking like a regular civilian. If possible, spend the extra money for an optics-ready version of your handgun, and mount a cheap Riton or Crimson Trace red dot sight from Palmetto State Armory on it. For aiming and shooting fast, it is like cheating.

I do not think we will be rolling around decked out like US Marine infantry on deployment to Iraq, in full battle rattle. We will want that level of protection and lethality, but you will want to appear harmless, in plain civilian clothes. The civil war I think is coming will be a covert guerilla war, fought in quick hit and runs, as citizen vs surveillance in the beginning, to degrade the ground surveillance, which is our biggest adversary.

Now between your kit and your knowledge of the surveillance, you are dangerous, our leaders will fear you, and in enough numbers, that alone will change how they act.

None of these measures, adapting your thinking to the intelligence-driven wartime environment, or preparing in the event things get hotter, or spreading the word about the surveillance is illegal to take now. You do not need to make sacrifices at this stage. All are prudent actions to take, and advance our position. I suspect the time is coming when you will want your brain adapted, and the tools required, to be able to operate in such an environment, and when that time comes, we will need everyone aware of the surveillance. Things are not decelerating. The trajectory now is clear. Either America falls, or we expose the surveillance and deal with it.

Surveillance is going to be exposed at some point, and America will either be ground beneath its boot, or it will eradicate it completely. When it is revealed, those will be the two choices.

Those in the surveillance will face ruin within a nation which will hate them with a passion, or their conspiracy will seize total control. In our ideal outcome, surveillance does not come out of the other side of whatever is coming. Adapt your brain to that reality, but know it will intend to avoid that outcome, by forcing you under its boot.

For decades we have espoused platitudes like freedom isn't free, or the tree of liberty needs to be watered with the blood of tyrants. And then we sat back and did nothing as politicians imported millions of third world savages, sank our nation into debt, announced criminals were going to be let free after committing crimes, and Police would be prosecuted for doing anything to stop crime. Now patriots like Bill Binney, and just regular citizens like myself, who have never transgressed against any fellow citizen, and who have held faith and loyalty with the nation we love, are prisoners in our own homes, assaulted freely with The Beam, by an enemy we cannot yet engage in any meaningful way in response.

We have been running up the tab for our expensive freedom as we sat back complacent, and now that bill is coming due. It will be paid by all of us in what is to come, in one way or another. Either Americans will step up and do incredibly unpleasant things, and allow others to do the even worse which will be necessary, or we will no longer have any freedom.

I have seen what awaits, if Americans prove unworthy. Bill Binney speaks openly about a criminal intelligence operation which is zapping people with energy beams to torture them in their own homes. He himself now cannot leave his basement, as energy beams rain down on him, blasting holes through steel sheeting he installed to try and keep from getting killed. The government is no help, and just ignores his pleas.

I have seen this with my own eyes, and felt The Beam wake me at night. Even I am getting hit. You would not believe what I have to do just to remain vaguely functional while facing that. I am not even sure I will make it to see the revolution that frees America from this thing, and I am so worn down, I really don't even care. If I do, it will be solely through God's will.

And it is getting worse. My being hit by The Beam is a progression, which began with the titan which is Bill, made its way to regular me, and now is working its way down toward you and your children. You and your children will one day know The Beam too, unless we take affirmative action now to see that does not happen.

While a recognition of the threats posed by this operation is vital to your own competitiveness, it is even more vital to that of your children. As much as the American Stasi is stalking the adults of your community, it is even more aggressive in monitoring and intervening in the lives of children.

Among children, in the eyes of this conspiracy, an ounce of prevention when a child is 12 or 13 can yield a lifetime of protection from the threat that child could have posed to the criminals who are running the nation. Childhood monitoring and interventions, both in the schools and from within their social circles, offers a much greater return on investment, for almost no risk, as parents are entirely unable to even conceive such an operation could exist. The operation is keenly aware of that.

If your child has potential, and especially if your child scores highly on standardized tests, you need to know that your child has been flagged, and there are trained adult domestic intelligence officers who know your child, are watching your child, and who have infiltrated children of the domestic surveillance operators in your locality around your child.

I have seen this myself with my own eyes, in my own childhood, and I have witnessed them derail other honors program kids around me. They are out there, in the schools, with a dedicated unit assigned to each school, and they are operational, and aggressive. They can simply surround your disciplined child with children who are undisciplined and nonacademic, or they can introduce them to alcohol, drugs, pornography, sex, or criminal behavior. All the good you try to do as a parent, if successful, will cause trained intelligence officers and your child's friends to begin working in tandem to undo your efforts.

None of these operations are their first time trying something. They are a sophisticated, mature intelligence operation with the support of psychological professionals and decades of experience, at least. As a parent, it is very difficult to meet them head to head and compete, especially when they surround your child with "peers" who are executing plans crafted by psychological professionals trained in intelligence operations and designed to manipulate your child's own reward circuitry to make them weaken themselves.

It is difficult to say what a parent should do. If you tell your child the full scope of the problem, that they are being watched and stalked, their online activity tracked, their social circles infiltrated, everything listened to and recorded in their own homes, and their neighborhood, and even fellow students targeting them, you rob them of their childhood.

I was a bold kid who liked fighting, especially with evil. Had I known the extent of the evil surrounding me, I might have decided to fall on my sword as a kid, just to take out as many of those traitors as possible. The world of intelligence is inherently toxic. I hate to expose children to it at an early age, before their minds have developed, and rob them of their innocence.

But if your child is empathetic and moral, as well as high functioning, and you do not warn them this operation is stalking them, you leave them at the mercy of some real psychopaths, who will strive to tear them down mercilessly, while they are at their most trusting, vulnerable, and naive. They will stand no chance.

I have seen, firsthand, kids who were raised in exemplary fashion by capable parents, who were straight "A" students, derailed by an ingratiating social circle which espoused a more undisciplined, non-academic, norm of behavior. I have even seen the introduction of a "bad boy" boyfriend who took a lovely girl off her academic path to drugs and alcohol. I actually saw that "bad boy" boyfriend taking part in surveillance of me at one point prior to that, in retrospect, before we had ever even officially crossed paths. As a parent it is tough to deal with that, without being completely honest with your child.

The bottom line is you are raising your child in a wartime environment, under incredibly adverse conditions, because we failed to rigorously keep our house clean, and we partook of the propaganda that those who wanted to keep our house clean were somehow "extremist." With these criminals, there can literally be no extremism. There is only an assent to slavery, or an aspiration of freedom. You will align with one or the other, for yourself and your children.

The propaganda even established a mindset in the populace where we all assumed everything was fine, nobody would attempt to seize any sort of undue advantage corruptly, and we dismissed, even denigrated, anyone who implied there was any sort of organized conspiracy, or that anyone might take extreme measures to seize or hold on to power.

Not only would doing something to secure freedom be wrong, even thinking anything could ever be so amiss in government would be wrong. It is incredible anybody fell for it, let alone a whole nation. The results of our apathy were the wartime conditions we now face, even in our grade schools.

Under these wartime conditions, extremism is just common sense, and anything less is the mindset of a loser who will spend the remainder of their days under a totalitarian dictatorship, living every moment in fear of The Beam.

Adapting our children to that more extreme mentality may be the only proper course of action. I wish I had known what was targeting me, though I also must concede, I probably was not mentally ready back then. But perhaps I would have risen to the challenge. Without the opportunity, it can never be known.

Home schooling is obviously the ideal. In such a case I would place my child in other socializing environments where surveillance would not be likely to be, such as rougher marital arts clubs, and I would keep track of any new students which showed up to subsequent classes, as they would have a high likelihood of being "surveillance kids," sent in by their parents as infiltrators to gather intelligence on your child for their file. I actually think that kid whose leg I broke, way back as a child, was a surveillance kid, sent to the club right after I began attending it. God works in mysterious ways.

Finally, for those who might one day plan a more kinetic, direct-action oriented revolution against this criminal conspiracy, it is vital to first be aware of the degree to which you are already observed, and the degree to which your monitoring will increase if you begin to look "interesting," through the people you associate with, the purchases you make, even the thoughts you begin voicing in the workplace or writing online.

You are already being watched, and if you become interesting, you will be watched even closer. Strive to be the grayman now in every facet of your existence if you want to play in the games to come.

Nothing you do will be unobserved, unless you take extreme measures – or you eliminate the surveillance through political means first.

I would not waste time organizing into groups, either. Almost none of the people who read this will be sophisticated enough in intelligence operations to cope with the process of infiltration. Any groups will rapidly be targeted, infiltrated, and subverted and controlled by this conspiracy. It is too good and has been doing this too long.

In the civil war I foresee, if it is ever to succeed, it will begin as a tsunami of lone wolves, who all activate when the moment is right, and deal with the surveillance operatives in their own communities first, putting surveillance on its heels, forcing it to move out of its assigned sectors, and eliminating it wherever it is not willing to be put in flight.

This will not be a war of massed enemies in uniforms, especially at first. It will be a vigilante, civil war of quick hit and run guerrilla tactics, pitting freedom-loving neighbor against surveillance neighbor, emphasizing high-gain-low-risk hit-and-run engagements, designed to move the surveillance, and prevent it from remaining in the communities in which it has been embedded.

You will have to get rid of the surveillance first. It is the only Achilles heel in this operation I see. So long as it is in place, our side will simply be Beamed to death each night if we offer any other form of resistance.

Your elections are rigged, your news media compromised, your means of communicating online controlled and censored, and the politicians and political leaders you see are almost all just easily replaced puppets. The people really running this operation from the top, are still unknown to us, and unable to be identified so long as the local surveillance is in play. There will be only one first step to take, and it will need to be taken aggressively, all at once, in overwhelming fashion. Take down the surveillance.

This operation's compromisation of the government is near

complete. Even among many Police departments, the conspiracy has now provoked a shift away from the older Civil Service exams which tested mathematics and reading/writing ability, as well as Policing skills like observation and reasoning. In those older tests, there were objectively clear right and wrong answers on the tests, they were marked in a clear and transparent fashion, and making it onto the Police force was a meritocracy where any citizen could become an officer.

Now the conspiracy is driving departments to adopt the newer "psychology/personality" tests, which have no right or wrong answers, and which are simply graded within a black box, utilizing proprietary criteria, in secret by a company which is selected by agents of the American Stasi in government. There is no transparency in, or oversight of the grading, and nobody is able to question the final decisions of the company, on who is hired.

Under this new scheme, the list of Civil Service applicants seeking to join the Police force is sent to the company along with their tests, the company claims it "grades" the tests in a way nobody can ever confirm or corroborate, using unknown proprietary criteria, and it simply returns a list of applicants to be hired by the municipality, with no oversight or questioning.

Here are some quotes from this article,[371] describing the process in two Police Departments which were forced by the compromised Justice Department, using "consent decrees," to adopt these new personality tests to ameliorate "racial disparities" in hiring, which the Justice Department claimed were present in the Departments:

"With the approval of the U.S. Justice Department, Nassau

and Suffolk counties issued no-bid contracts to testing companies that developed and scored written exams... for candidates trying to land one of Long Island's most coveted government jobs.

A primary focus of these tests is that they are not discriminatory toward any race or ethnic group, a mandate of the federal consent decrees that have guided police hiring in both counties since the 1980s...

... Nassau Police Commissioner Patrick Ryder and former Suffolk Police Commissioner Geraldine Hart said that the testing firms control how exams are prepared and scored. Hart called the process "a frustration" and said the department is "just kind of left to a very arbitrary process."

The companies closely guard the types of questions faced by would-be officers...

... Candidates were asked to agree or disagree with statements such as:

"I prefer to read short articles or summaries rather than lengthy documents," and, "People say that I'm flexible and open to change."

What's the right answer about a candidate's reading habits? Testing experts interviewed by Newsday disagreed.

Hough chose short stories because the response "likely reflects a preference for being more active rather than sedate, more practical than theoretical." She said that "police work is more active than passive, with quick decision making rather than slow and deliberate."

McKay saw the question as trying to pinpoint candidates who exhibited an "openness to experience" and would be less likely to be biased. He said preferring long stories revealed a more curious, open-minded candidate."

So the federal government forces these departments to issue no-bid contracts to a testing company, set up by the American Stasi, which supplies tests with no right or wrong answer, it never tells anyone what the right or wrong answers are on the test, so nobody can study for the test, or argue their grade. Once the tests are issued, the company simply takes back the tests and gives the departments lists of candidates it says must be hired, and lists of names which did not pass and are not to be hired.

In an intelligence-driven environment, you can see how in ten to twenty years, the local Police forces will all be filled with criminal American Stasi agents, dedicated to subverting the Constitution on behalf of the dictatorial conspiracy. All of them will be running cover for the local surveillance teams, as they assault innocent citizens within their homes, for resisting this coup of our government, or perform other criminal activities.

Obviously being a dissident in any form, opposed to anything your Stasi masters are doing will be frowned upon. You, and your children, will get The Beam, and there will be no governmental agency to which you will be able to turn. You will be entirely on your own.

As I have said, we do not have long to resist the takeover of the government by the American Stasi. Very soon there will be no choice but to endure under the rule of an all-powerful version of the Italian mafia – a fully criminal conspiracy - which will control every facet of government, as well as your life, and the lives of your children, as it openly steals everything you work for. You can see by Bill Binney, and the ever-increasing numbers of "Targeted Individuals," we are already well on the path there. They are working their way to you, and your children.

Making matters more complicated, is the fact that this operation's technology is beyond belief. I will delve into this more later, however it is important to understand for the last sixty to eighty years, the American Stasi, through our intelligence services, has been classifying select technologies which it officially deemed of national security interest, but which it has really retained to secure its own power in the world.

As Bill Binney described, and as I have seen with my own eyes, these technologies allow the application of energy and force to amazingly precise, highly focused positions in space, over incredible distances, from highly obscured origins, through mechanisms which are difficult to detect, discern, and shield against or counter.

The Havana Syndrome, where intelligence agencies and the highest levels of federal law enforcement, have proven unable to discover exactly how individuals have had damage inflicted on specific neural structures, is but one technology of likely several this conspiracy possesses. Of the specific details surrounding the Havana cases, a panel of 16 scientists from the Cuban Academy of Sciences, which the Cuban government assembled to examine the evidence in the cases, wrote, *"No known form of energy can selectively cause brain damage (with **laser-like spatial accuracy**) under the conditions described for the alleged incidents in Havana."[372]*

I can attest to the laser like accuracy of the impulse weapon the American Stasi employs. I cannot explain how it works either. I have scanned EMF field readings, Electric Field readings, spectral analysis of radio frequency emissions from zero to 12 GHz, employed a Geiger counter to look for ionizing radiations, and even measured ultrasound and infrasound readings. Only one meter showed energetic enough readings in the RF space to possibly be responsible, while another superior meter disagreed, and did not see such energies.

Understand, this conspiracy knows how the brain works. It knows what brain structures produce what functions. And it has a weapon capable of damaging specific brain structures, with "laser-like precision," from concealed positions in other residences which cannot be directionally located.

I suspect that project is in some way related to the old MK Ultra research projects on mind control,. Now the conspiracy is probably working toward a spot where it may be able to change your personality – change who you are, by altering your brain structure physically from a distance.

In theory, the day may come when it could cause your sex drive to overwhelm you, or damage your moral centers, lower your IQ or ability, even destroy your ability to remember what you are fighting for, or selectively wipe out memories, abilities, or motivational factors in your personality. It could eliminate your empathy, imbue an anger, even make you a psychopath. It could even make you compliant psychologically by changing who you are, to make you a better, more willing slave. "You will have nothing, and be happy," may have been an oblique reference to your brain being physically changed, so you accept being a slave.

As bad as this book has presented things so far, I have downplayed my own assumptions of how bad it will get, for fear they would never be believed. We are in a bad spot.

For a primer on the subject of this conspiracy's technological advancement, I have found one excellent book to read, despite the fact it is written in almost comical style, would be the book *Chameleo: A Strange but True Story of Invisible Spies, Heroin Addiction, and Homeland Security*, by Robert Guffre.[373]

Guffre was a professor of English, whose childhood friend, through a series of seemingly random misfortunes, became a sort of test subject which the American Stasi used to develop its tech, and train its agents.

In a rather comedic style, Guffre relates the stories he was told, as his friend, besieged by the Stasi, purchased a van and fled across the country, pursued by the conspiracy and assailed with its most advanced technologies at every turn, some of which almost mimicked the supernatural. From items in his house jumping as if impacted by some force, to a high-pitched sonic weapon, to operatives donning suits made of flexible, fabric-like LED TV screens which projected the image behind them over their body, so seamlessly they became almost invisible (something also reported by radio host Tom Bauerle[374]), I have seen many of the technologies he described. I believe his account, and assume the technologies he describes which I have not seen, exist as well.

We are in a bad spot. The criminal conspiracy already controls most facets of our government, rigging our elections to place its agents in power. It is taking over local law enforcement and it is very advanced technologically. However the surveillance is a key element in all of that. The conspiracy needs that ground surveillance network, to see what everyone is up to, run cover and overwatch for its election rigging and other criminal operations, and to protect the vulnerable, soft, fleshy parts of the conspiracy which deploy its directed energy technology to punish recalcitrant patriots like us.

That ground network of overweight couch potatoes, limping geriatrics, and Paris-Hilton-princess-types, as well as other misfits and troglodytes - who so feared competition they jumped at a chance to overthrow the Constitution, and see a rigid mechanism of complete control substituted in its place - is the weak link. Too weak to compete on its own in freedom, and from what I see mostly unarmed and violence-averse, it will offer no resistance to any attack.

Eliminate the ground surveillance, and The Beam will disappear with it, for almost all cases. Suddenly, the public-facing agents of the conspiracy in government will once again fear the American people's ire, because they will become vulnerable, absent the Stasi's constant, all-seeing, protective overwatch. Even worse for the enemy, they will cease to know what all of us are up to. That will terrify them. Under conditions of fear, errors increase, and conciliation becomes a more attractive option.

It is then you will begin to gain leverage over the machine, through legitimate government mechanisms. You could get the ground surveillance outlawed, get law enforcement allowed to investigate claims of wrong doing. You might even be able to begin electing your leaders again.

These strategies are all temporary strategies, to cope with

an operation, the scale and scope of which, and ruthlessness of, is unimaginable to normal Americans. Ultimately you will need to eradicate every last vestige of the conspiracy from the nation.

However there is only one path which can lead to where we need to go right now, and that is the broader exposure of this criminal domestic surveillance operation, to every single American, and its total destruction, at all costs, at the hands of real Americans who are not for sale.

I hope you will join me in this noble effort.

Chapter Nineteen

Civil Wars Will Not Be Like You Think

Before we finish, I want to prepare you for any potential hot conflict with the conspiracy which may arise, and look at where we will want to guide events, should the opportunity present itself.

First, I want to demonstrate to you how the presence of a surveillance operation such as this, in a theater of operations, would dramatically change the nature of any potential civil war, and how it would need to be fought by the citizenry, if we were to have a chance of prevailing.

Then we will discuss some of the more exotic weaponry I have seen wielded by the conspiracy, and how you should alter your strategy to confront this new form of warfare.

First, how would the presence of surveillance affect a civil war battlefield? In its essence, waging war against the conspiracy which has subverted our government would be similar to committing a criminal act in America today. While surveillance appears to not care about crimes, it still monitors them aggressively, probably looking for blackmail - and other citizens it can turn into its agents within our society.

So if we examine the performance of a criminal act, and how surveillance would operate around it, we can get an idea of how surveillance will be operative around any attempts by our kind to unseat the conspiracy, and reestablish a proper, Constitutional government, which we elect.

So lets examine a real criminal act. We are going to look at someone who murdered three people in the privacy of their home.

You and I now know how that would work. Long before the crime began, in a house nearby, which looked like any other house, but which served as the local neighborhood observation post, a surveillance monitor sat at a computer, looking bored, holding one headphone to an ear, like the sonar tech of a nuclear sub. They flipped through the various mechanisms in place to listen in houses nearby as if flipping through radio stations.

On the computer, they selected the Johnson's house, kitchen Alexa microphone. They had the soap opera General Hospital on, and you could hear the sounds of sizzling bacon in the background at two in the afternoon. Not a surprise the wife weighs 220lbs.

On the computer screen, he clicked a drop down menu, and selected the Schwartz house, downstairs, smart TV mic. A rhythmic sound, soft subtle, almost inaudible. He opened the drop down menu again, and clicked the upstairs, bedroom Ooma phone mic, and heard the sounds of a flexing bed frame, and a couple having sex. He listened for a bit, the couple finished, the wife got up, trotted away, and the bathroom door closed. He can hear the local postal worker yell to her he needed to finish his rounds. Nothing more there, but both files will get annotations and attached recordings.

He goes to the drop down, and opens up the O'Brian house, downstairs. He can hear keyboard keys clacking and the clicking of a mouse, and opens up his mirroring program in another window. He selects the O'Brian's husband's home desktop computer screen. Nothing. He flips the mirroring program to the husband's work laptop. Looking at what the husband is looking at on the computer screen, he is reading something about accounting practices for small businesses. That could be a problem, and will need to be investigated. He may be forming some kind of small business.

The monitor opens up O'Brian's file, adds a flag, and attaches a file with a screen mirroring video of what he has been looking at on the computer this morning, and then sends it on to analysis.

If he is thinking about forming a small business, command will need to see if it's allowed. Another asset might already have the same type of business, there may be important intelligence about something flowing from that which the conspiracy needs, and the conspiracy cannot be allowed to lose access to that data. Or somebody important may already occupy that space, and have the pull to use the conspiracy to maintain their control of the market. Whether his fledgling business will need to be sabotaged is above the monitor's paygrade, so he sends the file off to analysis and then selects the Haskell house.

Immediately he hears the arguing. Sam Haskell, the son of a big LA agent is cursing out his wife's parents, calling them deadbeats, sucking away his money. His wife chimes in, calling him a loser, and then there is the sound of something thrown, hitting a wall.

The fighting escalates for five or six minutes, before there is the sound of forks and knives all clanging together, as if a drawer were thrown open quickly, and then there is the first scream, which sounded like it was the mother-in-law. Footsteps suddenly fall like raindrops as people yell, and there is the sound of a struggle. It sounds like multiple people are trying to wrestle with each other, before there is a male voice groaning, and the wife screams, "No! How could you?" She then says, "No, No," before a groan is heard and everything goes silent. The surveillance monitor is motionless, and riveted.

Haskell is the son of a prominent LA celebrity agent. If there was just a murder, as it sounded like, this was big. City command would need to be immediately notified. The monitor immediately sends them word over an encrypted messaging system. They message back in a few moments they are taking over control remotely, and the monitor is released to continue to scan through the different houses in the neighborhood for anything else of interest, as all feeds from the Haskell house are rerouted to city central monitoring and control.

City command reviews what was just heard, and immediately tasks two aviation units which had been circling over LA in a holding pattern to the house. Flying at 20,000 feet, the planes are nearly silent and invisible, as they bank toward the target residence and begin circling. City surveillance command also has all communications, phone, internet, email, and text messaging from Haskell mirrored and routed to their big screen in the control room they have just assigned to this event. Meanwhile, the tech division taps into all webcams, nanny cams, surveillance cams, cell phone cameras, and any other imagery devices at the home's IP address, using the backdoors installed in all of those technologies by domestic surveillance agents which were employed by the companies which made them. Those employees really worked for domestic surveillance, and were sent to those companies specifically to covertly install those backdoors in the products. A monitor in City command is assigned to review them and put any feeds of significance up on the big screen in the control room assigned to this event.

City also commandeers thirty vehicular surveillance units which had just been roaming LA and sends them all text alerts on their surveillance apps, moving them to box positions around the residence, stashing some in parking lots and others off side streets with sightlines to exit paths from the target residence. All are sent pictures of Haskell, the family members who live at the residence, and their cars. Fifteen units are instructed to pick up foot surveillance units who had been roaming the city, as they drive toward their staging points around the house, and keep them on standby, waiting to be dropped off and guided to the target.

Looking up who in the neighborhood is surveillance, City sees the house across the street is owned by an electrician who was raised in surveillance, and is still a member today. He was given free residence in the house, but part of the deal was surveillance command got priority usage of it, if needed. The electrician was out at work anyway, so surveillance sends a technical team to the house to open it up. They will try to get additional data feeds out of the target house, seeing if WiFi clutter can be resolved to offer any sort of imagery showing the interior of the house, deploying a thru-wall microwave system, scanning the rf spectrum for any interesting signals, and setting up better camera feeds of the outside of the target residence. It is not clear if they will get set up in time, but they will go as fast as they can.

In addition, two other houses, farther away, but with sightlines to sides of the house, are similarly commandeered from their surveillance-owners, and techs are sent to set up imagery feeds and boom microphones pointing at the target residence.

By now, an hour after the initial flagging of an event, the operation has mobilized under sixty-five people in total from the three to four thousand active operators on call at any time, and the 300,000 total pool of civilians who could be called to set their lives aside and join operations, if the need arose. (Under the pilot program of Operation TIPS, which was created, before being supposedly disbanded, the surveillance network of available assets it was budgeted to recruit, just for the pilot program in New York City alone, amounted to 330,000 citizen-agents, monitoring everyone else – all for a pilot program (1 in 24 out of 8 million citizens equals 333,000, bigger than the real Stasi)[375]. And the program had gotten up and running, so most, if not all of those agents were recruited before it was supposedly shut down. At maturity, it probably would have had 800,000-900,000 people on call, just for one city.).

City control now has rough thru-wall imagery from inside the house, and visuals from all three front sides. Vehicular units are all staged around the house, but drivebys are being held back to not spook Haskell, in case he looks outside. It sounds extreme, but all of these assets would just have been loitering, doing nothing, had this event not occurred.

After a few minutes the control room fills with the sounds of groaning with physical exertion and dragging, then there is a clomping noise as something large and heavy seemingly drops into something, and then a bathtub faucet turns on. Shortly afterward, the sounds of a Sawzall, or similar reciprocating saw begins to be heard, followed by items being dropped in a plastic bag, maybe a garbage bag, which sounds like it might be being tied off immediately after. Thru-wall microwave imagery shows Haskell kneeling next to the tub, apparently dismembering bodies.

Fast forward, and one of the houses radios that Haskell is outside, bringing his Tesla back, closer toward the house. He is exiting with a large, heavy, black plastic bag, which appears to contain something solid, perhaps more likely a torso, than an array of loose limbs.

Immediately control over the vehicular units is handed to one of the aviation teams overhead, who will guide all pass-bys, and all of the surveillance cars get ready to begin a high priority follow.

Haskell exits his driveway in the Tesla and begins to head for a dumpster he knows of, near his house. Surveillance immediately begins a complex dance around him, designed to record everything of significance, without him noticing, or being spooked. As you have seen with the Google car, as he reaches every intersection, there will be someone to call his direction of travel, as he is tracked to the dumpster.

This is what you should know, after reading this book, or, at the very least suspect, is out there. Haskell, however has no idea. He is still among the clueless plebes, who thinks he is entirely alone, and nobody is paying any attention to him, or has any idea what he is up to.

Now we are going to show you what Haskell saw as he dumped the torso of his wife in the dumpster near his home. This is actually a real story, and we have the real surveillance video of the body dumping, which will show you the surveillance swarming around him at the critical moment. This is what preceded that, and how they had him buried under coverage as he went to dump the torso. Notice, regular law enforcement did not close on him to catch him in the act, with the torso. What you will see here, is the domestic surveillance of the American Stasi, gathering blackmail after discovering a crime through their own typically criminal means. This is not law enforcement, or even really US intelligence. For most purposes, this is best characterized as an off-the-books, foreign-controlled, non-state intelligence operation manned by Americans it has recruited to work against our nation, funded by the elites of the world and tasked with maintaining their control of the West.

Were you to identify any of these people involved in the surveillance here, they would not be official government agents, but rather would likely have regular office jobs somewhere, and they would live seemingly nondescript lives in regular homes in a neighborhood just like your's, where they would help fill out the files on their neighbors for the conspiracy. All of us have those files, and you would be shocked at the details in your's.

They live essentially in their own little secret society, patronizing conspiracy-member's businesses preferentially on orders of command, to help the businesses survive the competition with businesses owned by people who are not in the secret society. As a result, their people will own most, if not all of the local small businesses, and have access to the intelligence from them. They see each other around town on follows, and nod and wave, as they gather intelligence on all of those of us who are not in the conspiracy.

Their children would go to school with your's and report everything they observed about your children, as they are operating under some type of command authority that is actually assigned to the school your children attend, building the files on your children, and attempting to mold the human terrain the conspiracy will operate on in ten to fifteen years, by stifling some children who seem too promising and moral while elevating others who they think will appreciate their corrupt, criminal, and arbitrary system, and fight to protect it to preserve their own benefits from serving the conspiracy, when the time comes.

These people will never admit to anyone that they are involved in anything like surveillance. They will pretend to be horrified by things like 9/11. They will pretend to respect and love the American Constitution and the free, democratic republic it governs, as well as the supposedly honest meritocracy its freedom generates. However every night they spy on everyone else to line their own pockets, they revel in the fact the conspiracy elevated them and suppressed anyone in society who they might have been in competition with, and it is essentially a certainty they have gangstalked and gaslit regular innocent citizens, even assaulted them with directed energy weapons, just because the machine decided it did not like those citizens for some reason or other.

I assume if you went up their chain of command, at some point you would discover a CIA-linkage, and this would be officially identifiable as some sort of "training" operation just in the unlikely event it got exposed, though the intelligence it gathers is very real, and used operationally to control the course of events in the nation, as well as who succeeds and who fails.

From what I have seen, the account so far is as close to the reality in our country as you are going to see discussed. Only actual surveillance operators could give you a better account. But if anything, I think their's would show even more penetration, and the assignment of far more manpower, and more shocking technology. I scaled back what I think was really called into play here, simply because I think to the newcomer, the reality would be entirely unbelievable. I will bet while reading my toned-down account you were thinking, *"No way, this guy is nuts, it could not possibly be that bad..."* It is, sadly. I've seen it with my own eyes.

I have been under this for over a decade overtly. I am afraid this is normal to domestic surveillance. It is now normal to me, and I am repulsed by it. It is how it would have gone down in an East German apartment, where one apartment was run by the Stasi to watch all the others nearby, and it is how it works in America, where they imported that Stasi model, and adapted it to our suburban neighborhood residence structure, with one house monitoring all the others nearby.

In truth it is easier here, where people buy Alexas that hear and record everything in the house and wireless nanny-cams the neighbors could catch the signals from and watch freely with the right equipment, and smart TVs with microphones right in the TV remote in your hand, and cameras on the TV pointing at you and the rest of the room, and computers and cellphones with microphones and cameras, and Ring doorbell cameras, all connected to the internet and monitoring everything inside your house. None of this is unusual to exploit, to intelligence people. It is only you who were deceived about the world you lived in. You were lied to and deceived, to make you weak and helpless.

Now here are some photos from the actual surveillance video of the body-dump, or rather, torso-dump (the full video of which is located here),[376] showing how surveillance documented the body dump, with captions explaining the events. Look at the stills below, to see what is significant, and then cruise over and check out the video.

Understand the advanced training you are receiving here. There are Tier One Special Forces operatives who will not be as operationally capable as you will be when you finish this book.

Now the analysis.

Target Vehicle,
Torso Inside

Target vehicle enters the parking lot, aviation has all vehicular units fall back outside the target's visual perimeter to not spook him. One foot operator (out of view behind cars), is at the other side of the lot, out of sight of this camera, feigning distraction, looking in a backpack. You will see him when we examine the second angle of video which captured this event.

Target Has Opened Doors To Dumpster One Final Check For Witnesses

25 seconds into the video, no vehicles, no pedestrians, target feels secure, aviation has all ground assets on standby to swoop the moment the target commits to action. Count to 25 and look at how long that is. That is how long this place was deserted.

39 seconds in, no cars, no pedestrians in view, target has committed to action, aviation issues "Swoop" command, all assets move to target scene as rapidly as possible, and execute a skit to explain why they had to loiter there. Count to 39, and imagine that for that entire period, there was nobody there. And then this happened:

Two seconds after target commits to action, carrying the torso to the dumpster, a contractor van swoops into the scene at the top of the screen, and drives close to the target vehicle.

Simultaneously, an SUV with an open driver's side window enters the scene from the bottom. Despite both vehicles entering a parking lot, neither simply heads to a spot and parks, but rather they meet in the middle, create a traffic jam, and loiter.

One minute, two seconds in, White Van is trapped by SUV, which is itself trapped off to the left side by another pickup which you will see in the second angle of video presented shortly, which forces White Van to keep the hidden video camera pointing out his back window pointed at the target, videoing what is happening.

Even after SUV moves, White Van sits, until the target vehicle backs up to leave, at which point White Van begins rolling.

The moment the target vehicle finishes backing up, White Van clears the scene rapidly, so the target will not see him as he exits. It is better for a paranoid target, about to exit their crime scene, to look around and feel like they are alone, so they will think nobody noticed them. Clearly Haskell thinks he just dumped that torso, and nobody has any idea.

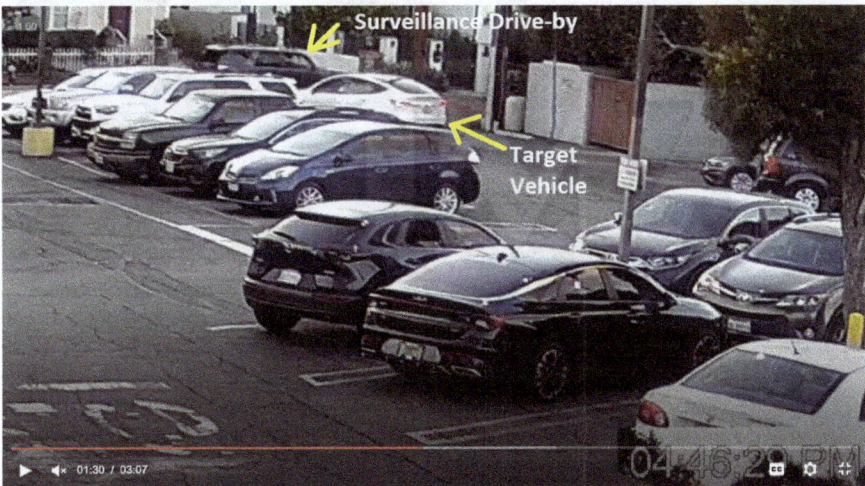

Just as the target vehicle gets to the exit to depart the scene, the surveillance SUV from the beginning drives right in front of it, hidden camera capturing a final frontal shot of the driver and documenting the occupancy of the vehicle as he leaves.

You can get a better look at the little traffic jam in the second angle of the video, which shows you a different view.

Target vehicle just parked.

A single walker enters the picture, and is sure to elaborately pantomime his distraction to ease target suspicion, digging through his backpack as he walks. Remember, dedicated foot surveillance frequently carries backpacks to house their costume kit, clothes change, comm gear, cameras, binoculars, audio gear, and other surveillance equipment.

At the crucial moment, surveillance walker stops looking in his bag and observes closely as the target commits to picking up the torso on his shoulder to carry it. Something this important almost certainly had aviation, however it's possible the walker made the primary call to the vehicular units to swoop in.

Surveillance walker returns to digging through his bag, completely engrossed, and not looking as if he is noticing the target offload a torso in the dumpster, as the target fully commits.

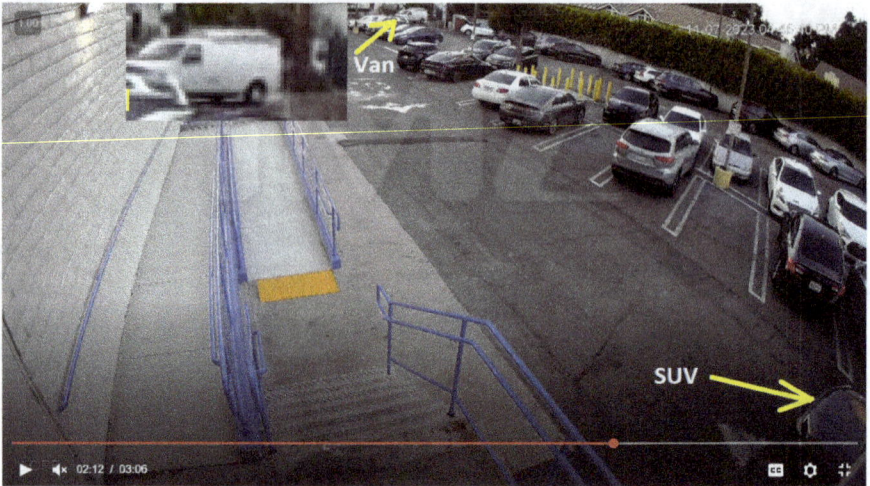

White Van and SUV both enter the parking lot at exactly the same moment, from opposite sides. Notice how slow SUV moves.

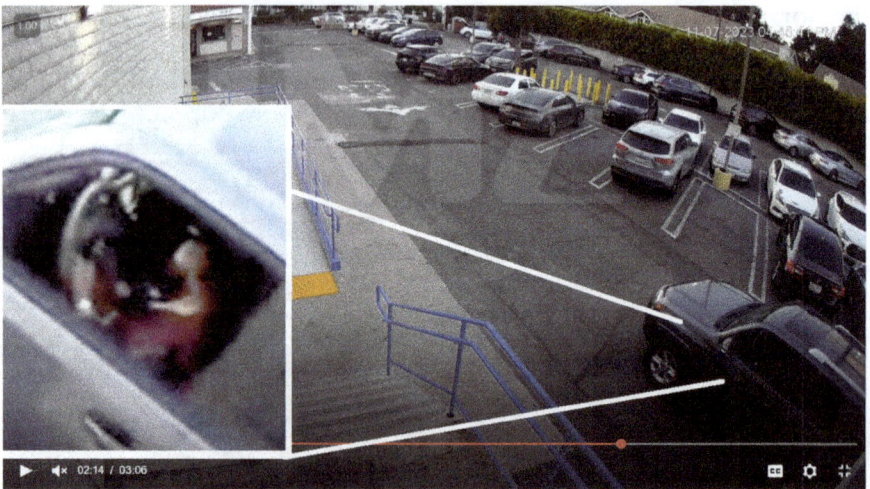

Just to enhance your capabilities, notice the SUV is being driven by a woman. In the United States, surveillance appears to be a matriarchal organization. Women are the least suspected as threats, and thus appear to be used in the most sensitive operations, and get promoted to the most powerful positions as a result. This appears to lead to the organization as a whole being organized around a matriarchy, both in work-hierarchy, and in family life, where it appears surveillance females preferentially select mates using the op's surveillance files and then aggressively pursue a relationship commitment from them using inside information to arrange "chance" meetings, arrange to have similar interests, disrupt other potential suitors, etc. This leads to couples consisting of a bossy alpha female and a more passive beta male. That is a dynamic which is probably only exacerbated should the female involve her husband in her surveillance duties.

When you are being followed regularly while shopping, you will notice an inordinate number of couples where the female is charging forward through the store as a dominating force, while a man follows meekly behind, seemingly unsure of what they will be doing next, as he assiduously follows his wife's lead.

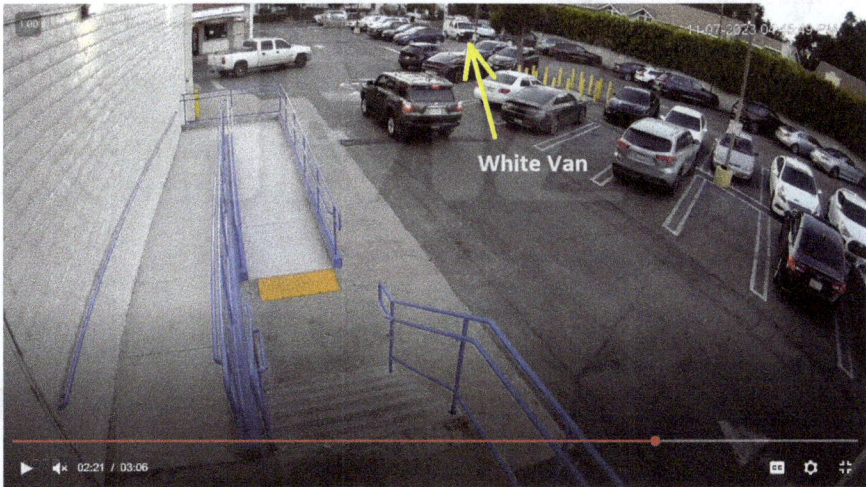

Enter White Pickup, which has entered the third entrance to the parking lot simultaneously with White Van and SUV. It is the simultaneous confluence of all three cars on the same point which initially causes a traffic jam, and allows White Van to loiter, taking video of the target out of the back of his van. The little traffic jam was planned, and indeed it is probably a rehearsed technique. Remember, for 39 seconds there was nothing here, then three cars, simultaneously swooped in, one each for each entrance to the lot.

SUV begins to drive in front of White Van, and then gets confused and hits her brakes, rather than continue, and White Van gets to loiter longer, with his back window pointed at the target.

SUV began to drive, but now a new pedestrian has inexplicably exited the building on the left, and walked in front of SUV, forcing it to hit its brakes and stop again, further delaying White Van. The pedestrian walks in front of SUV as if about to cross in front, but then stops, and walks back to the building.

Notice close foot position of the pedestrian, as if walking slowly.

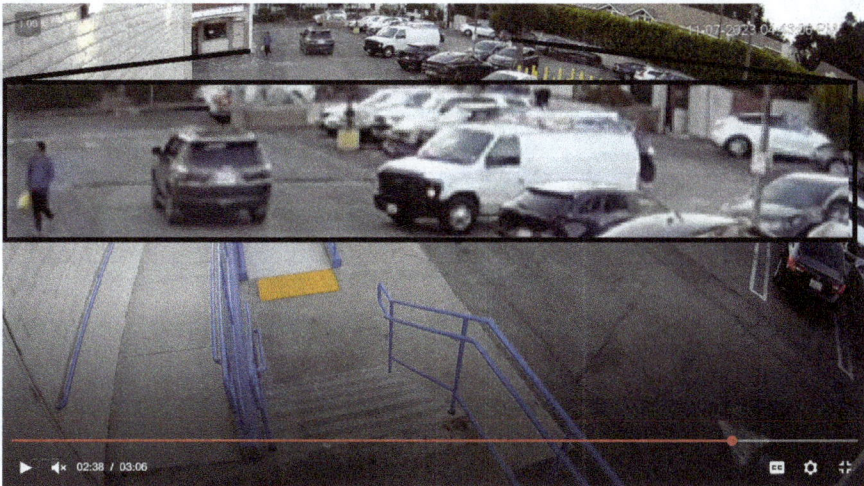

At 2:38, pedestrian has turned and is now walking in a totally different direction. Exactly as SUV begins to move, the target vehicle begins to back up. Both vehicles move at the exact same moment. The target has completed his operational activity, and now surveillance can clear the scene.

Target vehicle on the right has turned around, SUV is heading for the exit, where she will pass in front of the target vehicle and get final imagery, pedestrian has increased his walking pace as judged by his stride, and White Van is exiting the scene.

Your final scene, SUV exits in front of the target, and then another car comes through to lead him out in a cheating command position. SUV did not enter the parking lot to park, just as White Van and White Pickup did not enter the lot to park. All three, simultaneously, entered the lot, one from each entrance, drove through, paused in the critical spot, at the critical moment, and then exited by another entrance and drove off.

The final car will now lead the target vehicle out, probably to the next intersection, where it and SUV will take paths heading away from where they think the target is heading, call the target's decision at that intersection while driving off, and other cars will head to the next intersection to call the decision there.

Understand, the video taken there by the white van, of him dumping the body, will never see the light of day in a court. It is not evidence. Those are not Police, and they have no care of whether he is convicted or not. Every car there knew he was dumping his wife's torso, and none ever even thought to call the

Police so they could catch him in the act, because what they are a part of is a death-penalty-level, treasonous operation, contrary to every tenet of our Constitutional republic, that entirely violates the Fourth Amendment, and which the entire nation would fight to the death, if it is revealed.

It is just like on 9/11, when as the towers were burning, all of them knew, their operation had to have been on top of the 9/11 hijackers, and let that happen, at best - and at worst, making sure that happened could have been their conspiracy's objective. It is even possible that all of these ground surveillance knew how when intelligence is operative in a theater, what you see is what was intended, especially given the scale of the American Stasi's ground operations and how absolutely intelligence controls the outcomes you see. If so, they would have assumed 9/11 was their operation's mission, and it apparently was a success. Personally, I suspect this operation was in fact, the hidden hand behind all of the missed opportunities to stop the hijackers. They wanted those planes to hit those towers, because of how all of us united and gave them even more power.

I have dealt with this thing for years now, and can say with certainty, these are all very weird people who work for this thing. Things we cannot imagine are common banalities to them. They think in ways we are not designed to even dream other people might think in terms of, and they routinely, as a matter of course, do things we would never even consider doing ourselves.

What you see in these photos is purely the American Stasi, making sure it knows everything, and gets everyone's dirty little secrets for blackmail. It has that many assets on standby everywhere, at all times, and it is monitoring inside houses, just as the Stasi monitored inside apartments.

You saw them following the Google car of all things, and I guarantee you here, they were listening in Haskell's house when the murder happened, and a recording of it exists in some archive. You can tell yourself they were listening by chance, but I know this thing is designed to catch everything, and it is professional – it doesn't do "chance." They made it this way, and this thorough, just like the Stasi in East Germany, so they would not miss any critical detail and their control would be absolute.

I have been in my house, with relatives, speaking disparagingly of surveillance, only to have surveillance respond by having cars which were assigned to my neighborhood immediately begin driving back and forth in front of my house revving their engines, to register their displeasure with my lack of respect for their organization. My family has also had several other experiences, going back long before my harassment began, where people said things and knew things they could only have known if they were listening in my house, and I am not a criminal, nor could there be a reason for them to have legal justification to be listening inside my house. If they were doing it to my family, they were doing it to everyone.

Internalize the fact that even you are being listened to, in the privacy of your home, by somebody right in your neighborhood, whose job it is to perk up if anything interesting happens, or is discussed in any of the houses they are assigned to monitor. This operation knows where you will most let your guard down and discuss your secrets, and it has worked to get ears in there.

You must also understand the professionalism of the enemy. When Haskell exited his house to dump that torso, surveillance likely did not know where he was heading. Was it a forest in a national park? Was he heading to the marina, to board a friend's boat with the torso, some chain, and some cement blocks?

Most likely, when he entered that parking lot, out of the blue, there was a mad dash at central control to look up all the businesses within walking distance of the lot. Maybe he wasn't even there to dump the body.

If there was a lawyer's office, they would need to open up ears in the office. It could be the lawyer's cell phone, or their computer, or they could send somebody into the office with a super-sensitive directional mic. Or they could use some other device from outside, if they could get a sightline to the room. It is not even impossible that there is a procedure whereby all lawyer's offices, shortly after starting business, are surreptitiously entered and have listening devices installed in every room, hardwired into the power and the internet, just so if need be, local teams can quickly get ears in the office, since there could be very important intelligence in there at some point.

I suspect that is already the case with almost all confessional booths in churches, which I assume all have dedicated agents monitoring the eavesdropping equipment this thing has installed nearby to hear inside them, and which are recording during all open hours. Once you have an intelligence operation working in a theater, the rules are only there to weaken the idiots who think there are still rules.

They would not bother with a warrant for any of this, as

nothing they gather will ever see the inside of a court, unless it was mailed anonymously to a prosecutor. Their assets in the media, many of whom got their jobs due to participation in illegal surveillance themselves, will never even broach the subject. They are purely gathering blackmail. Wherever Haskell was going, they would need to be on top of him.

Given the fact he pulled in and went to the dumpster, I would say they saw him park by the dumpster on the aerial overhead of the scene from aviation above, looked at the car positions in the lot, and then arranged that little skit to film whatever he was doing in the lot right that moment, on the fly.

They got one foot surveillance in, and then choreographed one car entering each entrance simultaneously, all meeting at the center with a pedestrian, and creating a traffic jam. They designed it so the back of the van would be pointing at the dumpster, they decided what units would be assigned what roles in the skit (probably by looking at all unit cell-phone-GPS positions on a live map on the big screen, and picking the units closest to each entrance of the lot), and they then sent out the orders, and rushed those cars into staged positions - all within the space of 39 seconds.

That is very fast work to be done on the fly, and speaks to a lot of practice doing it. It also shows how saturated the environment in the US is with their vehicular units, that they could assume they would have some right near all three entrances, who could be given orders and deploy within moments, because after rudimentary analysis of the site and choreography, they would have only seconds to get cars into position and execute.

This all sounds quite ridiculous. However I have come to conclude, this is how power works. Whenever elites get into power, building something like this, to hold onto power, is essentially a normal procedure. It only sounds ridiculous because you have been so lied to and deceived all your life that you cannot imagine how things really work in the world, when dealing with intelligence agencies or those sharks who run the world. The powers that be tell you that in America, you are their boss, you are free, you can be anything you want, do anything you want, and nobody spies on anyone else, and intelligence cannot operate domestically. You could be President, or a billionaire, or a top news reporter, it is all up to whether you chose to follow that path.

Most comically, it is one of domestic intelligence's psyops agents in the establishment who tells you that, on orders from the powers that be, to try and blind you to your own surveillance, and discourage you from running any surveillance yourself, keeping you entirely helpless and under control.

Now, imagine if what I say is true, and this is a foreign intelligence operation, funded by elites so wealthy and powerful they are entirely unknown to us. Suppose it has subverted our beautiful Constitutional Republic, turning it into a shadow dictatorship run by this intelligence op, on orders from foreign elites, absent any resistance from a people who are entirely unaware such a thing could even be possible.

It is OK, we have been told. There is one final safeguard. The Second Amendment means when all else fails, we can reinstall our Constitutional Republic, by taking up arms and overthrowing the tyrannical government.

Imagine, as a former Army Ranger, you are up to the task. You've hooked up with some of your Ranger buddies, and have been scraping the rust off on weekends, training out in the woods, and you have a killer plan. You have been using online databases to track a bunch of George Soros-like elites who run the criminal intelligence operation subverting the American government. You have discovered they have a little pow-wow this weekend at a resort a hundred miles away.

You pulled the blueprints from a website. It is a fairly hardened building, one of those massive 1900's brick and concrete block jobs, and they will have security, but you know what you are doing.

The building is powered by a small power station thirty miles away. One of your guys is going to head out there with a Barrett 82A1 50 caliber semi-auto and pop the transformers, killing power to the whole region. At the same time, you will chainsaw down a telephone pole and cut the communication lines, killing the internet connectivity and any landlines. One of your other guys already got a job at the resort, where he has planted a battery-powered signal jammer, to block all radio-comms out of the building. You have also planted one next to the Sheriff's office, so nobody can reach them once the landline comms and power are out.

Your man at the resort also has planted explosives all around the grounds, focusing on places where he has noted the elite's private security tends to post, so one click of a detonator, and most of the security there will be reduced to pink mist. In addition he has located the assigned rooms of the elites, and where all the elites will be on the floor plan, at the assigned hour.

One of your other guys has a job at a local concrete company. He is going to fill a concrete truck up with concrete ten hours before the hit, and he will let it harden.

That truck will get a brick on the gas pedal and handle the breach of the side of the building through which your main team will make entry, while two guys in front and two in the rear, each with FN M249S belt fed rifles you have converted to fully automatic, tear up the front and the back with full-auto fire. You did this a hundred times in the Rangers in Iraq, it is a great plan. You are guaranteed to take out all of the leadership of the Cabal which took over America, since obviously none of them have any idea you are preparing this surprise for them.

Or do they? You are a trained former Ranger, who dislikes the Cabal which took over our government, and you have the psychology to take action. Do you think your neighborhood archivist doesn't know that? Do you think he hadn't already flagged you for closer analysis years ago? Do you think he doesn't make it a priority to look at all your communications, everything, in and out? You think every first degree contact of your's isn't getting similar coverage from their neighborhood surveillance units? Your archivist has nothing better to do each night, and knowing you is what he is getting special perks for.

You are interesting to him – far more so than your CPA and high-school-math-teacher neighbors. You also hold the key to a big promotion, if you try something like this and he gets on top of it. Your archivist will keep a closer eye on you. In fact, you are why they sectorized domestic intelligence, spread it out into every community, and embedded archivists in every neighborhood, assigned to get to know everyone personally, and keep an eye on the problem children. That means you, and any geniuses who could have made it big in business or politics if the operation did not stay on top of them.

How did you reach out to your Ranger buddies? Email? Encrypted app? Either they penetrated the app and already have seen all your messages, or they saw they could not, and now you are REALLY interesting to them, because you are hiding something. They know you are up to something, and they are going to find out what. You are Navy SEAL DEVGRU operator Thomas Mixon, about to rob your first bank. You have no idea of how the machine knew you were interesting, and what it placed, just out of sight, and entirely on top of you. And it is not just you. Every one of your Ranger buddies has the same monitoring, so even if they missed you, they would be guided to you by the buddies you reached out to.

Their's is a system bolstered by numerous redundancies, all designed to guide them to the homes of individuals with interesting intelligence data surrounding them. They have been doing this a long time.

Ever talk about your plan in a house? A car? I have been in a car on a highway, mentioned I wanted to take an exit to stop off somewhere unexpected, and seen two vehicular units in the passing lane up ahead both cut across three lanes of traffic to catch the exit ahead of me. No kidding.

They are listening in your car. And mine was an older car, without all the tech, and I use an archaic Samsung Galaxy S4 specifically because I can take the battery out. They were not using my tech to eavesdrop.

They have a device, which I think they install in the front or rear of some surveillance cars, which can hear in your car from inside the car behind you or in front of you, even over the engine, while driving at highway speeds. And they use it.

It is not surprising. The rolling meet was an age-old way operators would try to overcome the surveillance and eavesdropping of meetings, since unlike in a building, surveillance could not predict where you would be. You would get in a car with the other participants and drive, and they would have to follow you to listen in. So you could sweep the vehicle and then hold the meeting while your driver conducted countersurveillance detection routes, to expose if you had people trying to follow you.

When they encounter a successful technique like that, intelligence will have rafts of highly intelligent technicians work night and day, seeking a technical solution. They will be desperate to get ears in that rolling meet, because now they know, that is where you will reveal your most important, sensitive intelligence.

It was inevitable they would come up with something. Now, you could drive for hours, seeing only the random cars of normal traffic spending but minutes behind you before turning off and going their own way - and every minute of your rolling meeting would be recorded and transcribed piecemeal, by all of those vehicles, one after another.

When you went shooting, were you followed? Was somebody already out there, hiding in the woods in a Ghillie suit when you got there? Did you arrange the shooting trip over the internet, the phone, or in person inside your house? If so, surveillance heard what you were doing, and was there before you got there, and hid. And now they know you have four illegally converted belt-fed squad autos, and you are REALLY, REALLY interesting. Now they are really going to find out what you are up to.

How did you get the floor plan of the resort's main building? How were you tracking the elites? Did you ever look anything up online, which if someone were mirroring your computer screen in their observation post down the street, they might have seen you were up to something? How do you communicate with your Ranger buddies? Ever use a phone? Email? In person in one of your houses? In a car? In a public place, with other people around, like a bar?

Your op would probably be comped. Because this operation is professional, and does not screw around, it has procedures in place to make sure it can monitor communications via all of those methods, and it is not one over-worked, underfunded person in a basement at Langley trying to cover 40,000 people. It is a naturally nosy woman down the street in your neighborhood, who has been assigned to monitor 150 people, and of them 147 are boring beaten-down Melvins with cubicle jobs, who have never been in a fistfight, and know nothing of politics. Those remaining three, are both, interesting, and a potential goldmine for her if she can catch them while they are up to something.

Speaking from firsthand experience, it becomes very difficult to communicate once the local surveillance decides to flood the coverage in to cover you. You almost have to use a trusted courier, giving him the message, written in code, from within a secure SCIF and having him deliver it inside a SCIF at the destination.

It gets even weirder than that. Did any of your Ranger buddies meet a new girl he might have mentioned something to? Maybe a hard-core anti-government girl who constantly says she hates the Cabal which took over America, and who dragged him into bed on the first date, she was so in love with him?

That girl will be an agent. In surveillance culture, within their Secret Society, I think a girl who will not sleep with someone for the job is judged somehow weak and disloyal to the group. And from what I have seen, any girl who will drag a target into the sack and then utterly betray him later is seen as a goddess of surveillance culture. If you ever want to research it, simple Police infiltrators have actually married, and had children with surveillance targets, raising families with them, in numerous cases.[377] And that is Police intelligence. What I have seen here is a level of intelligence operation which is orders of magnitude worse in terms of morals and mores. Your buddy's wife could very well be reporting back on him.

You see what I'm trying to show you. Civil resistance, even Civil War, will not work the way you were taught, once you realize this surveillance machine is in theater, and already on top of everyone interesting. Even the most elite Tier One Navy SEALs are not capable of facing off with it, as Thomas Mixon showed. That is the way the elites wanted it, and they made it that way.

So yes, you have an AR and Level IV plates, and NODs, and an IR laser/illuminator, and Thermal, and two platoons of former Rangers, and explosives, and Squad Autos, and 50 cals, and armored vehicles, and training, and practice, and planning, and target intelligence, and everything you would have needed in the military to pull off this op flawlessly.

However, you are like elite DEVGRU/Red Cell/Navy SEAL veteran and bank robber Thomas Mixon. Your entire op is being torn apart before you even launch it by some 95lb tattooed millennial hipster girl, with blue hair and a nose ring, drinking soy lattes, who has never shot a gun, would defecate in her pants in a fistfight, and who is a total coward, completely incapable of violence. She probably still has nightmares about being hung from the lockers by her underwear in elementary school by the pretty girls.

She is a coward, with no morals, or mores, or anything she would die for, and no impressive capabilities to speak of. She may be completely pathetic - and they may even have recruited her because that pathetic quality left her with no options but to be loyal to the conspiracy to compete in society.

Despite all of that, she has completely tooled your op because the "government" (whatever that is, or has become, in the United States) has her watching your internet, reading your encrypted text messages, listening in your home, and assigning physical surveillance to put an eavesdropping car behind you when you tried to hold rolling meetings on the highway to discuss your plans.

She knows everything, and the dude you sent to the power station with the 50 cal was already killed in an ambush 20 miles out when he stopped in front of a staged five car pile-up on the way, and FBI HRT took him out on orders of this thing before he knew what happened, and you will not make it to the target, because while you were meeting with your buddies for the final target briefing yesterday, they entered your house and spiked your morning coffee. You will be dead from a heart attack in ten minutes.

I absolutely do not want to demoralize you. You can defeat this surveillance, easily, but you have to take it on directly, first of all, beginning in the information warfare space where striking is higher gain and lower risk. Then move on to engaging it through government and politics, doing what damage you can do to it there through shaming our leaders into action. Then have the citizenry move on to the legal realm to drain its resources with lawsuits, if we can get control of our courts so they will honestly enforce the law, and then you would probably finish it off kinetically in some fashion only later on, once it has been weakened to the greatest degree possible.

If you chose to go toe to toe with this thing right now kinetically, targeting the soft fleshy underbelly in your own communities, the citizenry could win if everyone went at once, but the risk-and-cost to damage-inflicted ratio would be quite high. Following the path above is a low to no-risk path which the conspiracy will have great difficulty resisting without exposing the greater conspiracy beyond the surveillance. I suspect the elites at the top would choose to shed the surveillance, and let it be destroyed, as they sought to flee into the shadows, living to rebuild it again later.

You cannot reinstall a Constitutional Republic if this one gets subverted by foreign powers, as it has, so long as that surveillance is still rolling. You have to get rid of it first. It is just too big an advantage for the other side.

I will explain what we need to do, but understand, as of now, you must assume you are totally owned by the surveillance.

You cannot operate against it indirectly, by trying to avoid it while launching another op against another wing of this conspiracy. I have been playing this game for a decade, and have probed their capabilities extensively in that time. Their tech is to die for, their numbers are astonishing, and you will not succeed targeting something else while the surveillance is on top of you.

You will need to play this the way I will explain, and tackle the war targeting the surveillance directly, in the informational warspace first, if you want to take down the surveillance, defeat the conspiracy, and have a chance at reinstalling a Constitutional republic, elected by Americans.

Now, I will need to stretch my credibility with you, by explaining what I have seen. This conspiracy and I have gone back and forth for some time now, as they have sought to prevent me from publicizing this material, and as I have ignored them and pressed forward regardless.

In the course of that, they have exposed me to some of their most advanced technologies, as they used them on me freely. As you can see from this book, from their perspective I am quite a pain in the ass, and they have expended quite some effort trying to wrangle me.

I remember what it was like to be unaware any of this was even possible, as you most likely are presently. I was told over and over things like I have seen are impossible, and people who claim to have seen such must be mentally ill.

I believed it myself, so I know how outlandish what I have experienced will sound to you. Still, I have no choice but to recount my experiences, as what I have seen must be known to our side, if we are to prevail in the battles to come. You need to know the enemy's capabilities.

All I can say is, for decades this thing has been studying the sciences, and developing technologies for use in these control and harassment operations. Where it has made technological advances, it has immediately hidden them, and kept them from the public. Decade after decade, advance after advance, its capabilities have progressed to a degree which will defy the belief of regular Americans today.

I have watched the needle on a compass in my house make a full 180 degree rotation, as I was bathed in some weird electrical sensation. I have awoken at night, in my house, a hundred feet from the nearest house, bathed in a different sensation of pulsating electricity, as my heart rate has exceeded 160 beats per minute, and I have felt myself breathing as if I were running a 100 yard sprint during it, even though I had only been sleeping.

I have laid in bed, a hundred feet from the nearest house, and felt a vibrating ball, floating in space, six inches in diameter, enter my legs and move up them to my abdomen, feeling as if it were shaking everything inside me within that sphere at a precise 4 shakes per second, only to continue to my head, where I felt the unmistakable sensation slowly grow in my sinuses which in full form, you get when punched in the face the first time during a sparring session. I have seen a clear degradation in my cognition from the vibration ball passing through my brain, and I have felt my heartbeat become rapid and irregular after it passed through my heart area.

I have laid under a lead dental apron, which shielded me

from the vibrations of my body, and listened as a spatter of what sounded like particles rained down on the apron. I believe now, they were a spatter of force-impulses, where point after point on the blanket experienced a point-force suddenly which caused it to jump, as if impacted.

I laid a sheet of aluminum foil over me, assuming the "impacts" would confer thermal energy on the foil, as their kinetic energy was halted, and I recorded a video of this using a thermal camera. You can see it at AmericanStasi.com, where I am laying out, and after eight minutes in the video of nothing, suddenly the beam turns on and a spot on the foil rapidly heated and became white hot on the thermal video available at the url in this endnote.[378]

I then began being "tapped," on the lead apron, while laying in bed, as if by an invisible finger tapping the lead apron to awaken me, demonstrating the ability, most likely from another residence a hundred feet away, to create a disturbing vectored force on a point on a piece of matter in another house, through the walls.

I recorded audio of the tapping, also available on AmericaStasi.com, at the same url. Interestingly the audio also captured an inaudible humming, similar to the charging of an MRI machine, which appeared to be due to some EM effect on the microphone. Also available on the site is a recording of some kind of static electric discharging, which occurs on surfaces of materials in the room, at the outset of these episodes. It is as if they have some way of charging surfaces in the room with static electricity, and these charges are then being struck with an electric field, which causes the charged material to jump.

My working theory is the humming is an effect on the microphone of some sort of broad swath of energy beam, which charges materials in the target location with electrical energy, like static. The force is then generated by applying some kind of focused electrical-field "beam" or point of constructive interference of fields, of some sort, which when it passes over the charged materials, creates a transversely-vectored inductive force in them, by pushing the charges, and the material holding them.

Alternatively, the humming is a massive electric field, applied to the whole area, and the beam is designed to somehow create an electric charge, as if a static charge, on one point, which then immediately experiences a force-effect and jumps.

The effect on the target surface of the combination of a charge and an electric field is similar to what would occur if the charged molecules and atoms were impacted by an object traveling along that vector-line. In one case the force causing the point to jump is field generated, while in the case of an impact, it is conservation of momentum-generated.

I have had a force of about 20 pounds, I would estimate, applied as a push, to a large metal frying pan I had placed over me to block what I had back then assumed were some kind of particles from a particle beam impacting me. In the audio recording at the link above, you can hear the frying pan hit the ground, after the push, which itself is preceded by a crescendo of the humming.

More disturbingly, I have felt the tapping within my body, and most disturbingly felt it inside my head, where they attempted to apply it for hours on a single point on my brain as I slept. I awoke to the sensation of vibrations throughout my skull, and a decided grogginess, along with a dull ache through the backs of my eye sockets. On moving my head on the pillow, I must have moved my eardrum into the point in space being tapped, and could hear the tapping in my head on my ear drum, with the same irregular cadence as the "spatter" of particles/impulses in the recordings above.

Unfortunately, over time, after moving around to different spots to sleep, I found no area within my home which was shielded from this head vibration/tapping.

In an effort to prevent the targeting of a specific point in my skull, and based off the observation they only applied it as I slept, implying I needed to be immobile, I purchased a motorized swinging hammock. I felt they could not focus the tapping as you would think, if I remained moving all night.

I laid in it, with my head as close as possible to the center of the hammock to maximize its movement as the automatic swinging mechanism swung it. My head was moving back and forth somewhere between 24 and 30 inches, on the arc of the hammocks' swing, at a rate of about one cycle per second.

Even as the hammock swung, I awoke to the buzzing sensation, indicating a point in my head was being "tapped," and as I slid my head forward on the pillow to try to get my head out of the bubble of vibration surrounding it, (as the hammock continued to swing), the point being targeted passed into my ear canal, and I could "hear" the "tapping" again. It sounded like the sound of fingers, drumming irregularly on a tympani drum, inside my head.

Judging by the movement of my head on the pillow, prior to

my moving it, that point would have been roughly on my Inferior Temporal Gyrus, a structure in the brain a few inches in front of the ear canal, which when damaged, will produce an inability to differentiate between reality and fantasy, such as in schizophrenia.

I think this thing is advanced enough technologically that it attempted to induce schizophrenia in me by damaging that brain structure, so as I presented this material, I would present other material which would clearly not be based in reality. That inability to differentiate reality from fantasy, probably similar to a dream state where all sorts of weird things can happen and you just accept them, would then discredit all of my work here. They may even have hoped to produce a diagnosed schizophrenia which would have rendered me unable to continue on this path, and perhaps even allowed me to be committed.

So you face an enemy capable of creating physical damage on a precise point within the brain within a skull, with, as the Cuban experts noted in the Havana Syndrome, a "laser-like precision" which presently is not possible with known technology,[379] and I have found that even when that head is moving back and forth 24-30 inches, at a rate of about one cycle per second, on an arc, they can precisely target a moving spot in the brain. This enemy can even precisely target a specific brain structure within that moving skull with an eye to producing a specific mental dysfunction. And they have the technology to do that from within another house, hundreds of feet away. I would assume this is some sort of AI controlled mechanism, but it is still impressive.

They are incredibly advanced technologically, and obviously as purely evil as any despot in history. The despots of old merely declared dissidents mentally ill and forcibly committed them to mental institutions. The despots today actually have developed the technology to engender the actual mental illness by damaging specific brain structures.

Of course I think back to dissidents like Mohammed Ali, who opposed the Vietnam War, refused the draft, spent his time in jail, and then suffered a deterioration of what was, in his youth, a flawless brain structure of incredible ability. We are told it was due to boxing, even though he had an above-average ability to avoid being hit, and other boxers with less intelligence and less evasiveness, suffered no such malady. With this, there is no telling where it was involved. From Ronald Reagan to Margaret Thatcher, it seems we lose a lot of our best to dementia and brain deterioration.

Although I assume my experiences are probably somewhat unique, and their present ability to roll out such technology to such a degree is limited, there is evidence they are rolling out some sort of beaming technology more widely as time goes on. Part of the strategy of this conspiracy is to degrade those who are not members of it, to reduce their ability to rise in society. I suspect to that end, this thing is broadly targeting large swaths of the population with some sort of degrading radiant technology.

Studies have recently found there is a measurable correlation between the overflights of aircraft at night, and heart attacks. From one article summarizing a study here:[380]

"Late night and early hour aircraft sound may disturb sleep in locals, which could temporarily increase blood pressure and activate the sympathetic nervous system—responsible for

adrenaline and the 'fight or flight' response—potentially leading to increased risk of cardiovascular issues. Longer term studies have found much larger risks associated with airplane noise."

Do you believe the noise from an airplane flying overhead would give you a heart attack? Why would it not do it during the day?

After being beamed in the night myself, and awaking numerous times with a heartbeat as high as 160 beats per minute, I could see a beam, being widely applied to a population to degrade them physically, from an aircraft flying overhead, causing an increase in heart attacks across the population, as it occasionally hit people with compromised cardiac function, which could not handle the added stress.

It surprises me the signal would be so large as to still be measurable when diluted by all of the other normal air traffic in the nation, but given this is late night when flights are reduced in number, it is plausible a small number of "Beaming" aircraft would produce a statistical signal which was still detectable when diluted by a relatively few other innocent aircraft each night.

It is also possible areas with higher surveillance activity on the ground get higher levels of aviation support, and it is a ground-based emissive technology being deployed on neighborhoods by observation posts in houses, which is being conflated with the aircraft overflights which accompany them.

Another summary of the findings of another, different study here:[381]

"For the first time, a study led by researchers at Swiss TPH

667

found that acute noise from airplanes during the night can trigger cardiovascular deaths within two hours of aircraft noise exposure. The study published today in the peer-reviewed European Heart Journal found that the risk of a cardiovascular death increases by 33% for night-time noise levels between 40 and 50 decibels and 44% for levels above 55 decibels."

Again, it could be that you are sleeping and a plane flies over and you have a heart attack from the noise, and the louder the noise, the greater the risk. Or it could be they are beaming something out of planes, into broad swaths of the populace, and it is causing racing hearts - and in some with weaker hearts, those hearts cannot take the extra stress. Perhaps, the louder the noise, the closer The Beam, and the more powerful the stimulus. Or the more planes are flying over the higher the surveillance activity, and the more thru-wall microwave radiation you are being exposed to from the neighbor's observation post.

Possibly supporting this as a broader exposure of the populace to some technology, would be the common phenomenon of people all waking up at around the same time in the middle of the night, every night, inexplicably, as described here:[382]

"But what's behind this collective wee-hours waking? If you regularly find yourself staring at the ceiling at 3 or 4 am, you're in good company: it's a phenomenon reported by around one in three of us, and probably more since the pandemic started."

It could be random chance those people are all waking at the same time each night. Or their neighborhood coverage could be activating a Beam at the same time each night, when they are deemed least likely to notice it due to being in the deepest phase of their sleep. It is possible 9/10ths of the population is being hit and degraded, and one in three are awoken by it. I awake when they hit me with the Beam on full force, but other times, I suspect I sleep through lower-level applications of it. Perhaps many do not awake at lower wattages per meter squared.

Remember Bill Binney's neighborhood where every other house had at least one case of cancer? The same monitoring unit operating on his street has an analogous unit present in every moderately populated neighborhood in the US, and all are technologically equipped with the latest thru-wall monitoring and harassment tech, which gives off this radiation, and they are using those devices.

The enemy you face is immensely technologically sophisticated, and it deploys its technology. However it appears this enemy has not been able to recruit the high fliers of our population into its grassroots ranks, as most high fliers would prefer freedom, and standing on their own two feet in a meritocratic society. It appears it has recruited lower performing individuals, probably using some assertion that in a meritocracy, the random presence of innate ability is an unfair means of allocating tangible success. Thus joining this conspiracy, which seeks to undo the natural meritocracy of freedom, is somehow a morally acceptable method of competing in an "unfair" world.

Even though the conspiracy is technologically sophisticated, we vastly outnumber it. Its beaming devices are probably limited in number as well, and its fewer members will tend to be incapable of free competition and afraid of it. As a result, despite its technological advancement, I believe it is fully defeatable. However you will need to follow specific steps to do

669

so.

Presently you are in the first, crucial phase of the war. This is the information warfare stage. To take part in this stage, you will need to apply your powers of observation to witness the ground surveillance of the American Stasi in your town and neighborhood yourself.

Once having seen it, your job will be to make others aware of its existence. At the very end of this book will be several copies of a chain letter guiding people to the AmericanStasi.com website. There, this book is available free, it will point to how to purchase this book in physical printed form, should the website be shut down, as I expect it will be, and we will offer additional Google Streetview surveillance detection case studies.

You will take a photo of the letter with a camera or cell phone, print out as many copies as you can, ideally twenty to one hundred or more, if you are willing, and you will drop them in random postal mail drop-boxes, addressed to random people as well as some people you know, while out in your travels, mailing them in groups of two or three. This is the future of our nation, and our children's freedom, so I beg you to act as aggressively as you can in spreading this. The faster this spreads, the less ability the conspiracy will have to shut it down.

The goal is to not have the text of the letters enter your computer, and to mail the letter anonymously, using random local return addresses other than your own on the envelope, to make the tracking of the spread of the idea as difficult as possible. You only mail two or three to not appear unusual to the postal worker who empties the mail dropbox. 50 letters, all mailed at once, in one dropbox might spark suspicion, as the potential spread of an idea by a motivated individual, and trigger further investigation of what the letters say. Having your real return address on the letters, in that case, would be very bad.

The US Postal Service maintains a massive database with photographs of all mailed letters, which includes a text entry for the destination address as well as the return address.[383] By randomizing the return addresses, it should make tracking the idea's origin of spread using conventional tools as difficult as possible.

My hope is the letter will persuade those who receive it to visit the site, and then continue the process, sending more letters to others. It is my hope we can spread this material offline virally, in real life, using physical chain letters.

I have tried spreading these ideas online, however the mechanisms of control are too formidable. The conspiracy discovered very quickly that the internet, by allowing free communication between individuals, was the most dangerous technology it had ever encountered.

I do not know exactly how it is done, but I have had reports at my website of readers who cannot find me online through various means, as well as reports from readers who discovered that they, and other people they encountered, were somehow quarantined in different "silos" of online individuals. In those cases, one reader's computer cannot see another person's Facebook account, even when that person is trying to find their own Facebook page, using the reader's home computer.

Through some mechanism, those people were quarantined

671

away from each other on the internet into isolated cells – isolated so they could not see each other, or share information with each other. I suspect that is more common than we think, though expertly hidden from us. I know trying to spread an idea online which the conspiracy wants suppressed is nigh impossible. Add in the overt censorship in social media, and spreading this online is practically impossible, especially as well known to them as I am now.

If you are willing to shoulder some risk in this, and want to print out copies and hand them out at political rallies, or concerts, or just around town, I would appreciate the help. However once having done this, you will be monitored, and mailing letters will be of little use, so please mail the anonymous copies first, before the machine figures out you are a threat.

So for now, we are back to the old ways of our forefathers - pamphleteering in real life. It would be fitting if the Second Revolutionary War began that way. I cannot help but think wherever they are, the Founders would laugh.

Once sufficient awareness has been built of the American Stasi, the war will need to enter a new phase. The problem is the conspiracy has taken over our government. This is why politicians refuse to put the interests of their constituencies first anymore. They are almost all carefully selected, compromised and controlled members of this conspiracy, serving its interests, and being rewarded with electoral successes which have nothing to do with the sentiments of their electorates. Do not make the mistake of thinking any politician is on your side. If they are in Congress, or "elected" to office, they almost certainly are owned by the conspiracy. Those who are not owned, are not allowed in the door, and if they persist, they will get nightly Beamings, as I now do.

If we elected them, they would serve us, and would seek to please all Americans. Instead the traitorous vipers nest which is our Congress and Executive branch cannot give our money away fast enough, as they free criminals to prey upon us, start forever wars we don't care for, and flood our nation with illegal alien criminals we neither asked for, nor want to support financially, while our intelligence community spies on every aspect of our lives.

There are curious indications something may be changing on that front. Mainly, information the conspiracy would never want to become public has become more widely known, and power structures the conspiracy would not want weakened have been degraded in some instances, and destroyed in others.

One of the most important facets of the conspiracy's control, and the most illegal, is the control of elections. It would never have wanted even a vague public assertion that any election might not have been 100% legitimate, for fear it might trigger suspicion in the populace, and investigation.

However, in the 2020 election, Joe Biden, the most anemic of candidates, barely campaigned with among the most unimpressive of vice-presidential nominees, and yet supposedly they won more votes than Barack Obama, Donald Trump, and Hillary Clinton, following a number of anomalies, including the complete cessation of vote counting on election night in several jurisdictions.

In response Donald Trump and numerous surrogates have asserted the election was rigged, and many of his followers see no other way Biden could get more votes than Obama. That being said publicly is unusual, and a state of affairs the conspiracy would never have allowed, if it held the control it held twenty years ago under George W. Bush's administration.

The news media, which has been given the moniker the "mainstream news," lest anyone think it represented less than the well established beliefs of everyone, saw its legitimacy destroyed under the first Trump campaign. The conspiracy, were it in full control, would never have allowed its chief propaganda machine to lose its legitimacy in the eyes of the public. And yet nobody takes the professional news media seriously anymore.

The intelligence agencies, which we were always told were forbidden from operating on American soil, were shown to have not only spied on the Trump campaign, but to have initiated a full fledged, multi-national intelligence operation to first, attempt to control the outcome of a US national election, and then, having failed to do that, delegitimize the elected administration once it took office.

The Jeffrey Epstein saga showed not only that there were intelligence agencies running underaged pedophile sex-trafficking/blackmail operations targeting our elites and politicians, but that they were being protected by the US government.[384] The Epstein case even created a belief in the public that it was possible a conspiracy behind it could assassinate the ring leader, even in the most secure prison facility in the country, while he was under the closest level of monitoring. The conspiracy wants everyone lulled into complacency, thinking conspiracies are impossible. This being revealed, also, is a change.

In short, the conspiracy penetrating America requires absolute secrecy, and yet over the past seven to eight years, one revelation after another has peeled away its secrecy and destroyed the influence of structures it needs to be influential. Even today, if you look on dissident websites, the presence of the American Stasi on the streets of our nation, harassing people for political beliefs under the rubric of "gangstalking," is well accepted as a fact of life in the circles of the politically active. Even here, look at how exposed the surveillance operations are in reviewable records like Google Streetview, where I can show it to you clearly. None of these things should be so exposed.

There are a few theories among observers. One is there is some American intelligence counter-conspiracy seeking to thwart the takeover of America, perhaps utilizing the Donald Trump phenomenon as a tool to expose the conspiracy. The "Q-anon" phenomenon is the most prominent group among these theorists, though you can see it as well simply among those who speak of a "Deep State" conspiracy.

Another theory, not entirely different from the first, is there is some sort of power struggle occurring between different factions of elites. The weaker faction, which does not control these elements, is exposing these things to weaken the dominant faction, with an eye to seizing power from it at some point.

Others think the conspiracy accidentally grew too large, and has decided to stage a mock execution of itself, shedding most of its machinery in a fake exposure and elimination, while the key elements remain in position, hidden, allowing it to continue to wield power from the shadows.

The fact that thus far, the domestic ground surveillance seems to have escaped exposure could be consistent with that, given it is the most important element of the conspiracy, which it would want to protect above all else. Certainly it is the element I would have destroyed before all else, as I sought to lay waste to everything about the conspiracy. That it remains, and its secret is protected, makes me dubious of all other theories.

Regardless, there is some unknown event taking place in the nation, and where the battle goes after exposure of the surveillance, would depend on whether or not America is honestly electing its leaders.

Once the surveillance is widely known, the best strategy forward would consist of a hybrid approach, beginning with the utilization of political shaming of politicians, to drive them to act against the surveillance using the power of government, combined with lawsuits against every element of the conspiracy, from compromised companies, which lent support to the conspiracy as it operated against citizens, to compromised government agencies, to drain their budgets and defund them, to regular ground level surveillance in your neighborhood.

What the surveillance has been doing is clearly illegal, and every compromised entity, complicit government agency, and member of it can be sued for their actions.

The lawsuits will be complicated by the fact the American Stasi has almost certainly compromised our court systems. I strongly suspect the issuance of juror-summonses and the assignment of judges is not in fact randomized, and can be compromised by this machine, using corrupted agents it has placed in critical positions of power, to yield entirely compromised jury pools and court proceedings. You would ideally want to have an honestly functioning court system for the lawsuit phase.

To that end shaming political leaders first, in an effort to get them to utilize government authority to purge the conspiracy from such things as the court system would best be done prior to initiating the lawsuit phase.

Even corrupted politicians will want to appear as if they are not compromised by the conspiracy. It is possible you can create, if not an honestly functioning court system, a court system which will temporarily function honestly, in an effort to fool you into thinking it is not compromised, and thereby take pressure off the elected leader-assets which the conspiracy will also want to preserve.

The lawsuits will then be the next vital step, as it appears the conspiracy hides much of its resources by allowing it to be owned by regular civilian surveillance people on paper. Stripping the individual members of the surveillance from the resources they own on paper will defund the intelligence operation presently seeking to destroy the United States.

We need every American to understand how vital it is, that if called to serve on such a jury, they award everything possible from anyone in surveillance, to anyone not in surveillance, as a means of defunding this machine.

I would expect at least one catch-all class action lawsuit, waged against everyone and everything which was associated with the surveillance in any way, by a class of litigant which would be best described as anyone not in surveillance.

This might work even if the conspiracy retained control over the courts, as the leaders of the conspiracy may seek to hide, or try to convince the broader public there is no conspiracy remaining. To do that, they may have to let the system work as we were told it would. The conspiracy may allow itself to endure damage, in the hopes it could weather the storm and then reconstitute itself later.

Even if the conspiracy stifles such legal actions, or forces politicians to not do anything to constrain the conspiracy, then the public will only be more certain of the conspiracy's subversion of the government, which would result in the masses rejecting the government's authority and delegitimizing it, robbing the conspiracy of a major source of power - the consent of the people to the government's authority.

However if the conspiracy chooses not to force its agents to stymie the government's moves against it, it will then endure the damage to its operational capabilities and the morale of its agents due to the lawsuits, which should prove quite prolific, from individual lawsuits over individual incidents of gangstalking and harassment surveillance, to broader class action suits in which every citizen not in the surveillance sues every citizen and entity in the surveillance for loss of privacy, loss of business or career opportunities, harassment, infliction of cancers through the deployment of radiant surveillance technologies on neighborhoods, and subversion of the lawful government honest citizens were paying for.

That flood of lawsuits promises to be the largest transfer of wealth, from all facets of the conspiracy, to regular America, in history. It will both immeasurably weaken the conspiracy, as it strengthens the position of regular America against it by giving them the resources to resist.

This phase will be crucial, and citizens should recognize any leader who seeks to prevent it, is in fact operating for the surveillance, and looking to keep its covert operational slush-funds intact so it can continue to operate. Hopefully a recognition of that by the populace would force even compromised leaders to allow the lawsuit phase to move forward unimpeded.

If we cannot get to a point where we are electing our leaders, or at least able to coerce them into serving our interests enough to defund the surveillance through lawsuits, then the leaders will surely never deal with the surveillance, and worse, I suspect you will be firmly on a path to a place where, after suitable expansion of the technology's rollout, every American will live in fear of being hit by The Beam™ at night, should they say or do anything which displeases their masters.

At that point the only path to freedom would lie in open, violent rebellion. However I would caution any would-be rebels, familiarize yourself as much as possible with the operating procedures of the surveillance, and its capabilities, both in observation, and infiltration of social/operational groups.

It vastly complicates any potential revolutionary strategy, when there is no room in anyone's private residence where the machine is not actively listening, and maybe watching through cameras installed during a prior break-in. I have even seen indications that when targeted to a sufficient degree, they may be able to "read" written notes in a residence, possibly through remote imaging using some form of through-wall radiation emissions.

As a result, any revolution launched, utilizing our plan, or through any other means, will absolutely have to begin with a swift elimination of the entirety of all local surveillance operations, by any means necessary. Either eliminate it entirely, or make it so it can not remain in place and will have to flee, disrupting its localization and organization.

You can leave no part of the surveillance operational before beginning to oppose the greater conspiracy. It is simultaneously the conspiracy's weakest and most exposed link, and its most vital element.

To that end, it is worth noting much of its technology relies on the power grid, and thus eliminating power to a sector would disable at least some of its technology, and make any remaining functional technology locatable through the sound produced by backup power generation at the undercover observation posts established in residences, or other detection means.

On the bright side, from what I see, the neighborhood Gollums who conduct the ground surveillance tend to be individuals who joined due to a desire to not engage in the open competitions of freedom, and thus they have little in the way of combat capability, a lack of competitive spirit, and they are often unarmed and incapable of combat. They will flee.

If we are able to advance to the point we are electing our leaders, the nature of the battle to be fought will then enter the final phase. It would also mean other governmental functions which are likely presently controlled by the conspiracy, such as the selection of jury pools, would become influenced by citizen participation, rendering them more honest. Once entering this final phase, a two-part strategy will become appropriate.

First, regular Americans will need to unite in agreement to deny the conspiracy members any facet of government service or protection, as well as discriminate against them personally. If there is a trial, criminal or civil, regardless of the facts or merits of the case, the conspiracy members will need to be voted against by any jury.

Regular citizens should also identify businesses run by conspiracy members, and refuse to do business with them. Employers would need to be convinced through boycotts to not employ conspiracy members. In short, what the conspiracy is presently doing to regular Americans from the shadows as part of the "gangstalking" phenomenon, would need to be done openly to them, in an effort to encourage them to leave the country.

The problem is for the last fifty to eighty years, at least, the conspiracy's entire schtick has been to tell every American it would never betray them, so they will let down their guard - as the conspiracy betrayed everyone at every turn as much as possible.

The idea you will allow it to remain in the United States, even afford it the loyalty of a fellow citizen again, with a belief that it will not betray anyone going forward from now on, is laughable. It is akin to Charlie Brown believing Lucy will not pull away the football if he tries to kick it. This organization's entire culture is based around the principle of betraying the rest of the nation for personal gain, and it always has been.

As long as they remain in the nation, they will seek to re-establish their criminal conspiracy, and begin depriving fellow

681

citizens of their freedom for personal gain. You will not be rid of this cancer until you are rid of those who sought to create it, and betray all of their fellow Americans.

The second element of the revolution in this case would be a more forceful stimulus. Elect former Targeted Individuals to political offices, both governorships and the Presidency, on a non-partisan platform promising to offer full and immediate pardons to anyone who commits any crime against any member of the conspiracy, pardoning them for all state and federal laws which were broken.

Some former targets would see that environment as akin to a no-tags/no-limits hunting season, and they would begin pursuing their former harassers as game, just as they were once hunted and targeted. Meanwhile, regular criminals would see a way to ply their criminal trade, without running afoul of the law, or at least being shielded from the consequences of it. If you could put TIs in control of the Presidency and all fifty state governorships, this would make remaining in America impossible for members of the conspiracy.

Technically called outlawry, this is a process which has been used throughout history, where those who held themselves outside and beyond the law of the land were then denied any protections afforded by the laws they rejected. You are basically not allowing them to use your own system to protect themselves, while attacking you outside of it. This process has a rich history in the United States, stretching back to the Old West.

Targeted Individuals, or TI's, as they call themselves, will have dealt with the conspiracy for some time, and will understand

682

its ruthless nature, as well the necessity to make sure it never reinfects the nation. By electing them to office with such a mandate, the conspiracy would likely be forced to move overseas, leaving the nation to be united in freedom, absent any internal strife or betrayals, or governmental skulldugery, in a way this nation has not been free of such negativity in some time.

That is basically what the Secret Society has been doing to regular Americans for decades now. It would only be fair to turn the tables, and let them see what it is like.

This will sound radical to you now, however you must understand I have seen far more of this operation than you have, for my entire life, and I cannot overstate the danger these individuals pose to simple freedom and democracy. There are children who were molested as part of active intelligence operations designed to curtail the threat they could pose to the conspiracy later in life. Invariably, the reason for such a child to be judged to pose such a threat would be heightened empathy or decency, or increased senses of fairness and loyalty to nation. For merely possessing those laudable qualities, they would be judged by this conspiracy to be in need of some horror like molestation.

Jeffrey Epstein was but one of many pedophile blackmail operations the conspiracy runs, which will traffic innocent children to pedophiles. In some similar cases, like the Finders Cult, which was referenced by the CIA as an "internal matter,"[385] it would appear the CIA was choosing children to traffic who lacked official records, and who would not be missed, were they to die in the course of their operations.

Additionally, I believe there will be few people who read

683

these words, who have not had opportunities in their life curtailed by the ground network of the American Stasi, to prevent them from possibly becoming too successful, and thus a threat to its control. There will even be parents who labored mightily to raise their children properly, and create a future for them, who have seen their children corrupted by peers on the orders of this conspiracy, going on to fall into lives far below that which they had been on track to enjoy. There will even be some whose children succumbed to drug or alcohol addictions engendered by the conspiracy specifically to clip the child's wings while they were young and vulnerable.

They do not want the world of freedom and opportunity you want, and they will gladly crush you, and enslave you and your children, should you be foolish enough to extend them any measure of loyalty or trust again. They are trained, capable, experienced in such operations, they have already formed a command structure to organize their operations, and they have shown they have the desire and the motivation to launch such operations. They are uniquely dangerous.

Only a fool, looking at those circumstances, and aware of what they have already done, would chose to embrace them as fellow citizens, and continue to allow them to live amongst you. By their history, they have shown they will reform their command structure, begin their operations to betray you, and then seek to enslave you and your children - and they will do anything, even launch an operation like 9/11, killing hundreds of selfless firefighters and police officers like those who rushed into the towers, and then drive the nation to needless wars which will kill and maim tens of thousands of the best Americans our nation produces, to manipulate your emotions and divert your focus from your true enemy – them.

I cannot overstate the evil the American Stasi represents, or the degree to which you cannot allow such a snake to remain within your home. They will gladly destroy you and your children, for little more than trinkets and crumbs tossed at their feet by the elites they serve.

This final phase of the battle will be crucial, and citizens should recognize any leader who seeks to prevent it, or calls for moderation, or tolerance, or forgiveness, is in fact operating as an agent of the American Stasi, seeking to preserve the ability of the conspiracy to reform its network. Hopefully, if that is understood widely among the citizenry, even compromised leaders will be forced to allow the lawsuit phase, and the subsequent outlawry phase to move forward unimpeded, lest they be revealed as agents of the conspiracy and see the nation turn upon them as well. One benefit of dealing with this conspiracy – its members are not courageous, nor are they loyal, and unwilling to cut anyone who is a burden, loose to suffer their own fate.

With over 90% of the nation on our side, constant discrimination, and a raft of former targets given full legal authority to act violently against conspirators at will, as well as criminals focusing the crimes of the nation on the conspirators, it would not take much in the way of notable events from that to convince the majority of former conspirators to move overseas and leave the United States, absent the need for a hot physical war.

It would also create a lesson going forward, that pursuing a conspiracy such as the American Stasi, or joining it if approached, will have stiff repercussions, thereby dissuading anyone who might think of creating or joining something similar in the future from doing so.

To do this however, you will need a roster of members of the conspiracy. The most obvious source of such a roster would be the National Security Agency. It clearly could identify anyone so involved through its analysis of electronic communications, which are used extensively during harassment and surveillance operations. You would have to, of course, be careful in trusting any work product offered by the Agency. In this war, most of the nation's spies will be enemies, and members of the conspiracy.

The Russian government could potentially be a second source of intelligence. It has doubtless flown satellites over the United States. If it has acquired video of traffic patterns, then it is highly likely an AI analysis of the traffic could identify vehicles engaging in surveillance follows within the videos. Once identified as surveillance, those vehicles could be tracked to their residences, from where identities could be extracted. I would be shocked if the Russians had not already done this.

To that end cell phone geolocation data likely could similarly be used. It would not surprise me if the Russians have already purchased it from advertising companies, and used it to gather the identities of US domestic surveillance personnel, by identifying individuals whose movements were coordinated with others, as they were part of a team involved in surveillance of a target.

Donald Trump has proposed creating a "reconciliation commission," which would absolve those who engaged in illegal surveillance of any liability, in return for acknowledging what they did for the historical record.

You can expect a more aggressive push toward something like this if we get close to exposing the network. That is what they did in East Germany when the Stasi security service's spying on the citizens of East Germany was exposed. All of the citizens who had betrayed their fellow citizens, even torturing them with "Zersetzung" operations designed to drive them crazy or get them to commit suicide, were given immunity for their crimes in return for simply admitting to them, for the historical record.

The real goal of "reconciliation commissions" is to make having been involved in such a conspiracy free of any cost, and to allow members to continue to hold the resources of the conspiracy, to aid reforming it in the future. The only reason the powers that be will wish to make it free of any cost is so they can rebuild the network at a later date.

Presently in the United States, the network has likely recruited nearly every citizen with the lack of moral fiber and absence of loyalty to their fellow citizens required to engage in this type of operation. If these citizens were to refuse to rejoin such an operation in the future, or even be taken out of circulation now through imprisonment or being forced to flee the US, there would be no pool of potential recruits left, and the United States would actually not be able to form another American Stasi to spy on and harass its citizens.

If the perpetrators are subject to the full civil and criminal penalties which the law would normally apply to a citizen such as us, the next time domestic intelligence approaches these people

687

about forming a criminal conspiracy to spy on everyone and illegally harass or assault innocent citizens, with an eye to subverting the lawful United States government, potential recruits will be hesitant to join, fearing a future exposure might ruin their lives all over again.

If, however, the political leadership can institute a "reconciliation commission," then there will have been no cost to having taken part in this conspiracy, and these people will jump at the chance to pick up operations where they were left off, once enough time has elapsed, and domestic intelligence believes it can begin to reassemble the network.

Having been assaulted in my house through the use of The Beam^{TM} by this thing, I can understand the perception that those who engaged in such treasonous crimes against American freedom should pay a price. I would prefer they did. It is patently clear to me, that every member of domestic surveillance is fully aware that the 9/11 hijackers were fully covered by surveillance, surveillance knew the details of the 9/11 plot, and yet it, at the least, allowed the hijackings to occur, likely to gain greater surveillance power over the country. "Americans" who willingly joined a group which allowed 9/11 really do not belong in the country, nor are they really Americans.

In addition, I have seen them operating against me. Every one of them knows their harassment operations are criminal, and are being directed against innocent citizens, and they still continue to engage in them. This thing does not belong in a nation as beautiful as America, to say nothing of its deployment of directed energy weapons against citizens, to physically assault innocent citizens in the sanctity of their own homes.

However the biggest step in ridding us of this plague would be getting the full roster of all of those involved. The reconciliation commission idea would be an excellent means of acquiring a full roster of everyone involved, confirmed by their own admission of involvement.

Even if they were absolved of all civil and criminal penalties, it would not shield them from a future electorate electing TI's to governorships and the Presidency, who would pardon anyone who acted, violently or otherwise, to remove them from our society.

There are people who would immediately set about hunting them in retaliation for what happened before the conspiracy lost its power. They would have to leave the country.

The end goal of every real American must be to remove those who would engage in these actions from the country. So long as they remain, there will be a very potent enemy within America's gates, and we will never escape this hell of partisan acrimony, and politicians who refuse to carry out their duties, or serve the people who elected them. Worse, we will eventually end up at a point where every American is forced to live their lives in fear of The Beam^{TM}.

The United States could be a utopia of love, harmony, and blinding success - but you will have to get rid of the domestic surveillance first. So long as it is here you have as much as ten percent of your population which wants to gaslight, torture, and beam their fellow citizens for an all-powerful conspiracy subverting the government.

I cannot emphasize enough, I have seen this thing operate.

Its people take sadistic pleasure in gaslighting targets, and trying to put them in fear and spin them up into a frenzy. There is something really wrong with these people on a deep, psychological level. I believe either they must not view regular Americans as fellow human beings, or they have some strange sadistic aspect to their psychologies which makes them inhuman.

You will have to remove them, or the conspiracy will reform spontaneously. Whoever has sold Trump on the reconciliation commission idea, is already thinking in those terms. The people involved want to see this dictatorial shadow conspiracy of despots running the nation with an iron fist again, and parceling out a few extra crumbs to them in return for their eager betrayal of everyone else and their Beaming of their neighbors.

You will never be able to have a nation united in freedom, living in peace and harmony, where every American is blindly loyal to every other American, and where things just make sense in the nation, with the remnants of this conspiracy contained within its borders. It will always be seeking to foment strife, and Beam anyone seeking to strive, and spy on everyone to make sure nobody has any visions of accomplishing anything impressive in their lives.

And given its training and experience in these fields, as well as its established willingness to engage in these actions, it is dangerous, in a way which can not be easily addressed within the boundaries of a Constitutional government. Ridding our nation of it by any means, and at any cost, is the only way forward and would constitute the great noble war of our time.

The election of TIs would have the additional benefit of

confirming if the public was actually electing its leaders, as the conspiracy would never allow the election of a TI Governor or TI President who was pledging to offer any such pardons to citizens for acting against the former members of the conspiracy. If, despite strong public sentiment, the public proved unable to elect a former TI to office under such conditions, it would be a strong indication the conspiracy remained in the shadows, rigging elections, and merely tried to feign its own elimination, to buy time to regroup and rebuild.

You have a long road ahead, and in truth I do not know exactly what path it will follow, or even if I will be there to see where it leads myself. Obviously I am out on a ledge in issuing this warning to the populace. Still, I hope to be a part of whatever will come, but I will be there with you in rebellion against this conspiracy, at the very least, in spirit.

Whatever happens, have no illusions. You face a highly technologically advanced enemy, which will be ruthless in its attempts to hold onto power. It presently controls the government, both political parties, the news media, the entertainment industry as well as much of the business sector in the United States, and there is good evidence it crosses numerous national boundaries. Your only advantage will be every citizen who is not in the conspiracy rising up to destroy the surveillance at the grass roots.

This conspiracy is acting with such impunity it has launched directed energy attacks against FBI Agents in their homes, as well as against White House Cabinet-level officials in their homes, and other White House officials on White House grounds, while they were under the protection of Secret Service. It has even struck a sitting US Senator. To say nothing of what it has been doing below that level to regular American citizens for decades, neighborhood by neighborhood.

I suspect when you finally rid the nation of it, one of the most dramatic measures will be the fall in cancer rates, once energy beams are no longer freely flying through neighborhoods. But from the reduced car pollution and traffic that will come from shutting down the vehicular surveillance units (which may be responsible for as much as 20% of traffic in many towns), to just the reduction in animals killed from being hit by cars, there will be no facet of this operation anyone will miss.

In your favor, it has not recruited the cream of the crop to its ranks, you vastly outnumber its ground forces, and from what I have seen, its ground surveillance forces have little to no real combat capability and would be no match for the warriors within the American citizenry if a real, hot war were to begin.

We have something worth dying for. They have crumbs, dropped from a table they are not even allowed to dream of sitting at. When the time comes, for those who know, move quickly, violently, and show no mercy. Do not mistake them for human beings, let alone fellow Americans.

You will need to be as ruthless as this conspiracy has been, and settle for nothing short of a complete eradication and removal of the conspiracy from American society, executed as swiftly and completely as possible. You will get no second chance, if you even get a first. Do not be fooled by the protestations of the guilty that they thought they were serving the country, or that they didn't know. They all know.

Whatever happens, if you are up for the battle, do whatever

you must to be rid of this thing. And if you are not up for the battle, stay out of the way of those who are, and let them do what they must. Because America cannot go on with this thing continuing to advance technologically, developing its tools against the citizenry, and deploying them with ever more frequency and ruthlessness. I have seen where that leads, I experience it every night now, and it is horrific.

You must be rid of it, whatever it takes, or you and your children will be enslaved.

The road ahead is long and difficult, but it leads to a true utopia – an America where we all, including our children, are free, united as a single team, devoted loyally to each other, and able to do whatever we want, rising as high as we chose in society, in peace.

I look forward to one day exploring that utopia with you.

Godspeed, and God Bless Real America and the patriots within her who have held loyalty - with the noble ideals of our Constitution and our free republic, and with their fellow real Americans.

We will win.

Epilogue

What Do I Do Now?

So you have made it this far, and want to help rid America of the American Stasi. Following will be the first phase of steps to follow.

At the end of the book will be five copies of our chain letter, asking Americans to visit our website or check out the book, and learn to spot the surveillance. We then ask that they help us to warn other Americans about it, and the risk to our health and freedom it presents. The letter is also available in 8x10 format in two images at the bottom of every page on our website, or at the archives we will list in it.

However if you have a printed book, it would be best not to pull the online files, or visit the website, as your neighborhood archivist, who loosely skims everyone's internet activity in their sector, will see you visited the web address, which is flagged, and they will assign surveillance to take a closer look at you. If you are reading the book, do not visit the website until after you finish the covert phase of spreading the work.

If you are working from the book, you need to make copies of the letter, either scanning it, making photocopies, or taking pictures of it with your phone, and printing them out. I would try to use a USB cable for the printer, as any WiFi signals from a print spooler floating in the air will be grabbed and reviewed by your neighborhood monitor. Alternately you can make copies at work or

695

at the library.

Now you have copies of the letter. Our first phase of spread is a covert phase. You are going to visit any mapping site online like Google Maps, or any online directory where you could procure mailing addresses, or even an old phone book and map, or even in your drives around, note mailing addresses on mail-boxes. You are going to select houses not located close to intersections (with higher likelihoods of being surveillance people), and you will mail the chain letters out to them. Do not dedicate a trip to finding addresses, or stop to write them down every 200 feet. Do this covertly.

For now, I would focus on areas which tend to be politically rightward-leaning. The right has an inherent distrust of government and natural paranoia with respect to government over-reach, which will be more open to these ideas, and be more likely to see the surveillance. They already accept our elections are likely rigged. A Stasi-like surveillance operation is not that much farther a reach.

Due to the nature of the political left's foundational concepts, and its inherent trust of government and authorities, it may take much longer for the grassroots political left to grasp it could face an enemy outside of the political right, let alone share a common enemy with the political right - let alone that such an enemy could be so dangerous and such a threat that it would be worthwhile to unite with the political right to eliminate it. They will eventually arrive there, but it will take time, so to speed the spread of this, it may be best for now to focus on dissemination in areas which are more rightward-leaning.

Address the envelopes by hand, use stamps, and do not include your real return address on them, to stymie any tracking of where these letters are coming from. Use real return addresses for other people and businesses, as fakes will be flagged in the database as they travel through the system, and allow the letters to be grabbed out. Like Mao's revolutionaries, we want these letters to move through the mail system like fish through water, making no waves.

You will drop them, in groups of two to five, in random postal drop boxes while you are out on other business, to avoid having a mailman (who very well could be surveillance) notice fifty identical letters in the box when he empties it, and grow curious about what they say, and maybe crack one open. I would only drop such a group of three once per day, to avoid having any surveillance following you see you make multiple stops to different drop boxes. For that reason you also do not want to drive out just to visit drop boxes, and then return home. Your neighborhood monitor is watching who comes and goes at all hours from the neighborhood, and they will get curious and look into where such frequent and repetitive trips are going.

When you use a drop box, you want to look like a regular person dropping normal mail. You may want to take measures to not leave fingerprints on the letters or envelopes, but do so in such a way it will not be obvious to any surveillance posted at the Post Office or watching the mail drop box. I would not lick any glue on any envelopes to avoid leaving DNA, which is used much more widely by surveillance than you would think.

They may send foot surveillance to do a close approach as you mail it, probably someone who comes up behind you, feigning waiting to mail their own letters. Act normal, and do not worry. A watcher assigned to the drop box to watch it will do that a lot, just to gauge reactions of people using the drop box, in the event you are mailing something in an effort to avoid scrutiny or commit a crime. If you looked surprised or fearful they might investigate your letters later, but if you act normal, and it is just letters, it should not be an issue.

If you know people who would be receptive to this, you can send a letter to them during the covert phase, but do not tell them you sent them the letter. As well as you think you know them, they may be surveillance, and they will then be forced to alert their command, and you will no longer be able to spread this covertly.

Surveillance is designed to be everywhere, and just by being the type of person to act in this situation, they have probably noticed you, and assigned extra coverage to you, including several "friends," who are in reality keeping an eye on you for the machine. If so, those friends who you "click" the most with will be the agents they sent in, with specific orders to "click" with you at all costs, as much as possible. Be aware, they may approach you and ask directly, looking to get you to admit you sent the letter, on orders of their command, which may suspect you. Admit nothing, deny everything, and then ask for the web address, saying you overheard somebody talking about that while you were out, and are curious to read the site.

I would try to only spread this covertly, and continue to send letters until such time as the movement goes public. Covert spread through the mailing of chain letters will be the most effective means of spread, the most difficult for the machine to thwart, and the least likely to endure any adverse consequences from the American Stasi.

Unfortunately we really need those willing to send letters to send a lot of them. Initially it will be slow going building the chain of sent letters, since simply to keep letters being mailed, even without exponential growth, would require every person who sends letters to find one more person who will first read the site and then learn how to spot surveillance, apply that knowledge, see their surveillance, and then mail enough letters themselves to find another such person.

Doing work is not as common as you would think, even when the risks involve theoretically getting cancer from some radiation beam which nobody can see when it is being used, or someone's children being hooked on drugs or molested for having ability and morality.

I would estimate initially it will take each person sending between twenty and fifty letters to find that one person, especially since in many cases, people trying to send letters will be under surveillance they did not know about, and it will see what is happening and intercept the letters before any are delivered. Those letters will simply be lost in the mail, and the sender will never know.

If we can ignite growth however, and get to the point letters are flying all over in every direction, once a person receives two or three letters from different people, it may be easier to motivate them to look into this. Our goal is to have masses of random people, who the machine does not know to watch, sending surges of letters which will lead to those who are unaware receiving five or six letters, which will both make them wonder what the fuss is about, and lend social proof to the idea this operation exists, and is targeting everyone. But it will be slow going at first. Do what you can - every letter, even just a single mailed copy counts.

Once you have sent as many random letters as you intend to, you should then progress to the overt spreading phase. Here you will begin telling people you know and trust that the website at AmericanStasi.com is interesting, and they should check it out, or they should check the book out of the library.

We would also appreciate any other forms of spreading these ideas you can think of, from telling your church about it, to spreading it at your book club, to putting up flyers on telephone poles, to taping chain letters to front doors of homes, to stickers placed around while you are out, to wearing our T-shirts, to putting bumper stickers on your car, to handing out chain letters at political rallies, concerts, or other gatherings. If you wanted to purchase a billboard and had the resources, or invested in a print ad somewhere, we would not argue.

We do not presently accept donations, and while we make some small amount from book purchases, due to the cost structure of printing 800 some-odd pages, we cannot make much and keep the book affordable enough to further the spread. We will make some small amount from merchandise like T-shirts and bumper stickers. However some of that may need to first be spent on countermeasures to the beaming, which has been growing more powerful and which I expect will have serious adverse health consequences, if I cannot, at some point, find a way to deal with it. Nevertheless, we are committed to the spread of this and will spend whatever resources we can on the promotion of this work, and revealing this conspiracy to our fellow Americans.

This is the first step to being rid of this abomination, and we would like to go as quickly as possible. We need every American to know this is out there, operating against them. A revolutionary like yourself, when spreading the knowledge of this, is both helping to strengthen your social circles, and helping to free the nation from a force which increasingly appears bent on destroying the entire country.

Presently this conspiracy is crashing the West, including the United States. Most likely they have positioned investments to profit off the collapse, and the bigger the collapse, the bigger the profits. In a decade or so those profits will probably then get invested in the rebuilding, so they can profit again. However by then, there is no telling what will be left to rebuild, or if we will even be alive to see it happen.

As we speak, a half million Ukrainian refugees are being given Social Security benefits they have no right to, to crash that program. Immigrants from the third world are being given hundreds of billions we do not have, in everything from free food and housing, to medical care, to educations for their kids, and even debit cards loaded with taxpayer dollars, so they can have spending money around town. Fentanyl is pouring into our communities as part of this organized plan to destroy the nation, homelessness is skyrocketing, crime is exploding as criminals are freed over and over, and it is all heading to a debt collapse which will crush our nation, and our entire way of life. Some even think they plan a world war with Russia, to further decimate the population of principled patriots who would oppose them by sending them off to die.

Your family, your loved ones, your children, your entire

community, your very way of life is, right now, on track for total destruction, if you do not attempt to stop it - and this is the only way which stands a chance to expose, and ultimately destroy this conspiracy.

Until the nation grasps that we have been infiltrated by a hostile intelligence operation, that none of what is happening is misguided empathy, that all of it is malicious, hostile action, by a well trained and organized enemy, and until the nation sees the scope of the surveillance overwatch this conspiracy has deployed on all of us, we have zero chance of stopping this. Nobody even recognizes that all of our political leaders, on the right and left, are enemies of the entire United States, installed by the conspiracy in rigged elections - let alone do they see the surveillance tracking them, making any moves toward resistance to what is coming, futile.

If you are reading this, the entire fate of the nation, your life, and your loved one's lives, rest on your shoulders now.

I would gladly do all of this myself, but I am now known, and watched closely. All of my neighbors were suddenly gone over a period of a week when I began this path, and literally every neighbor is now surveillance. I get beamed nightly to degrade me, with steadily increasing force. I am followed everywhere, and any letters I try to send will be noticed and get "lost in the mail," or "misdelivered" to surveillance personnel.

I am now burned as an operative in the information warfare phase of this war. This book, and my hope you are one of my kind, and are ready and willing to finally stand up and fight for your own way of life and your freedom, is the only path forward I see in this war. If I can find enough lone wolves like you to spread this knowledge, simply mailing chain letters, we will get a revolution, and we will win. Americans will allow no less, if we can open their eyes and show them the truth.

Thank you for your time and effort in examining this material, as well as any help you might offer.

704

This is the American Stasi Chain Letter. I've sent you this letter after reading the book American Stasi, available free at AmericanStasi.com. You may also request a library acquire it, or, if banned, you can purchase it at any bookstore, read it, and return it.

Since reading the book, I've seen the domestic surveillance operation it describes. I've sent you this letter as a warning, from one patriotic American to another.

Our government has created a massive domestic surveillance machine to spy on all of us, modeled on the East German Stasi. It has recruited an unbelievably massive civilian informant network made up of seemingly fellow citizens assigned to watch the people in their neighborhood, for the purpose of limiting our ability to succeed in society, so the elites who run America will never have to compete with us. The neighborhood units we all have, are listening in your house at times, and running their children in our schools, to limit the ability of your children to succeed, and compete with their operation as adults. There, those children spies, under the command of adult domestic intelligence officers assigned to the schools, will expose successful children to influences, from drugs, to sex, to alcohol, or other means, to stifle them, to prevent them from succeeding, and being a threat to the operation.

None of us are free, so long as this operation is running, and none of us can resist, if nobody knows it exists, or can even believe such a thing is possible. I am hoping after reading this, you will visit AmericanStasi.com, to read the book for free. It

will show you photos of actual covert surveillance personnel captured on Google Streetview, in Russia, in Bulgaria, and in America. It will show video of surveillance children talking about spying for this machine, and highlight interviews with luminaries like Bill Binney, the 4th in command of NSA on 9/11, explaining this thing has been built and is operating against all of us in secret, shielded by the fact none of us would believe it possible such a thing could happen in the US.

More troubling, Bill will explain the neighborhood units assigned to monitor each sector of our country are given thru-wall radio-emissive technologies to monitor us in our homes which are painting neighborhoods with microwave, X-ray, and other rf radiations, which are causing cancers. As an intelligence expert, he has detected these emissions.

As a leader in the NSA, Bill noted his house was a focus of these technologies, and as a result half of the people on his street got cancer, including his son, and his wife, who passed from it. The surveillance units assigned to each neighborhood have, and are deploying, those technologies, without regard to people's safety, and with no government oversight. Bill's interview is at the website AmericanStasi.com.

We are a non-partisan, non-ideological movement composed solely of people who love America, and do not want cancer, seeking to expose this scandal, and warn our fellow Americans. But we need help. This cannot spread online, the censorship is too great and too well controlled. We're forced to resort to real-life pamphleteering, like our Forefathers, using this chain letter, to spread word of this.

We need heroes willing to sacrifice to save our nation. Please join us. Visit the website AmericanStasi.com, directly, or at the archives listed below, take its free course on spotting surveillance, and look for the units in your neighborhood. Once you know what to look for you will see them in your area. When you see it, for the good of America, as well as your own health and safety, and that of your loved ones, please copy this letter and send it on to other Americans with a random return address on the envelope. The more letters each of us send, the faster this will spread virally, and the sooner we can break this story open nationally, and begin to trigger action to rid us of this operation. Alternatively if you wish to print these out as flyers and distribute them by hand at political rallies, concerts, or other venues, every bit helps.

Please note, this domestic intelligence operation is a huge threat to every single American. It has nothing to do with the right or left, conservatives or liberals, Republicans or Democrats, or any other label or issue. We ask everyone to put their conflicts in those regards on pause, so we may temporarily join together as one America to collectively battle this pox on our nation. This battle holds the possibility of freeing all of us to succeed as we would, protecting our children from malign influences, eliminating many cases of cancer each year, and perhaps joining our nation together in one common cause. Our common enemy is solely the psychopaths of the American Intelligence Community who have done this.

But this movement needs old fashioned American heroes who will just blindly love and support their fellow Americans,

regardless of everything else, and work together against the biggest common enemy our nation will ever face. It will only cost you a few photocopies, and some stamps, if you are willing to help, and you could be a part of something which will change the course of American History, as well as free you to succeed in life however you want. And given this operation is the source of most of the strife in our country, you could even make American culture fun and pleasant again, instead of constantly acrimonious and strife-riven, if we can get rid of it.

Thank you for your consideration. Please visit AmericanStasi.com, or if it has been shut down see one of the archive links below:

https://web.archive.org/web/20240917204019/https://americanstasi.com/

or:

https://archive.ph/wRc6K

This is the American Stasi Chain Letter. I've sent you this letter after reading the book American Stasi, available free at AmericanStasi.com. You may also request a library acquire it, or, if banned, you can purchase it at any bookstore, read it, and return it.

Since reading the book, I've seen the domestic surveillance operation it describes. I've sent you this letter as a warning, from one patriotic American to another.

Our government has created a massive domestic surveillance machine to spy on all of us, modeled on the East German Stasi. It has recruited an unbelievably massive civilian informant network made up of seemingly fellow citizens assigned to watch the people in their neighborhood, for the purpose of limiting our ability to succeed in society, so the elites who run America will never have to compete with us. The neighborhood units we all have, are listening in your house at times, and running their children in our schools, to limit the ability of your children to succeed, and compete with their operation as adults. There, those children spies, under the command of adult domestic intelligence officers assigned to the schools, will expose successful children to influences, from drugs, to sex, to alcohol, or other means, to stifle them, to prevent them from succeeding, and being a threat to the operation.

None of us are free, so long as this operation is running, and none of us can resist, if nobody knows it exists, or can even believe such a thing is possible. I am hoping after reading this, you will visit AmericanStasi.com, to read the book for free. It

will show you photos of actual covert surveillance personnel captured on Google Streetview, in Russia, in Bulgaria, and in America. It will show video of surveillance children talking about spying for this machine, and highlight interviews with luminaries like Bill Binney, the 4th in command of NSA on 9/11, explaining this thing has been built and is operating against all of us in secret, shielded by the fact none of us would believe it possible such a thing could happen in the US.

More troubling, Bill will explain the neighborhood units assigned to monitor each sector of our country are given thru-wall radio-emissive technologies to monitor us in our homes which are painting neighborhoods with microwave, X-ray, and other rf radiations, which are causing cancers. As an intelligence expert, he has detected these emissions.

As a leader in the NSA, Bill noted his house was a focus of these technologies, and as a result half of the people on his street got cancer, including his son, and his wife, who passed from it. The surveillance units assigned to each neighborhood have, and are deploying, those technologies, without regard to people's safety, and with no government oversight. Bill's interview is at the website AmericanStasi.com.

We are a non-partisan, non-ideological movement composed solely of people who love America, and do not want cancer, seeking to expose this scandal, and warn our fellow Americans. But we need help. This cannot spread online, the censorship is too great and too well controlled. We're forced to resort to real-life pamphleteering, like our Forefathers, using this chain letter, to spread word of this.

We need heroes willing to sacrifice to save our nation. Please join us. Visit the website AmericanStasi.com, directly, or at the archives listed below, take its free course on spotting surveillance, and look for the units in your neighborhood. Once you know what to look for you will see them in your area. When you see it, for the good of America, as well as your own health and safety, and that of your loved ones, please copy this letter and send it on to other Americans with a random return address on the envelope. The more letters each of us send, the faster this will spread virally, and the sooner we can break this story open nationally, and begin to trigger action to rid us of this operation. Alternatively if you wish to print these out as flyers and distribute them by hand at political rallies, concerts, or other venues, every bit helps.

Please note, this domestic intelligence operation is a huge threat to every single American. It has nothing to do with the right or left, conservatives or liberals, Republicans or Democrats, or any other label or issue. We ask everyone to put their conflicts in those regards on pause, so we may temporarily join together as one America to collectively battle this pox on our nation. This battle holds the possibility of freeing all of us to succeed as we would, protecting our children from malign influences, eliminating many cases of cancer each year, and perhaps joining our nation together in one common cause. Our common enemy is solely the psychopaths of the American Intelligence Community who have done this.

But this movement needs old fashioned American heroes who will just blindly love and support their fellow Americans,

regardless of everything else, and work together against the biggest common enemy our nation will ever face. It will only cost you a few photocopies, and some stamps, if you are willing to help, and you could be a part of something which will change the course of American History, as well as free you to succeed in life however you want. And given this operation is the source of most of the strife in our country, you could even make American culture fun and pleasant again, instead of constantly acrimonious and strife-riven, if we can get rid of it.

Thank you for your consideration. Please visit AmericanStasi.com, or if it has been shut down see one of the archive links below:

https://web.archive.org/web/20240917204019/https://americanstasi.com/

or:

https://archive.ph/wRc6K

This is the American Stasi Chain Letter. I've sent you this letter after reading the book American Stasi, available free at AmericanStasi.com. You may also request a library acquire it, or, if banned, you can purchase it at any bookstore, read it, and return it.

Since reading the book, I've seen the domestic surveillance operation it describes. I've sent you this letter as a warning, from one patriotic American to another.

Our government has created a massive domestic surveillance machine to spy on all of us, modeled on the East German Stasi. It has recruited an unbelievably massive civilian informant network made up of seemingly fellow citizens assigned to watch the people in their neighborhood, for the purpose of limiting our ability to succeed in society, so the elites who run America will never have to compete with us. The neighborhood units we all have, are listening in your house at times, and running their children in our schools, to limit the ability of your children to succeed, and compete with their operation as adults. There, those children spies, under the command of adult domestic intelligence officers assigned to the schools, will expose successful children to influences, from drugs, to sex, to alcohol, or other means, to stifle them, to prevent them from succeeding, and being a threat to the operation.

None of us are free, so long as this operation is running, and none of us can resist, if nobody knows it exists, or can even believe such a thing is possible. I am hoping after reading this, you will visit AmericanStasi.com, to read the book for free. It

will show you photos of actual covert surveillance personnel captured on Google Streetview, in Russia, in Bulgaria, and in America. It will show video of surveillance children talking about spying for this machine, and highlight interviews with luminaries like Bill Binney, the 4th in command of NSA on 9/11, explaining this thing has been built and is operating against all of us in secret, shielded by the fact none of us would believe it possible such a thing could happen in the US.

More troubling, Bill will explain the neighborhood units assigned to monitor each sector of our country are given thru-wall radio-emissive technologies to monitor us in our homes which are painting neighborhoods with microwave, X-ray, and other rf radiations, which are causing cancers. As an intelligence expert, he has detected these emissions.

As a leader in the NSA, Bill noted his house was a focus of these technologies, and as a result half of the people on his street got cancer, including his son, and his wife, who passed from it. The surveillance units assigned to each neighborhood have, and are deploying, those technologies, without regard to people's safety, and with no government oversight. Bill's interview is at the website AmericanStasi.com.

We are a non-partisan, non-ideological movement composed solely of people who love America, and do not want cancer, seeking to expose this scandal, and warn our fellow Americans. But we need help. This cannot spread online, the censorship is too great and too well controlled. We're forced to resort to real-life pamphleteering, like our Forefathers, using this chain letter, to spread word of this.

We need heroes willing to sacrifice to save our nation. Please join us. Visit the website AmericanStasi.com, directly, or at the archives listed below, take its free course on spotting surveillance, and look for the units in your neighborhood. Once you know what to look for you will see them in your area. When you see it, for the good of America, as well as your own health and safety, and that of your loved ones, please copy this letter and send it on to other Americans with a random return address on the envelope. The more letters each of us send, the faster this will spread virally, and the sooner we can break this story open nationally, and begin to trigger action to rid us of this operation. Alternatively if you wish to print these out as flyers and distribute them by hand at political rallies, concerts, or other venues, every bit helps.

Please note, this domestic intelligence operation is a huge threat to every single American. It has nothing to do with the right or left, conservatives or liberals, Republicans or Democrats, or any other label or issue. We ask everyone to put their conflicts in those regards on pause, so we may temporarily join together as one America to collectively battle this pox on our nation. This battle holds the possibility of freeing all of us to succeed as we would, protecting our children from malign influences, eliminating many cases of cancer each year, and perhaps joining our nation together in one common cause. Our common enemy is solely the psychopaths of the American Intelligence Community who have done this.

But this movement needs old fashioned American heroes who will just blindly love and support their fellow Americans,

regardless of everything else, and work together against the biggest common enemy our nation will ever face. It will only cost you a few photocopies, and some stamps, if you are willing to help, and you could be a part of something which will change the course of American History, as well as free you to succeed in life however you want. And given this operation is the source of most of the strife in our country, you could even make American culture fun and pleasant again, instead of constantly acrimonious and strife-riven, if we can get rid of it.

Thank you for your consideration. Please visit AmericanStasi.com, or if it has been shut down see one of the archive links below:

https://web.archive.org/web/20240917204019/https://americanstasi.com/

or:

https://archive.ph/wRc6K

This is the American Stasi Chain Letter. I've sent you this letter after reading the book American Stasi, available free at AmericanStasi.com. You may also request a library acquire it, or, if banned, you can purchase it at any bookstore, read it, and return it.

Since reading the book, I've seen the domestic surveillance operation it describes. I've sent you this letter as a warning, from one patriotic American to another.

Our government has created a massive domestic surveillance machine to spy on all of us, modeled on the East German Stasi. It has recruited an unbelievably massive civilian informant network made up of seemingly fellow citizens assigned to watch the people in their neighborhood, for the purpose of limiting our ability to succeed in society, so the elites who run America will never have to compete with us. The neighborhood units we all have, are listening in your house at times, and running their children in our schools, to limit the ability of your children to succeed, and compete with their operation as adults. There, those children spies, under the command of adult domestic intelligence officers assigned to the schools, will expose successful children to influences, from drugs, to sex, to alcohol, or other means, to stifle them, to prevent them from succeeding, and being a threat to the operation.

None of us are free, so long as this operation is running, and none of us can resist, if nobody knows it exists, or can even believe such a thing is possible. I am hoping after reading this, you will visit AmericanStasi.com, to read the book for free. It

717

will show you photos of actual covert surveillance personnel captured on Google Streetview, in Russia, in Bulgaria, and in America. It will show video of surveillance children talking about spying for this machine, and highlight interviews with luminaries like Bill Binney, the 4th in command of NSA on 9/11, explaining this thing has been built and is operating against all of us in secret, shielded by the fact none of us would believe it possible such a thing could happen in the US.

More troubling, Bill will explain the neighborhood units assigned to monitor each sector of our country are given thru-wall radio-emissive technologies to monitor us in our homes which are painting neighborhoods with microwave, X-ray, and other rf radiations, which are causing cancers. As an intelligence expert, he has detected these emissions.

As a leader in the NSA, Bill noted his house was a focus of these technologies, and as a result half of the people on his street got cancer, including his son, and his wife, who passed from it. The surveillance units assigned to each neighborhood have, and are deploying, those technologies, without regard to people's safety, and with no government oversight. Bill's interview is at the website AmericanStasi.com.

We are a non-partisan, non-ideological movement composed solely of people who love America, and do not want cancer, seeking to expose this scandal, and warn our fellow Americans. But we need help. This cannot spread online, the censorship is too great and too well controlled. We're forced to resort to real-life pamphleteering, like our Forefathers, using this chain letter, to spread word of this.

We need heroes willing to sacrifice to save our nation. Please join us. Visit the website AmericanStasi.com, directly, or at the archives listed below, take its free course on spotting surveillance, and look for the units in your neighborhood. Once you know what to look for you will see them in your area. When you see it, for the good of America, as well as your own health and safety, and that of your loved ones, please copy this letter and send it on to other Americans with a random return address on the envelope. The more letters each of us send, the faster this will spread virally, and the sooner we can break this story open nationally, and begin to trigger action to rid us of this operation. Alternatively if you wish to print these out as flyers and distribute them by hand at political rallies, concerts, or other venues, every bit helps.

Please note, this domestic intelligence operation is a huge threat to every single American. It has nothing to do with the right or left, conservatives or liberals, Republicans or Democrats, or any other label or issue. We ask everyone to put their conflicts in those regards on pause, so we may temporarily join together as one America to collectively battle this pox on our nation. This battle holds the possibility of freeing all of us to succeed as we would, protecting our children from malign influences, eliminating many cases of cancer each year, and perhaps joining our nation together in one common cause. Our common enemy is solely the psychopaths of the American Intelligence Community who have done this.

But this movement needs old fashioned American heroes who will just blindly love and support their fellow Americans,

regardless of everything else, and work together against the biggest common enemy our nation will ever face. It will only cost you a few photocopies, and some stamps, if you are willing to help, and you could be a part of something which will change the course of American History, as well as free you to succeed in life however you want. And given this operation is the source of most of the strife in our country, you could even make American culture fun and pleasant again, instead of constantly acrimonious and strife-riven, if we can get rid of it.

Thank you for your consideration. Please visit AmericanStasi.com, or if it has been shut down see one of the archive links below:

https://web.archive.org/web/20240917204019/https://americanstasi.com/

or:

https://archive.ph/wRc6K

This is the American Stasi Chain Letter. I've sent you this letter after reading the book American Stasi, available free at AmericanStasi.com. You may also request a library acquire it, or, if banned, you can purchase it at any bookstore, read it, and return it.

Since reading the book, I've seen the domestic surveillance operation it describes. I've sent you this letter as a warning, from one patriotic American to another.

Our government has created a massive domestic surveillance machine to spy on all of us, modeled on the East German Stasi. It has recruited an unbelievably massive civilian informant network made up of seemingly fellow citizens assigned to watch the people in their neighborhood, for the purpose of limiting our ability to succeed in society, so the elites who run America will never have to compete with us. The neighborhood units we all have, are listening in your house at times, and running their children in our schools, to limit the ability of your children to succeed, and compete with their operation as adults. There, those children spies, under the command of adult domestic intelligence officers assigned to the schools, will expose successful children to influences, from drugs, to sex, to alcohol, or other means, to stifle them, to prevent them from succeeding, and being a threat to the operation.

None of us are free, so long as this operation is running, and none of us can resist, if nobody knows it exists, or can even believe such a thing is possible. I am hoping after reading this, you will visit AmericanStasi.com, to read the book for free. It

721

will show you photos of actual covert surveillance personnel captured on Google Streetview, in Russia, in Bulgaria, and in America. It will show video of surveillance children talking about spying for this machine, and highlight interviews with luminaries like Bill Binney, the 4th in command of NSA on 9/11, explaining this thing has been built and is operating against all of us in secret, shielded by the fact none of us would believe it possible such a thing could happen in the US.

More troubling, Bill will explain the neighborhood units assigned to monitor each sector of our country are given thru-wall radio-emissive technologies to monitor us in our homes which are painting neighborhoods with microwave, X-ray, and other rf radiations, which are causing cancers. As an intelligence expert, he has detected these emissions.

As a leader in the NSA, Bill noted his house was a focus of these technologies, and as a result half of the people on his street got cancer, including his son, and his wife, who passed from it. The surveillance units assigned to each neighborhood have, and are deploying, those technologies, without regard to people's safety, and with no government oversight. Bill's interview is at the website AmericanStasi.com.

We are a non-partisan, non-ideological movement composed solely of people who love America, and do not want cancer, seeking to expose this scandal, and warn our fellow Americans. But we need help. This cannot spread online, the censorship is too great and too well controlled. We're forced to resort to real-life pamphleteering, like our Forefathers, using this chain letter, to spread word of this.

We need heroes willing to sacrifice to save our nation. Please join us. Visit the website AmericanStasi.com, directly, or at the archives listed below, take its free course on spotting surveillance, and look for the units in your neighborhood. Once you know what to look for you will see them in your area. When you see it, for the good of America, as well as your own health and safety, and that of your loved ones, please copy this letter and send it on to other Americans with a random return address on the envelope. The more letters each of us send, the faster this will spread virally, and the sooner we can break this story open nationally, and begin to trigger action to rid us of this operation. Alternatively if you wish to print these out as flyers and distribute them by hand at political rallies, concerts, or other venues, every bit helps.

Please note, this domestic intelligence operation is a huge threat to every single American. It has nothing to do with the right or left, conservatives or liberals, Republicans or Democrats, or any other label or issue. We ask everyone to put their conflicts in those regards on pause, so we may temporarily join together as one America to collectively battle this pox on our nation. This battle holds the possibility of freeing all of us to succeed as we would, protecting our children from malign influences, eliminating many cases of cancer each year, and perhaps joining our nation together in one common cause. Our common enemy is solely the psychopaths of the American Intelligence Community who have done this.

But this movement needs old fashioned American heroes who will just blindly love and support their fellow Americans,

regardless of everything else, and work together against the biggest common enemy our nation will ever face. It will only cost you a few photocopies, and some stamps, if you are willing to help, and you could be a part of something which will change the course of American History, as well as free you to succeed in life however you want. And given this operation is the source of most of the strife in our country, you could even make American culture fun and pleasant again, instead of constantly acrimonious and strife-riven, if we can get rid of it.

Thank you for your consideration. Please visit AmericanStasi.com, or if it has been shut down see one of the archive links below:

https://web.archive.org/web/20240917204019/https://americanstasi.com/

or:

https://archive.ph/wRc6K

Notes

01 Koehler, John O. (2000). Stasi: The Untold Story of the East German Secret Police. Westview Press.. p. 8-9. ISBN 978-0-8133-3744-9.

02 Lenzenweger, Mark F.; Lane, Michael C.; Loranger, Armand W.; Kessler, Ronald C. (September 2007). *"DSM-IV Personality Disorders in the National Comorbidity Survey Replication."* Biological Psychiatry. 62 (6): 553–564.

03 https://www.kxan.com/news/local/austin/ex-navy-seal-allegedly-behind-austin-bank-robbery-spree/

04 https://www.youtube.com/watch?v=Ksb4YZSarl0

05 https://en.wikipedia.org/wiki/Operation_TIPS

06 https://www.google.com/maps/
@56.1183833,40.3354038,1311a,35y,315.17h/data=!3m1!1e3?entry=ttu
If typing it in to a browser, you can use the shorturl:
https://tinyurl.com/ycy7pj2j

07 https://www.google.com/maps/
@56.1194826,40.3408723,3a,75y,332.68h,91.43t/data=!3m6!1e1!3m4!
1sw4DxcGeJaOKznugAohuMyw!2e0!7i13312!8i6656?entry=ttu

08 http://rogerpbrown.com/spy/fs017.html

09 https://www.google.com/maps/
@56.1193792,40.3413791,3a,75y,262.74h,69.05t/data=!3m7!1e1!3m5!
1sA2VMR58ZEYWUwDqMd2AJpw!2e0!5s20120801T000000!7i13312!
8i6656?entry=ttu

10 https://www.google.com/maps/
@56.1193866,40.3410604,3a,75y,277.21h,81.52t/data=!3m6!1e1!3m4!
1sBUE0IxVYy4P0H3PIoFTgzw!2e0!7i13312!8i6656?entry=ttu

11 https://www.google.com/maps/https://www.google.com/maps/
@56.1194826,40.3408723,3a,15y,207.02h,88.51t/data=!3m6!1e1!3m4!
1sw4DxcGeJaOKznugAohuMyw!2e0!7i13312!8i6656?entry=ttu
If typing it in to a browser, you can use the shorturl:
https://tinyurl.com/4jvxp5ty

12 https://www.google.com/maps/
@56.1194826,40.3408723,3a,60y,327.75h,84.44t/data=!3m6!1e1!3m4!
1sw4DxcGeJaOKznugAohuMyw!2e0!7i13312!8i6656?entry=ttu
or
https://tinyurl.com/4m9p9rt3

13 https://www.google.com/maps/
@56.1210208,40.3364676,3a,15y,266.31h,84.47t/data=!3m6!1e1!3m4!
1sU3RgBaBjIHf-3g86pHa4Dg!2e0!7i13312!8i6656
https://tinyurl.com/3azfvvc6

14 https://www.google.com/maps/
@56.1211843,40.3351576,3a,30y,229.9h,87.21t/data=!3m6!1e1!3m4!
1s42OwVN3nuRdwkg7lN3lVrQ!2e0!7i13312!8i6656
https://tinyurl.com/357k469c

15 https://www.google.com/maps/
@56.1213031,40.3328369,3a,15y,320.4h,80.42t/data=!3m6!1e1!3m4!

1sYzZOYJ8fEMyOkT_Fmv9YRw!2e0!7i13312!8i6656?entry=ttu

16 https://www.google.com/maps/
@56.1212823,40.3326869,3a,15y,336.61h,81.9t/data=!3m6!1e1!3m4!
1scq5SYuLRav6stYIvrUJXiA!2e0!7i13312!8i6656?entry=ttu

17 https://www.google.com/maps/
@56.1201966,40.3359132,3a,75y,88.05h,66.26t/data=!3m6!1e1!3m4!
1sybPiYmi9jlhhitYYhT4A-A!2e0!7i13312!8i6656
https://tinyurl.com/mvfawnfu

18 https://www.google.com/maps/
@56.1200169,40.3385284,3a,37.5y,359.61h,78.36t/data=!3m6!1e1!3m4!
1sFA0BJn7acCT2Kqpw75OR7w!2e0!7i13312!8i6656?entry=ttu
https://tinyurl.com/46cwddtx

19 https://www.google.com/maps/
@56.1199342,40.3396091,3a,15y,208.43h,86.82t/data=!3m6!1e1!3m4!
1sdCmvO9CtO13BIm-ENw0-nQ!2e0!7i13312!8i6656
https://tinyurl.com/mryzup8n

20 https://www.google.com/maps/
@56.1199151,40.3399516,3a,75y,275.63h,78.02t/data=!3m6!1e1!3m4!
1s5qD25zitNLjr0CIrOFpL3w!2e0!7i13312!8i6656?entry=ttu
https://tinyurl.com/5xt4hayf

21 https://www.google.com/maps/
@56.1199759,40.3390485,3a,75y,188.14h,97.25t/data=!3m7!1e1!3m5!
1s1YpeNOwfJdmKoRGQCpwEig!2e0!6shttps:%2F%2Fstreetviewpixels-
pa.googleapis.com%2Fv1%2Fthumbnail%3Fpanoid
%3D1YpeNOwfJdmKoRGQCpwEig%26cb_client%3Dmaps_sv.tactile.gps
%26w%3D203%26h%3D100%26yaw%3D3.0621588%26pitch
%3D0%26thumbfov%3D100!7i13312!8i6656?entry=ttu
https://tinyurl.com/2s3szh46

22 https://www.google.com/maps/
@56.1199494,40.3394422,3a,15y,149.89h,122.33t/data=!3m6!1e1!3m4!
1sqbOjKTs5d2TwJNTLTKWKZw!2e0!7i13312!8i6656?entry=ttu
https://tinyurl.com/2p8mvyru

23 https://www.politico.com/magazine/story/2018/05/19/michael-mcfaul-book-
excerpt-218408/

24 https://www.google.com/maps/
@56.1193866,40.3410604,3a,15y,157.13h,89.81t/data=!3m6!1e1!3m4!
1sBUE0IxVYy4P0H3PIoFTgzw!2e0!7i13312!8i6656?entry=ttu
https://tinyurl.com/yz8uz62t

25 https://www.google.com/maps/
@56.1193503,40.3411823,3a,15y,286.8h,90.66t/data=!3m6!1e1!3m4!
1sMSp9xwXl7YRpJVT29d9SOA!2e0!7i13312!8i6656?entry=ttu

26 https://www.google.com/maps/
@56.1199328,40.3415237,3a,15y,61.06h,86.45t/data=!3m6!1e1!3m4!
1sFEVN6W2TkICt7eNQW6WpRw!2e0!7i13312!8i6656

27 https://www.google.com/maps/

@56.1191345,40.3413083,3a,15y,21.88h,88.34t/data=!3m6!1e1!3m4!
1szX4ix8goUFUOTJm_v3_eig!2e0!7i13312!8i6656
28 https://www.google.com/maps/
@56.1201738,40.3418173,3a,75y,182.62h,78.76t/data=!3m7!1e1!3m5!
1slywuZ6aUDj1FNxRerbHfFQ!2e0!5s20170701T000000!7i13312!8i6656?
entry=ttu
29 https://www.google.com/maps/
@56.1197929,40.3415198,3a,75y,136.91h,73.84t/data=!3m7!1e1!3m5!
1s0HL8WE5XGbF7sIH6BNaLBA!2e0!5s20170701T000000!7i13312!
8i6656?entry=ttu
30 https://tinyurl.com/vja644hc
31 https://www.google.com/maps/
@42.4393044,25.7139024,3a,75y,72.99h,75.5t/data=!3m8!1e1!3m6!
1s4FyrEa12xuSvg2m7LqafyA!2e0!5s20150801T000000!6shttps:%2F
%2Fstreetviewpixels-pa.googleapis.com%2Fv1%2Fthumbnail%3Fcb_client
%3Dmaps_sv.tactile%26w%3D900%26h%3D600%26pitch
%3D14.503147980064995%26panoid%3D4FyrEa12xuSvg2m7LqafyA
%26yaw%3D72.98845937719142!7i13312!8i6656?
coh=205410&entry=ttu&g_ep=EgoyMDI0MTAwNy4xIKXMDSoASAFQAw
%3D%3D
https://tinyurl.com/mr2883s9
32 https://www.google.com/maps/
@42.4392167,25.7135654,3a,15y,354.15h,63.15t/data=!3m6!1e1!3m4!
1stDwOCeLvT-RWoU8dOKqJ5g!2e0!7i13312!8i6656
https://tinyurl.com/3zs69bx9
33 https://www.google.com/maps/
@42.4388292,25.712038,3a,37.5y,356.79h,63.09t/data=!3m6!1e1!3m4!
1sUpuhsnfAcIAExotE5a64hw!2e0!7i13312!8i6656
https://tinyurl.com/ye2xznry
34 https://www.google.com/maps/
@42.4384891,25.7106734,3a,15y,74.6h,88.77t/data=!3m7!1e1!3m5!
1syT9WalLxYxZHga4dtVwb9A!2e0!5s20150801T000000!7i13312!8i6656?
entry=ttu
35 https://www.google.com/maps/
@42.4384662,25.7105512,3a,15y,350.63h,87.87t/data=!3m6!1e1!3m4!1sm-
Op-mk_4NQ9jEFYSggROQ!2e0!7i13312!8i6656
https://tinyurl.com/4dxyf3ac
36 https://www.google.com/maps/
@42.438006,25.7087923,3a,25.8y,20.38h,66.45t/data=!3m6!1e1!3m4!
1szuXxSu6-CZ8e2UDBoQAYGg!2e0!7i13312!8i6656
https://tinyurl.com/25kaxb99
37 https://www.google.com/maps/
@42.4375102,25.7068252,3a,15y,0.62h,84.4t/data=!3m6!1e1!3m4!
1s_OG_rweyMovwt3P9emYl8Q!2e0!7i13312!8i6656
https://tinyurl.com/3rzsewjp

38 https://www.google.com/maps/
@42.4374866,25.7067302,3a,37.5y,15.78h,64.63t/data=!3m6!1e1!3m4!
1s0kBpqygy6sXkluYw6JmQSg!2e0!7i13312!8i6656
https://tinyurl.com/mumezbwk

39 https://www.google.com/maps/
@42.4375188,25.7068441,3a,15y,353.28h,65.48t/data=!3m6!1e1!3m4!
1s_OG_rweyMovwt3P9emYl8Q!2e0!7i13312!8i6656?entry=ttu

40 https://www.google.com/search?
q=Tucker+Carlson+delivered+an+urgent+warning%3A+
%E2%80%9CBe+prepared.+The+grid+is+going+down.
%E2%80%9D&sourceid=chrome&ie=UTF-8
http://tinyurl.com/yau7tc3d

41 https://www.google.com/maps/
@42.4366382,25.7032423,3a,15y,17.82h,78.38t/data=!3m7!1e1!3m5!
1skXUEob6dthG832W7xWMUkg!2e0!5s20150801T000000!7i13312!
8i6656?entry=ttu
http://tinyurl.com/3xtjyrk5

42 https://www.google.com/maps/@42.433939,25.6923449,3a,75y,256.57h,90t/
data=!3m6!1e1!3m4!1sMO2vNaUM_sf2zCgvYw5ndw!2e0!7i13312!8i6656?
entry=ttu
https://tinyurl.com/ms2htdm8

43 https://www.google.com/maps/
@42.4339281,25.6921829,3a,15y,249.53h,89.03t/data=!3m6!1e1!3m4!
1sMTBOf4Q-uuCbDFfxe_W89A!2e0!7i13312!8i6656
https://tinyurl.com/565w5mme

44 https://www.google.com/maps/
@42.4337064,25.691623,3a,75y,306.97h,75.04t/data=!3m7!1e1!3m5!
1sLLQE-E714MP9_jeSKb_TfA!2e0!5s20150801T000000!7i13312!8i6656?
entry=ttu
https://tinyurl.com/3e8xfv7j

45 https://www.google.com/maps/
@42.433517,25.6914366,3a,15y,85.53h,87.19t/data=!3m6!1e1!3m4!
1sMyaP2JlfXdn_52jtcOz5GQ!2e0!7i13312!8i6656
https://tinyurl.com/44yvzcym

46 https://www.google.com/maps/
@42.4335871,25.6911217,3a,75y,5.07h,71.78t/data=!3m6!1e1!3m4!
1sjhnAaAgoaWLNNdRV9LCRaw!2e0!7i16384!8i8192?entry=ttu
https://tinyurl.com/kyt5z3w9

47 https://www.google.com/maps/
@42.4336596,25.6920066,3a,15y,348.69h,90.51t/data=!3m6!1e1!3m4!
1sIFsSVlyj91sn9NtzG1ZtwA!2e0!7i13312!8i6656
https://tinyurl.com/5bx5b5zp

48 https://www.google.com/maps/
@42.4339522,25.6920776,3a,15y,209.92h,89.13t/data=!3m6!1e1!3m4!
1saBU79CymROPD6xSjM8hNwg!2e0!7i13312!8i6656

https://tinyurl.com/2yakjb9y

49 https://www.maptiler.com/maps/
#style=hybrid&mode=2d&position=15.19/42.433379/25.690093
https://tinyurl.com/4fr9n6zj

50 https://www.google.com/maps/
@42.4339281,25.6921829,3a,15y,339.49h,90.77t/data=!3m6!1e1!3m4!
1sMTBOf4Q-uuCbDFfxe_W89A!2e0!7i13312!8i6656
https://tinyurl.com/y63w78bw

51 https://www.google.com/maps/
@42.4340117,25.6919938,3a,15y,344.18h,87.72t/data=!3m7!1e1!3m5!
1sGQh6RT0TJL_tusM8CVnezg!2e0!5s20120301T000000!7i13312!8i6656?
entry=ttu
https://tinyurl.com/euw5ncyw

52 https://www.google.com/maps/
@42.4347797,25.6917478,3a,15y,336.77h,88.05t/data=!3m6!1e1!3m4!
1sVLqLZ3d_FwESt9HOE0yECg!2e0!7i13312!8i6656?entry=ttu
https://tinyurl.com/333xfe97

53 https://www.google.com/maps/
@42.4348691,25.691719,3a,15y,252.96h,70.79t/data=!3m6!1e1!3m4!
1swv2BoPAgjQPLHSXxVAGWqw!2e0!7i13312!8i6656
https://tinyurl.com/yc8cjjvp

54 https://www.google.com/maps/
@42.4353214,25.6916063,3a,30y,251.66h,80.06t/data=!3m6!1e1!3m4!
1sGf9dMu-eTWQg8Qj_G5BkXA!2e0!7i13312!8i6656
https://tinyurl.com/bdhk76zy

55 https://www.google.com/maps/
@42.4340171,25.6920086,3a,15y,345.07h,89.05t/data=!3m7!1e1!3m5!
1sGQh6RT0TJL_tusM8CVnezg!2e0!5s20120301T000000!7i13312!8i6656?
entry=ttu

56 https://www.google.com/maps/
@42.4353182,25.6916063,3a,75y,210.78h,80.68t/data=!3m6!1e1!3m4!
1sGf9dMu-eTWQg8Qj_G5BkXA!2e0!7i13312!8i6656?entry=ttu
https://tinyurl.com/2bse9zhk

57 https://www.google.com/maps/
@42.4339556,25.6925317,3a,15y,332.07h,88.83t/data=!3m7!1e1!3m5!
1syPc1kTvwo_pN1VO96NnWVg!2e0!5s20120301T000000!7i13312!
8i6656?entry=ttu

58 https://www.google.com/maps/
@42.4348691,25.691719,3a,15y,166.58h,85.14t/data=!3m6!1e1!3m4!
1swv2BoPAgjQPLHSXxVAGWqw!2e0!7i13312!8i6656
https://tinyurl.com/5a9n5rmt

59 https://www.google.com/maps/
@42.4356525,25.691509,3a,15y,289.03h,89.13t/data=!3m6!1e1!3m4!
1sFi90lqVjBOtkXDdGTYKjfg!2e0!7i13312!8i6656
https://tinyurl.com/mrxka4a6

60 https://www.google.com/maps/
@42.43568,25.6914992,3a,75y,338.27h,79.51t/data=!3m6!1e1!3m4!
1sFi90lqVjBOtkXDdGTYKjfg!2e0!7i13312!8i6656?entry=ttu
61 https://www.google.com/maps/
@42.43568,25.6914992,3a,15y,165.72h,87.25t/data=!3m6!1e1!3m4!
1sFi90lqVjBOtkXDdGTYKjfg!2e0!7i13312!8i6656?entry=ttu
62 https://www.google.com/maps/
@42.4362879,25.6925265,3a,75y,87.19h,82.08t/data=!3m7!1e1!3m5!
1s5AmpDBRapF4Px8IL-HcvcA!2e0!5s20120301T000000!7i13312!8i6656?
entry=ttu
63 https://www.google.com/maps/
@42.4362808,25.692657,3a,30y,68.8h,85.24t/data=!3m6!1e1!3m4!
1sacbDCfyoOJLHJjhFNqK7rw!2e0!7i13312!8i6656
https://tinyurl.com/bdhvw5t3
64 https://www.google.com/maps/
@42.436283,25.6926302,3a,15y,250.22h,86.22t/data=!3m6!1e1!3m4!
1sacbDCfyoOJLHJjhFNqK7rw!2e0!7i13312!8i6656?entry=ttu
https://tinyurl.com/3pjhbmu5
65 https://www.google.com/maps/
@42.4365672,25.6937446,3a,15y,252.32h,91t/data=!3m6!1e1!3m4!
1s7ntPO7Rf9NWx3_W5KdI8qw!2e0!7i13312!8i6656?entry=ttu
https://tinyurl.com/bdh2bf5k
66 https://www.google.com/maps/
@42.4394564,25.7024999,3a,60y,58.6h,84.39t/data=!3m6!1e1!3m4!1sD-
IhGwYZNzlWliIww852qg!2e0!7i13312!8i6656
https://tinyurl.com/n7kzdfm3
67 https://www.google.com/maps/
@42.4393436,25.7023979,3a,15y,23.17h,90.83t/data=!3m7!1e1!3m5!
1sWMcXwcNLtN4plmOwcr23tQ!2e0!5s20120301T000000!7i13312!8i6656?
entry=ttu
68 https://www.google.com/maps/
@42.4397013,25.7026636,3a,75y,278.09h,83.82t/data=!3m6!1e1!3m4!
1sYXK3DAnYfZJ7mtDInmgqoQ!2e0!7i13312!8i6656
https://tinyurl.com/5fa7s5j6
69 https://www.google.com/maps/
@42.4396645,25.7026371,3a,15y,341.34h,97.58t/data=!3m7!1e1!3m5!
1slUHSWv4uVxQe_eHWGvrnfw!2e0!5s20120301T000000!7i13312!
8i6656?entry=ttu
70 From https://en.wikipedia.org/wiki/Operation_TIPS , 2/12/2024: "Operation
TIPS, where the last part is an acronym for the Terrorism Information and
Prevention System, was a domestic intelligence-gathering program designed
by President George W. Bush to have United States citizens report suspicious
activity. The program's website implied that US workers who had access to
private citizens' homes, such as many cable installers and telephone repair
workers, would be reporting on what was in people's homes if it were deemed

"suspicious." It came under intense scrutiny in July 2002 when the Washington Post alleged in an editorial that the program was vaguely defined, and investigative political journalist Ritt Goldstein observed in Australia's Sydney Morning Herald[1] that TIPS would provide America with a higher percentage of 'citizen spies' than the former East Germany had under the notorious Stasi secret police... The program's website implied that US workers who had access to private citizens' homes, such as cable installers and telephone repair workers, would be reporting on what was in people's homes if it were deemed "suspicious."... Operation TIPS was accused of doing an "end run" around the United States Constitution... the reports by citizens on fellow citizens would be maintained in government databases. While saying that the information would not be in a central database as part of Operation TIPS, he maintained that the information would still be kept in databases by various law enforcement agencies.... various civil liberties groups (on both the left and the right)... felt that such databases could include false information about citizens with no way for those citizens to know that such information was compiled about them, nor any way for them to correct the information, nor any way for them to confront their accusers."

71 https://www.google.com/maps/
@42.4398748,25.7027606,3a,75y,2.07h,93.85t/data=!3m6!1e1!3m4!
1sCm5hplFESAmjWGaXoTK3VQ!2e0!7i13312!8i6656
https://tinyurl.com/35nech8n

72 https://www.google.com/maps/
@42.4404007,25.7030302,3a,26y,54.63h,78.18t/data=!3m6!1e1!3m4!1s-
h1ImPynpHmuCL2l611d0g!2e0!7i13312!8i6656
https://tinyurl.com/23rymu7j

73 https://www.google.com/maps/
@42.4400433,25.7028552,3a,75y,15.39h,72.77t/data=!3m6!1e1!3m4!
1szIdEykEKA8nKwb7mNw8LAw!2e0!7i13312!8i6656
https://tinyurl.com/44b38yc9

74 https://www.google.com/maps/
@42.4410429,25.7032593,3a,15y,190.65h,84t/data=!3m7!1e1!3m5!
1sfaykiGjrlYjbG9_GBXBgzA!2e0!5s20120301T000000!7i13312!8i6656?
entry=ttu
https://tinyurl.com/4u6shcp4

75 https://www.google.com/maps/
@42.4402833,25.702957,3a,60y,139.75h,74.23t/data=!3m7!1e1!3m5!
1sErS_LN3a74LcRaUBsUiUhg!2e0!5s20120301T000000!7i13312!8i6656?
entry=ttu

76 https://www.google.com/maps/
@42.4412531,25.7032227,3a,15y,238.11h,66.78t/data=!3m6!1e1!3m4!
1sq9u4FAi-lX1NYtZRYv4MZA!2e0!7i13312!8i6656
https://tinyurl.com/yvb9k3fr

77 https://www.google.com/maps/
@42.4423214,25.7029443,3a,15y,268.39h,90.07t/data=!3m7!1e1!3m5!

1samomwlS_0FlqkXn7-erTUA!2e0!5s20120301T000000!7i13312!8i6656?
entry=ttu
https://tinyurl.com/3r8857uf

78 https://www.google.com/maps/
@42.4440942,25.700013,3a,15y,293.45h,84.65t/data=!3m6!1e1!3m4!
1sQQwe6KDukZuRy42Ej3zqmQ!2e0!7i13312!8i6656
https://tinyurl.com/fhdv4uxd

79 https://www.google.com/maps/
@42.4435662,25.7006348,3a,15y,317.96h,89.3t/data=!3m7!1e1!3m5!
1se_25kir2PunUPrChXzOj2A!2e0!5s20120301T000000!7i13312!8i6656?
entry=ttu
https://tinyurl.com/y5xdubrs

80 https://www.google.com/maps/
@42.4442573,25.6998981,3a,15y,253.01h,86.97t/data=!3m7!1e1!3m5!
1sTwL0eQgeNJMHRuq-QRl_3A!2e0!5s20120301T000000!7i13312!8i6656?
entry=ttu
https://tinyurl.com/2vs9kdtb

81 https://www.google.com/maps/@42.444931,25.6994202,3a,15y,251.57h,85t/
data=!3m7!1e1!3m5!1s5UeBNjgntOefAwONx5MYvw!2e0!
5s20120301T000000!7i13312!8i6656?entry=ttu
https://tinyurl.com/2p9d84kc

82 https://www.google.com/maps/
@42.445566,25.6989269,3a,15y,147.53h,88.04t/data=!3m7!1e1!3m5!
1sArSQonJ5ke1Pnw_JbmjCWQ!2e0!5s20120301T000000!7i13312!8i6656?
entry=ttu
https://tinyurl.com/2s4zh9jw

83 https://www.google.com/maps/
@42.4456158,25.6986869,3a,15y,9.15h,87.17t/data=!3m7!1e1!3m5!
1s_J4_xvlKsyUa8SdOJyffFA!2e0!5s20120301T000000!7i13312!8i6656?
entry=ttu
https://bit.ly/3GZMNSL

84 https://www.google.com/maps/
@42.4455794,25.6987137,3a,25.8y,10.28h,88.25t/data=!3m6!1e1!3m4!
1ssn759zA9KHyb0lbvV5g9SA!2e0!7i16384!8i8192?entry=ttu

85 https://www.google.com/maps/
@42.4456598,25.6988962,3a,15y,94.17h,84.89t/data=!3m6!1e1!3m4!1s0l-4-
123fSj8xcy2mi7YeA!2e0!7i16384!8i8192?entry=ttu

86 https://www.google.com/maps/
@42.4407854,25.6937148,3a,15y,38.37h,90.83t/data=!3m7!1e1!3m5!
1ser93YnxVSCudiXEo2J-rAA!2e0!5s20120301T000000!7i13312!8i6656?
entry=ttu
https://tinyurl.com/sas3xnty

87 https://www.google.com/maps/
@42.4367835,25.6926048,3a,15y,11.18h,90.87t/data=!3m7!1e1!3m5!
1sVnagWmJXxcDHeOv5CAhilw!2e0!5s20120301T000000!7i13312!8i6656?

entry=ttu

https://tinyurl.com/5cyv55ut

88 https://www.google.com/maps/
@42.4361795,25.6920425,3a,15y,62.83h,86.38t/data=!3m7!1e1!3m5!
1sREakWJ3lA8UxazC5v9JbWA!2e0!5s20120301T000000!7i13312!8i6656?
entry=ttu

89 https://www.google.com/maps/
@42.4359024,25.6911887,3a,25.8y,87.17h,90.46t/data=!3m6!1e1!3m4!
1slC3gXbZrOVvjrDiktMEelg!2e0!7i13312!8i6656?entry=ttu
https://tinyurl.com/yv2286rt

90 https://www.chicagotribune.com/2002/07/23/beware-of-cable-guys-snooping-
around-the-neighborhood/

91 https://www.google.com/maps/
@42.4360528,25.6895694,3a,75y,313.94h,91.79t/data=!3m6!1e1!3m4!
1sKgxK8Soajo13CFO3wK5NRA!2e0!7i13312!8i6656?entry=ttu

92 https://www.google.com/maps/
@42.4373285,25.6895375,3a,75y,0.2h,96.01t/data=!3m6!1e1!3m4!
1sblV8gbhXPYj0SUaAmpcWAg!2e0!7i13312!8i6656?entry=ttu

93 https://www.google.com/maps/
@42.4366769,25.6894798,3a,15y,0.2h,96.01t/data=!3m6!1e1!3m4!
1sLZ_PS3xFpTkYtlu1ckP7Ng!2e0!7i13312!8i6656?entry=ttu
https://bit.ly/3vrzZlq

94 https://www.google.com/maps/
@42.4360615,25.689423,3a,60y,325.51h,84.59t/data=!3m6!1e1!3m4!
1se9mCJsaeF9Wtc1ePCAf_Rw!2e0!7i13312!8i6656?entry=ttu

95 https://www.google.com/maps/
@42.4362484,25.68918,3a,15y,62.47h,88.85t/data=!3m6!1e1!3m4!
1s7zKIolQo_kNxyVTApUI04Q!2e0!7i13312!8i6656?entry=ttu
https://bit.ly/41H7218

96 https://www.google.com/maps/
@42.4369156,25.6857633,3a,15y,274.92h,90.68t/data=!3m6!1e1!3m4!
1sQQJixevoLn4V-2DoWt68vA!2e0!7i13312!8i6656?entry=ttu

97 https://www.google.com/maps/
@42.4375615,25.6894119,1010a,35y,286.36h,44.69t/data=!3m1!1e3?
entry=ttu
https://bit.ly/48fAZYC

98 https://www.google.com/maps/
@42.4359556,25.6895886,3a,75y,202.37h,71.1t/data=!3m6!1e1!3m4!
1sPhTaRM0qMS1BtqfYSHtk9g!2e0!7i13312!8i6656?entry=ttu
https://bit.ly/3tDwg3V

99 https://www.google.com/maps/
@42.4358656,25.6899191,3a,15y,267.27h,84.41t/data=!3m6!1e1!3m4!
1sNqjfXus-9mVA6HE2URluUQ!2e0!7i13312!8i6656?entry=ttu
https://bit.ly/3RJeKmK

100https://www.google.com/maps/place/Kalispell,+MT+59901/@48.1746056,-

114.314634,15z/data=!4m5!3m4!
1s0x536650959ceac247:0xaf1fbdda1d5abb62!8m2!3d48.1919889!4d-
114.316813
https://bit.ly/47hWLcW
101https://www.google.com/maps/@48.16986,-
114.3093425,3a,15y,2.94h,88.44t/data=!3m7!1e1!3m5!
1s2eUdEj9kBmfyIdrpfzRf9w!2e0!5s20080901T000000!7i3328!8i1664?
entry=ttu
https://bit.ly/3vgJ1Sq
102https://www.google.com/maps/@48.1717231,-
114.3093334,3a,15y,88.97h,81.96t/data=!3m7!1e1!3m5!
1sQiUu_8JpgIqmIvn1z_vAcQ!2e0!5s20080901T000000!7i3328!8i1664?
entry=ttu
https://bit.ly/47k1qeg
103https://www.google.com/maps/@48.1719813,-
114.3093361,3a,75y,311.94h,75.02t/data=!3m6!1e1!3m4!
1sdXwx_1uRjqpfSDStgS3p5A!2e0!7i3328!8i1664?entry=ttu
https://bit.ly/3tBgAOB
104https://www.google.com/maps/@48.171065,-
114.309334,3a,15y,359.33h,89.09t/data=!3m6!1e1!3m4!
1srPvObfEmzlfLCnCD_80ByQ!2e0!7i3328!8i1664?entry=ttu
http://tinyurl.com/2a7uumr5
105https://www.google.com/maps/@48.1720859,-
114.3093167,3a,30y,276.88h,90.48t/data=!3m6!1e1!3m4!
1s6cYJAfq3foGBrmRzXzC_OQ!2e0!7i16384!8i8192?entry=ttu
106https://www.google.com/maps/@48.1720593,-
114.3115381,3a,15y,89.46h,88.53t/data=!3m6!1e1!3m4!
1sYuR0QhR06uPNH_boDEv_YA!2e0!7i3328!8i1664?entry=ttu
http://tinyurl.com/yzxxhu5j
107https://www.google.com/maps/@48.1720937,-
114.3101279,3a,15y,210.36h,86.13t/data=!3m6!1e1!3m4!
1s0FQFySBp5xywK-JkkQul2A!2e0!7i3328!8i1664?entry=ttu
http://tinyurl.com/33jxm8r7
108https://www.google.com/maps/@48.1720692,-
114.3111515,3a,37.5y,333.07h,85.83t/data=!3m6!1e1!3m4!
1s_09SSJvIqCd6d0seBufdTQ!2e0!7i3328!8i1664?entry=ttu
http://tinyurl.com/mwdb4tdu
109https://www.google.com/maps/@48.1724537,-
114.3113611,3a,15y,279.52h,88.35t/data=!3m6!1e1!3m4!
1s1oFHuOdjZKzwV6PTzkIUhQ!2e0!7i3328!8i1664?entry=ttu
http://tinyurl.com/y3aty99f
110https://www.google.com/maps/@48.1721769,-
114.3159994,3a,75y,68.08h,82.61t/data=!3m6!1e1!3m4!
1sfWqBsy93wct9Z8BH8DrmOQ!2e0!7i3328!8i1664?entry=ttu
https://bit.ly/3RBCAkm

111https://www.google.com/maps/@48.1723449,-
114.315988,3a,15y,302.95h,87.4t/data=!3m6!1e1!3m4!
1sLG8cL8SwObaNn9Qk7QqkXA!2e0!7i3328!8i1664?entry=ttu
http://tinyurl.com/3ewbcnpm
112https://www.google.com/maps/@48.1743219,-
114.3093912,3a,30y,284.55h,79.52t/data=!3m7!1e1!3m5!1sS0tvUSG-O-
qdrvYm89-NQA!2e0!5s20080901T000000!7i3328!8i1664?entry=ttu
http://tinyurl.com/44k98xae
113https://www.google.com/maps/@48.1767625,-
114.3093406,3a,75y,342.2h,81.02t/data=!3m6!1e1!3m4!
1sbJ9GN13pSFRfQrHITUodJg!2e0!7i3328!8i1664
http://tinyurl.com/5n8a8m2z
114https://www.google.com/maps/@48.1766333,-
114.3093371,3a,30y,332.47h,84.79t/data=!3m7!1e1!3m5!1s2kstBhPgQ-
7bfOd5dzCAFQ!2e0!5s20190901T000000!7i16384!8i8192?entry=ttu
115https://www.google.com/maps/@48.1767775,-
114.3093924,3a,75y,309.63h,70.44t/data=!3m7!1e1!3m5!
1s2LBR4T56ebKFxTMLPCP7aw!2e0!5s20080901T000000!7i3328!8i1664?
entry=ttu
116https://www.google.com/maps/@48.1783048,-
114.3225744,3a,60y,350.46h,77.44t/data=!3m6!1e1!3m4!
1sq9c5Fb0kJuZnpdsFHA8Haw!2e0!7i3328!8i1664?entry=ttu
http://tinyurl.com/3r8ypkkw
117https://www.google.com/maps/@48.1786748,-
114.322569,3a,75y,267.99h,84.49t/data=!3m6!1e1!3m4!1s-
KdECXN5QTL1uT1G8o6oJA!2e0!7i3328!8i1664?entry=ttu
118https://www.google.com/maps/@48.1782163,-
114.3225702,3a,30y,345.28h,84.4t/data=!3m6!1e1!3m4!
1slNUkK2mAso3GLCbAOa6zyA!2e0!7i3328!8i1664?entry=ttu
http://tinyurl.com/y794swz2
119https://www.google.com/maps/@48.1782877,-
114.321708,3a,15y,267.92h,87.76t/data=!3m6!1e1!3m4!
1sBWtSgqP9RC2K_mMGPk0OYg!2e0!7i3328!8i1664?entry=ttu
http://tinyurl.com/2uc7b57j
120https://www.google.com/maps/@48.6309973,-112.3383633,12.67z?entry=ttu
121https://www.google.com/maps/@48.6248407,-
112.3048448,3a,75y,132.68h,80.42t/data=!3m7!1e1!3m5!1sJh1h-
nSH1t2EUAuUMvmKnw!2e0!5s20080801T000000!7i3328!8i1664?entry=ttu
http://tinyurl.com/4ytuuy78
122https://www.google.com/maps/@48.6248407,-
112.3048448,3a,75y,311.84h,68.02t/data=!3m7!1e1!3m5!1sJh1h-
nSH1t2EUAuUMvmKnw!2e0!5s20080801T000000!7i3328!8i1664?entry=ttu
http://tinyurl.com/4byc2r2z
123https://www.google.com/maps/@48.6271459,-
112.3094216,3a,75y,319.86h,73.48t/data=!3m7!1e1!3m5!

1sriwWDx6GV4OWxayDRDXh4g!2e0!5s20080801T000000!7i3328!8i1664?entry=ttu

http://tinyurl.com/4ef6ecrn

124https://www.google.com/maps/@48.6272118,-112.3095331,3a,75y,284.94h,80.01t/data=!3m7!1e1!3m5!1sXf_7hu4I3d8-DfBHkmyqQQ!2e0!5s20080801T000000!7i3328!8i1664?entry=ttu

http://tinyurl.com/vfm4bfdk

125https://www.google.com/maps/@48.6272393,-112.3096755,3a,37.5y,115.44h,84.23t/data=!3m7!1e1!3m5!1s9unwkPl6Q7gj7P8-RwIhKA!2e0!5s20231001T000000!7i16384!8i8192?entry=ttu

http://tinyurl.com/36fk5suw

126https://www.google.com/maps/@48.6273219,-112.3094508,3a,75y,210.59h,73.48t/data=!3m7!1e1!3m5!1sq0iHOOKvVw8wAiwBwDre8Q!2e0!5s20230901T000000!7i16384!8i8192?entry=ttu

http://tinyurl.com/cccw2pru

127https://www.google.com/maps/@48.6272188,-112.3098261,3a,26.4y,66.56h,81.91t/data=!3m7!1e1!3m5!1swB0E1eNBSEVO--Q_maO1Bw!2e0!5s20231001T000000!7i16384!8i8192?entry=ttu

http://tinyurl.com/mr2xk6ye

128https://www.google.com/maps/@48.6292553,-112.3156862,3a,37.5y,285.44h,82.9t/data=!3m7!1e1!3m5!1stBqMc6mRc1ZkhOdSMS9akQ!2e0!5s20080801T000000!7i3328!8i1664?entry=ttu

http://tinyurl.com/bdk9bjwp

129https://www.google.com/maps/@48.6292388,-112.3156999,3a,30y,289.74h,84.54t/data=!3m7!1e1!3m5!1ss1Fr4QrMBL1nhUXilw1Uaw!2e0!5s20231001T000000!7i16384!8i8192?entry=ttu

http://tinyurl.com/bdzbww8d

130https://www.google.com/maps/@48.629988,-112.3196021,3a,75y,299.27h,71.85t/data=!3m7!1e1!3m5!1sciy-bXHH4CBrmVjgjz_5mw!2e0!5s20080801T000000!7i3328!8i1664?entry=ttu

http://tinyurl.com/mtvj2vub

131https://www.google.com/maps/@48.6300541,-112.3203929,3a,75y,106.08h,66.96t/data=!3m7!1e1!3m5!1sfaWMNJMJrBLg2Lxjy0KvTQ!2e0!5s20080801T000000!7i3328!8i1664?entry=ttu

http://tinyurl.com/3d3xn5mx

132https://www.google.com/maps/@48.6298195,-112.3201647,3a,75y,354.5h,64.85t/data=!3m6!1e1!3m4!1sCeimmA519p9hOl9HgjgTOQ!2e0!7i3328!8i1664?entry=ttu

http://tinyurl.com/yfsru7aj

133https://www.google.com/maps/@48.6395412,-112.3388637,3a,75y,216.32h,67.58t/data=!3m7!1e1!3m5!1sFYjFQ5hI6aSdx2AoaL4Qaw!2e0!5s20231001T000000!7i16384!8i8192?entry=ttu
http://tinyurl.com/3razdwts
134https://www.google.com/maps/@48.6395412,-112.3388637,3a,30y,315.87h,81.83t/data=!3m7!1e1!3m5!1sFYjFQ5hI6aSdx2AoaL4Qaw!2e0!5s20231001T000000!7i16384!8i8192?entry=ttu
http://tinyurl.com/5n6wfxw4
135https://www.google.com/maps/@48.6393678,-112.3381177,3a,75y,72.68h,89.63t/data=!3m6!1e1!3m4!1sxdfWLRAvcILIVnzequJ3Pw!2e0!7i16384!8i8192?entry=ttu
136https://www.google.com/maps/@48.6394725,-112.33985,3a,37.5y,200.57h,79.24t/data=!3m7!1e1!3m5!1s9kRlAFN3U8bjDhx64w_rzw!2e0!5s20231001T000000!7i16384!8i8192?entry=ttu
http://tinyurl.com/2nrtxet3
137https://www.google.com/maps/@48.6306202,-112.3543239,3a,30y,62.49h,84.12t/data=!3m6!1e1!3m4!1sPOPsCJwT9afmbwkvMZmzSQ!2e0!7i16384!8i8192?entry=ttu
http://tinyurl.com/2ba6ajnw
138https://www.google.com/maps/@48.6309818,-112.3535951,3a,75y,180.4h,74.14t/data=!3m6!1e1!3m4!1sBeCfLUn4dx-nmW9G4pkXxQ!2e0!7i16384!8i8192?entry=ttu
http://tinyurl.com/scwp5m8j
139https://www.google.com/maps/@48.6302934,-112.3555038,3a,15y,250.99h,90.17t/data=!3m6!1e1!3m4!1sp0z_dYIoBit2-CTVsBJWOA!2e0!7i16384!8i8192?entry=ttu
http://tinyurl.com/27fwkwft
140https://www.google.com/maps/@48.6294594,-112.3590366,3a,75y,208.58h,80.34t/data=!3m6!1e1!3m4!1s9Hps9tGJhr3IJqBJ627Edg!2e0!7i16384!8i8192?entry=ttu
http://tinyurl.com/2a84yt2y
141https://www.google.com/maps/@48.6289944,-112.3616077,3a,75y,50.81h,89.16t/data=!3m6!1e1!3m4!1sSqdL43f-wRm7ncb6gZNNyw!2e0!7i16384!8i8192?entry=ttu
http://tinyurl.com/3zz3mwu8
142https://www.google.com/maps/@48.628936,-112.3593848,3a,30y,6.79h,90.33t/data=!3m6!1e1!3m4!1sJpAQB2u5ELDKrlCW0cimZw!2e0!7i3328!8i1664?entry=ttu
http://tinyurl.com/4eepwkjn
143https://www.google.com/maps/@48.6284737,-112.3644352,3a,15y,254.54h,91.25t/data=!3m6!1e1!3m4!1sgiBscfgTi69R7Is-9SAZYQ!2e0!7i16384!8i8192?entry=ttu

144https://www.google.com/maps/@33.7447585,-118.1130378,17.15z?entry=ttu
http://tinyurl.com/bd4rpx2d

145https://www.google.com/maps/@33.7439749,-
118.1125303,3a,15y,188.65h,85.18t/data=!3m7!1e1!3m5!
1sxgoWxSDPTIixSgrEOZAxwA!2e0!5s20180401T000000!7i16384!8i8192?
entry=ttu
http://tinyurl.com/y9ddj3wv

146https://www.google.com/maps/@33.7446195,-
118.1120597,3a,26.4y,135.38h,83.47t/data=!3m7!1e1!3m5!
1sEV1WHfi_v9I6DUg5GfjOXg!2e0!5s20180401T000000!7i16384!8i8192?
entry=ttu

147https://www.google.com/maps/@33.7454325,-
118.1115992,3a,75y,19.46h,76.87t/data=!3m7!1e1!3m5!
1sk_pdWbEYGkweDd7YlHKabQ!2e0!5s20180401T000000!7i16384!
8i8192?entry=ttu
http://tinyurl.com/2tusw64a

148https://www.google.com/maps/@33.7463666,-
118.1111161,3a,27.3y,270.7h,82.9t/data=!3m6!1e1!3m4!
1srKegVNSeMdMHrdYffFdJJA!2e0!7i16384!8i8192
http://tinyurl.com/ykt8jddt

149https://www.google.com/maps/@33.7456834,-
118.1114415,3a,15y,147.5h,86.91t/data=!3m7!1e1!3m5!1sg2X0N5ZtWEynz-
qk1AgRog!2e0!5s20180401T000000!7i16384!8i8192?entry=ttu
http://tinyurl.com/ysrb2vrm

150https://www.google.com/maps/@33.7434781,-
118.1129432,3a,26.1y,105.99h,91.25t/data=!3m6!1e1!3m4!
1sn5K0eFuYt_50qjoDGTc3Kg!2e0!7i16384!8i8192
http://tinyurl.com/3xxjk7xv

151https://www.google.com/maps/@33.7430569,-
118.1135155,3a,15y,252.11h,85.35t/data=!3m6!1e1!3m4!
1sKrtifZnodUyvX8wfKLg6QQ!2e0!7i16384!8i8192
https://archive.is/8Plpl

152https://www.google.com/maps/@33.7427946,-
118.1140163,3a,15y,253.9h,88.1t/data=!3m6!1e1!3m4!
1s9JdrdWcN9uQyvVHiF6mOOQ!2e0!7i16384!8i8192?entry=ttu

153https://www.google.com/maps/@33.7428716,-
118.1141936,3a,75y,256.85h,73.12t/data=!3m6!1e1!3m4!
1scnJUI3ohHoyCsGnifbVW8g!2e0!7i16384!8i8192?entry=ttu

154https://www.google.com/maps/@33.7427218,-
118.1143094,3a,75y,109.58h,65.46t/data=!3m7!1e1!3m5!
1s8coSBboTIwycPgEJvsIsig!2e0!5s20170601T000000!7i13312!8i6656?
entry=ttu

155https://www.google.com/maps/@33.7426412,-
118.1138675,3a,37.5y,315.3h,67.13t/data=!3m7!1e1!3m5!1sxOw2zU4F-
1XW0ROIpoiUnQ!2e0!5s20070601T000000!7i3328!8i1664?entry=ttu

156https://www.google.com/maps/@33.7433782,-
118.1129486,3a,75y,39.85h,86.96t/data=!3m7!1e1!3m5!1sib5Tr-
Aqkm4KEBrJmSzAMQ!2e0!5s20180401T000000!7i16384!8i8192?entry=ttu
157https://www.google.com/maps/@33.743429,-
118.1128196,3a,75y,139.34h,88.9t/data=!3m6!1e1!3m4!
1sD3juxHcVA54Ucq8pLV3dCw!2e0!7i16384!8i8192
http://tinyurl.com/4ptc7zam
158https://www.google.com/maps/@33.743429,-
118.1128196,3a,75y,339.5h,80.34t/data=!3m6!1e1!3m4!
1sD3juxHcVA54Ucq8pLV3dCw!2e0!7i16384!8i8192
http://tinyurl.com/sebrtdus
159https://www.google.com/maps/@33.7432761,-
118.1125154,3a,15y,296.41h,85.17t/data=!3m7!1e1!3m5!
1skcbGznRYcd0Od9JGmWGeqw!2e0!5s20180401T000000!7i16384!
8i8192?entry=ttu
160https://www.google.com/maps/@33.7465188,-
118.1125325,3a,15y,135.13h,85.86t/data=!3m7!1e1!3m5!
1sE8dUzAaXmEZ_hqYb-fjI2w!2e0!5s20180401T000000!7i16384!8i8192?
entry=ttu
http://tinyurl.com/2t8cp7nj
161https://www.google.com/maps/@33.7457044,-
118.1115191,3a,15y,143.58h,87.79t/data=!3m6!1e1!3m4!
1s83wl_UwAKI0CaiB3io1Rkg!2e0!7i16384!8i8192?entry=ttu
http://tinyurl.com/mwjkchtj
162https://www.google.com/maps/@33.7457066,-
118.1115224,3a,60y,177.39h,91.31t/data=!3m6!1e1!3m4!
1s83wl_UwAKI0CaiB3io1Rkg!2e0!7i16384!8i8192?entry=ttu
163https://www.google.com/maps/@33.7457034,-
118.1115244,3a,15y,188.58h,90.19t/data=!3m6!1e1!3m4!
1s83wl_UwAKI0CaiB3io1Rkg!2e0!7i16384!8i8192
http://tinyurl.com/wrn2hzz7
164https://www.google.com/maps/@33.7457044,-
118.1115191,3a,15y,190.62h,86.59t/data=!3m6!1e1!3m4!
1s83wl_UwAKI0CaiB3io1Rkg!2e0!7i16384!8i8192?entry=ttu
http://tinyurl.com/3crxcya4
165https://www.google.com/maps/@33.7466219,-
118.1107534,3a,15y,336.28h,84.73t/data=!3m7!1e1!3m5!
1s_67spK5nyfGSn1Z9SJ4mKQ!2e0!5s20180401T000000!7i16384!8i8192?
entry=ttu
166https://www.google.com/maps/@33.7455212,-
118.1113279,3a,15y,95.26h,87.52t/data=!3m6!1e1!3m4!
1sFOjcYZsKeJWHrIoq13ftaw!2e0!7i16384!8i8192
http://tinyurl.com/yzjpzhmu
167https://www.nydailynews.com/2019/01/24/see-it-man-accosts-wpix-reporter-
cameraman-in-their-van-slaps-cell-phone-from-his-hand/

168https://www.google.com/maps/@33.7455212,-
118.1113279,3a,15y,39.42h,80.51t/data=!3m6!1e1!3m4!
1sFOjcYZsKeJWHrIoq13ftaw!2e0!7i16384!8i8192
http://tinyurl.com/4f3ezjvh
169See:https://twitter.com/ShawnWitzemann/status/1495139454444519430
and
https://twitter.com/Truth_InMedia/status/1723011043734040939
170https://twitter.com/JamesOKeefeIII/status/1695857067104366975
171https://www.google.com/maps/@33.7437213,-
118.1127346,3a,30y,267.89h,85t/data=!3m6!1e1!3m4!
1sHSHWNeFb4cizsfQkqOxQ_Q!2e0!7i16384!8i8192
http://tinyurl.com/58st2szv
172https://www.google.com/maps/@33.7455169,-
118.1115508,3a,15y,281.92h,90.87t/data=!3m6!1e1!3m4!
1sHWd2wS2a9FnLopgAsXsVWg!2e0!7i16384!8i8192
http://tinyurl.com/54f2cahx
173https://www.google.com/maps/@60.194945,-149.3827686,14.61z
174https://www.google.com/maps/@60.1959639,-149.3783209,14.21z?entry=ttu
175 https://www.google.com/maps/@60.1919672,-
149.3743137,3a,75y,205.35h,92.63t/data=!3m6!1e1!3m4!1sZK5iV-
a9pxwemyhkYGVFiQ!2e0!7i13312!8i6656
176 https://www.google.com/maps/@60.1917829,-
149.3746934,3a,27.5y,206.44h,86.69t/data=!3m6!1e1!3m4!
1sMLN3Fru7QSiUENmMcDm_tg!2e0!7i13312!8i6656
177https://www.google.com/maps/@60.1932535,-
149.3757392,3a,75y,157.08h,104.94t/data=!3m6!1e1!3m4!
1szbUGEWmk9LEGbQ7QZfptPg!2e0!7i13312!8i6656?entry=ttu
178https://www.google.com/maps/@60.1950931,-
149.382793,3a,15y,183.02h,89.22t/data=!3m7!1e1!3m5!
1s96Yur2_nafy9rxZmvQv2lw!2e0!6shttps:%2F%2Fstreetviewpixels-
pa.googleapis.com%2Fv1%2Fthumbnail%3Fpanoid
%3D96Yur2_nafy9rxZmvQv2lw%26cb_client%3Dmaps_sv.tactile.gps%26w
%3D203%26h%3D100%26yaw%3D135.41245%26pitch%3D0%26thumbfov
%3D100!7i13312!8i6656?entry=ttu
179 https://www.google.com/maps/@60.1916858,-
149.3748152,3a,75y,200.66h,75.88t/data=!3m6!1e1!3m4!
1sG18Vu6Mwjse6gB7pLF2ajg!2e0!7i13312!8i6656
180https://www.google.com/maps/@60.1902274,-
149.3769995,3a,15y,171.36h,75.49t/data=!3m6!1e1!3m4!
1soKAleLzjiBwwsxBHDFecXg!2e0!7i13312!8i6656?entry=ttu
181https://www.google.com/maps/@60.1991866,-
149.3754032,3a,26y,351.1h,80.16t/data=!3m6!1e1!3m4!1sZ-
h5980vztAxHiRzJ4GRVw!2e0!7i13312!8i6656?entry=ttu
182https://www.google.com/maps/@60.2001281,-
149.3747583,3a,75y,99.18h,65.06t/data=!3m6!1e1!3m4!

1sxkwpwI4h4EWFFFFZ4gFixw!2e0!7i13312!8i6656?entry=ttu
183https://www.google.com/maps/@60.1867525,-
149.3823729,3a,15y,39.9h,89.57t/data=!3m6!1e1!3m4!1sPDxexk-
PuHG5Us5VJolf-A!2e0!7i13312!8i6656?entry=ttu
184https://www.google.com/maps/@60.1867525,-
149.3823729,3a,15y,217.39h,88.97t/data=!3m6!1e1!3m4!1sPDxexk-
PuHG5Us5VJolf-A!2e0!7i13312!8i6656?entry=ttu
185https://www.google.com/maps/@60.1857928,-
149.3805181,3a,15y,239.97h,74.63t/data=!3m6!1e1!3m4!
1sk_24oVhEEtBggnxwxQr7GA!2e0!7i13312!8i6656?entry=ttu
186https://www.google.com/maps/@60.1864797,-
149.3826465,3a,15y,31.74h,89.75t/data=!3m6!1e1!3m4!
1sZU_HLHvDgb8kd76mau6tvA!2e0!7i13312!8i6656?entry=ttu
187https://www.google.com/maps/@60.1864797,-
149.3826465,3a,15y,218.53h,91t/data=!3m6!1e1!3m4!
1sZU_HLHvDgb8kd76mau6tvA!2e0!7i13312!8i6656?entry=ttu
188https://www.google.com/maps/@60.1860742,-
149.3834012,3a,25.3y,215.69h,86.2t/data=!3m6!1e1!3m4!
1sctPJy6RPgYuN0cq-SmrsUA!2e0!7i13312!8i6656?entry=ttu
189https://www.google.com/maps/@60.1849296,-
149.3864417,3a,75y,139.87h,86.16t/data=!3m6!1e1!3m4!
1sQ94EYShh5UUjFoWgDv0JkA!2e0!7i13312!8i6656
190https://www.google.com/maps/@60.1845592,-
149.3858641,3a,15y,214.19h,88.75t/data=!3m6!1e1!3m4!
1sz6MRuvNQAuviEwQ8VJ_CUw!2e0!7i13312!8i6656
191https://www.google.com/maps/@60.1836748,-
149.3871239,3a,15y,214.19h,87.77t/data=!3m6!1e1!3m4!
1symnFLQsYa8RN6yAdy7_4jg!2e0!7i13312!8i6656?entry=ttu
192https://www.google.com/maps/@60.1828343,-
149.3883337,3a,25.3y,148.22h,88.13t/data=!3m6!1e1!3m4!
1sL5CoGXHCgZ0z6untG_wwqQ!2e0!7i13312!8i6656
193https://www.google.com/maps/@60.1822256,-
149.386734,3a,15y,178.52h,85.06t/data=!3m6!1e1!3m4!1sAkYiLi3k-
g6xMjodQbCufw!2e0!7i13312!8i6656
194https://www.google.com/maps/@60.1827569,-
149.3885457,3a,15y,219.67h,86.1t/data=!3m6!1e1!3m4!1s5-
Rkkcy9CUiA9Hn7ftWSNQ!2e0!7i13312!8i6656?entry=ttu
195https://www.google.com/maps/@60.1819956,-
149.3898396,3a,75y,217.02h,84.57t/data=!3m7!1e1!3m5!
1srPx40xtewQpAHICz_tlnFg!2e0!6s%2F%2Fgeo3.ggpht.com%2Fcbk
%3Fpanoid%3DrPx40xtewQpAHICz_tlnFg%26output%3Dthumbnail
%26cb_client%3Dmaps_sv.tactile.gps%26thumb%3D2%26w%3D203%26h
%3D100%26yaw%3D139.7278%26pitch%3D0%26thumbfov%3D100!
7i13312!8i6656
196https://www.google.com/maps/@60.1819956,-

149.3898396,3a,75y,45.31h,82.51t/data=!3m7!1e1!3m5!
1srPx40xtewQpAHICz_tlnFg!2e0!6s%2F%2Fgeo3.ggpht.com%2Fcbk
%3Fpanoid%3DrPx40xtewQpAHICz_tlnFg%26output%3Dthumbnail
%26cb_client%3Dmaps_sv.tactile.gps%26thumb%3D2%26w%3D203%26h
%3D100%26yaw%3D139.7278%26pitch%3D0%26thumbfov%3D100!
7i13312!8i6656

197https://www.google.com/maps/@60.1770747,-
149.3976854,3a,75y,243.52h,75.27t/data=!3m6!1e1!3m4!
1sMsE7ngoW7LUKIi79vIWHrQ!2e0!7i13312!8i6656

198https://www.google.com/maps/@60.1624484,-
149.4121343,3a,75y,174.88h,84.44t/data=!3m6!1e1!3m4!
1suQadeDUbWqLNHOXVrk4q3A!2e0!7i13312!8i6656?entry=ttu

199https://www.google.com/maps/@60.1652953,-
149.4099466,3a,26.2y,254.9h,82.74t/data=!3m7!1e1!3m5!
1sjuYaLjgOB5EdyLhLIYCCtA!2e0!6s%2F%2Fgeo0.ggpht.com%2Fcbk
%3Fpanoid%3DjuYaLjgOB5EdyLhLIYCCtA%26output%3Dthumbnail
%26cb_client%3Dmaps_sv.tactile.gps%26thumb%3D2%26w%3D203%26h
%3D100%26yaw%3D217.16196%26pitch%3D0%26thumbfov%3D100!
7i13312!8i6656

200https://www.google.com/maps/@60.1676791,-
149.4142075,3a,30y,254.14h,86.81t/data=!3m6!1e1!3m4!
1sX_YzPHbzFyY2wP3cd24Ptw!2e0!7i13312!8i6656

201https://www.youtube.com/watch?
time_continue=3&v=x65LUeAvt_s&embeds_referring_euri=https%3A%2F
%2Fwww.anonymousconservative.com%2F

202https://www.heraldnet.com/news/detectives-mum-on-deadly-home-invasion-
case-near-everett/

203https://irahsokimages.com/ or https://archive.is/28faa

204https://www.google.com/maps/@47.8779375,-
122.2101737,3a,15y,230.34h,88.55t/data=!3m6!1e1!3m4!
1sm2oLpmvjw7mmgLanioUNOw!2e0!7i16384!8i8192

205https://www.google.com/maps/@47.8779404,-
122.2103771,3a,15y,166.33h,83.13t/data=!3m6!1e1!3m4!
1sybOV16CHGYvM6s3xV09zfA!2e0!7i16384!8i8192

206https://www.google.com/maps/@47.8779404,-
122.2103771,3a,60y,179.89h,58.79t/data=!3m6!1e1!3m4!
1sybOV16CHGYvM6s3xV09zfA!2e0!7i16384!8i8192

207https://www.google.com/maps/@47.877934,-
122.210039,3a,37.5y,249.2h,86.47t/data=!3m6!1e1!3m4!
1s6ytOVT7dzdLOeZzNlwo6jg!2e0!7i16384!8i8192?entry=ttu

208https://www.google.com/maps/@47.8779286,-
122.210653,3a,15y,88.38h,88.12t/data=!3m6!1e1!3m4!
1s_RwBWNV4WkpThTWMeZkqVw!2e0!7i16384!8i8192?entry=ttu

209https://www.google.com/maps/@47.8779576,-
122.2098366,3a,90y,350.18h,93.42t/data=!3m6!1e1!3m4!1sowiBEnk-

FUahQ1SKgLOdag!2e0!7i16384!8i8192?entry=ttu

210https://www.google.com/maps/@47.8776762,-
122.2106992,3a,37.5y,195.21h,80.25t/data=!3m6!1e1!3m4!
1swlkCjESzThpRmkuqTXrexw!2e0!7i16384!8i8192?entry=ttu

211https://www.google.com/maps/@47.877531,-
122.2104378,3a,15y,268.72h,87.53t/data=!3m6!1e1!3m4!
1sc1O93Ylh0Vf7uGdSmqCVKA!2e0!7i16384!8i8192?entry=ttu

212https://www.google.com/maps/place/2613+96th+St+SE,+Everett,
+WA+98208/@47.9109804,-122.1966745,18z/data=!4m5!3m4!
1s0x5490072fc87981e1:0x8890c7769623e3db!8m2!3d47.9111894!4d-
122.196947

213https://www.google.com/maps/@47.9111697,-
122.1984002,3a,75y,129.68h,73.04t/data=!3m6!1e1!3m4!
1sF2GUc3kRnjZghY_-FCvqGA!2e0!7i16384!8i8192?entry=ttu

214https://www.google.com/maps/@47.9110383,-
122.198287,3a,75y,97.91h,86.92t/data=!3m6!1e1!3m4!1sCzxJH4iY-
xwUe3k5h_lAnw!2e0!7i16384!8i8192?entry=ttu

215https://www.foxnews.com/us/dog-filleted-skinned-weeks-4-idaho-college-
students-brutally-murdered-report

216https://www.google.com/maps/@46.7554377,-
116.9858552,3a,75y,288.46h,86.27t/data=!3m6!1e1!3m4!
1sgI9F7Quhl7h5JAC5n3m6Yw!2e0!7i13312!8i6656

217https://www.youtube.com/watch?v=0jCKcrXc7II

218https://www.google.com/maps/@32.9293557,-
96.7694064,3a,75y,336.5h,84.66t/data=!3m6!1e1!3m4!
1sqQPKKqrZ99qJOPwplRPfSw!2e0!7i16384!8i8192

219https://www.whitepages.com/name/Makara-Sok/Everett-WA/Po3jZlmaE37
To confirm Irah Sok's husband's name, see: https://www.latintimes.com/30-
year-old-filipina-shot-dead-alleged-home-invasion-washington-524768

220https://www.google.com/maps/@47.9110156,-
122.1970572,3a,90y,92.31h,48.84t/data=!3m6!1e1!3m4!
1sOSP4ISA5CQ3pkESsOOeSmA!2e0!7i16384!8i8192

221https://www.youtube.com/watch?v=dIvc31sxZtY

222https://youtu.be/20G1jjZxXM8?si=mtKhdmfnaY1fhpE7

223https://www.google.com/maps/@47.9109833,-
122.1962023,3a,30y,42.6h,85.26t/data=!3m6!1e1!3m4!
1sWFcOfb5wtTGQuNml5CxusQ!2e0!7i16384!8i8192

224https://www.google.com/maps/@47.9110757,-
122.1961212,3a,15y,258.78h,90.89t/data=!3m6!1e1!3m4!1sF-
4ts4I2PezmjHpOT4FJzg!2e0!7i16384!8i8192?entry=ttu

225https://www.google.com/maps/@47.9108148,-
122.1961062,3a,75y,334.85h,80.7t/data=!3m6!1e1!3m4!
1s0oweUk7R64ojjEiN2E5YuA!2e0!7i16384!8i8192?entry=ttu

226https://www.google.com/maps/@47.9109782,-
122.1958621,3a,25.8y,270.35h,84.62t/data=!3m6!1e1!3m4!1saqAT_LV-

BjtKfC04pCBd0w!2e0!7i16384!8i8192
227https://www.google.com/maps/@47.9109884,-
122.1960398,3a,30y,251.57h,82.09t/data=!3m6!1e1!3m4!
1s_21OMbC4pR_5MaXsrueivg!2e0!7i16384!8i8192?entry=ttu
228https://www.google.com/maps/@47.9110012,-
122.1963588,3a,75y,202.31h,71.69t/data=!3m6!1e1!3m4!
1shDcCitnvFIk2fSJ13sIcLw!2e0!7i16384!8i8192?entry=ttu
229https://www.google.com/maps/@47.9110178,-
122.1973286,3a,15y,98.19h,86.78t/data=!3m6!1e1!3m4!
1stf87kQ14L4wt8mlxnoBOsw!2e0!7i16384!8i8192?entry=ttu
230https://www.google.com/maps/@47.9110757,-
122.1961212,3a,37.5y,234.58h,89.04t/data=!3m6!1e1!3m4!1sF-
4ts4I2PezmjHpOT4FJzg!2e0!7i16384!8i8192?entry=ttu
231https://www.google.com/maps/@47.9109884,-
122.1960398,3a,75y,306.45h,85.54t/data=!3m6!1e1!3m4!
1s_21OMbC4pR_5MaXsrueivg!2e0!7i16384!8i8192?entry=ttu
232https://www.google.com/maps/@47.9112811,-
122.1961019,3a,30y,138.73h,76.15t/data=!3m6!1e1!3m4!
1sKKAlBUEzEFilhNpCVNeEfw!2e0!7i16384!8i8192?entry=ttu
233https://www.google.com/maps/@47.9109629,-
122.1957065,3a,25.1y,273.26h,88.96t/data=!3m6!1e1!3m4!1s4Il-
COrO3CLsrSODJn57zg!2e0!7i16384!8i8192
234https://www.google.com/maps/@47.9120749,-
122.196071,3a,15y,349.29h,87.14t/data=!3m6!1e1!3m4!
1sOnjwaeilVXe53v5RY4oCjw!2e0!7i16384!8i8192
235https://www.google.com/maps/@47.912287,-
122.1960733,3a,15y,183.35h,87.67t/data=!3m6!1e1!3m4!
1sfN8gbsGVf2ML6GifnLlJ1g!2e0!7i16384!8i8192
236https://www.google.com/maps/@47.9124705,-
122.196069,3a,37.5y,342.28h,87.2t/data=!3m6!1e1!3m4!
1sglVVFhW3B1gki7txL4hm3A!2e0!7i16384!8i8192
237https://www.google.com/maps/@47.9126356,-
122.1962295,3a,15y,177.15h,86.33t/data=!3m6!1e1!3m4!
1sJVaHUcNVD7TOpYPLdq_Rig!2e0!7i16384!8i8192
238https://www.google.com/maps/@47.9126398,-
122.1963807,3a,75y,27.99h,73.35t/data=!3m6!1e1!3m4!1s5YF4RKzsvH-
4ys8YCOarGA!2e0!7i16384!8i8192
239https://www.google.com/maps/@47.9125804,-
122.1992922,3a,15y,85.59h,87.57t/data=!3m6!1e1!3m4!
1s7P8SOM0bDJO__lSzf9jcPg!2e0!7i16384!8i8192
240https://www.google.com/maps/@47.9125699,-
122.1987799,3a,15y,298.57h,91.33t/data=!3m6!1e1!3m4!
1sORoSUOyzvJ0YN2tL3Borxg!2e0!7i16384!8i8192
241https://radaronline.com/p/prince-andrew-lady-victoria-hervey-jeffrey-epstein-
role-9-11/

242https://www.ktvb.com/article/news/crime/moscow-murders-one-month-since-stabbing-near-university-of-idaho-campus/277-d22cbda4-b03c-4958-a54e-a4ee308bad06

243https://www.newsweek.com/moscow-police-identify-idaho-murder-victims-potential-stalker-1764823

244https://rumble.com/v4u6tn5-idaho-college-student-grubtruck-livestream.html

245https://twitter.com/ShawnWitzemann/status/1495139454444519430

246https://www.dailymail.co.uk/news/article-11461727/Retracing-murderers-steps-Blueprints-Idaho-student-stabbed-death.html?ico=related-replace

247https://www.dailymail.co.uk/news/article-11550099/Kaylee-Goncalves-Maddie-Mogen-heard-new-audio-hours-University-Idaho-slayings.html

248https://www.youtube.com/watch?v=wnVqpYRhyXs

249https://www.anonymousconservative.com/blog/wp-content/uploads/2022/12/Kaylee.gif

250https://abcnews.go.com/US/university-idaho-murders-house-demolished-despite-mixed-feelings/story?id=105771204#:~:text=Interest%20Successfully%20Added-,Idaho%20college%20murders%3A%20House%20demolished%20despite%20some%20families'%20objections,torn%20down%20before%20the%20trial.&text=The%20off%2Dcampus%20house%20where,mixed%20feelings%20from%20victims'%20families.

251https://www.newsnationnow.com/crime/idaho-college-killings/idaho-college-killings-moscow-house-now-boarded-up-guarded/

252https://www.newsnationnow.com/banfield/demolished-university-idaho-home-buried-deep-underground/

253https://www.dailymail.co.uk/news/article-11549353/Idaho-murder-victim-Kaylee-Goncalves-terrified-stalker-whod-follow-town.html

254https://www.newsweek.com/kaylee-goncalves-warned-about-stalker-three-weeks-before-murder-1767803

255https://www.newsweek.com/kaylee-goncalves-injuries-suggest-killers-target-ex-fbi-profiler-1765289

256http://nymag.com/news/features/long-island-serial-killer-families-2011-6/

257https://www.oxygen.com/true-crime-buzz/lost-girls-what-happened-to-dr-peter-hackett#:~:text=Peter%20Hackett%2C%20The%20Mysterious%20Doctor,Mari%20Gilbert%2C%20after%20Shannan's%20disappearance.

258https://www.denofgeek.com/culture/lost-girls-long-island-serial-killer-true-story/

259https://unresolved.me/the-long-island-serial-killer

260https://nypost.com/2016/07/25/shannan-gilberts-death-drove-sister-to-kill-mom-lawyer/

261https://www.oxygen.com/crime-news/shannan-gilberts-911-call-lawyer-claims-it-contradicts-previous-story

262https://art19.com/shows/lisk/episodes/81dae889-44a3-4d56-b6e8-fd61cf0e0646

263https://unresolved.me/the-long-island-serial-killer

264https://www.google.com/maps/dir/40.7172519,-

73.3116914/100+Ocean+Pkwy,+Babylon,+NY+11702/@40.6950931,-
73.3290133,13.25z/data=!4m8!4m7!1m0!1m5!1m1!
1s0x89e9d26c0314c0fb:0xaa5968a69c6cc02a!2m2!1d-73.2935857!
2d40.6398904

265https://unresolved.me/the-long-island-serial-killer

266https://www.nytimes.com/2011/04/09/nyregion/09bodies.html

267https://www.huffingtonpost.com/2013/03/19/natasha-jugo-identified-missing-
queens-woman-gilgo-beach_n_2905653.html

268https://archive.is/jm29k

269https://www.longislandpress.com/2015/12/13/48290/

270https://www.dea.gov/press-releases/2020/07/15/ms-13-gang-members-
indicted-six-murders-long-island

271https://www.dea.gov/press-releases/2020/07/15/ms-13-gang-members-
indicted-six-murders-long-island

272https://www.cbsnews.com/newyork/news/mother-ms-13-victim-killed/

273https://www.youtube.com/watch?
v=OQwhIDmbYeE&embeds_referring_euri=https%3A%2F
%2Fwww.websleuths.com
%2F&source_ve_path=OTY3MTQ&feature=emb_imp_woyt

274http://abc7ny.com/news/bail-denied-...-in-alleged-revenge-beating-cover-up/
1118786/

275https://www.nbcnewyork.com/news/local/oxycodone-pills-found-prison-cell-
convicted-suffolk-police-chief-james-burke/129430/

276http://archive.is/IMSoX

277http://casebycase.solutions/murder-cases/long-island-serial-killer/

278https://unresolved.me/the-long-island-serial-killer

279https://people.com/crime/long-island-serial-killer-gilgo-beach-fbi-profilers-
experts/

280https://www.rightrasta.com/rex-heuermann-wikipedia/

281https://thehill.com/regulation/court-battles/4468586-epstein-victims-accuse-
fbi-enabling-sex-trafficking-lawsuit/

282https://www.youtube.com/watch?v=cabcQA5gokE

283https://www.reddit.com/r/UnresolvedMysteries/comments/6wfqoc/
long_island_serial_killer_theories/

284https://youtu.be/V46U-hiu5Yc?si=h_-TxkOy_TMOMhDe

285https://www.newsday.com/long-island/crime/da-thomas-spota-s-wiretap-of-
robert-macedonio-new-details-of-probe-a12534
Archive : https://archive.ph/eee4r

286https://www.longislandpress.com/2016/03/12/feds-suffolk-da-spota-quashed-
investigations-into-conservative-party-chair-ed-walsh/

287https://www.cnn.com/2010/CRIME/07/28/ny.paterson.investigation/
index.html

288https://tbrnewsmedia.com/motion-to-sue-ex-suffolk-police-chief-burke-over-
1-5m-settlement-tabled/

289https://www.nytimes.com/2023/07/14/nyregion/gilgo-beach-murders-long-island-suspect.html

290https://www.cbsnews.com/newyork/news/james-burke-arrested-soliciting-sex/

291https://www.nbcnewyork.com/news/local/crime-and-courts/two-charges-dropped-against-former-suffolk-county-police-chief-arrested-in-sex-sting/4639762/

292https://medium.com/true-crime-addiction/was-the-orange-socks-girl-killed-by-cult-member-henry-lee-lucas-9c235a9d7f54

293https://english.elpais.com/elpais/2013/10/15/inenglish/1381856701_704435.html

294https://www.neonrevolt.com/2021/01/06/at-the-highest-levels-part-2-of-3/

295https://www.cambridge.org/core/journals/advances-in-psychiatric-treatment/article/confederacy-of-dunces-mental-illness-in-the-life-and-work-of-john-kennedy-toole/D9DA205C358EDB5D2B31F3D78B504E08

296https://infogalactic.com/info/John_Kennedy_Toole

297https://abcnews.go.com/blogs/headlines/2014/05/why-has-this-man-been-honked-at-over-5000-times

298https://www.youtube.com/watch?v=r9-3K3rkPRE

299https://rumble.com/v2std78-bill-binney-and-katherine-horton-directed-energy-weapons-4117.html?start=283

300https://www.cbsnews.com/baltimore/news/former-nsa-codebreaker-i-tried-to-tell-people-about-government-spying/

301https://web.archive.org/web/20180224165306/https://www.biggerthansnowden.com/
https://is.gd/lSBsfj

302https://twitter.com/Bill_Binney/status/1343396427431628800
https://is.gd/q5gSkJ

303https://ny1.com/nyc/all-boroughs/politics/2022/02/21/former-national-security-officials-report--havana-syndrome--attacks-in-washington

304https://twitter.com/bfcarlson/status/1631703749021270027

305https://americanstasi.com/wp-content/uploads/2024/05/Gunderson.pdf

306For a sanitized analysis of this, see:
https://www.vice.com/en/article/7x53vg/the-finders-cult-from-the-80s-was-patient-zero-for-epstein-and-pizzagate-conspiracies
For a more thorough analysis of this Epstein-like case, see:
https://www.mintpressnews.com/finders-cult-us-government-worked-keep-cia-connection-secret/277948/
It is perhaps even more instructive, once understanding the details of the Finders case better, to then perform a Google search and note how all of the earliest returned results assure readers there was no conspiracy, everything was debunked, and the CIA and intelligence had nothing to do with the Finders, which was just an innocent, misunderstood social club. This conspiracy behind the surveillance, as well as the Epstein-like blackmail operations, extends deeply into, and exerts incredible control over, everywhere you would look to try and gain insight into it.

307https://archive.is/1jiq0 or http://gothamist.com/news/gov-paterson-says-state-police-drove-him-to-confess-affairs-drug-use

308http://nymag.com/daily/intelligencer/2018/05/four-women-accuse-ny-ag-eric-schneiderman-of-physical-abuse.html

309https://archive.is/JL3Y2 or https://www.newsmax.com/Newsfront/andrew-napolitano-antonin-scalia-obama-spied/2017/05/16/id/790439/

310https://archive.is/k9eys or https://nymag.com/news/features/michael-hastings-2013-11/

311https://www.heraldsun.com.au/news/world/reporter-michael-hastings-sent-panicky-email-hours-before-sudden-car-crash-death/news-story/d8a07712abbcb79451b928c722931df6

312https://www.military.com/video/law-enforcement/police/raw-michael-hastings-car-crash/2575505618001

313https://www.huffpost.com/entry/michael-hastings-car-hacked_n_3492339

314https://archive.is/u0NJq or https://www.dailymail.co.uk/news/article-3417745/If-read-committed-suicide-don-t-believe-Dramatic-warning-Clinton-mistress-claims-Hillary-s-associates-harassed-1980s-affair-Bill.html

315https://archive.is/AMMaO

316https://canadafreepress.com/article/vindicated-talk-show-radios-true-patriot-tom-bauerle or https://archive.is/EQPpL

317https://www.bitchute.com/video/t2Z2f1SEqAlU/ or https://files.catbox.moe/c92u1b.mp4

318https://www.barrons.com/articles/jeffrey-epstein-was-no-market-wizard-his-returns-lagged-behind-the-market-51563381839

319https://www.moroccoworldnews.com/2024/01/359973/court-documents-raise-suspicion-on-jeffery-epstein-maxwells-links-to-israeli-mossad

320 Alternately there is a copy at https://files.catbox.moe/c92u1b.mp4

321https://www.deepcapture.com/2020/10/finale-the-deep-states-hillary-clinton-bribery-blackmail-sting-the-maria-butina-rape-murder-gambit/

322https://www.youtube.com/watch?v=JFdk-6rbrdU

323https://www.youtube.com/watch?v=SkktSQNP5-g

324https://www.fresnobee.com/news/local/crime/article69339482.html

325https://theamericansun.com/2019/04/30/how-the-illuminati-fucked-up-my-life/

326https://www.youtube.com/watch?v=U0mjwAPtcRY

327https://www.the-sun.com/news/1940981/brandy-vaughan-anti-vaccination-dead/

328https://www.youtube.com/watch?v=fuTXlCGjqMc

329https://www.independent.com/2021/02/18/santa-barbara-coroner-concludes-anti-vaxxer-brandy-vaughan-died-of-natural-causes/

330https://twitter.com/MN_CRIME/status/1704312449359380859

331https://web.archive.org/web/20190526061632/https://www.biggerthansnowden.com/

332https://en.wikipedia.org/wiki/William_Binney_(intelligence_official)

333https://rumble.com/v2std78-bill-binney-and-katherine-horton-directed-energy-weapons-4117.html (Starting at 04:43)

334https://www.youtube.com/watch?v=o7hsJAaJjR4

335https://americanstasi.com/gently-rapping-at-my-chamber-door/

336I actually recorded these events with a microphone (which appears responsive to electromagnetic effects not audible to the ear). A written account, the audio file, as well as a separate thermal video showing the heat signature suddenly emerge on my chest on being "beamed" with a microwave beam from the neighbor's house, are here: https://americanstasi.com/gently-rapping-at-my-chamber-door/

337 https://www.politico.com/story/2013/09/navy-yard-gunman-blamed-radio-waves-097378

338https://discover.hubpages.com/education/Infrasound-Weapons-Silent-But-Deadly

339https://www.cbsnews.com/news/havana-syndrome-white-house-cabinet-60-minutes-2022-06-26/

340https://www.anonymousconservative.com/blog/flashback-the-story-of-aaron-alexis-and-the-cuban-and-chinese-sonic-attacks/

341https://www.cbsnews.com/news/havana-syndrome-white-house-cabinet-60-minutes-2022-06-26/

342https://www.independent.co.uk/news/world/americas/us-politics/us-officials-sonic-attacks-america-havana-syndrome-symptoms-b1208414.html

343https://wislawjournal.com/2023/09/27/havana-syndrome-hits-cia-congress-in-wisconsin-russia-takes-credit/

344https://www.youtube.com/playlist?list=PLl9lnK9XQ94rDGgTHlLeqN44ik-3ROy4p

345https://www.youtube.com/watch?v=a1vIkUZjRl4

346https://www.pbs.org/wgbh/pages/frontline/government-elections-politics/united-states-of-secrets/the-frontline-interview-william-binney/

347https://www.pbs.org/wgbh/pages/frontline/government-elections-politics/united-states-of-secrets/the-frontline-interview-thomas-drake/

348https://www.americanstasi.com/followed

349https://archive.4plebs.org/pol/thread/383497959/#383530840

350https://www.reddit.com/r/AskReddit/comments/3wuxau/people_of_reddit_how_were_you_first_exposed_to/

351https://www.reddit.com/r/britishproblems/comments/1i0kmp/i_think_the_woodland_porn_fairy_may_now_be_extinct/

352https://www.reddit.com/r/AskUK/comments/16ky1ky/why_was_there_always_porn_in_the_woods/

353https://reason.com/2002/04/03/porn-and-politics-in-palestine/

354https://www.americanstasi.com/followed

355https://en.wikipedia.org/wiki/United_States_Foreign_Intelligence_Surveillance_Court
http://archive.is/gJFbq

356http://www.tabletmag.com/jewish-news-and-politics/256333/fisas-license-to-hop
http://archive.is/w2M7V

357http://archive.is/r4xVj

358https://www.cbsnews.com/newyork/news/bronx-nypd-officer-killed-investigation/

359https://www.latimes.com/california/story/2023-09-18/la-deputy-attack-killing-suspecte-heard-voices-attempted-suicide-mother-says

360https://www.cnn.com/2019/01/13/us/davis-police-officer-corona-sonic-waves-letter/index.html

361https://www.wusa9.com/article/news/local/dc/noah-green-suspect-in-capitol-attack-suffered-delusions/65-93b1c6e8-325c-4e82-bc18-91039bb39310

362https://infogalactic.com/info/Project_MKUltra

363https://www.theadvocate.com/acadiana/news/why-didnt-bizarre-behavior-block-man-accused-in-lafayette-police-officers-death-from-buying-a/article_cc214bc4-603a-11e8-af22-7b683c089491.html

364https://www.nytimes.com/2016/07/20/us/gavin-long-baton-rouge-targeted-individuals.html

365https://www.nytimes.com/2021/03/27/us/boulder-gunman-alissa.html

366https://nypost.com/2021/03/25/boulder-cop-eric-talleys-dad-my-son-was-a-gun-rights-advocate/

367https://www.youtube.com/watch?v=ikujTMetrUk&rco=1

368https://twitter.com/Michael_Yon/status/1764214765860085821

369https://americanstasi.com/epilogue-what-do-i-do/

370https://americanstasi.com/epilogue-what-do-i-do/

371https://projects.newsday.com/long-island/police-hiring-written-tests/
https://archive.is/tJwvL

372https://web.archive.org/web/20210913172206/https://news.yahoo.com/cuban-scientists-reject-havana-syndrome-164820841.html

373Guffey, Robert *"Chameleo: A Strange but True Story of Invisible Spies, Heroin Addiction, and Homeland Security,"* OR Books, 2015

374https://buffalonews.com/news/local/the-engineer-and-ex-cop-who-stand-behind-bauerles-invisibility-cloak-theory/article_6eb79c4d-dcfc-58e9-9d08-9c39946782f2.html
https://archive.is/iEWfw

375https://www.smh.com.au/world/us-planning-to-recruit-one-in-24-americans-as-citizen-spies-20020715-gdfgbq.html

376https://ovp.tmz.com/video/bf/o/2023/11/12/bf4f394e20c748d39f32b7f4ca4b835a.mp4

377https://www.theguardian.com/uk-news/2021/apr/22/fourth-officer-allegedly-fathered-child-after-meeting-woman-undercover

378https://americanstasi.com/gently-rapping-at-my-chamber-door/

379https://apnews.com/article/science-cuba-havana-physics-4316989d278ae353c42ef78033d9b2a5

380https://medicalxpress.com/news/2023-07-airplane-noise-linked-day-heart.html

381https://medicalxpress.com/news/2020-11-airplane-noise-night-trigger-cardiovascular.html

382https://www.iflscience.com/why-do-some-people-always-wake-up-at-3am-or-4am-every-night-72200

383https://infogalactic.com/info/
Mail_Isolation_Control_and_Tracking#:~:text=Mail%20Isolation%20Control%20and%20Tracking%20(MICT)%20is%20an%20imaging%20system,processed%20in%20the%20United%20States.

384 When US Attorney Alex Acosta was undergoing screening for the position of Labor Secretary, he told the Trump administration he cut the deal with Epstein when he was a US Attorney because he was told Epstein "belonged to [US]intelligence," and that the issue was above his "pay grade." https://www.newsweek.com/alex-acosta-epstein-sex-trafficking-department-labor-1448568

385https://www.mintpressnews.com/finders-cult-us-government-worked-keep-cia-connection-secret/277948/

www.ingramcontent.com/pod-product-compliance
Lightning Source LLC
Chambersburg PA
CBHW060540280326
41932CB00011B/1356